Reading the Times

Reading the Times

Temporality and History in
Twentieth-Century Fiction

Randall Stevenson

EDINBURGH
University Press

Edinburgh University Press is one of the leading university presses in the UK. We publish academic books and journals in our selected subject areas across the humanities and social sciences, combining cutting-edge scholarship with high editorial and production values to produce academic works of lasting importance. For more information visit our website: edinburghuniversitypress.com

© Randall Stevenson, 2018

Edinburgh University Press Ltd
The Tun – Holyrood Road, 12(2f) Jackson's Entry, Edinburgh EH8 8PJ

Typeset in 11/13 Adobe Sabon by
IDSUK (DataConnection) Ltd

A CIP record for this book is available from the British Library

ISBN 978 1 4744 0155 5 (hardback)
ISBN 978 1 4744 0156 2 (webready PDF)
ISBN 978 1 4744 3234 4 (epub)

The right of Randall Stevenson to be identifiedastheauthorofthisworkhasbeen asserted in accordance with the Copyright, Designs and Patents Act 1988, and the Copyright and Related Rights Regulations 2003 (SI No. 2498).

Contents

List of Illustrations	vi
Preface	vii
1. Introduction: Picnic Time, Prime Time, Story Time	1
2. 'All Those Figures': Joseph Conrad and the Maritimes	27
3. 'Wheels within Wheels': D. H. Lawrence, Industrial Time and War Time	47
4. Times in the Mind: Modernism in the 1920s	73
5. Not Like Old Times: The 1930s to Mid-Century	124
6. 'Time is Over': Postmodern Times	160
7. Conclusion: Millennial Times, Perennial Times	220
Bibliography	239
Index	251

List of Illustrations

1.1	The Great Western Railway's clock workshop.	10
1.2	The Corn Exchange clock, Bristol.	12
2.1	Longitude by daily reckoning.	30
2.2	Longitude by chronometry and astronomical observation.	32
2.3	Meridians and divisions to be identified in Board of Trade navigation examinations.	43
3.1	Clocking-in.	54
3.2	Charlie Chaplin in *Modern Times* (1936).	60
3.3	Home Office Summer Time poster, 1916.	69
4.1	*The Times*, 7 November 1919.	92
4.2	Wyndham Lewis, *Portrait of the Artist as the Painter Raphael* (1921).	115
6.1	The town clock in *Back to the Future* (1985).	207
6.2	Greenwich and the Millennium Dome.	219

Preface

> Mending the clock. Mending the clock – that was the idea.
> Joseph Conrad, *Lord Jim* (1900)

> A clock has always struck me as something ridiculous, a thoroughly mendacious object, perhaps because I have always resisted the power of time.
> W. G. Sebald, *Austerlitz* (2001)

Appearing in novels a hundred years apart, these comments characterise a century of fiction which amended regularly – often radically – temporalities ticked out by the clock, or measured out by the broader evolution of history.[1] *Reading the Times* assesses these amended narrative temporalities in relation to historical pressures, throughout the twentieth century, which compelled the modern novel's resistance to 'the power of time'. It also outlines origins of these pressures in the nineteenth century, and considers in conclusion their continuing consequences for the twenty-first.

Eminent commentators on the area might differ in their assessment of the scale of enquiry this aim demands. In *Time and Narrative* (*Temps et récit*, 1983–5), Paul Ricoeur identifies fiction in which temporality is unmistakeably an issue: novels such as Virginia Woolf's *Mrs Dalloway* (1925), which ensure that 'it is the very experience of time that is at stake'. Ricoeur distinguishes fiction of this kind from the majority of novels: ones which offer 'tales about time' only in the straightforward sense that as their narratives develop, 'the structural transformations that affect the situations and characters take time'.[2] In *About Time* (2007), on the other hand, Mark Currie considers that

---

[1] Joseph Conrad, *Lord Jim: A Tale* (1900; Harmondsworth: Penguin, 1968), 193; W. G. Sebald, *Austerlitz*, trans. Anthea Bell (2001; Harmondsworth: Penguin, 2002), 143–4.

[2] Ricoeur, *Time and Narrative*, II, 101. Ricoeur is following the views of A. A. Mendilow in *Time and the Novel* (1952).

fiction's 'structural transformations' not only *take* time, but inevitably entail perceptions about the *nature* of time and its passage, suggesting that 'all novels should be viewed as tales about time'.³

Reading the Times mediates between these positions, acknowledging that temporality is fundamental to the structuring of all fictional narrative – in ways outlined in Chapter 1 – but that certain novels make this structuring particularly conspicuous, sometimes also discussing explicitly the nature of time and its measurement. Novels of this kind – highlighting in subject or structure the measures of the clock, or the influence of wider movements of history – are the ones principally discussed in the chapters that follow. These discussions might nevertheless be supposed much more widely relevant, as Currie indicates, since issues which are manifestly 'at stake' in the novels analysed may also be at work, covertly or implicitly, throughout all contemporary fiction. While focusing on a particular set of novels, in other words, *Reading the Times* may be considered to have implications for any literary history of twentieth-century fiction, and consequently for the period's life and imagination generally.

The choice of novels discussed also relates to questions of space – in several senses – or geography, rather than only time. Even focused on temporality in the ways suggested, it would be difficult to contain a study of *all* twentieth-century fiction in the space of a single volume. There are other reasons to restrict the scale of enquiry. As Chapters 1 and 6 explain, attitudes to temporality did not develop, globally, in the same way or at the same pace during the twentieth century, even towards its end. Pressures exercised on these attitudes by advancing technology and industrialisation – by modernity generally – were long experienced fairly exclusively within the industrialised nations of the West. Many of the pressures concerned were initially encountered particularly sharply within Britain, the first country to experience an industrial revolution, and still, in the early decades of the twentieth century, a principal victim or beneficiary of its influences. In examining time in twentieth-century fiction, and historical factors that made it a key issue, discussion therefore concentrates on novels published in Britain – starting with two authors, Joseph Conrad and D. H. Lawrence, whose work is illuminating about the century's opening decades, then looking at broader movements in later chapters. Many further examples, though, are drawn from elsewhere in Europe and the United States – also, in Chapter 6, from other parts of the world.

---

³ Currie, *About Time*, 4.

Even delimited in these ways, analysis of a century or more of fiction remains a demanding task: one that has benefited greatly from the help of wise and generous advisers, going back to the 1990s and beyond. Chapter 2, and in a way the study as a whole, originated in the determined research of Alexandra Lawrie, and she remained a well-informed adviser throughout, along with the inexhaustibly knowledgeable Jonathan Wild. Jackie Jones was another initiating influence, and a key one in encouraging and supporting every stage. As might be expected of someone so loyal to Nottingham Forest, Greg Walker was likewise a committed supporter of the whole project, commenting insightfully on chapters as they were completed and regularly persuading the author to persevere. Ryan Edwards was an equally generous, thoughtful reader and commentator, adding illuminating suggestions throughout.

Thanks, too, to many others for help with particular areas or issues: to Bill Bell, Janet Black, Clare Brennan, Keith Carabine, Sarah Carpenter, Emilie Chazelle, Paul Crosthwaite, James Dale, David Denby, Ian Donaldson, Hugh Epstein, Alice Ferrebe, Abbie Garrington, Susanne Greenhalgh, Sarah M. Hall, Tom Handley, Mike Hill, John Hocking, Alan Hood, Vassiliki Kolocotroni, James Loxley, Rebecca Mackenzie, Brian McHale, Churnjeet Mahn, Simon Malpas, Ken Millard, Martin Mülheim, Colin Nicholson, Emma Nicolson, Katy Price, Caroline Root, Niklas Salmose, Roger Savage, Jonathan Sawday, Laura Scott, Allan H. Simmons, Andrew Stevenson, Anna Stevenson, Matthew Stevenson, Kate Stratton, Andrew Taylor, Alex Thomson, Peter Womack and Neil Young.

I'm also grateful to the National Maritime Museum in Greenwich, to the School of Literatures, Language and Cultures in the University of Edinburgh, to all at Edinburgh University Press, and as always, to the helpful staff of the National Library of Scotland. Thanks also to the Moray Endowment Fund, whose support allowed the inclusion of illustrative material, and to Faber for permission to quote from T. S. Eliot's *Four Quartets*. Chapter 2 first appeared in a shorter version in *The Conradian* (40 (2)), and some of Chapter 5 likewise in *Novel: A Forum on Fiction* (43 (1)) and in *The Legacies of Modernism* (2012), ed. David James. I'm grateful to be allowed to redeploy some of the material concerned in this volume.

Details of editions of literary works from which quotations are taken appear in footnotes throughout. Titles of other texts quoted appear in footnotes, with the editions used listed in the Bibliography.

Chapter 1

Introduction: Picnic Time, Prime Time, Story Time

On 14 July 2000 – the millennial Bastille Day – headlines and reports throughout the French press featured 'l'incroyable pique-nique'. Plans for this 'incredible picnic' – a main event on the national holiday – had filled a special supplement in *Le Monde* the previous day. Huge numbers of French citizens, *Le Monde* explained – around 3 million – had been invited to sit down to lunch along a line spanning France from sea to sea: from Dunkirk on the Channel, southward through Paris, all the way to Prats-de-Mollo on the Mediterranean. Sections of pink-and-white chequered table-cloth – more than 600 kilometres of it – would mark out much of this picnic line. Extensive tree-planting, begun well in advance of the July holiday, would ensure that the line remained visible permanently, even from space, along its entire 960-kilometre length.

Le Monde also explained the motives shaping this 'incredible', nation-spanning celebration. According to one of the organisers, it was intended to 'mobilise a whole family of memories', celebrating liberty and the French Republic in general, and highlighting particular national triumphs in science and in the creation of the metric system. Those trees and tablecloths were obviously not placed at random, but strategically aligned in order to 'matérialiser le méridien de Paris': to revive and make visible the old meridian, centred on the Paris Observatory, running north–south throughout France.[1] Established in 1667, the Paris Observatory and its meridian had acquired

---

[1] 'Entretien avec Paul Chemetov: "La table, quintessence de la solidarité"', *Le Monde Supplement*, 13 July 2000, v. 'La méridienne verte' soon featured as a tourist attraction in the designated areas of the French countryside.

much-expanded roles a century or so later, contributing crucially to attempts to delineate a new world – through science, measurement and standardisation, as much as social and political change – following the Revolution of 1789. Early governments in the new French Republic sought to reform both the calendar and time-measurement generally – renaming the months, redefining weeks, and decimalising hours into 100 minutes, each made up of 100 seconds. These initiatives were discarded within a few years, but standardisations of spatial measurement were more successful. Despite the turbulence of the post-revolutionary period, surveyors were able to make observations, throughout France, which allowed them to determine the length of the Paris meridian – running from the Equator, through Paris, to the pole – and to establish a standard metre, equivalent to one ten-millionth of this length.[2]

Responsibility for this standard – and for other new measures, including the kilogram – eventually passed on to France's Bureau of Weights and Measures, set up in 1875. By that date, another legacy of early Republican governments – the Bureau des Longitudes, established in 1795 – was reaching the height of its powers. From the early 1880s, it took on an expanding role, not only in the determination of longitudes, but in the global standardisation of time, including, from 1910, the broadcasting of time-signals from the top of the Eiffel Tower. Shortly afterwards, in 1912, an international conference at the Paris Observatory agreed to establish yet another bureau: the Bureau International de l'Heure. Still based in the Paris Observatory, this Bureau continued from January 1920 to coordinate global time measurement and the increasingly meticulous calculation of 'l'heure définitive'.[3]

As *Le Monde* suggested, there was therefore good reason for French citizens to look back with pride on more than two centuries of technical advances and rationalisations, in areas often centred on the Paris Observatory and meridian, and initiated through the revolutionary fervour Bastille Day commemorates. Yet as lunch was served on that pink-and-white tablecloth, on 14 July 2000, pride might also have been tinged with regret. As the British press smugly suggested, a dominant flavour at that incredible *pique-nique* might well have been *pique*, resulting from the disappointing fate of the Paris meridian, both within

---

[2] In his novel *The Measure of the World* (*La Mesure du monde*, 1987), Denis Guedj provides a full account of this demanding operation, undertaken during the 1790s by the surveyors Pierre Méchain and Jean-Baptiste Delambre. See also Chapter 6.
[3] See Howse, *Greenwich Time and the Longitude*, 155–6.

France and worldwide.[4] Hints of this eventual fate were discernible even before the French Revolution. Though established several years in advance of its Greenwich equivalent, the Paris Observatory and its meridian were already losing ground to British competition by 1789. Ever since the British Astronomer Royal, Nevil Maskelyne, published his *Nautical Almanac* in 1766, navigators had relied increasingly on Greenwich as the base point for their calculations. A century or so later, by the 1880s, Greenwich Mean Time (GMT) and charts based on Greenwich were employed by 72 per cent of the world's shipping, with only 8 per cent relying on Paris.

Prime Time

Inevitably, this was a decisive factor in the deliberations of the Prime Meridian Conference, an international gathering of scientists and diplomats convened in Washington in 1884. Delegates were charged with completing the work of other international conferences, earlier in the 1880s, which had stressed the necessity of a world standard of time and an internationally agreed meridian of zero longitude. In principle, the Washington conference could have based this Prime Meridian on any city or landmark. As Umberto Eco records in his novel *The Island of the Day Before* (1994), more than a dozen benchmark meridians had been employed in earlier centuries. At least ten remained in use on navigational charts in the 1880s, with preferences for Cadiz and Naples, as well as Paris, sometimes still resisting the majority choice of Greenwich. French delegates to the 1884 conference naturally maintained a stiff rear-guard action against ratification of this choice, seeking to postpone any final decision in Washington, then advocating a neutral meridian, perhaps running through the Bering Strait, or the Azores. Legitimately enough, since the conference was convened to establish global standards, they also recommended worldwide adoption of the metric system – another, covert, advocacy of the Paris meridian, on which the system was partly based. None of these arguments proved sufficient to resist Greenwich's already established position. Only San Domingo's delegates voted against its nomination as the world's Prime Meridian, though Brazil and France abstained. With less unanimity, and another abstention by France,

---

[4] See, for example, the account of French plans in 'Look Out Greenwich as French Revive Paris Mean Time', *Guardian*, 28 June 1999, 1.

Greenwich was also accepted as the point of origin for calculations of time, the 'universal day', and the hour-long time-zones, twenty-four in number, established to span and delineate the globe.⁵

Contemporary reports in *The Times* celebrated the 'good sense' of these resolutions – particularly, of course, from the British point of view. In terms of national pride, *The Times* considered, it was 'flattering' that 'the line running through the Observatory at Greenwich' had been selected by '21 representatives of the chief States of Europe and America'. This choice, the newspaper diplomatically suggested, was 'not a question of science, far less of politics'.⁶ Yet as the French evidently understood, the conference's favouring of Greenwich both advertised and consolidated the pre-eminence of British power, trade and navigation. Not surprisingly, there are signs that this confirmation appealed quite strongly to the British public at the time. In Arthur Wing Pinero's *The Magistrate*, first performed a few months after the Conference, a character records the time of day unusually cheerfully, remarking 'Hurray! . . . Just half-past ten. Greenwich mean, eh Guv?' In Joseph Conrad's *The Secret Agent* (1907), set around 1886, a character notes that 'the whole civilized world has heard of Greenwich. The very boot-blacks in the basement of Charing Cross Station know something of it'.⁷

There were nevertheless limitations to Greenwich's newly confirmed powers, both within and beyond the 'civilized world'. Though establishing global systematisation of time and space in principle, the Prime Meridian Conference could not ensure its immediate, worldwide implementation in practice. Like climate-change conferences in the early twenty-first century, it merely made recommendations – neither binding on governments, nor even, in some cases, apparently very influential. Practicalities of navigation ensured that the Greenwich meridian consolidated its well-established influence on global positioning, but acceptance of Greenwich Mean Time (GMT) often followed more slowly. In the supposedly 'uncivilised' world – areas

---

⁵ Howse, *Greenwich Time*, 138–40. See also 131–8.
⁶ 'The Decision of the Prime Meridian Conference', *The Times*, 15 October 1884, 9–10.
⁷ Arthur Wing Pinero, *The Magistrate* (1885), in *The Magistrate and other Nineteenth-Century Plays,* ed. Michael R. Booth (Oxford: Oxford University Press, 1974), 315; Joseph Conrad, *The Secret Agent: A Simple Tale* (1907; Harmondsworth: Penguin, 1967), 37. As the next section notes, anyone working in a station – even in its basement – would have been especially alert to the standardisation of time.

and nations not included among 'the chief States of Europe and America' – it was often several decades before Greenwich-centred systematisation had full effect.[8] Among the 'chief States' represented in Washington, the USA and Canada were already using time-zones based on the Greenwich standard before 1884, but other nations were sometimes slow or reluctant in its adoption, even after 1900.

France, not surprisingly, was one of these. Speculating about motives for a bomb attack on Greenwich Observatory, ten years after the Prime Meridian Conference – the episode Joseph Conrad developed into *The Secret Agent* – *The Times* remained concerned about the kind of *pique* described above. Noting the nationality of the man who had carried the bomb, Martial Bourdin, the newspaper remarked that 'the reputation of Greenwich Observatory is world-wide, and . . . Frenchmen have rather an objection to its pre-eminence'. Even when triumphantly reporting the outcome of the Conference in 1884, *The Times* had noted with disdain the diversionary tactics employed by French delegates in Washington, and feared that France might prove 'very reluctant to put the name of Greenwich on her charts'.[9] Reluctance of this kind did remain in evidence, well into the twentieth century, in France's determination to keep 'the name of Greenwich' away, if not necessarily from charts, at least from the nation's clocks. Consequences for continental life and travel, even three decades after the Washington conference, are vividly described in later fiction. When one of Thomas Pynchon's characters in *V.* (1963) – the appropriately named Mélanie l'Heuremaudit – arrives in Paris on a summer's day, shortly before the Great War, she encounters oddities of a kind perplexing travellers across Europe in earlier decades, and still affecting journeys into France:

> The clock inside the Gare du Nord read 11:17: Paris time minus five minutes, Belgian railway time plus four minutes, mid-Europe time minus 56 minutes. To Mélanie, who had forgotten her traveling clock – who had forgotten everything – the hands might have stood anywhere. She hurried through the station.[10]

---

[8] See Ogle, *The Global Transformation of Time*, esp. chs 3–6, and Nanni, *The Colonisation of Time*.
[9] 'The Anarchists', *The Times*, 27 February 1894, 8; *The Times*, 15 October 1884, 9.
[10] Thomas Pynchon, *V.* (1963; New York: Bantam, 1973), 369. Mélanie arrives in either July or August 1913 – the text is unclear about which – and Pynchon ascribes to 1913 conditions probably prevailing only until 1911.

As Mélanie might have deduced, France's capital and the rest of the country still maintained the time defined by the Paris Observatory. This was nine minutes ahead of clocks in Belgium, where GMT had been adopted in 1892. Austro-Hungary, Romania and Bulgaria had followed during the next two years, sharing with much of 'mid-Europe' a time-zone one hour ahead of Belgium's.

France had begun legal moves to accept GMT as its official time in 1896, only a few years after Belgium, but without decisive effects on the nation's clocks until 1911. Even then, lost ambitions for the Paris meridian were discreetly obscured, and any reference to external standards carefully effaced. Legislation in 1911 named France's new national standard not as Greenwich Mean Time, but as 'Paris Mean Time, retarded by 9 minutes 21 seconds'.[11] The figures reflect the exact longitudinal difference between the Greenwich and Paris observatories, calculated with some difficulty by astronomers, using new devices of telegraphy, towards the end of the nineteenth century.[12] Descriptions of the French national standard remained in this reticent, Greenwich-denying form for many decades, until France moved onto a new system – consistent with GMT, but based on caesium clocks and named as Co-ordinated Universal Time – in 1978.[13] Published the following year, Jean Echenoz's novel *Le Méridien de Greenwich* mentions the accuracy of atomic clocks, while also seeming to express a final phase of French exasperation with the whole issue of meridional calculation. The scepticism of one of its characters extends beyond the eponymous Greenwich meridian to encompass the function of meridians generally:

> This meridian is a scandal . . . it's a disgrace that time can be made to run on a globe only through recourse to a kind of intellectual artifice, an abstract and arbitrary meridian, employed in slicing up at a stroke both time and the earth . . . without this line, time has neither form, norms, nor a rate of passage.[14]

---

[11] Howse, *Greenwich Time*, 150.
[12] See Galison, *Einstein's Clocks, Poincaré's Maps*, 180–2, 206–7.
[13] 'Universel Temps Coordonneé', relying on atomic clocks rather than only celestial observation, had been in increasingly widespread use since 1960. See also Chapter 6.
[14] My translation of Jean Echenoz, *Le Méridien de Greenwich* (1979; Paris: Editions de Minuit, 2012), 273–4, 322. Like Eco's *The Island of the Day Before*, the novel is set on an *anti*-prime meridian – a 180° meridian, on the opposite side of the world from Greenwich. In the early 1880s, this meridian – relatively neutral politically – had often been suggested as a Prime one. See Blaise, *Time Lord*, 187.

New Lines

Picnicking along that pink-and-white tablecloth on 14 July 2000, French citizens were thus resuming a long history of world standardisation, and of Franco-British achievements, ambitions, and mutual envies which had shaped developments involved. *L'incroyable pique-nique* offers in this way evidence of obvious interest for historians of technology, science, society or international relations – also, in at least two ways, for literary critics. The picnic shows, straightforwardly, that 'intellectual artifice', slicing up time and the earth – and its history – still had a place in popular awareness at the end of the twentieth century. Pervasive in its effects on the timing and conduct of daily life, this 'artifice' could hardly have avoided influencing writers, and imagination generally, throughout the century just completed – especially in its opening decades, when temporalities were still a matter of ongoing, sometimes confused negotiation both within and between nations. Another interest centres on that term 'matérialiser', employed by the organiser of *l'incroyable pique-nique*. As he explained in *Le Monde*, the Bastille Day event attempted to make palpable on the surface of the earth, whether as tablecloth or trees, the kind of abstract, intellectual line Echenoz mentions – invisible in the experienced world, despite strongly influencing its affairs. This attempt offers an apt metaphor for the aims of *Reading the Times*, which seeks to make more visible and accessible to critical attention certain lines, divisions and dissections – specifically within the dimension of time – which shaped and often troubled the life and literary imagination of the twentieth century.

Before these aims can be developed – before Mélanie's perplexities in the Gare du Nord can even be fully explained – other sets of lines need to be considered. The Prime Meridian Conference and its centring of world time on Greenwich were obviously not the only factors shaping the temporality of the century that followed. Nor were its resolutions consequent only on the needs of shipping and navigation – or the intellectual preferences of scientists and astronomers – for firmer ordering of global space and time. On the contrary, the conference's deliberations responded principally to growing demands from globalised systems of communication, commerce and transport, on land as well as sea – from material interests steadily expanding their influence throughout the nineteenth century. Pre-eminent among such influences were those shaped by a very visible new set of lines – railways. First scoring their way across the physical landscape in the 1820s and 1830s, these soon imposed on Britain – and before long the wider world – challenging new delineations and precisions within the dimension of time.

Mélanie's arrival in Paris highlights some of the challenges concerned. Simple arithmetic clarifies the nine-minute – or really nine-minute-and-twenty-one-second – disparity she encounters between Parisian and Belgian time. The five-minute difference between the Gare du Nord and the rest of Paris is also easily explained. At one stage of the nineteenth century, the French railway system had operated on the basis of Rouen time, five minutes behind clocks in the capital. Even after the system generally adopted Paris time, in 1889, a five-minute retardation was retained in *l'heure de la gare* (station time). This offered clemency to tardy travellers, relieved to find train departures lagging behind city clocks they might have observed while rushing to the station. These straightforward explanations nevertheless highlight other complications. The first of these is the discrepancy between exact railway timetabling and unpunctual railway customers – a conflict between mechanical system and human disposition of a kind often explored in twentieth-century literature, as later chapters will discuss. Another intriguing complication appears in the disclosure that French cities – in this case Paris and Rouen – evidently maintained disparate versions of the time of day.

Before the rapid spread of the railways in the 1830s and 1840s, disparities of this kind would hardly have surprised anyone, and were certainly just as widely evident in Britain. Travel between towns was still not rapid enough to demand mutual adjustment of the time of day followed in each, usually defined – sometimes only loosely – by local church clocks, or public ones. As a result, much of the British population shared the kind of conditions illustrated in Thomas Hardy's fiction. *Tess of the d'Urbervilles* (1891) recalls an era when 'one-handed clocks sufficiently subdivided the day', and *The Return of the Native* (1878) demonstrates that even in the 1840s, when the novel is set – and two-handed timepieces were the norm – punctuality remained a matter of very uncertain negotiation:

> 'Twenty minutes after eight by the Quiet Woman . . .'
> 'Ten minutes past by Blooms-End.'
> 'It wants ten minutes to, by Grandfer Cantle's watch.'
> 'And 'tis five minutes past by the captain's clock.'
> On Egdon there was no absolute hour of the day. The time at any moment was a number of varying doctrines professed by the different hamlets . . . West Egdon believed in Blooms-End time, East Egdon

in the time of the Quiet Woman Inn. Grandfer Cantle's watch had numbered many followers in years gone by, but since he had grown older faiths were shaken.[15]

Variation in 'doctrines' of this kind – between towns, as well as Hardy's different hamlets – was in a way entirely natural. The sun rises, sets, and passes its highest (noon) altitude at varying times throughout Britain, with several minutes of difference for locations any distance east or west of each other. Just as noon at Greenwich – more than two degrees of longitude west of the French capital – occurs nine minutes and twenty-one seconds later than at the Paris Observatory, so Plymouth lags a further sixteen minutes behind London. A position still further to the west explains why Ireland was one of the last areas of Europe to adjust to GMT, despite the whole island remaining part of Great Britain in the early twentieth century. A difference of nearly twenty-five minutes – obviously still greater in the west of Ireland – separates Dublin from London, encouraging the retention of a separate time-zone until 1916; ironically, the year in which movements towards Irish independence were most violently in evidence. Thirty years earlier, a *Times* report on early stages of the Prime Meridian Conference mentioned the 'familiar story' of an Irishman who forgets to reset his watch on arrival on the mainland, and turns up half an hour late for a meeting in Liverpool. Consequences of Ireland's separate time-zone continue to figure complicatedly in James Joyce's *Ulysses* (1922) – in Leopold Bloom's confusions, in 1904 Dublin, about whether the Ballast Office time-ball falls according to Greenwich reckonings or those of the nearby Dunsink Observatory.[16]

Within mainland Britain, incentives toward conformity gathered force much earlier. As long as towns maintained their own time, even when quite close together, it remained technically possible for railway travellers to arrive at a nearby destination at a time apparently earlier than the one at which they had set out. Oddities of this kind – no doubt leading travellers to wonder, like Mélanie, whether their watch-hands 'might have stood anywhere' – were further highlighted by the nationwide timetables first published towards the end

---

[15] Thomas Hardy, *Tess of the d'Urbervilles: A Pure Woman* (1891; London: Macmillan, 1974), 52; *The Return of the Native* (1878; London: Macmillan, 1981), 154.
[16] *The Times*, 2 October 1884, 9; see James Joyce, *Ulysses* (1922; Harmondsworth: Penguin, 1992), 194, 211, and Warner, 'The Ballast-Office Time Ball', 861–4.

of the 1830s. Among other confusions regarding local and railway time, the new timetables easily led passengers to believe that trains travelled faster from east to west than in the opposite direction – an impression of a kind sometimes still troubling air-travellers in the twenty-first century.[17] Near-instantaneous communication by means of another set of lines – telegraph lines, often set up alongside the railways during and after the 1830s – made still more essential the move the railway historians Jeffrey Richards and John M. Mackenzie describe, towards 'standard national time and not solar time'.[18] This transition gathered pace at the start of the 1840s, when the Great Western Railway began keeping London time on all its lines, though

Fig. 1.1 The Great Western Railway's clock workshop. Most railway companies established workshops of this kind, ensuring the maintenance and accuracy of clocks throughout their systems. British Railways continued to employ a Horology Department in the latter half of the twentieth century. Getty Images.

---

[17] The situation remained still more confusing in the United States, where numerous railway times were in operation, even in the 1870s, often including several different ones in the same station. See Ogle, *Global Transformation*, 25; Blaise, *Time Lord*, 72–4.

[18] Richards and Mackenzie, *Railway Station*, 94.

still announcing to passengers differences from local clocks in towns along its routes. Similar tactics spread steadily across the network throughout the decade, with railway staff sometimes employed to travel up and down the lines with a chronometer, checking and adjusting clocks at each station.

By 1847, GMT was employed almost throughout the railway system, increasingly directing pressure on civic authorities to conform to this 'Railway Time', as it was often called, adjusting their town clocks to match those in their local stations. When the Statutes (Definition of Time) Act was eventually passed by Parliament in 1880, making GMT the nationwide legal standard, it might have seemed no more than a ratification of changes which were sensible, practical, inevitable, and in any case already widely implemented. To borrow a judgement *The Times* offered four years later, concerning the outcome of the Prime Meridian Conference, the railways' influence might simply be considered to have 'put an end to ... worse than useless diversity', eliminating the kind of rustic dithering exemplified by life on Egdon Heath.[19] New travel arrangements were often presented in this way: naturally enough, by Thomas Cook, for example. *Cook's Excursionist* in July 1854 offered the cheerful – though inaccurate – conclusion that 'Railway time is London time, and London time is the sun's time, and the sun's time is common time; and Railway time all must keep'.[20]

Railway time and its relations with the sun were not always viewed with such enthusiasm. 'Railway time observed in clocks' simply made it seem 'as if the sun itself had given in', Charles Dickens comments when describing a dreary London scene in *Dombey and Son* (1848).[21] Reluctance to 'give in' to railway clocks remained widely apparent. In areas distant from the railways' influence, the habits of Egdon still survived – the Astronomer Royal mentioning that clocks in neighbouring villages, in the later 1880s, often still differed by more than half an hour.[22] From the late 1840s, pocket watches were sometimes produced with a third hand, indicating railway time only as an alternative to the truer measures of solar time, or local time, displayed by the other two. Similar tactics were adopted for public clocks, particularly in cities furthest from the Greenwich Meridian – Plymouth and Bristol in the west, or Norwich in the east – and

---

[19] *The Times*, 15 October 1884, 10.
[20] Quoted in Brendon, *Thomas Cook*, 16.
[21] Charles Dickens, *Dombey and Son* (1848; Oxford: Oxford University Press, 1999), 185.
[22] See Ogle, *Global Transformation*, 68.

therefore with the strongest motives for rejecting equations of 'London time' with solar time. In Bristol, a three-handed public clock of this kind remained in operation throughout the twentieth century (Fig. 1.2). Even in towns closer to the Meridian, public resentment of the new temporality was often vehemently expressed. In the year *Dombey* appeared, *Blackwood's Edinburgh Magazine* published a double-columned, eight-page complaint – half-facetious, half-vituperative – about the loss of the sun's influence, following the town council's recent imposition of Railway Time on Edinburgh. Attributed to W. E. Aytoun, Edinburgh University's Professor of 'Rhetoric and Belles Lettres' – essentially literary criticism – the article inveighed against an interference 'with the arrangements of Providence' which perversely required that clocks 'ceased to be regulated by the sun' and were instead 'made to lie [by] . . . civic jurisdiction'. It would be better, the article asserted, 'to see every railway throughout the kingdom torn up or battered down', rather than accept 'a confused notion that the motions of the sun are regulated by an observatory at Greenwich'. Local or unregulated temporality is further endorsed through reference to Shakespeare's *Henry IV* – to Falstaff's claim to have fought 'a long hour by Shrewsbury

Fig. 1.2 The Corn Exchange clock, Bristol. © RichardHayman13/istockphoto.com

clock', while laudably omitting any reference to the mean standards of Greenwich.[23]

Appropriately, the *Blackwood's* article approves Falstaff's tactics when commenting on the constraints imposed by pub closing times. As licensing came to be increasingly regulated nationally rather than municipally, during Aytoun's time and the following decades, drinkers often sought to lengthen opening hours by referring to some convenient local clock – obviously with particular scope for fluid interpretation if, as in Bristol, it happened to have three hands. National sobriety, public order and Victorian propriety required a more watertight system. Along with the need to ratify the railways' influence, a factor motivating Parliament's 1880 confirmation of GMT as the nationwide standard was the opportunity this offered to restrict intoxicating freedoms the public might hitherto have enjoyed. As Richards and Mackenzie describe, 'the station, with its timetables, tickets, uniformed staff, and ubiquitous clocks, is an inherent supporter and encourager of discipline and order' (14). The legislation of 1880 finally institutionalised this kind of order for the entire civic community: for the nation as a whole.

As the same commentators suggest – along with others quoted above – the resulting order seemed logical, essential and often convenient, yet sometimes unnatural, or even against the dictates of heavenly spheres. Even in emphasising the railways' need for 'national time and not solar time', Richards and Mackenzie nevertheless regret that 'God's time, or natural time, the time dictated by the sun's progress through the heavens and the countryman's age-old rhythm of life, was superseded by Man's time' (94). As other historians have pointed out, regrets of this kind may in one way be romantic, or exaggerated. By the opening decades of the nineteenth century, or earlier, life even for country dwellers may already have been extensively controlled by the clock, rather than only 'age-old rhythm' or the sun's progress in the sky.[24] Even Hardy's views of Egdon suggest as much, albeit with slender prospects of punctuality offered by the clocks concerned.

---

[23] 'Greenwich Time', *Blackwood's Edinburgh Magazine*, March 1848, 354–6; *Henry IV*, pt 1, V, iv. Ten years earlier, Edgar Allan Poe had offered a still more disturbing view of Edinburgh horology. His short story, 'A Predicament' – originally entitled 'The Scythe of Time' – parodies Gothic fiction often published in *Blackwood's* by describing an unwary visitor, beheaded by a clock's huge minute-hand while viewing the city's splendours from a cathedral tower.

[24] See Glennie and Thrift, *Shaping the Day*.

Yet the changes imposed by the railways – nationwide in their scale, minute and precise in their demands – did introduce genuinely new and more exigent apprehensions of temporality into everyday life. These new exactitudes continued to be viewed critically, in literature and contemporary opinion generally. As that tardy *l'heure de la gare* indicates, new disciplines and orders often seemed contrary not only to a wider natural world, but to the nature of individuals caught up in the new systems. At the very least, new demands for punctuality and precision necessitated new forms of attentiveness to the clock, as Marcel Proust's narrator notes in *Remembrance of Things Past* (*À la recherche du temps perdu*, 1913–27). 'Since railways came into existence', Marcel remarks, 'the necessity of not missing trains has taught us to take account of minutes, whereas among the ancient Romans . . . the notion not only of minutes but even of fixed hours barely existed'.[25] As he suggests, long before digital clocks displayed exactly-numbered hours and minutes, later in the twentieth century, travellers had learned to read clock-faces more minutely, with Mélanie's passage through the Gare du Nord at 11.27 – not 11.25, 11.30, or half-past eleven – indicative of the change.

For one of Proust's Parisian contemporaries, the eccentric composer Erik Satie, such minute exactitude in daily life seemed not only unnatural but risible. In the year the first volume of *À la recherche du temps perdu* appeared – *Swann's Way* (*Du côté de chez Swann*, 1913) – Satie published a 'precise timetable of my daily acts', recording that

> I rise: at 07.18; inspired: from 10.23 to 11.47. I lunch at 12.11 and leave the table at 12.14 . . .
>
> Various activities (fencing, reflection, immobility, visits, contemplation, dexterity, swimming etc.): from 16.21 to 18.47 . . .
>
> I retire with regularity at 22.37. Once a week, I wake up with a start at 03.19 (on Tuesdays).[26]

---

[25] Marcel Proust, *Remembrance of Things Past*, trans. C. K. Scott Moncrieff and Terence Kilmartin (Harmondsworth: Penguin, 1983), II, 853. Subsequent references are to this edition.

[26] Erik Satie, 'Memoirs of an Amnesic (Fragments): The Musician's Day' (1913), in *A Mammal's Notebook: The Writings of Erik Satie*, ed. Ornella Volta, trans. Antony Melville (London: Atlas Press, 1996), 112.

In *Swann's Way*, Proust also suggests incongruities between minute timetabling and everyday life. Marcel generally welcomes new opportunities for rapid travel offered by the railways, describing

> The fine, generous 1.22 train, whose hour of departure I could never read without a palpitating heart on the railway company's bills or in advertisements for circular tours: it seemed to me to cut, at a precise moment in every afternoon, a delectable groove, a mysterious mark. (I, 418–19)

Yet Marcel's vocabulary suggests some uneasiness about new precisions cutting across his languid afternoons – especially in the original French, in which 'cut' appears as the more surgical 'inciser'. His 'palpitating heart' resonates with troubled views of rail travel – and of newly stringent temporalities generally – also expressed in medical journals during the nineteenth century, as well as by several of Proust's contemporaries, among authors of modernist fiction, in the early decades of the twentieth. By the 1850s and 1860s, medical practitioners were regularly recording concerns about railway travel's general 'effect on the nervous system' and the particular risks of 'excitement, anxiety, and nervous shock consequent on the frequent efforts . . . to be in time for the fearfully punctual train'. There were even 'cases of sudden death' thought to have been occasioned by the stresses involved.[27] Milder versions of such concerns still echo through modernist fiction in the 1920s, particularly in Gudrun's fears of 'terrible bondage' to 'the eternal, mechanical, monotonous clock-face of time' in D. H. Lawrence's *Women in Love* (1921). Nightmarish visions of this bondage centre on her experience of railway stations, where 'still she could see, with her very spine . . . the great white clock-face', even if she tries to ignore it – an awareness which makes 'her heart palpitate with a real approach of madness'.[28]

Gudrun's experience of a palpitating heart – more alarming than Marcel's – resembles the 'great shock to the nervous system' Virginia

---

[27] 'Influence of Railway Travelling on Public Health', *The Lancet*, 4 January 1862, 15; *The Association Medical Journal*, 1854, quoted in Harrington, 'The Railway Journey and the Neuroses of Modernity', 241. For a fuller view of nineteenth-century concerns about 'The Pathology of Railroad Travel', see ch. 5 of Schivelbusch, *The Railway Journey*.

[28] D. H. Lawrence, *Women in Love* (1921; Harmondsworth: Penguin, 1971), 522–3. See also Chapter 3.

Woolf's heroine experiences when hearing a clock strike in *Orlando* (1928).[29] It also recalls threats of approaching madness Woolf describes in her earlier novel, *Mrs Dalloway* (1925). These threats are directly associated with reductive, intrusive, aspects of temporality, envisaged cutting across daily life still more incisively than those Marcel envisages in *À la recherche du temps perdu*. 'Shredding and slicing, dividing and subdividing', in the novel's description, 'the clocks of Harley Street nibbled at the June day, counselled submission, upheld authority, and pointed out in chorus the supreme advantage of a sense of proportion'. Confidence in the authority of this 'time ratified by Greenwich' is undermined not only by the reductive 'shredding' the novel's many clocks impose on the June day, but also by the disastrous effects – on the shell-shocked mental patient, Septimus Smith – of any 'proportion' they might offer.[30]

For Woolf's original audience, doubts about this proportion and the clock's authority would have been firmly focused by the name of the Harley Street expert – Bradshaw – principally responsible for Septimus's treatment. Comprehensive railway guides were first published by George Bradshaw in 1839, offering essential information about the network throughout the country, though sometimes adding to the confusions between railway time and local times mentioned earlier. These guides continued to appear under his name for almost a century, until the 1930s, their ubiquitous use soon making 'Bradshaw' synonymous with railway timetables.[31] When urgently planning a train journey in Arnold Bennett's *Clayhanger* (1910), Hilda simply asks Edwin 'Have you got a Bradshaw?' In Arthur Conan Doyle's *The Valley of Fear* (1915), Sherlock Holmes describes *Bradshaw*, along with the Bible, as the kind of 'very common book . . . which any one may be supposed to possess'.[32] Possession of a *Bradshaw* also figures crucially in Bram Stoker's *Dracula* (1897) and in Max Beerbohm's *Zuleika Dobson* (1911), as well as

---

[29] Virginia Woolf, *Orlando* (1928; Harmondsworth: Penguin, 1975), 216. Subsequent references are to this edition.
[30] Virginia Woolf, *Mrs Dalloway* (1925; Harmondsworth: Penguin, 1976), 113. See also Chapter 4.
[31] Bradshaw's guides recovered some of their fame in the twenty-first century through Michael Portillo's reference to them in his *Great Railway Journeys* series on BBC2.
[32] Arnold Bennett, *Clayhanger* (1910; Harmondsworth: Penguin, 1976), 280; Arthur Conan Doyle, *The Valley of Fear* (1915; London: John Murray and Jonathan Cape, 1974), 22. Holmes – the name of Septimus's other doctor in *Mrs Dalloway* – extends the significance of 'Bradshaw' in invoking a rigorously orderly, rationalising mentality.

in other Sherlock Holmes stories, and is noted as an essential prerequisite for travel in Woolf's earlier novel, *Night and Day* (1919).

For Woolf's readers, the name of Bradshaw would therefore have succinctly recalled the railways' role in disseminating 'time ratified by Greenwich' throughout contemporary society. The influence of this exigent temporality had been further consolidated by factors in later nineteenth-century life considered in Chapter 3 – principally the advancing industrialisation which Dickens considers, in *Hard Times* (1854), to have ensured that time 'went on . . . like machinery'.[33] The Prime Meridian Conference of 1884 thus extended – globally and officially – powers already allowing the clock to shred and subdivide life within individual countries, Britain in some ways particularly. As the vocabulary of authors quoted above suggests, by the end of the nineteenth century and in the twentieth these powers rarely figured in literature as congenial, often appearing instead as incompatible with the kind of freer, flowing experiences of time or 'age-old rhythm' earlier periods supposedly enjoyed.

Pynchon's *V.* thus offers an emblem for modern literary imagination not only in mentioning that five-minute gap between station clocks and city time. Pynchon's Mélanie also sums up a disposition in twentieth-century literature simply in her second name: 'l'Heuremaudit', the accursed hour. As later chapters will discuss, much of the century's fiction – in earlier decades especially – seems to consider *l'heure définitive* as synonymous with *l'heure maudite*. In James Joyce's *A Portrait of the Artist as a Young Man* (1916), 'the ticking of a great clock' even figures as a key feature in a vision of hell.[34] In many other novels, though less extremely, a minutely, globally regulated temporality seems more of a curse than a blessing. The legacies of late nineteenth-century standardisation and systematisation might even be summed up by comparing Pinero's 1885 *The Magistrate* with a novel published a century later, William Gibson's futuristic *Neuromancer* (1984). 'A readout chipped into [her] optic nerve' places a digital clock permanently in the field of vision of Gibson's heroine, Molly. With an accuracy that might have amused Eric Satie, this allows her to inform her lover, Case, that their first sexual encounter began at '2:43:12 AM'. Later in the novel, another of Case's questions about the time receives a reply far removed from Pinero's cheery 'Hurray! . . . Greenwich

---

[33] Charles Dickens, *Hard Times* (1854; Harmondsworth: Penguin, 2003), 90.
[34] James Joyce, *A Portrait of the Artist as a Young Man* (1916; Harmondsworth: Penguin, 1992), 143.

mean, eh guv?' – Molly reporting glumly that 'it's eight twenty-five, PM, Greenwich fucking Mean'.³⁵

In *Time and Literature* (1955), Hans Meyerhoff remarks that in the twentieth century 'time . . . ceased to be a friendly medium', seeming instead 'neutral, indifferent, and hostile to man's works and values'. Theodore Ziolkowski likewise sums up *maudite* or accursed attitudes Gibson's novel highlights when noting that in general 'clocks in modern literature seem to exist only to be ignored, dropped, shattered, deformed, or improved upon'.³⁶ As he remarks, 'modern literature' – modernist fiction particularly – demonstrates more than merely passive resentment of the clock's divisions and constraints. It also explores ways these constraints may be resisted, regularly suggesting possibilities for attitudes to temporality to be reshaped or improved. Strategies for doing so are suggested in Thomas Mann's *The Magic Mountain* (*Der Zauberberg*, 1924), for example, when Hans Castorp vigorously dissents from his cousin Joachim's conventional views of time. Joachim remains blandly content to rely on 'watches and calendars', accepting that 'a minute is as long – it *lasts* as long – as it takes the second hand of [his] watch to complete a circuit'. Hans argues instead that 'our units of measurement are purely arbitrary, sheer conventions', and that a minute takes 'a varied length of time – to our senses'. Time, he concludes, '*isn't* "actual". When it seems long to you, then it *is* long; when it seems short, why, then it is short'.³⁷

Similar views are advanced in *Orlando*. Woolf's novel proposes that

> an hour, once it lodges in the queer element of the human spirit, may be stretched to fifty or a hundred times its clock length; on the other hand, an hour may be accurately represented in the timepiece of the mind by one second. This extraordinary discrepancy between time on the clock and time in the mind is less known than it should be and deserves fuller investigation. (69)

Castorp's arguments and Orlando's experience indicate that, by the early decades of the twentieth century, the heightened 'shock to the

---

³⁵ William Gibson, *Neuromancer* (1984; London: Grafton, 1986), 44, 300.
³⁶ Meyerhoff, *Time in Literature*, 104; Ziolkowski, *Dimensions of the Modern Novel*, 188.
³⁷ Thomas Mann, *The Magic Mountain*, trans. H. T. Lowe-Porter (1928; London: Vintage, 1999), 66. Subsequent references are to this edition.

nervous system' delivered by striking clocks had also highlighted alternative and less exigent versions of temporality. As references in *Orlando* and *The Magic Mountain* to 'the 'human spirit' and 'our senses' suggest, private, personal forms of temporal experience, emotion or memory offer a range of alternatives and resistances to the official, exact, public measures of the clock. Woolf's contrast of 'time on the clock' with 'time in the mind' offers a succinct formulation – convenient for several of the chapters that follow – of antitheses between these subjective and objective versions of temporality. Factors considered in the previous two sections ensured that the promise of freer, subjective temporal experience appealed strongly to the twentieth century generally: it obviously also offered a particular opportunity for literature – one given the 'fuller investigation' *Orlando* invites in many novels during the period. This is the opportunity to free not only characters but *readers* from conventional temporality, by means of narrative forms which displace the clock's constraints in favour of the expansive imagination offered by 'time in the mind'.

Story Time

In developing this opportunity, twentieth-century authors in some ways only extend potentials which are inherent in all narrative, and deployed in fictional forms dating back, as Chapter 7 suggests, even beyond the eighteenth-century 'invention' of the novel in English. Of all inventions, then or since, the novel may be the best equipped to resist or reorient the relentless, measured passage of time. In its bound, printed form, it may be the only artefact ever devised whose physical shape allows its users to keep the dimension of time so firmly under their thumb, or thumbs. The past of the story safely remains mostly under the reader's left thumb, in the section of the novel already read, while the future waits placidly under the right.[38] As the novel's pages are turned, the present unfolds at a pace – unlike that of other narrative forms, such as film – largely at the reader's discretion. New habits of on-screen scrolling through e-books, or other forms of electronic text, may eventually alter this sense of control during the twenty-first century. Even radical changes in the novel's outer, published form should nevertheless leave intact its profound

---

[38] Narrative anachronies of course sometimes partly infringe this containment.

inner potentials for reshaping time. As Georg Lukács concludes in *The Theory of the Novel* (*Die Theorie des Romans*, 1920), the 'entire inner action of the novel is nothing but a struggle against the power of time' – against 'its sluggish, yet constant progress'.[39]

A brief survey of twentieth-century commentary on this struggle may further delineate the novel's potential to improve upon the clock, while also introducing ways this potential will be assessed in later chapters. Many commentators in the area develop the kind of views offered by one of the earliest of them – at any rate in English-language criticism – E. M. Forster. In *Aspects of the Novel* (1927), Forster offers a critical or theoretical version of some of the ideas Mann and Woolf were discussing in fiction around the same time. Extending Hans Castorp's views of the flexibility of 'time in the mind' – and in fiction – Mann points out in *The Magic Mountain* that

> a narrative which concerned itself with the events of five minutes, might, by extraordinary conscientiousness in the telling, take up a thousand times five minutes, and even then seem very short ... On the other hand, the contentual time of a story can shrink its actual time out of all measure. (542)

In *Aspects of the Novel*, Forster outlines conditions allowing this kind of flexibility, suggesting that – rather than easy correspondence with any 'chronological chart' – there seems

> something else in life besides time, something which may conveniently be called 'value', something which is measured not by minutes or hours, but by intensity, so that when we look back at our past it does not stretch back evenly but piles up into a few notable pinnacles ... all dreamers, artists, and lovers are partially delivered from [time's] tyranny ... when the clock collected in the tower its strength and struck, they may be looking the other way. So daily life, whatever it may be really, is practically composed of two lives – the life in time and the life by values – and our conduct reveals a double allegiance. 'I only saw her for five minutes, but it was worth it'. There you have both allegiances in a single sentence.[40]

Frank Kermode, in *The Sense of an Ending* (1967), and Peter Brooks, in *Reading for the Plot* (1984), further analyse narrative in

---

[39] Lukács, *The Theory of the Novel*, 122, 121.
[40] E. M. Forster, *Aspects of the Novel*, 36.

terms of the fundamental opposition that Forster indicates between measured time and, on the other hand, significance, desire or value. Brooks describes how narrative responds to 'our refusal to allow temporality to be meaningless', and to desires for the 'rescue of meaning from passing time'. In *The Sense of an Ending*, Kermode likewise analyses how narrative fictions 'meet a need' for structure and meaning by offering to do 'what Bacon said poetry could: "give some show of satisfaction to the mind, wherein the nature of things doth seem to deny it"'.[41]

This analysis extends into Kermode's distinction between contrary apprehensions of temporality which he defines as '*chronos*' and '*kairos*'. For Kermode, *chronos* is the 'purely successive, disorganized time' of daily life (45), measured out by the unrelenting tick of the clock – the kind of time summed up by Lukács as 'sluggish, yet constant', or later described in one of Don DeLillo's novels as 'sheer and bare, empty of shelter'.[42] *Kairos*, on the other hand, reflects imaginative attempts to make the clock 'talk our language' – translated into 'the time of the novelist' by means of 'organization that humanizes time by giving it form' (44, 45, 46). Working towards this humanised time, novelists exploit immense, varied and flexible formal possibilities offered by narrative imagination. 'Satisfaction to the mind' accumulates from – among other devices – narratives' concentration on coherent, causally connected 'pinnacles' of experience, highlighted by re-orderings, abbreviations and extensions which ensure that the sluggish, petty pace of clock and calendar is thoroughly 'improved upon'.

Though supposedly *un*improved, or 'sheer and bare', ordinary life obviously does exhibit elements of form and meaning of its own – personal or institutional plans and routines; patterns of eating, work and sleep; rhythms inherent in heartbeat, breath, the cells of the body, or the suprachiasmatic nuclei in the brain. For commentators such as David Carr, these and other features of ordinary experience offer a 'richness and complexity of . . . structure' less distant from the orderly nature of narrative forms than Kermode and others suggest.[43] Yet in one way at least, the experience of ordinary life cannot provide fully the *kairos* Kermode describes, unless possibly for the deeply

---

[41] Brooks, *Reading for the Plot*, 321, 323; Kermode, *Sense of an Ending*, 62–3.
[42] Don DeLillo, *The Body Artist* (London: Picador, 2001), 92.
[43] Carr, *Time, Narrative and History*, 43. Carr does also discuss the implications of authorship, 57–62.

religious. As well as keeping fictional time under their own thumbs, readers remain aware that the events they encounter in the novel – however apparently random – have been shaped by the controlling hand of an author. For Kermode, Brooks, and later commentators such as Mark Currie, this contributes a particular 'satisfaction to the mind' – a unique appeal in fiction, drawing simultaneously on two worlds, or two perspectives. Though written most often in the past tense, fictional narratives engage readers, along with characters, in a vivid, continuous present, an unfolding of events as immediate and challenging as life itself, or often more so. Yet the novel also offers a superintendent security, missing from lived experience in any present moment – a confident sense (Kermode's 'sense of an ending') that experiences encountered will eventually be satisfactorily contained within overall pattern and closure, structured through the controlling vision of the author.[44]

Kermode's *chronos* and *kairos* also correspond to distinctions – contributing to a methodology for analysing 'the time of the novelist' – developed by the work of the Russian Formalists, some years before Forster published *Aspects of the Novel*. Critics involved used the term *fabula* to refer to the sequence of events in a story as these might be supposed to have occurred in reality – in Boris Tomashevsky's terms, in 'the actual chronological and causal order of events'.[45] The Formalist term *sjuzet*, on the other hand, refers to events imaginatively rearranged into the time of the novelist – into the form and order of the narrative text readers encounter. This distinction might seem to flirt with tautology – imagining, in *fabula*, a strictly chronological version of narrative texts, then used as a basis for analysing their imagination. Yet it might also be considered merely to extend long-established critical distinctions between content and form, or linguistic ones between signified and signifier, or more profound divergences between lived experience and imagination or desire. It has at any rate proved extensively useful to narrative analysis. In studying the practices and potentials of novelistic imagination, an ordinary, 'sheer and bare' version of events – *fabula* – offers a convenient template, highlighting contrastively authors' reshapings of the petty pace of everyday life, and suggesting specific motives for its reconfiguration in their narratives.

---

[44] See Currie, *About Time*, 5, etc. As he explains, the grammatical tense of the narration does not much affect the sense of an unfolding present inherent in reading fiction.

[45] Tomashevsky, 'Thematics', 67.

In assessing the present chapter, for example, a critical reader might consider that it could have begun more logically, or chronologically, in the 1840s, with the railways' mid-nineteenth-century consolidation of a standardised, nationwide temporality. A generous appraisal might nevertheless acknowledge advantages in the anachronic tactics followed instead – 14 July 2000 offering a picturesque place to start, with subsequent analepses filling in the history of chronology in ways that emphasise the continuing influence of nineteenth-century industrialisation and standardisation on later ages.

Terms just employed – 'anachronic' and 'analepses' – indicate ways narrative analysis moved on, later in the twentieth century, from the work of the Russian Formalists, or Forster or Kermode. French critics in the 1970s and later usually favoured their own terms, *histoire* and *récit*, over the Formalists *fabula* and *sjuzet*, though Anglophone commentators often retained Forster's 'story' and 'plot', or story and narrative, to refer to the same sort of distinctions. In the work of Gérard Genette and his successors, French criticism also extended the range and subtlety – and the terminology – of analyses tracing the anachronic, time-warping transformations of *fabula* or *histoire* into finished narrative texts. As well as examining relations between observers, or narrators, and events, Genette's *Narrative Discourse* (*Discours du récit*, 1972) categorised aspects of narrative temporality sometimes little considered previously. These included the relative frequencies of occurrence, and of narration, of events – repeated tellings of a single event, or single accounts of repeated ones. Genette also discusses questions of duration, categorising the capacities Mann identifies when noting narratives' potential to expand or shrink 'actual time out of all measure'. *Narrative Discourse* covers more familiar ground in discussing the ordering of events, though coining new terms – 'analepsis' and 'prolepsis' – useful in discussing departures from the narrative present more sustained than the older terminology of 'flashback' or 'flashforward' might suggest.

Genette's work offers in this way a kind of user's manual for what Brooks calls 'the infinitely variable gearbox that links the told to the ways of its telling'(20). Yet neither Genette, nor the other commentators mentioned, much examine factors motivating changes of gear – at any rate in historical terms that might illumine the nature, and origins, of patterns of anachrony distinguishing particular periods of fiction. Like the dreamers, lovers and artists he mentions, E. M. Forster seems ready to turn his own back on the clock – and on history, when he describes the 'idea of a period' as one he is merely 'hoping to avoid'.

He extends instead T. S. Eliot's recently expressed conclusions about literary works composing a simultaneous order – defining time in *Aspects of the Novel* as 'our enemy' and envisaging authors 'all writing their novels simultaneously'.[46] Genette likewise pays very limited attention to variations in narrative strategies between periods, or to historical influences which might occasion them. Kermode is readier to consider such issues, acknowledging that 'the pressure of reality on us is always varying' – and that in seeking 'satisfaction to the mind', 'fictions must change' as a result – but *The Sense of an Ending* does not have scope to analyse processes involved in any detail (24).

This analysis is central to *Reading the Times*, which considers novels rather as Elizabeth Bowen describes her central characters in *The Heat of the Day* (1949) – as 'the creatures of history . . . of a nature possible in no other day'.[47] For analysis of this kind, potentials supplementing those described above seem promised by the Russian Formalists, or at any rate by one of their successors, Mikhail Bakhtin. Offering 'notes . . . toward a historical poetics', his essay 'Forms of Time and of the Chronotope in the Novel' (1938) seems to offer a promising term even in its title. Bakhtin coins the term 'chronotope' to describe a literary 'time space', specific to 'historical situations' and configured by the 'temporal and spatial relationships' shaping literary forms and genres prevalent at the time. Unlike commentators considered above – mostly concerned with perennial, transhistoric potentials for the 'rescue of meaning from passing time' – Bakhtin thus at least acknowledges that a certain literary 'form of time' may be specific to an individual period, and widely shared among contemporary authors.[48] Yet the idea of 'chronotope' is not altogether straightforwardly applicable to the twentieth century, whose rapidly changing social and literary idioms require more specific, concentrated forms of analysis than Bakhtin provides in his essay, which is mostly concerned with long-extended literary periods in the distant classical past. The productive principles he establishes are worth adopting, but also adapting for modern periods and for fuller concentration on issues specifically of chronology. The term 'chrono*type*' will be used in later chapters to do so: to refer to narrative structurings of temporality – particular relations of *fabula* and

---

[46] Forster, *Aspects*, 16; see also T. S. Eliot, 'Tradition and the Individual Talent' (1919).
[47] Elizabeth Bowen, *The Heat of the Day* (1949; Harmondsworth: Penguin, 1983), 194–5.
[48] Bakhtin, 'Forms of Time and of the Chronotope in the Novel', in *The Dialogic Imagination*, 84–5, 206.

sjuzet – sometimes distinguishing relatively short literary periods within the twentieth century.[49]

Bakhtin's principles are worth extending in a further, related direction – towards fuller analysis than he offers of ways that historical pressures shape the characteristics of literary periods, including the distinctive 'form of time' which may be discernible in their fictional narratives. For analysis of this kind, Fredric Jameson's work provides a productive guide – through his mantra 'always historicize', and ways this is developed in *The Political Unconscious: Narrative as a Socially Symbolic Act* (1981). As its subtitle's mention of symbol suggests, *The Political Unconscious* examines how 'pressures of reality' can be recognised configuring narrative imagination not only directly, but in oblique or subtler ways. Jameson identifies one of these when he describes fiction as 'a weaker form of myth', imaginatively reconfiguring social stresses into more manageable or comprehensible narrative forms – though ones perhaps less universally relevant or compelling than myth. Rather like Kermode, Jameson explains in this way the novel's commitment to 'substitute gratifications' – to finding, in imagination and the consoling forms and orders of fiction, 'satisfaction to the mind' even when dealing with stresses unresolvable within society itself. Literature, in other words, may be unable directly to alter historical conditions, but it can offer alternative and less troubling ways of configuring them imaginatively – forms of 'Utopian compensation' which *The Political Unconscious* explores throughout.[50]

Like most of the theorists discussed above, Jameson concentrates in this way on literary form. This emphasis further delineates strategies to be followed, in later chapters, in analysing the novel's response to historical stresses of the kind identified in the previous two sections. As those sections began to demonstrate, there are many instances in twentieth-century literature of clocks *maudites* – clocks cursed, badly spoken of, dropped or ignored, as Ziolkowski describes. There are also many examples, such as appear in *Orlando* or *The Magic Mountain*, of direct advocacy of alternative and less exacting temporalities – or of merely looking the other way, whenever the clock strikes. Contemporary pressures of history and horology are conveniently highlighted by explicit evidence of this kind, which later chapters will continue

---

[49] An adaptation employed in Bender and Wellerby, *Chronotypes*. The volume's introduction explains the modification of Bakhtin's term to focus specifically on 'the concept of temporality', and to refer to 'models or patterns through which time assumes practical or conceptual significance' (3–4).
[50] Jameson, *The Political Unconscious*, 9, 70, 266, 42.

to provide. Yet as Jameson suggests, narrative also offers a profound resistance to these pressures *implicitly*, through renegotiating or reconfiguring them into compensatory styles, forms and structures favouring 'time in the mind'. Understanding the imaginative processes involved and their historical motivations depends on a straightforward recognition. The measured pace of clock and calendar – the steady chronological order on which *fabula* depends – remains unaltered throughout all literary periods. Attitudes to this pace, measure and order do not – varying, instead, according to the degree of exigency of the clock's rule over contemporary experience, and the extent to which its measured orderliness seems compatible with the life of the times. As a result, the gap between *fabula* and *sjuzet* opens and closes like an accordion, while historical events call the tune – shaping and re-shaping chronotypes required to reorient their shifting pressures into forms offering 'satisfaction to the mind'. This is especially recognisable in the opening decades of the twentieth century, when Utopian compensation for the age's exigent, recently standardised temporalities required modernist narrative to depart unusually decisively from the chronological orderliness of *fabula*. Yet fiction in later decades often continues to bear comparison with those clocks, in Bristol and elsewhere, duly displaying time ratified by Greenwich, while also maintaining another hand, still pointing towards alternative values or older rhythms, resistant to the exacting demands of a mechanised modern age. Reading the times expressed in this way, throughout twentieth-century fiction, is the aim of the chapters that follow.

Chapter 2

'All Those Figures': Joseph Conrad and the Maritimes

Reminiscing about their profession, mariners in Joseph Conrad's *Chance* (1913) recall sharp disparities between the 'glamour' and 'romantic associations' promised by a career at sea and the 'rational and practical grounds' of the work actually involved. In *Lord Jim* (1900), Conrad's narrator Marlow likewise highlights difficulties awaiting anyone whom 'cherished glamour' has attracted towards a career in the Merchant Navy. 'In no other kind of life is the illusion more wide of reality', Marlow remarks, 'the disenchantment more swift – the subjugation more complete'. Troubling the novel's central figure, first attracted to the sea by 'a course of light holiday literature', disenchantment of this kind may also have been experienced by the author himself.[1] According to his friend Ford Madox Ford, Conrad 'always declared that it was reading *Peter Simple* and *Midshipman Easy* that made him wish to go to sea', and that he considered the author of these popular 1830s stories, Captain F. Marryat, 'the greatest English novelist since Shakespeare'.[2]

Conrad at any rate recalls in one of his *Last Essays* (1926) how sharply some of his own values – including romantic or imaginative ones required in his second career, as a novelist – conflicted with the 'rational and practical grounds' of his years of work in the Merchant Navy. In the intriguingly entitled memoir, 'Outside Literature' (1922), he reflects on how thoroughly this work depended on

---

[1] Joseph Conrad, *Chance: A Tale in Two Parts* (1913; Harmondsworth: Penguin, 1984), 16; Joseph Conrad, *Lord Jim: A Tale* (1900; Harmondsworth: Penguin, 1968), 101, 11. Subsequent references are to this edition.
[2] Ford Madox Ford, *Memories and Impressions* (1971; Harmondsworth: Penguin, 1979), 256. In *Joseph Conrad*, Ford explains that Marryat enjoyed 'incredible popularity' (252–3) in Poland around the time of Conrad's early youth.

'fidelity to ... the ideal of Perfect Accuracy', vividly encapsulated in the Board of Trade's 'Notices to Mariners'. Used to communicate crucial information to ships and sailors, these Notices offered 'good prose', but in a 'language expounding the truth', whose aims and style could hardly have been further outside literature. The Notices, Conrad emphasises,

> don't belong to imaginative literature ... all means of acting on man's spiritual side are forbidden to that prose ... all suggestion of Love, of Adventure, of Romance, of Speculation, of all that decorates and ennobles life, except Responsibility, is barred.[3]

Among the rational, practical grounds and responsibilities Conrad encountered at sea, the pursuit of 'Perfect Accuracy' in chronometry and navigational systems – based comprehensively on Greenwich's Mean Times and meridians – would inevitably have occupied a central role. As the historians of horology Paul Glennie and Nigel Thrift emphasise, long before Greenwich-centred systems had much influence within Britain, the importance of 'clock times on ships' – of 'routines and drills' requiring 'clear allegiance to temporal measurement' – had made of 'seafarers ... [a] time-obsessed community'.[4]

For Conrad himself, this allegiance to temporal measurement inevitably gained force as his maritime career continued and he pursued the navigational skills and qualifications required for work as an officer. As 'Outside Literature' records, this involved several other encounters with the Board of Trade – not only with its Notices, but with its stringent examinations for the certificates of competency, or 'tickets', required for service at the various officer ranks of the British Merchant Navy. Conrad's difficulties with these examinations are worth considering in detail. They offer clear indications of how far the new lines, temporalities and constraints which the previous chapter identified developing outside literature eventually impacted within it – in Conrad's own writing, when he began his literary career, and in the wider modernist movement his work helped to initiate. 'I am *modern*', Conrad insisted in a letter of 1902.[5] As this chapter will show, his nautical experience, and his Board of Trade examinations in particular, played key roles in ensuring the truth of that judgement – in establishing a modern style, in Conrad's work, which proved usefully exemplary for many writers in the years that followed.

---

[3] Joseph Conrad, 'Outside Literature', *Last Essays*, 33, 30.
[4] Glennie and Thrift, *Shaping the Day*, 304, 318–19.
[5] Letter to William Blackwood, 31 May 1902, *Collected Letters*, II, 418.

Conrad Re-examined

Another reason for considering these exam ordeals is that they have so seldom been assessed by critics – though this neglect may be understandable, given Conrad's efforts to suppress or obscure some of the details involved. In *A Personal Record* (1912), he offers only partial versions of his encounters with the 'august academical body of the Marine Department of the Board of Trade' – with agreeable but long-winded examiners faced when acquiring his Second Officer's ticket, in 1880, and his certificate as Master, or Captain, in 1886.[6] *A Personal Record* also describes a briefer but challenging examination for his First Officer's ticket – likewise successful, but involving an examiner who hypothesises a ship with innumerable parts damaged or missing, then reminds Conrad that if his proposed remedies fail, he still has the option of saying his prayers. Though entertaining, these accounts – and a similar, fictional, one in *Chance* – omit to mention that the Board of Trade required two written papers, in 'Seamanship' and in 'Navigation and Nautical Astronomy', in addition to the oral examinations described. Conrad failed the latter examination when seeking his First Officer's ticket, on 17 November 1884 – requiring a resit around two weeks later – and again when applying for his Master's certificate in July 1886, passing only that November.

Failures in each case occurred in 'The Day's Work' section of the Navigation and Nautical Astronomy paper, with further deficiencies in 'Arithmetic' in July 1886.[7] Conrad sought to improve his performance with help from a navigation school – a 'crammer' for the Board of Trade examinations, run by John Newton at the Sailors' Home in Dock Street, London. Described by Conrad as 'my only teacher', Newton also published a handy guide to the examinations and the skills they required.[8] Its seventh edition might have seemed a useful purchase to Conrad in 1884, if he had not already acquired a copy of the sixth, when studying to pass as Second Officer, in 1880. Along with similar manuals in circulation at the time, Newton's *Guide* at any rate makes the demands of the Board of Trade fairly clear – particularly in its completed examples and model answers for the 'Day's Work' section of the navigation paper. This work required calculation of a vessel's location either through 'dead reckoning' – based

---

[6] Conrad, *Mirror of the Sea* and *A Personal Record*, 112.
[7] See van Marle, 'Plucked and Passed', 99–108.
[8] Letter to Vernon Watson, 26 May 1896, *Collected Letters*, I, 283; Newton, *Newton's Guide to the Board of Trade Examinations of Masters and Mates of Sailing Ships and Steam Ships in Navigation and Nautical Astronomy*.

on the bearing, speed and duration of courses travelled in the previous twenty-four hours, and recorded in the ship's log (Fig. 2.1) – or by means of chronometry and astronomical observation (Fig. 2.2).

	23
	EXAMPLE.

Bearing E by N
Reversed W by S
7 pts.=78° 45' RS
Dev.   9 18 L
69 27 RS
Var. 22 30 R
91 57 RS
Or.   88 3 LN
1st Co.73° 7' RS
9 18 L
63 49 RS
22 30 R
86 19 RS
2ndCo.84° 22' LN
11 12 L
95 34 LN
22 30 R
73 4 LN
3rdCo.67° 30' RS
6 58 L
60 32 RS
22 30 R
83 2 RS
4thCo.28° 7' RS
0 47 L
27 20 RS
22 30 R
49 50 RS
5thCo.90° 0' LN
11 50 L
101 50 LN
22 30 R
79 20 LN
6thCo.73° 7' LN
11 10 L
84 17 LN
22 30 R
61 47 LN
Current Co.
WSW=67°30'RS
Var. 22 30 R
90 0 RS
Or.   West

H.	Courses.	K.	½/10	Winds.	L.	Deviation.	Remarks.
1	W.S.W.	8	5	S.	½	9°18'W.	A point lat. 44° 20' S. long. 176° 49' W., bearing E. by N. by compass, distant 16 miles. Ship's head W.S.W. Deviation as per log.
2		9	5				
3		9	5				
4		10	5				
5	W. ½ S.	10	5	S.S.W.	1	11°12'W.	
6		9	5				
7		8	9				
8		8	1				
9	S.W.½W	8	4	S. by E.	1½	6°58'W.	
10		7	6				
11		7	5				Variation 22° 30' E.
12		7	5				
1	S. ½ W.	7	7	S.E.½E.	2	0°47'W.	
2		7	3				
3		8	0				
4		8	0				
5	W.	9	6	E.	0	11°50'W.	
6		10	6				
7		10	6				
8		11	2				A current set the ship W. S. W., correct magnetic, 28 miles during the day.
9	W. by N.	10	5	S.W.byS	½	11°10'W.	
10		10	4				
11		10	1				
12		9	0				

Courses.	Dist.	N.	S.	E.	W.
N. 88° W.	16	00.6			16.0
S. 86 W.	38		02.7		37.9
N. 73 W.	37	10.8			35.4
S. 83 W.	31		03.8		30.8
S. 50 W.	31		19.9		23.7
N. 79 W.	42	08.0			41.2
N. 62 W.	40	18.8			35.3
West.	28				28.0
		38.2	26.4	00.0	248.3
		26.4			00.0
	D. Lat.	11.8		Dep.	248.3

Lat. left............ 44° 20' S.   Long. Left .. 176° 49' W.
D. Lat. ....   12 N.   D. Long. 347=   5 47 W.
Lat. in .... 44 8 S.   182 36 W.
                                                      360 0
Sum of Lats......... 88 28
                                        Long. in...... 177 24 E.
Half sum or mid. Lat. 44 14

Course N. 87° W.   Dist. 249 miles.

Fig. 2.1 Longitude determined by daily reckoning, from John Newton's *Guide*. Reproduced with the permission of the Trustees of the National Library of Scotland.

Though familiar enough to experienced navigators, each method involves substantial challenges. In Conrad's day, measurement of a ship's speed was hardly straightforward, in any sense. It depended largely on the apparatus of 'log-and-line': on dropping a float behind the ship, then observing how fast a cable attached to it reeled out, though generally without knowing how much the float might itself be moved by wind and current. Ships themselves – sailing ships especially – were obviously also subject to winds and currents. These often imparted a lateral drift –'leeway' – requiring calculation of how far the ship might have been deflected from moving ahead directly along the course it was attempting to follow. Determination of this course was also made uncertain by the unreliability of compasses. These were subject both to 'deviation' – due to the magnetic attraction exercised by ships themselves, iron-hulled ones especially, and differing in the extent of its influence according to the course followed – and to 'variation', occasioned by divergences between true and magnetic north. These change over time, and were especially problematic during Conrad's seagoing years, when the magnetic pole was only 70° north of the equator, rather than around 85°, as in the twenty-first century. Had Conrad headed for arctic waters, instead of the tropics or antipodes in which he mostly plied his trade, he might have had to deal with a magnetic north pole actually to the south of his ship's position.

Standard devices were available to assist with the calculations involved, such as 'Napier's Diagram', to help make adjustments for the effects of deviation. Yet dead reckoning was never likely to be dead easy, or dead accurate, and other factors made still more challenging the second method of calculation, based on astronomical observation (Fig. 2.2). A sextant reading of the sun's angle above the horizon at its highest (noon) altitude should allow straightforward determination of a ship's latitude. Once effective marine chronometers became available in the later eighteenth century, the more difficult matter of determining longitude also became relatively straightforward, at least in principle. A chronometer keeping Greenwich Mean Time indicates how much earlier, or later, noon occurs at the ship's location than at the Prime Meridian, and correspondingly how far its position lies to the east or west of Greenwich: 15° of longitude per hour of difference.[9] Yet in a popular account of John Harrison's development of chronometers, *Longitude* (1996), Dava Sobel risks obscuring some of the practical

---

[9] A further, chart-based strategy for determining a ship's position, 'Sumner's Method by Projection' – extending the principles described above – had been included in Board of Trade Examinations by the 1880s, and is described in Newton's *Guide*, 82–9.

To find the longitude.—Below the mean time at ship place the mean time at Greenwich, taking care always to have the day as well as the hours, &c.; then subtract the less from the greater. The remainder brought into degrees, &c., is the Longitude of the ship.

The Long. is East if the Greenwich time is less than the mean time at ship.

The Long. is West if the Greenwich time is more than the mean time at ship.

The following rhyme is often used to tell the name of the Long. :—

" Greenwich Time least Long East,

Greenwich Time best Long West."

EXAMPLE.

1885.—February 6th.—A.M. at Ship in Latitude 28° 40' N. The observed altitude of the sun's lower limb 42° 50' 10"; height of eye 15 feet. Time by a chronometer, February 6^d 7^h 2^m 0^s which was 1^m 0^s fast for mean noon at Greenwich on November 10th, 1884, and on January 2nd, 1885, it was 0^m 9^s *slow* for mean noon at Greenwich. Required the Longitude.

From Nov. 10 1^m 0^s fast   Feb. 6^d .. 7^h 2^m 0^s *From* Jan. 2
To Jan. 2   0 . 9 slow   2nd error   + 9   *To* Feb. 6

```
    Nov. 20      1   9         6..7  2  9      Jan. 29
    Dec. 31     60          Loss   +46         Feb.  6
    Jan.  2     —
    ———       53)69(1.3     G.M.T.6 ..7 2 55    35.3
     53         53                               1.3
                                                          h
                160                             1059   24)7.0(3
                159                              353     .72
                                                —
                                                45.89
```

Altitude.   H. diff. Eqn. Time. H. diff.
   42° 50' 10" Dec. Feb. 6th 15° 28' 0" S.   46".56 14^m 20s.28   .144
Dip. —3 42 Cor. .... —5 28   7.05   1.01   7.05

   42 46 28   15 22 32   23280   14 21.29   720
Ref. —1 1   90   325920   10080
                                             To be added to
   42 45 27 Pol. dist..... 105 22 32   6,0)32,8.2480   *App. Time*, 1.01520
Sem. + 16 15
Par. + 7   5' 28"

T Al. 43 1 49

Note.—*In " Chronometer" all Logs. must be taken out to seconds.*

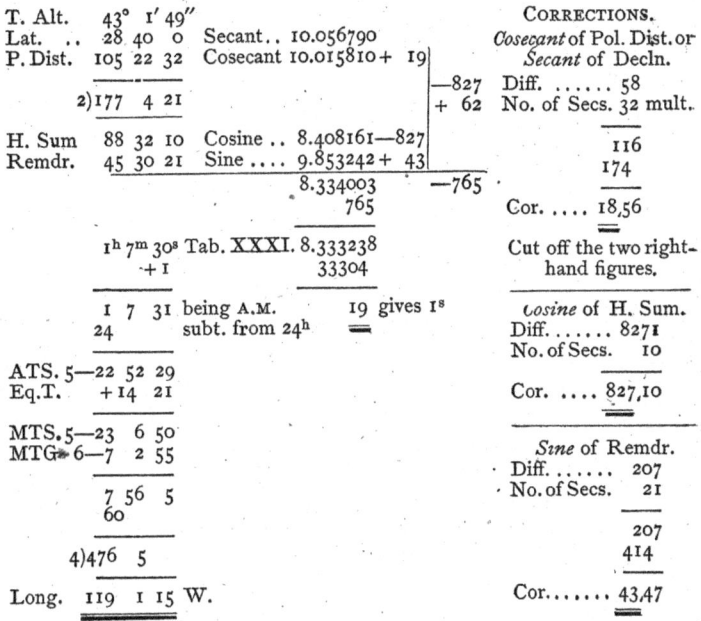

Fig. 2.2 Longitude determined by chronometry and astronomical observation, from John Newton's *Guide*. Reproduced with the permission of the Trustees of the National Library of Scotland.

difficulties involved in this method – at any rate in her confident subtitle, 'The Story of a Lone Genius Who Solved the Greatest Scientific Problem of his Time'. Harrison's wonderfully accurate chronometers did offer a solution to the problem of determining longitude at sea, but later manufacturers could not always match his level of 'genius'. Marine chronometers generally ran at least slightly fast or slow, and ships usually carried two, or sometimes three, rested on gimbals to reduce disturbance to their mechanisms, and daily compared with each other by the captain or his officers. The need for these checks is explained at length in a section devoted to 'Management of Chronometers' in *Captain Alston's Seamanship* (1871), a book Conrad kept all his life, and passed on to his son Borys. Conrad also emphasises the duties involved in *The Nigger of the 'Narcissus'* (1897), describing his central figure, Captain Allistoun, disembarking after a disastrous, exhausting voyage, yet still remembering to tell his Mate to look after the chronometers next morning.

As the worked example in Figure 2.2 shows, based on a chronometer '1m 0s fast for mean noon at Greenwich on November 10th, 1884', inaccuracies established by regular checking had to be carefully factored into calculations. These were further complicated by difficulties in establishing the true position of the sun. Refraction of its light by the earth's atmosphere causes its apparent and actual positions to diverge. Other disparities result from the earth's movement around its orbit, placing the sun, at noon, in a position in the sky which differs slightly from day to day. As this orbit is elliptical, such changes are not regular, and nor is the sun's apparent size, complicating the reduction of its disc to the precise point required for navigational computations. These also need to take account of the irregular shape of the earth – an imperfect, oblate sphere, slightly fatter at the equator – and the position from which observations are made, not usually exactly at sea level, but twenty or thirty feet above it, on a ship's deck or bridge.

As in dead reckoning, shortcuts and standard devices were available to help manage these complex factors in practice – such as the 'Equation of Time', dealing with the effects of the earth's orbit on the sun's apparent position, which figures in the latter stages of the example in Figure 2.2. Shortcuts might seem viable, or attractive, in other ways – some of the detailed adjustments outlined above perhaps seeming insignificant enough to be discarded in daily calculations. Nautical experts in the late nineteenth century occasionally expressed concern about how much *was* overlooked in daily navigational practice. They feared that officers relied too readily on casual 'rule-of-thumb', or deployed imperfectly the principles they had 'crammed' for their examinations.[10] There was some cause for their concern. The year before his First Officer's examination, Conrad had fortunately left a ship, the *Riversdale*, shortly before its Captain sailed sixty miles off course during the first hundred miles of a journey. Yet such errancy was unusual. For obvious reasons, even minor inaccuracies may prove disastrous at sea, particularly if their effects are allowed to accumulate during a long voyage. They were in any case wholly unacceptable to Conrad's august Board of Trade examiners. An 'ideal of Perfect Accuracy' shaped the Board's examinations as much as its 'Notices to Mariners'. Its 'Notice to Candidates' emphasised in 1880 that examinees were 'expected to bring their answers to all problems within, or not to exceed, a margin of one mile of position from a correct result'. Newton's *Guide* warned in 1884 that 'it is now well-known that at these Examinations the *strictest accuracy* is required in all calculations'.[11]

---

[10] See, for example, Allingham, *Board of Trade Examinations*, 116 et seq.
[11] The 'Notice to Candidates' is reproduced in Ainsley, *A Guide Book to the Local Marine Board Examination*, 8; Newton's *Guide,* iii.

The exacting nature of these demands, and the complexity of calculations required to meet them, suggest that Conrad might be judged to have done moderately well to fail his Board of Trade examinations on only two occasions – or even, as it turns out, very nearly three. Though omitting to mention in 'Outside Literature' that the successful examination for his First Officer's certificate was a resit, Conrad acknowledges that his performance did briefly 'endanger the course of [his] 'humble career at sea', and that he was saved from failure only by the intervention of a friendly examiner's assistant. In 'consideration ... of all [his] other answers being correct', this assistant was generous enough to inform him that he had 'fourteen minutes yet' in which to check his paper and eliminate an error. Conrad was nevertheless appalled at the scale of difficulties likely to be involved:

> I looked at the face of the clock; it was round like the moon; white as a ghost, unfeeling, idiotic. I sat down under it with the conviction of the crushing materiality of Time ... For no man could have gone over all those figures in fourteen minutes. (32)

A Personal Record mentions an oral examination taking as much as three hours: written examinations lasted for five or more. This was time enough, as Conrad emphasises, for more pages of calculation than could conceivably be checked in fourteen minutes. Fortunately, in his mention of the time remaining, the assistant had also hinted at where the error had occurred – minutes, of course, also being fractions of a degree, of longitude in this case. Taking the hint, Conrad spotted that he had written 'the letter W instead of the letter E at the bottom of a page full of figures', and quickly made the necessary correction (32).

Much evidence suggests that – after further struggles with his Master's examinations – Conrad went on to deploy the calculative, navigational skills outlined above thoroughly competently. As a letter of 1903 suggests, successful acquisition and exercise of these skills remained a lifelong source of pride, Conrad remarking that

> during my life as a seaman ... I was conscientious, passing all the necessary examinations, winning the respect of people (in my modest milieu) who ... attested to my being a 'good sailor and a trustworthy ship's officer'. In what it seems to me were pretty difficult situations, I think I always remained faithful to the traditions of the profession.[12]

---

[12] Letter to Kazimierz Waliszewski, 5 December 1903, *Collected Letters*, III, 89.

Pride in good seamanship remains in evidence two decades later, towards the end of Conrad's life, in 'Geography and Some Explorers' (1924) – another memoir included, like 'Outside Literature', in *Last Essays*. It recalls Conrad's unhesitating reliance on his navigational skills when using the Torres Straits, in 1888, as a route from Sydney to Mauritius for his first command, the *Otago* – 'very likely the first and certainly the last merchant ship that carried a cargo that way', he claims, though perhaps slightly immodestly.[13] His decision to risk sailing this way, two years after failure in his first Master's examination, at any rate suggests how confident he eventually became in the knowledge and skill the Board of Trade required. This, in turn, confirms how comprehensively he mastered the demands of the examinations described – in areas including geometry, trigonometry, chronometry, logarithms and navigational astronomy, as well as the perpetually repeated use of the global reference point of Greenwich to determine positioning in time and space.

All these areas of expertise – each manifestly 'outside literature' – obviously contrast comprehensively with the interests in adventure, romance, spirit and illusion shaping Conrad's second, literary career. Antinomies between the two sets of values might in one way be used just to consolidate conventional biographical judgements of Conrad as 'homo duplex'– a view he endorses in one of his letters,[14] and extends in *A Personal Record*, accepting summaries of his character as 'romantic . . . realist also' (111). In this view, Conrad was fated to sustain into later life values inscribed on his early years not only by Marryat's novels. His Polish childhood was shaped instead by antitheses between the romantic ideals of his father, or of his early reading, and the more realistic outlook favoured by his uncle and eventual guardian, Tadeusz Bobrowski. Divided careers, in this interpretation, naturally extended a divided self. 'All those figures', demanding perfect accuracy in Board of Trade Examinations, simply offer the best demonstration of how thoroughly Conrad was equipped to work outside literature – dealing with the 'rational and practical grounds' of life in the Merchant Navy – as well as within it.

Yet Conrad, obviously, did not simply swap selves when he ceased to work at sea, but continued in his writing career to negotiate con-

---

[13] *Last Essays*, 16. In *Joseph Conrad: Master Mariner*, Villiers describes the route as 'officially recommended' though also 'potentially dangerous' (85). It does seem to have been avoided at least by larger ships, and required the arrangement of extra insurance with the *Otago*'s owners, as well as the careful navigation 'Geography and Some Explorers' describes.

[14] Letter to Kazimierz Waliszewski, *Collected Letters*, 89.

flicts between the values of seamanship and of authorship, as 'Outside Literature' suggests. Tensions between responsibility and romance, calculation and glamour, are especially evident – and most illuminating for literary criticism, rather than only biography – in Conrad's early fiction, when his career at sea remained freshest in memory. Written early in 1897, and published in November of that year, his short story, 'Karain: A Memory', reproduces particularly clearly the antinomies defined in 'Outside Literature'. These are highlighted in contrasts between the extravagant imagination of the central figure, Karain, and the steadier views of the narrator, commander of a trading schooner. The dependable measures of Greenwich Mean Time, this narrator finds, reach what seem the ends of the earth, resisting the wildness of nature – and imagination – even in its remotest regions. In a calm moment following a deafening thunderstorm, he notes that 'the silence became so profound that we all could hear distinctly the two chronometers in my cabin ticking along with unflagging speed against one another'. Later, in a moment of respite from Karain's torrential imaginings, he notes that

> the silence was profound; but it seemed full of noiseless phantoms, of things sorrowful, shadowy, and mute, in whose invisible presence the firm, pulsating beat of the two ship's chronometers ticking off steadily the seconds of Greenwich Time seemed to me a protection and a relief.[15]

Descriptions of chronometers 'ticking along . . . *against* one another' incidentally confirm that ships carrying two could not count on them agreeing. But the passage and the story as a whole throw wider doubts on the 'unflagging' measures they provide. Their mechanical, systematic accuracies offer assurance of a solidly manageable, calculable world, dispelling the 'noiseless phantoms' and 'invisible presences' terrorising Karain. The story nevertheless hints that the exclusion of these elements may be as much a loss as a relief. A good deal of credence is accorded Karain's complaint that British sailors, the narrator included, might be people 'who live in unbelief; to whom day is day, and night is night – nothing more, because you understand all things seen, and despise all else' (59). The narrator himself begins to suggest an affirmative aspect in 'invisible presences' – in

---

[15] Joseph Conrad, 'Karain: a Memory' (1897) in *Heart of Darkness and Other Tales* (Oxford: Oxford University Press, 2008), 43, 56. Subsequent references are to this edition.

a stir invisible and living as of subtle breaths. All the ghosts driven out of the unbelieving West . . . all the homeless ghosts of an unbelieving world . . . all the exiled and charming shades of loved women; all the beautiful and tender ghosts of ideals . . . ghosts of friends admired, trusted, traduced, betrayed. (62)

By the end of the story, when the narrator returns to London, there is a strong suggestion that its solid, squalid city streets may not be 'as real' as the 'world of sunshine and illusions' he encountered in Karain's imaginative domain (67, 60).

Contrasts between reason and illusion, responsibility and romance, rarely recur quite so explicitly in Conrad's later fiction. Versions of them nevertheless figure in much of his writing. Similar conflicts might be discerned between another restrained, reliable, seaman-narrator, Marlow, and imaginative but erratic characters – the 'romantic' Jim, in *Lord Jim* (1900); even Kurtz, in *Heart of Darkness* (1899) – with whom he nevertheless feels some complicity (165). Similarly mixed feelings are shown disturbing the inexperienced, insecure captain in 'The Secret Sharer' (1912) – another 'homo duplex', gradually construing a guilty intruder on his ship as a second, alternate self. Conrad's fiction also contains several minor instances – and a major one – in which he re-examines doubts 'Karain' raises regarding orders imposed by Greenwich and its chronometries, or by navigational exactitudes more generally. In *Lord Jim*, this scepticism figures in contrasts between navigation's 'strictest accuracy' and errancies in human natures, or even in nature itself. Jim's enjoyment of the 'high peace of sea and sky' on the bridge of his ship is heightened by the reassuring proximity of navigational apparatus – 'parallel rulers with a pair of dividers'; a chart with 'the ship's position at last noon . . . marked with a small black cross'. A sense of security is further enhanced by the apparently seamless match between 'the white streak of the wake drawn . . . straight by the ship's keel upon the sea' and 'the black line drawn by the pencil upon the chart' (21–2). Yet this reassuring congruence between navigation, measurement and the sea soon proves wholly deceptive – the ship striking something unrecorded on any chart, precipitating the crisis which ruins most of Jim's illusions forever.

Later in the novel, Captain Brierly displays equally thorough competence in computation and navigation, yet to equally nugatory effect. His first mate recalls how Brierly checked the compass, reset the log-and-line apparatus, 'marked off the ship's position with a tiny cross and wrote the date and the time . . . seventeen, eight, four a.m.', and left precise instructions about a twenty-degree course change anticipated after thirty-two further miles (50–1). Yet none of this comprehensive nautical exactness – of just the kind examined in the 'Day's Work' section of Conrad's examinations in the 1880s – restrains Brierly from suicide. After ensuring everything is in strict order, he vanishes forever into the sea, leaving behind his fine chronometer watch, a reward for outstanding service, tied to the ship's rail. Hanging by its golden chain above the endless, timeless rolling of the waves, it suggests the limits or irrelevance of human agency in the midst of a waste of waters – a summary image of archetypal, unresolvable conflict between calculation and chaos, orderliness and the measureless immensities of the sea.[16]

Later episodes in *Lord Jim* extend some of these implications, particularly when chronometry is involved. While briefly imprisoned, Jim finds that it is only while tinkering with 'a nickel clock of New England make' that the 'true perception of his extreme peril dawned upon him'. He drops it 'like a hot potato' to seek his escape, yet finds that memories of his task – even the words, 'mending the clock. Mending the clock' – pursue him with nightmarish insistence as he flees (192–3). This equation of 'extreme peril' with the clock resembles Conrad's account of the last moments of that examination described in 'Outside Literature'. The examiner's notification of scant minutes available for corrections provokes much more than a nervous glance at the time. Instead, it leads into surprisingly intense, graphic reflections, focused on a strangely spectral yet animate clock – 'white as a ghost, unfeeling, idiotic' – and towards a wider horror of temporality itself, of 'the crushing materiality of Time'.

In Conrad's fiction generally – not only in *Lord Jim* – clocks and chronometry are often similarly associated with crisis, figuring in roles equally crushing, critical, or just peculiar.[17] Throughout much of his writing, a kind of nervous tick remains audible in Conrad's imagination – as troubling and inescapable as the clock in the crocodile pursuing the Captain in J. M. Barrie's *Peter Pan* (1904).[18] In *Nostromo* (1904), Captain Mitchell's interrogation by Sotillo's troops is oddly interrupted by Sotillo himself, first using his prisoner's 'sixty-guinea

---

[16] A comparable antinomy appears at the end of Conrad's *The Secret Agent: A Simple Tale* (1907; Harmondsworth: Penguin, 1967) when Winnie's wedding ring – another of the novel's 'innumerable circles' – is found 'stuck to the wood in a bit of wet' after she, too, has committed suicide by jumping overboard (45, 247). Subsequent references are to this edition.
[17] See Higdon, 'Conrad's Clocks'.
[18] Biographers suggest that the figure of Captain Hook might derive partly from J. M. Barrie's personal impressions of Conrad. See Stape, *The Several Lives of Joseph Conrad*, 132.

gold half-chronometer' – like Brierly's, a reward for outstanding service – as a means of threatening him, then becoming so mesmerised by its mechanism that he forgets Mitchell altogether. In *The Shadow-Line* (1917), the old Captain's powers – sinister or even supernatural – seem to include dying with a navigator's exactitude, 'as near noon as possible', while his mate is 'on deck with his sextant to "take the sun"'. In *Under Western Eyes* (1911), Razumov finds himself so unnerved by an encounter with Haldin that he drops his watch before he can see the time. Looking 'wildly about as if for some means of seizing upon time which seemed to have escaped him altogether' he fixes upon something he has never previously noticed. Though this is only 'the faint sounds of some town clock tolling the hour', he nevertheless finds that 'the faint deep boom of the distant clock seemed to explode in his head'.[19]

Holes in Space and Time

Clocks and chronology figure much more extensively in Conrad's *The Secret Agent* (1907) – in its account of Verloc's plot to blow up Greenwich Observatory, and in roles assigned to timepieces and time-measurement which are as odd as any to be found in fiction in English. Often endowed with animate, even human qualities, clocks are apparently able to 'steal through ... minutes' behind characters' backs, or to steal into the Verlocs' bedroom 'as if for the sake of company' – apparently disdaining any 'lonely' obligation merely to 'count off ... ticks into the abyss of eternity' (121, 149, 150). Murder as well as stealing seems within their powers – figuratively, at any rate, when Winnie Verloc misconstrues the sound of blood dropping from the knife used to kill her husband, hearing this not as dripping but as 'ticking growing fast and furious like the pulse of an insane clock' (214). Other characters further conflate temporal measurement with murder or destruction. The anarchist Ossipon reflects on the 'full twenty seconds' which would inevitably elapse between the Professor's activation of the detonator he always carries and the ensuing explosion (62). Chief Inspector Heat thinks with terror of a still shorter interval, reflecting that one of 'the mysteries of conscious existence' may be that 'ages of atrocious pain and mental torture

---

[19] Joseph Conrad, *Nostromo: A Tale of the Seaboard* (1904; Harmondsworth: Penguin, 1969), 278 – subsequent references are to this edition; Joseph Conrad, *The Shadow-Line: A Confession* (1917; Oxford: Oxford University Press, 2003), 47; Joseph Conrad, *Under Western Eyes* (1911; Harmondsworth: Penguin, 1975), 59, 61.

could be contained between two successive winks of an eye' (79). Above all, the great master clock of Greenwich apparently takes a terrible revenge for the failed plot to destroy it, looming unscathed above shattered fragments of the novel's most sympathetic character, Stevie, whose body-parts the explosion strews around the first meridian like 'the by-products of a butcher's shop' (79).

Threatening roles accorded these clocks, and to the Observatory, might invite a straightforward view of influences those career-endangering examinations exercised on Conrad's later imagination – particularly given the dominant role occupied by Greenwich in the computations they required, and in navigational duties throughout his maritime career. In the example in Figure 2.2, Greenwich figures eight times, in two pages, as a defining point in time and space. Much the same rate of reference is maintained throughout Newton's *Guide* and other primers available in the 1880s. Struggling with examination preparations at the time, and with navigational calculations during long years at sea, might not Conrad have dreamed vengefully himself, like Verloc's paymaster Vladimir, of 'having a go at astronomy', throwing 'a bomb into pure mathematics', even 'blowing up ... the first meridian' (36–7)? Mightn't the plot of *The Secret Agent*, in other words, represent a kind of wish-fulfilment – a long-deferred, imaginative revenge against strictest accuracies, defining meridians, and exigent astronomical and chronometric calculations filling all those pages of figures?

Neither *The Secret Agent*, of course, nor Conrad's life and work more generally, support any such interpretation – directly, at any rate. 'Fidelity to ... the ideal of Perfect Accuracy', and to norms and controls required by a maritime career, contributed to values sustained by Conrad not only in his work outside literature, but also within it. His writing is driven not by any simple rejection of commitments defining his shipboard responsibilities, but rather the exploration of their tensions and interactions with contrary factors – including, as in 'Karain', the potentials of imagination itself. After so many years at sea, Conrad could not have supported straightforwardly, even in fiction, an attack on Greenwich – the principal institution securing the safety of mariners, globally guaranteeing for them the accurate charting of lands, seas and hours. Conrad, in any case, makes clear his disgusted assessment of the original attack on the Observatory, in 1894, on which *The Secret Agent* is based. His 'Author's Note' describes it as 'a blood-stained inanity of so fatuous a kind that it was impossible to fathom its origin by any reasonable or even unreasonable process of thought' (9). Little more sympathy is directly apparent in the novel itself, which depicts Verloc and other so-called anarchists involved in the attack as gross, lazy and disreputable, treating them with unrelenting irony throughout.

At other levels of *The Secret Agent*, figural rather than explicit, different sympathies are nevertheless discernible – even covert complicities either with forms of anarchy, or at any rate with the 'unreasonable process of thought' Conrad ostensibly disdains. Scarcely capable of reasonable thought, Stevie relies instead on emotion to arrive at the most universal and reliable political conclusion *The Secret Agent* offers – 'bad world for poor people' (143). In some of his actions, he also proves himself a more effective anarchist than anyone in Verloc's circle, in one instance responding to supposed 'injustice and oppression' by setting off explosions, not at Greenwich, but by detonating fireworks in a City office. Description of the ensuing chaos – of 'silk hats and elderly businessmen . . . rolling independently down the stairs' – suggests at least minor disruption to capitalist enterprise (18). A more frequent activity, also anarchic in its way, is Stevie's use of 'compass and pencil' to draw 'innumerable circles, concentric, eccentric; a coruscating whirl of circles that by their tangled multitude of repeated curves, uniformity of form, and confusion of intersecting lines suggested a rendering of cosmic chaos . . . chaos and eternity' (18–19, 45–6, 193). In a novel so concerned with the institution of Greenwich, Stevie's chaotically drawn circles readily suggest themselves as parodies of the exactly defined meridians, centred on the Observatory, and precisely partitioning the world's space and time. Stevie's tangled, intersecting circles may also correspond to the kind of diagrams, requiring identification of meridians and other divisions inscribed on the terrestrial globe, which Conrad encountered so copiously in primers and examinations in the 1880s (Fig. 2.3).[20] These encounters with reasonable but exigent process of thought may have been demanding – or maddening – enough to have encouraged imagination of anarchic alternatives, in Stevie's chaotic circles, a quarter of a century later.

The Secret Agent demonstrates another reaction against Greenwich's rationalisations – of temporality, in particular – through its extraordinary narrative form. This is unconventional enough to have led one commentator to conclude that in *The Secret Agent* 'the true

---

[20] Board of Trade examinations often began by requiring candidates to identify various lines or meridians drawn across the globe. The example in Figure 2.3 is taken from Morris, *Answers to the Definitions*, 57–8, and reproduced by permission of the Trustees of the National Library of Scotland.

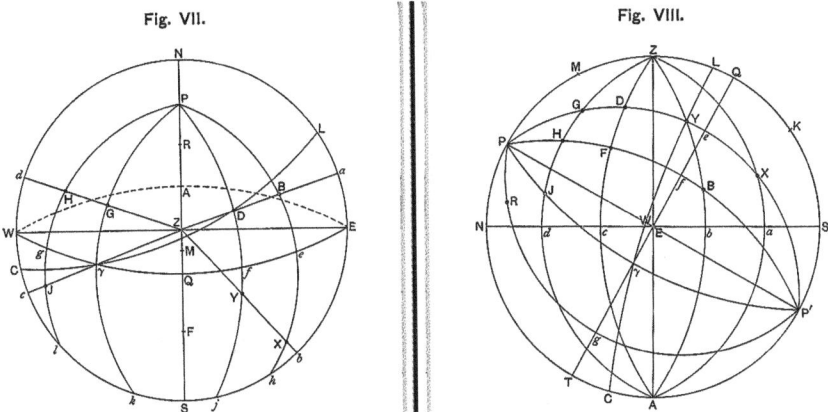

Fig. 2.3 Meridians and divisions to be identified in Board of Trade navigation examinations.

anarchist . . . is none other than the author himself'.[21] Conrad's strategies might be more appropriately defined not as altogether anarchic, but comprehensively anachronic, and aptly characterised by some of Inspector Heat's reflections about time and its relations to 'conscious existence'. Descriptions of his thoughts allude to 'unexpected solutions of continuity, sudden holes in space and time', and to Heat's inclination to rise 'above the vulgar conception of time' (76, 78). The novel regularly follows him in this direction, repeatedly engaging in 'solutions of continuity' of its own. News of the Greenwich explosion, for example, appears early, in chapter 4, but it is not until chapter 10 that details of it are provided, and only in the following chapter that the nature of the plot leading up to it is described. Such 'solutions of continuity' develop still more strikingly when the narrative is closest to the 'conscious existence' of characters – particularly in its account of Heat's thoughts during his uneasy conversation with the Professor. This inserts a seven-page analepsis – describing Heat's experiences earlier in the day, and earlier in his life – between successive remarks in the conversation; almost 'between two successive winks of an eye'. A later chapter likewise records of a conversation shortly before Verloc's murder that 'a few seconds only had elapsed since the last word had been uttered aloud', yet this interval proves sufficient for Winnie's recollection, not just of hours, but of years. Two pages of these recollections include memories not only of her

---

[21] Erdinast-Vulcan, '"Sudden Holes in Space and Time"', 210.

childhood and her marriage to Verloc, but also of the seven years of 'domestic feeling' that have ensued (198).

Strikingly deployed throughout *The Secret Agent* – especially in following the consciousnesses of characters – anachronies of this kind extend tactics that had been developing in Conrad's fiction since the turn of the century. *Heart of Darkness* (1899) and *Lord Jim* (1900) are presented largely as supposedly oral narratives – ordered by the idiosyncratic memory and associations of the narrator, Marlow – ensuring that each novel takes the form of a 'free and wandering tale'.[22] *Lord Jim*, in particular, is more faithful to the order in which Marlow first learns of events, or later recollects them, than the sequence in which these supposedly occurred. *Nostromo* (1904) wanders still more freely away from straightforward chronology, even without the sanction of an oral narrator. Instead, Captain Mitchell's 'relation of . . . "historical events"' in Part III, supposedly delivered directly and garrulously to a visitor to Sulaco, seems rather straightforward – 'stereotyped', in the novel's own description – in comparison to the extravagant anachronies shaping much of the rest of the novel (389). Reliant on repeated, extended analepses, especially in the opening section, Conrad's construction forces readers to share, unusually immediately and intimately, in a long history of barely coherent events, and in the ensuing struggles for political and social order in the chaotic South American republic the novel depicts.

As the previous chapter discussed, tactics of this kind are, of course, not altogether Conrad's invention, but extend instead narrative's perennial potential to open up gaps between *fabula* and *sjuzet*, and to wander imaginatively away from measured temporality. Yet anachronies are developed much more extensively and purposively in Conrad's writing than in most fiction in the nineteenth century or at the start of the twentieth. Their use contributed centrally to the innovativeness Ford Madox Ford claimed for Conrad's work, and his own, as a result of their collaboration in the first years of the new century. Ford recalls that 'it became very early evident' in their work together that the novel should not 'go straight forward', or 'work . . . life chronologically', but instead 'work backwards and forwards over [the] past'.[23] Later commentators have generally confirmed Ford's view of how early this conclusion was reached, and of how significant Conrad's writing proved – in this way and others – in the emergence of new fictional forms in

---

[22] Joseph Conrad, 'Author's Note' to *Lord Jim*, 7.
[23] Ford, *Joseph Conrad*, 129–30.

the years that followed. Fredric Jameson, for example, describes Conrad's work – *Lord Jim* particularly – marking a 'strategic fault-line' in the emergence of literary modernism, and of twentieth-century imagination and culture more generally.²⁴

Whatever Ford's share in originally establishing this 'fault-line', his later fiction aptly demonstrates ways modernist narrative continued to develop the complex structures of the kind that Conrad's novels introduced. *The Good Soldier* (1914) replicates a form of the supposedly oral narrative shaping *Lord Jim* – one which its narrator acknowledges 'goes back . . . goes forward' in 'a very rambling way'. In *Parade's End* (1924–8) – like many of his modernist contemporaries in the 1920s – Ford moves on to anachronous structures reflecting, like those in *The Secret Agent,* characters' recollections, mental processes and 'conscious existence' generally.²⁵ Modernist fiction follows Conrad not only structurally, in its treatment of this inner experience, but often explicitly, in its descriptions of characters' encounters with 'the crushing materiality of Time'. In finding that the striking hours and their 'great shock to the nervous system' resembles being 'violently struck on the head', Virginia Woolf's Orlando, for example, clearly shares some of Razumov's experience of a clock's chimes seeming to 'explode in his head' in *Under Western Eyes*.²⁶

Conrad's early-twentieth-century novels, in other words, offer 'very early' examples of a chronotype shaping much modernist fiction in the following three decades – one in which often-explicit hostility to the clock is matched by anachronies which liberate characters and readers from some of its constraints. Conrad's work, though, marks an especially distinctive 'fault-line' in literary history, not only in exemplifying new narrative forms, but in showing so clearly how and why they were made essential by the new pressures of the age. Conrad's examination ordeals and career at sea ensured that he encountered some of these pressures substantially earlier, and more acutely, than other modernist authors. Henry James sums up the effects of this sharp, early engagement with the 'rational and practical grounds' of modernity when suggesting, in a letter to Conrad, that 'the prodigy of [his] past experience' confers on him 'an authority that no one has approached'. James adds that 'no one has *known* – for intellectual use – the things you know', evidently discounting the possibility that other mariners might have made intellectual use of their experiences,

---

²⁴ Jameson, *The Political Unconscious*, 206.
²⁵ Ford Madox Ford, *The Good Soldier: A Tale of Passion* (1914; Harmondsworth: Penguin, 1977), 167. See also Chapter 4.
²⁶ Virginia Woolf, *Orlando* (1928; Harmondsworth: Penguin, 1975), 210, 216.

and thus overlooking the achievement of another seaman-novelist, his compatriot Herman Melville.[27] In *Pierre, or, the Ambiguities* (1852), Melville is as alert as Conrad to the advancing powers of Greenwich – to 'the great Greenwich hill and tower from which the universal meridians are far out into infinity reckoned'.[28] *Pierre* even compares Greenwich's chronological controls and world-spanning meridians with the ubiquitous powers of deity, envisaging the adjustment of chronometers under the central authority of GMT as equivalent to belief in an omnipotent and omnipresent God.

A certain uniqueness can nevertheless be ascribed to Conrad's work, not on account only of his maritime career, but of the timing of his most intense engagement with the computational competencies it required. Conrad's struggles with his Master's examinations, between July and November of 1886, might account for his setting *The Secret Agent* back in that year, rather than 1894, when the actual attack on Greenwich Observatory took place. A more epochal focus is offered by events late in 1884. Conrad's unsuccessful examination for his First Officer's ticket, on 17 November, followed five weeks after the Prime Meridian Conference's major resolutions had been publicised in the world's press – extensively in *The Times* on 15 October – and only a fortnight or so after the conference itself had ended. Conrad's examination, and his preparation for a second attempt two weeks or so later, coincided exactly with a period in which, as Vladimir remarks in *The Secret Agent*, 'the whole civilized world ha[d] heard of Greenwich' (37). In contemporary awareness generally, late in 1884 – and not only in the navigational guides Conrad found himself obliged to study yet more carefully – Greenwich's chronometries and meridians occupied a peculiarly pre-eminent position. Conrad's confrontation with 'the crushing materiality of Time', fourteen minutes before the end of his resit, on 3 December 1884, was therefore crucial not only for his personal life and imagination, but in encapsulating new global pressures, new emphases on computation and calculation, experienced by a whole age. Further factors contributing to this ubiquitous, calculative materiality of time are considered in the next chapter, along with, in the one following, the modernist chronotype they helped to shape.

---

[27] Letter to Conrad of 1 November 1906, concerning his memoir *The Mirror of the Sea*. *Henry James: Letters*, IV, 419.
[28] Herman Melville, *Pierre, or, the Ambiguities* (1852; New York: HarperCollins, 1995), 302.

Chapter 3

'Wheels within Wheels':
D. H. Lawrence, Industrial Time and War Time

The terrible bondage of this tick-tack of time, this twitching of the hands of the clock, this eternal repetition of hours and days – oh God, it was too awful to contemplate. And there was no escape from it, no escape . . .

How she suffered, lying there alone, confronted by the terrible clock, with its eternal tick-tack. All life, all life resolved itself into this: tick-tack, tick-tack, tick-tack; then the striking of the hour; then the tick-tack, tick-tack, and the twitching of the clock-fingers . . .

A horrible mechanical twitching forward over the face of the hours . . . always the great white clock-face . . . the eternal, mechanical, monotonous clock-face of time.[1]

Antipathies to the clock Gudrun Brangwen expresses are as vehement as any in English literature. Extending over several pages in *Women in Love* (1921), they suggest that 'bondage' to measured time gripped the society D. H. Lawrence portrays still more strongly than it had the world Joseph Conrad describes in *The Secret Agent* (1907). Factors contributing to this tightening grip – hardening the influence of those considered in the previous two chapters – can be traced throughout the writing Lawrence began in 1913, variously entitled 'The Sisters' or 'The Wedding Ring'. This was eventually divided into two long novels: *The Rainbow* (1915), following several generations of the Brangwen family in the nineteenth century

---

[1] D. H. Lawrence, *Women in Love* (1921; Harmondsworth: Penguin, 1971), 522–3. Subsequent references are to this edition.

and early in the twentieth, and the work Lawrence considered 'more or less a sequel', *Women in Love*, set in the troubled years around the Great War.² Analysis of this extended fictional history, and of differences in mood and structure between the two novels, helps suggest why 'the terrible clock' had come to seem so threatening by the time *Women in Love* was published – on the threshold of the 1920s, modernism's major decade.

Circle and Line

Early pages of *The Rainbow* record how the Brangwen family 'had lived for generations on the Marsh Farm': on 'horizontal land' in Nottinghamshire, beneath an 'empty sky' whose horizon is broken only by the distant church tower of a country town. Life for the family has long remained almost as featureless temporally as it is topographically, changing only through the kind of 'age old rhythms' or eternal circles considered in chapters 1 and 2 – natural, annual cycles of 'earth and sky and beast and green plants'. Until, that is,

> about 1840, a canal was constructed across the meadows of the Marsh Farm, connecting the newly-opened collieries of the Erewash Valley. A high embankment travelled along the fields to carry the canal . . .
>
> Then, a short time afterwards, a colliery was sunk on the other side of the canal, and in a while the Midland Railway came down the valley . . . and the invasion was complete. The town grew rapidly . . . red, crude houses plastered on the valley in masses.

'The rhythmic run of the winding engines' and 'the shrill whistle of the trains . . . announcing the far-off come near and imminent' leave the Brangwens feeling 'strangers in their own place'.³ Referred to as 'the cut', the canal separates them not only from part of their land. The changes it represents, bringing the once far-off world of industry into their valley, also cuts them off from the older cyclic rhythms of

---

[2] D. H. Lawrence, letter of 19 December 1916 to Lady Cynthia Asquith, *Letters*, III, 55. *Women in Love* generally leaves the date of its action unspecified, though an indication is offered in its closing pages when Ursula refers to a remark made by the Kaiser in 1915.

[3] D. H. Lawrence, *The Rainbow* (1915; Harmondsworth: Penguin, 1971), 7, 9, 11–13. Subsequent references are to this edition.

agricultural life and the almost unvarying conditions experienced by generations of their predecessors. Circling seasons of earth, sky, beast and plant give way to development instead of repetition – to linear, forward movements as marked on the temporal landscape as the new lines cut by railway and canal appear in the physical one.

Typically, too, of the experience of the nineteenth century – much as the Romantic poets had warned in its early decades – the 'forward' movement of industrial progress exercises more and more negative influences on this rural landscape and its inhabitants. The Brangwens of the 1840s begin to be troubled by the 'faint, sulphurous smell of pit-refuse burning': for later generations of the family, industrialisation takes on a more thoroughly infernal aspect (13). For Gudrun's sister Ursula, the town she visits in the Yorkshire coalfields suggests 'death rather than life' (345). Its miners seem 'not like living people, but like spectres', their 'bodies and lives subjected in slavery to that symmetric monster of the colliery [which] . . . held all matter, living and dead, in its service' (345, 350). 'Green meadows and rough country' are still just visible beyond the town, but within it nature and 'organic formation' are wholly subjugate to 'mechanical activity': to 'the great colliery, to the great machine' (345, 346, 350).

Yet green meadows and organic life do not disappear from *The Rainbow*, nor does the older temporality of recurrence and renewal entirely give way to development and change. As if keeping the distant church tower in view, characters remain tenuously in touch with perennial temporal cycles through the religious calendar and its annual festivals, even when finding some of these have grown 'flat and stale'. 'The year of Christianity, the epic of the soul of mankind' still offers a vestigial 'rhythm of eternity in a ragged, inconsequential life' – 'still it was there, even if it were faint and inadequate. The cycle of creation still wheeled in the Church year' (279, 280). *The Rainbow* also indicates cyclic aspects in secular experience, still shaped by recurrence as well as change. Each of the three generations the novel portrays moves on through growing challenges in the life of the times, but also conforms – though with dwindling surety – to fundamental, repeated patterns of marriage, procreation and renewal. These remain tenuously evident even in the experience of Ursula, the last of the Brangwens described in *The Rainbow*. She ends the novel troubled and isolated: distanced from family, friends and community; distressed by an unfulfilling relationship and the miscarriage which follows. Yet she still finds potential for continuity and renewal in the natural world, comparing herself with 'acorns in February lying on the floor of a wood', free 'to take new root, to create a new knowledge of Eternity in the flux of Time' (493).

Symbolic patterns in *The Rainbow* emphasise this potential, still to be found somehow circling around linear drives towards progress and change. Appropriately in a novel making up half of 'The Wedding Ring', semi-circular shapes figure prominently – rainbows and rounded arches often symbolising the dynamic integration achievable within a wholeheartedly successful relationship. By steadily inclining towards each other, disparate individuals establish stable mutual support, leaving their children secure as if beneath a 'span of the heavens' – between 'the pillar of fire and the pillar of cloud', with 'assurance on [their] right hand and the assurance on [their] left' (97). Symbol and biblical allusion of this kind add an element of transcendence to Lawrence's description of secular relationships, allowing them to figure in *The Rainbow* as a substitute for older forms of faith and the fading vision of the Church. The novel ends with 'the old church-tower standing up in hideous obsoleteness above raw new houses on the crest of the hill' (495). Yet renewed promise appears in the span of the heavens when Ursula notices an immense rainbow forming faintly in the clouds. It suggests to her a 'new architecture' – a wider, overarching form of the new creation offered by the acorns, revivifying 'the old brittle corruption of houses and factories' and a society of 'sordid people', 'colliers . . . buried alive' (495–6). Optimistically, or perhaps just mystically, Lawrence's concluding vision promises some redemption from the rising flood of industrialisation, which destroys – literally, when 'the cut' overflows – the old, secure life of the Brangwens and their land.

Little of this promise survives into the second part of 'The Wedding Ring'. *Women in Love* is much less optimistic in its view of relations between industry and the natural world, and between individuals in an increasingly disintegral society. One reason for this darker mood – another is considered later in this chapter – can be found in the changing priorities and growing powers of industrialisation which *Women in Love* envisages. In the coalfield that Ursula visits in *The Rainbow*, the colliers' subjugation to 'the great machine' and the destruction of 'organic formation' seem disastrous by-products of industrial development. In *Women in Love*, they appear instead as consequences of deliberate strategy – of radical new management policies imposed on his family's mines by Gudrun's lover, Gerald Crich. His father, Thomas Crich, had 'thought only of the men', seeking to 'benefit the men every time' (252). Gerald, on the other hand, has 'conceived the pure instrumentality of mankind', and is determined, in modernising the pits, to ensure 'the subordination of every organic unit to the great mechanical purpose' (250, 260).

In Gerald's new planning, 'individuals did not matter in the least', functioning merely as 'instruments', more or less efficiently, within a 'great and perfect system that subjected life to pure mathematical principles' (251, 259, 260). In 'The Industrial Magnate' chapter of *Women in Love,* these principles are shown steadily converting the colliery and its workers into 'a great and perfect machine, a system, an activity of pure order, pure mechanical repetition, repetition *ad infinitum*' (256). Perfect realisation of this system also offers Gerald – as owner-manager and 'God of the machine' – a kind of 'eternity' (256). He finds 'his eternal and his infinite in the pure machine-principle of perfect coordination into one pure, complex, infinitely repeated motion, like the spinning of a wheel . . . repetition through eternity, to infinity' (256).

This 'eternal and infinite' obviously contrasts as sharply as possible with the eternity Ursula finds among her February acorns. Gerald's 'productive spinning' banishes any of the rhythms or natural cycles still faintly turning through lives described in *The Rainbow* (256). Mechanical activity displaces organic formation. Infinite time passes from God or nature to the God of the machine; from wheeling seasons and their fertile, eternal renewals to the endless spinning of factory wheels. Before long, the same mechanism extends into Gerald's own nature, taking over 'his own pure will, his own mind' (257). The colliery is so thoroughly, systematically coordinated, it scarcely requires any further intervention: 'the whole system was now so perfect that Gerald was hardly necessary any more' (261). This leaves him with a sense of emptiness, even 'sterile horror' (262). Gudrun experiences this horror in a much sharper form – one integral to her intense dread of the 'eternal, mechanical, monotonous' tick-tack of the clock. She fears that 'the same ticking, the same twitching across the dial' is all that is offered by Gerald's 'body, his motion, his life' (523). Mechanical activity and mechanical repetition seem to her to have overtaken his entire enterprise, leaving Gerald himself merely its most complex, central component. Her nightmare vision of 'terrible bondage' to the clock concludes by extending still further her equation of measured time with the mechanisation of modern industry and, ultimately, of all who work within it. Managers and workers alike, she fears, have become merely 'wheels within wheels' –

> pure machines, pure wills, that work like clockwork, in perpetual repetition . . . the miner, with a thousand wheels, and then the electrician, with three thousand, and the underground manager, with twenty

thousand, and the general manager with a hundred thousand little wheels working away to complete his make-up, and then Gerald, with a million wheels and cogs and axles.

Poor Gerald, such a lot of little wheels to his make-up! He was more intricate than a chronometer-watch. (522, 524–5)

Clocking On

Gudrun's comparison of Gerald with a clock or 'chronometer-watch' offers several insights into the industrial age of the late nineteenth and early twentieth centuries. Chronometers' sophisticated mechanisms exemplified the precision achievable by manufacturing industry in this period. This made them appropriate, regularly chosen rewards for reliable employees – for Captain Brierly, in Conrad's *Lord Jim* (1900), for example, and Captain Mitchell, in *Nostromo* (1904).[4] As Gudrun suggests, clocks and chronometers also offer appropriate metaphors for the complex systems manufacturing industry required, particularly as chronometry and time-measurement were so crucial in the running of these systems themselves. Lewis Mumford highlights this combination of practical and emblematic roles when describing the clock, in *Technics and Civilization* (1934), as 'both the outstanding fact and the typical symbol of the machine'. He emphasises this outstanding role by suggesting that 'the clock, not the steam-engine, is the key-machine of the modern industrial age' – an indispensable device in 'synchronizing the actions of men' to ensure they work as efficiently and productively as possible.[5]

This key role dates back at least as far as the Industrial Revolution, but rapidly became more central with the further spread and fuller organisation of factory-based labour during the period represented in *The Rainbow* and *Women in Love*. In *The Condition of the Working Class in England* (1845), Frederick Engels noted of contemporary factory practices that

> The operative must be in the mill at half-past five in the morning; if he comes a couple of minutes too late, he is fined; if he comes ten minutes too late, he is not let in until breakfast is over, and a quarter

---

[4] The chapter entitled 'The Watch' (Bk III, ch.14) in Arnold Bennett's *Clayhanger* (1910) exemplifies another symbolic role for chronometers in the Victorian years and the early twentieth century – as valuable heirlooms, passed on from generation to generation as signifiers of familial wealth and patriarchal influence.

[5] Mumford, *Technics and Civilization*, 14.

of the day's wages is withheld, though he loses only two and one-half hours' work out of twelve. He must eat, drink, and sleep at command. For satisfying the most imperative needs, he is vouchsafed the least possible time absolutely required by them. Whether his dwelling is a half-hour or a whole one removed from the factory does not concern his employer. The despotic bell calls him from his bed, his breakfast, his dinner.[6]

After the 1840s, railway schedules forced much of the population to begin paying attention to individual minutes, in ways that Marcel Proust highlights in the remark quoted in Chapter 1. This kind of attention was made still more necessary for industrial workers, as Engels indicates, by their need to exchange labour-time for wages. As the century went on, and more and more of the population worked in factories, this exchange ensured that the expression 'time is money' became less a metaphor than an unrelenting condition of daily life and subsistence. As Mumford describes, employers' 'time-accounting' and 'time-rationing' strategies turned hours and minutes into 'a commodity in the sense that money had become a commodity' (14, 197). By the 1890s, labour-time could be quantified and commodified more accurately than ever, by means of 'clocking-on' or 'clocking-in' devices which stamped employees' cards with the exact hour and minute of their arrival and departure (Fig. 3.1).[7]

Clocking-in machines recorded only the length of time spent at work. The pace and duration of tasks undertaken within the workplace also came to be more stringently controlled by new measures, mostly introduced from the United States. These 'principles of scientific management' were developed during the last two decades of the nineteenth century, largely by Frederick Winslow Taylor, and disseminated in books and articles he began publishing in the mid-1890s. Taylor argued that 'the best management is a true science,

---

[6] Engels, *The Condition of the Working Class in England*, 205–6. Engels also notes that employers sometimes manipulated factory clocks so that they were 'a quarter of an hour slower than the town clocks at night, and a quarter of an hour faster in the morning', or defined the working day through a 'machine clock', registering the number of revolutions made by factory apparatus, rather than the time of day (207–8). See also Chapter 7.

[7] Practices that Mumford identifies in *Technics and Civilization* are also discussed in Marx's *Capital*, particularly in the sections on Surplus-value, vol. I, chs 11 and 12.

Willard Bundy took out a US patent for a clocking-in machine in 1890, though similar devices were being developed in Britain at the time. Bundy's International Time Recording Company was eventually absorbed into IBM, International Business Machines, in the 1920s.

Fig. 3.1 An office worker clocking-in during the 1920s. The homily at upper right proclaims an assumed equivalence of labour, time, money, and materials. Getty Images.

resting upon clearly defined laws, rules and principles' – ones formulated through 'accurate, minute, motion and time study'.[8] His 'minute study with a stop-watch' led him to conclude, for example, that heavily-loaded workmen could still walk 'at the rate of one foot in 0.006 minutes' (100, 61). Taylor also noted that workmen involved would rarely appreciate measurements of this kind, or any rules and principles developed from them, generally proving

---

[8] Taylor, *Principles of Scientific Management*, 7, 25.

'incapable ... of understanding this science' (41). In consequence, he suggested that whereas 'in the past the man has been first; in the future the system must be first' (7). Rather than being allowed to follow their own judgement, workers should be strictly regulated by the management, and if need be 'moved from place to place ... with elaborate diagrams or maps ... very much as chessmen are moved on a chess-board' (69). Taylor acknowledged that where the worker was concerned 'this all tends to make him a mere automaton', but considered any loss involved was outweighed by the promise of 'the greatest possible productivity of the men and machines' (125, 12).

Taylor's 'rules, laws, and formulae' impose constraints on working life of a different order to any Conrad experienced during his years working within the 'time-obsessed community' of mariners (37). Though precise and demanding, Conrad's calculations with maps and chronometers directly served his own interests, and those of his ship and crew, ensuring safe passage to their destination. Taylor's stopwatches and 'elaborate diagrams or maps' instead negate individual will and autonomy as far as possible. Increasing numbers of workers were affected, as the theories of Taylor and his disciples spread through Britain, and beyond, in the early years of the twentieth century. As *Women in Love* shows, Lawrence was clearly and critically aware of the changes involved. Conrad's career at sea made him thoroughly conversant with Greenwich-centred measures of time and space: childhood in Nottinghamshire, as the son of a miner, ensured Lawrence encountered contemporary industrial practices almost as directly. An early acquaintance recalls that children, Lawrence included, were regularly invited on Boxing Day to 'the home of the colliery owner, Mr. Barber, and were given one new penny and one large orange each'.[9] This benign regime resembles the paternalistic one which *Women in Love* describes Gerald Crich's father establishing. In his memoir of the period, 'Nottingham and the Mining Countryside', Lawrence recalls that at this stage of the industry's development – when miners were still allowed to work in small collaborative groups or 'butties' – 'the pit did not mechanize men'.[10] He was inevitably also aware of the contrasting effects of new machinery, management and efficiencies introduced into local

---

[9] Mabel Thurlby Collishaw's reminiscence, in Nehls, *D. H. Lawrence*, I, 31.
[10] Lawrence, *Phoenix*, 135.

pits by the old colliery owner's son, Thomas Philip Barber, using what he knew of this member of the family in his portrayal of Gerald in Women in Love. Changes that Barber made in modernising Barber, Walker and Co.'s collieries around 1905–7 are likewise reflected in the novel's account of Gerald's reforms – ones which ensure that, among many other moves towards mechanisation and profit, 'the butty system was abolished' (259).[11] Gerald's general determination that 'everything was run on the most accurate and delicate scientific method', with mathematical exactitude, and that 'educated and expert men were in control everywhere', clearly follows Taylorist principles – imported from the United States, along with new mining machines, described as 'great iron men' (259). Consequences for the workforce in Women in Love – with 'all the control ... taken out of the hands of the miners', who are 'reduced to mere mechanical instruments' – further recall Taylor's readiness to treat workers as mere 'chessmen' or automata (259).

Local factors might have added to Lawrence's fear that 'organic formation' would be overtaken by mechanisation – a threat particularly apparent in Nottinghamshire landscapes, in which collieries were juxtaposed with 'green meadows and rough country' in unusual proximity. Lawrence describes the locale of his childhood – also the setting of The Rainbow – as 'an extremely beautiful countryside' in which 'the mines were, in a sense, an accident in the landscape', contributing to 'a curious cross between industrialism and the old agricultural England'.[12] Local in some of their origins, Lawrence's concerns were nevertheless globally relevant by the time Women in Love was published. By the start of the 1920s, Taylorist principles had influenced not only Western capitalist economies, particularly those of Britain and the USA, but also manufacturing practices in the Soviet Union established by the Russian Revolution of 1917. A Taylorist 'Institute of Labour' was founded by Alexei Gastev, with the approval of the new Soviet leader, Vladimir Lenin, and associated with a 'League of Time' operating between 1923 and 1925. The Institute promoted comprehensive industrial efficiency, based on timings and calculations rigorous enough to allow workers to be operated as precisely as factory machinery.[13]

---

[11] See The First 'Women in Love', ed. John Worthen and Lindeth Vasey (Cambridge: Cambridge University Press, 1998), 483–5.
[12] Lawrence, Phoenix, 133, 135.
[13] See Stites, 'Utopias of Time', 141–54.

Robotic efficiency of this kind is satirised in Yevgeny Zamyatin's dystopian novel *We* (*My*, 1921), which describes a future world in which workers, and citizens generally, are rigorously organised 'in accordance with Taylor . . . keeping in time, like the levers of a single immense machine'. 'The whole of life', in Zamyatin's futuristic vision, is committed to 'mathematically infallible . . . Taylorized happiness' and to 'the great, divine, precise, wise straight line'. His 'chronometrically perfect' future society appropriately considers Taylor '*the* genius of antiquity', and – extending the resonance of the name 'Bradshaw', outlined in Chapter 1 – that the 'greatest of all monuments of ancient literature that has come down to us' is 'the *Railroad Timetable*'.[14]

Taylor's ideas were equally familiar to the Hungarian Marxist Georg Lukács. He criticises their consequences, and the effects of contemporary industrial practices generally, in an essay written the year after *Women in Love* was published, 'Reification and the Consciousness of the Proletariat'. Lukács traces the displacement of 'the qualitative, human and individual attributes of the worker' by forms of 'rational calculation' which leave him merely 'a mechanical part incorporated into a mechanical system'. He concludes that

> With the modern 'psychological' analysis of the work-process (in Taylorism) this rational mechanisation extends right into the worker's 'soul' . . .
> Marx puts it thus: 'Through the subordination of man to the machine the situation arises in which men are effaced by their labour; in which the pendulum of the clock has become as accurate a measure of the relative activity of two workers as it is of the speed of two locomotives . . . Time is everything, man is nothing; he is at the most the incarnation of time. Quality no longer matters. Quantity alone decides everything: hour for hour, day for day . . .'
> Thus time sheds its qualitative, variable, flowing nature; it freezes into an exactly delimited quantifiable continuum filled with quantifiable 'things' (the reified, mechanically objectified 'performance' of the worker, wholly separated from his total human personality).[15]

---

[14] Yevgeny Zamyatin, *We*, trans. Clarence Brown (London: Penguin, 1993), 81, 34, 3, 44, 4, 33, 12. Zamyatin was acquainted not only with Soviet working practices, but also, while working abroad during the Great War, with those employed in shipyards in Newcastle and Glasgow.
[15] Lukács, 'Reification and the Consciousness of the Proletariat', in *History and Class Consciousness*, 88–90.

Lukács's analysis of commodified time and labour strongly resembles Lawrence's, in *Women in Love* – not only in its ideas, but even in its vocabulary of 'mechanical part ... mechanical system' and 'subordination ... to the machine'. Similarities of outlook and terminology, shared by such otherwise disparate writers, confirm how comprehensively Taylorist influences shaped the working world by the early 1920s.

By that time, and increasingly in the following decade, further developments in industrial practice were extending the threat of 'rational mechanisation' to the worker's 'soul'. In the years shortly before the Great War, many of Taylor's strategies had been adapted into the assembly-line techniques developed in the factories of Henry Ford – appropriately, a successful watch-repairer in his youth – making factory labour still more thoroughly subordinate to the pace and demands of machines. 'We ourselves became machines ... along with the thousands of little wheels', Louis-Ferdinand Céline's narrator reports of work in a Ford plant in Detroit, after the Great War, in *Journey to the End of the Night* (*Voyage au bout de la nuit*, 1932).[16] Consequences of Ford's new techniques are explored more thoroughly in another novel published in 1932, Aldous Huxley's *Brave New World*. Like Zamyatin in *We*, Huxley projects current social stresses into a dystopian future, describing workplaces containing as many as 4,000 synchronised electric clocks, and workers – along with citizens generally – engaged in still more disturbing relations with machines and production lines. In Huxley's vision of future bioengineering, humans are not just subordinate to machinery, or cognate with its operations, but entirely manufactured by it: reproduced from bottled embryos, moved along production lines for 'two hundred and sixty-seven days at eight metres a day'.[17]

Committed to ensuring that 'the machine turns, turns and must keep on turning', this society has installed as its deity, appropriately, a 'God of the Machine' – specifically, of the production line (37). The God of Christianity has been replaced by 'our Ford', Big Ben has become 'Big Henry', and the tops of any surviving crosses have been trimmed off so that they commemorate the Model-T automobiles which first rolled off Ford's new assembly lines. Descriptions

---

[16] Louis-Ferdinand Céline, *Journey to the End of the Night*, trans. Ralph Manheim (London: Alma Classics, 2010), 186.
[17] Aldous Huxley, *Brave New World* (1932; London: HarperCollins, 1994), 9. Subsequent references are to this edition.

of Big Henry booming out 'Ford, Ford, Ford' over London, and of the ubiquitous 'click, click, click, click' of electric clocks, suggest a future world encountering 'the miseries of space and time' still more exactingly than the 1930s society Huxley satirises (70, 161). For his hyper-regulated future citizens, the only access to 'enormous, immeasurable durations . . . out of time' – to what their 'ancestors used to call eternity' (139) – is through mind-altering drugs: a synthetic or perhaps parodic version of the modernist 'time in the mind' assessed in Chapter 4 below.

Not even this respite is available to the production-line workers depicted in Charlie Chaplin's film *Modern Times* (1936). Clockwork and its powers had interested Chaplin twenty years earlier in a short film, *The Pawnshop* (1916), which shows the inner workings of a clock coming strangely alive and acquiring will and animacy of their own. For the workers in *Modern Times*, this transformation operates in reverse, exemplifying the deadening, reifying processes Lukács describes. The labour force in *Modern Times* figures not as individuals, but as an anonymous herd, marshalled by a huge clock – shown in close-up as the film opens – and by the clocking-in devices controlling entrance to the factory. Within it, assembly-lines ensure workers have no choice but to become mechanical parts in a mechanical system. The repetitive nature of their labour forces them to reduplicate mechanical movements so automatically that even their leisure periods continue to be marked by the 'horrible mechanical twitching' that Gudrun attributes to the hands of the clock. Thoroughly enthralled to the motion and rhythm of machinery, Chaplin is eventually swallowed up literally, as well as metaphorically, by the intricate cogs and wheels within wheels of the factory's production-line apparatus, as if ingested into the tortuous inner workings of a monstrous clock (Fig. 3.2).

Chaplin's descent into this mechanical underworld offers a vivid, summary image of the effects of industrialisation in the late nineteenth and early twentieth centuries, shown in contemporary literature steadily extending their grip over working life. As described above, *The Rainbow* offers a warning – familiar enough from Victorian fiction, and from Romantic poetry – regarding the destructive effects of a machine age on 'green meadows' and the natural world. Later in that novel, and in *Women in Love*, Lawrence moves on to focus on industrialism's threats not only to nature generally, but to human natures and behaviours. Highlighted in Gudrun's vision of the 'wheels within wheels' of Gerald and his workforce, *Women in Love* envisages an industrialised society in which attributes of individuals and machines have become readily interchangeable, much as Lukács describes.

Fig. 3.2 Charlie Chaplin in *Modern Times* (1936). Getty Images.

Clocks – machines disturbingly possessed of a face and hands – figure as perfect emblems, as well as agents, of this exchange.

Though *Women in Love* offers the most thorough examination of this interchange until Huxley's in the 1930s, similar concerns are widely apparent in literature earlier in the century. As Chapter 2 noted, clocks in *The Secret Agent* (1907) take on a sinister will and agency of their own, along with other machines Conrad describes, such as the pianola, which apparently chooses 'all by itself . . . with aggressive virtuosity' to accompany the anarchists' bar-room conversations. The anarchists themselves are often characterised, reciprocally, in mechanical terms – the Professor, determined to make of himself a living bomb; or Verloc, compared to 'an automaton . . . a mechanical figure . . . aware of the machinery inside of him'.[18] Comparable interchanges of human agency with machinery or the automatic continued to appear a few years later in T. S. Eliot's vision of modern city life, 'Rhapsody on a Windy Night', written around 1910. The poem's human characters appear either fragmented, figuring only as eyes or hands, or mechanical – the child empty behind the eyes, pocketing a toy in an apparently 'automatic' gesture. Objects meanwhile take on some of the animacy humans have forfeited. The toy seems readier

---

[18] Joseph Conrad, *The Secret Agent: A Simple Tale* (1907; Harmondsworth: Penguin, 1967), 58, 162.

than the child to run around. Doors, not people, seem to grin, and only street lamps speak aloud.

Their mode of speech and the information they deliver indicate another phase of industrialisation's suppression of the natural world, and of the clock's complicities in the processes involved. Their muttering and sputtering suggest that Eliot's street lamps rely not on electricity but on the older technology of gas lighting, first introduced early in the nineteenth century to allow factories to continue working throughout the night. Its use soon extended through city streets, partly effacing, by the end of the century, another natural temporal ordering – not the perennial cycle of the seasons, but the reiterated, diurnal succession of light and dark, night and day. According to Wolfgang Schivelbusch's history of the technologies involved, *Disenchanted Night* (1988) – gaslight in this way 'like the railway, reigned supreme as a symbol of human and industrial progress . . . a triumph over the natural order'.[19] Initially, rather than marking any such 'triumph', street lighting had carefully collaborated with the natural order. Several European cities – including Paris, where Eliot was living when he wrote the poem – used street lamps only when they were required as a substitute for the light of the moon, sometimes continuing to factor lunar phases into lighting schedules even in the early twentieth century.[20]

Moon and street lamp nevertheless figure as firm adversaries in 'Rhapsody on a Windy Night'. Fainter moonlight illumines areas between the lamps, whose artificial light measures out the length of the street in bright, regular, patches. The lamps divide up the night's temporal duration just as sharply and regularly. Like some dogged speaking clock, each lamp offers a firm notification of the time, contributing a 'fatalistic' beat to the poem, while in the darker moonlit intervals, these exact divisions dissolve into vaguer, inward spaces of memory. Eliot offers in this way another version of the antitheses, discussed in Chapter 1, which troubled the mid-nineteenth century. Conflicts between 'railway time' and 'the sun's progress though the heavens' seemed to offer, in those days, a paradigmatic antithesis between industrial progress and the natural order. 'Rhapsody on a Windy Night' delivers an updated, lunar version of the same conflict, offering – like Lawrence's fleeting vision of 'green meadows' beyond

---

[19] Schivelbusch, *Disenchanted Night*, 152–3. J. R. R. Tolkien likewise finds street lamps (though in their more modern, electric version) symbolic in this way, expressing 'disgust for so typical a product of the Robot Age' in *Tree and Leaf*, 56.
[20] See *Disenchanted Night*, 90; and Schlör, *Nights in the Big City*, 60 etc.

a colliery town – a pale reminder of phases and cycles of a natural world, still reaching across the artificially illumined, precisely timed life of modern cities.[21] Significantly, too, it is the inhabitants' memories and inner consciousnesses which this fragile, moonlit reminder seems most to touch. This emphasis on the inner life also prefigures modernism's flight from an industrialised world into the 'times in the mind' considered in Chapter 4 – ones through which more inviolate, unmechanised forms of selfhood might still be preserved.

Cracks and Chasms

By July 1915, when 'Rhapsody on a Windy Night' was first published, the effects of the Great War were greatly extending stresses that industrialisation imposed on individuals, on society, and on the natural world, while also reshaping apprehension of the passage of time itself.[22] Experience of conscription and military bureaucracy added to D. H. Lawrence's conviction that in wartime 'every man was turned into an automaton . . . turned into a mere thing' – a view of 'induration' strongly shared by many serving soldiers.[23] In a letter of July 1917, he also indicates some of the war's impact on literature, including his own – particularly on *Women in Love*, completed in a first version around six months earlier, after revisions during the Somme campaign, in the summer and autumn of 1916. His letter further explains the darkening mood that separates *Women in Love* from *The Rainbow*, remarking that the earlier novel

> was all written before the war, though revised during Sept. and Oct. of 1914. I don't think the war had much to do with it – I don't think the war altered it, from its pre-war statement . . . alas, in the world of Europe I see no Rainbow. I believe the deluge of iron rain will destroy the world here, utterly . . .
>
> *Women in Love* . . . actually does contain the results in one's soul of the war: it is purely destructive, not like *The Rainbow*, destructive-consummating.[24]

---

[21] Schlör suggests in *Nights in the Big City* that 'the need to adopt, to learn a *new attitude towards the night*, was also one of the new demands in the process of industrialization' (93).

[22] Entitled 'Rhapsody of a Windy Night', the poem first appeared in the second, 'War', number of Wyndham Lewis's radical journal, *Blast*.

[23] Lawrence, *Movements in European History*, 312–13; Edmund Blunden, *Undertones of War* (1928; Harmondsworth: Penguin, 2000), 53.

[24] Lawrence, letter of 27 July 1917 to Waldo Frank, *Letters*, III, 142–3.

The 'results' Lawrence mentions appear as much in the structure of *Women in Love* as in its 'statement', or in its darker mood. Neither the straight lines nor the circles of *The Rainbow* remain much in evidence in the later novel. *Women in Love* is so much less linear – reflecting much more fully 'a ragged, inconsequential life' – that its chapters and episodes seem at times only barely consecutive. More thoroughly than *The Rainbow*, it illustrates instead Lawrence's preference for 'rhythmic form', along with his reluctance to allow 'the development of the novel to follow the lines of certain characters', each equipped with a conventionally 'stable ego'.[25] Though some chapters in *Women in Love* do follow clearly and causally from previous ones, several focus instead on characters' fickle moods and feelings without much indicating how these unstable phases develop from each other. As a result, as Frank Kermode suggests, *Women in Love* sometimes 'proceeds by awful discontinuous leaps', with the chronology of individual chapters indicated only by unspecific formulations such as 'a school day', 'every year', 'one morning', or 'one day at this time'.[26] Especially in its early stages, *Women in Love* almost resembles a collection of short stories about the same group of characters, rather than a novel conventionally following cause and consequence in the steady development of their lives.

Differences of this kind between *The Rainbow* and *Women in Love* exemplify a growing readiness, more widely apparent during the 1920s, to move away from conventional nineteenth-century narrative structures. In following the experience of successive generations, *The Rainbow* continues to resemble chronicles of family life popular in the Victorian period, and still produced early in the twentieth century by authors such as John Galsworthy, in *The Forsyte Saga* sequence (1906–29). In tracing the development of individual lives, within successive generations, *The Rainbow* also shares some characteristics with another popular nineteenth-century genre, the *Bildungsroman*. Faith in the individual's capacity to develop, through time, towards maturity and a secure position within a stable society is central to mid-nineteenth-century examples of the genre, such as Charles Dickens's *David Copperfield* (1850). The same interests in personal development shape *Bildungsomane* continuing to appear in the early twentieth century, though sometimes – as in Lawrence's *Sons and Lovers* (1913) – with dwindling confidence in the possibilities of settled individual life or stable social integration. Such possibilities generally seemed much

---

[25] Letter of 5 June 1914 to Edward Garnett, *Letters*, II, 183–4.
[26] Kermode, *Lawrence*, 64.

more remote after 1914 – the Great War threatening social stability and, for many individuals, the expectation of a life long enough to allow maturity or personal fulfilment to be realised. In *Sinister Street* (1913–14), Compton Mackenzie provides a celebrated late example of the genre, but also a kind of epitaph for it. He recalls almost unconsciously doodling 'names like Louvain and Ypres' over his manuscript, when completing the second volume, while hearing of the Great War's opening military engagements.[27]

Even within a day of the war's outbreak, Henry James recognised how profoundly it had challenged longstanding ideas of continuity, progress or development in human affairs. In a letter written on 5 August 1914, he remarks that 'the plunge of civilization into this abyss of blood and darkness ... is a thing that so gives away the whole long age during which we have supposed the world to be, with whatever abatement, gradually bettering'. Thomas Hardy also reflects on the demise of 'bettering' in a poem about the war's ending, in November 1918. By that date, Hardy considers, 'old hopes that earth was bettering slowly,/Were dead and damned'.[28] Even contemporary authors less convinced of 'bettering' could hardly dissent from James's judgement of the war as a 'rupture with the past', and a 'breach ... with the course of history'. Lawrence himself considered in *Kangaroo* (1923) that 'it was in 1915 the old world ended', adding in *Lady Chatterley's Lover* (1928) that 'the cataclysm has happened ... there is now no smooth road into the future'.[29]

Several other authors used much the same image to describe radical change the war wrought in the experience of the age – even in its sense of the coherent movement of history itself. Virginia Woolf recalls in a later essay how in 1914 'suddenly, like a chasm in a smooth road, the war came' and 'cut into' contemporary lives. For Thomas Mann, in *The Magic Mountain* (1924), the war 'shattered its way through life and consciousness and left a deep chasm'. In *Parade's End* (1924–8), Ford Madox Ford describes it as a 'crack across the table of History'. Looking back across the twentieth century in an

---

[27] Compton Mackenzie, *Gallipoli Memories* (London: Cassell, 1929), 2.
[28] James, letter of 4/5 August 1914 to Howard Sturgis, *Letters*, II, 398; Thomas Hardy, '"And There Was a Great Calm"', *The Complete Poems of Thomas Hardy*, ed. James Gibson (1976; London: Macmillan, 1991), 589.
[29] James, letter of 18 June 1915 to Compton Mackenzie, *Letters*, II, 493; D. H. Lawrence, *Kangaroo* (1923; London: Heinemann, 1974), 220; D. H. Lawrence, *Lady Chatterley's Lover* (1928; Harmondsworth: Penguin, 1982), 5.

autobiography, *Margin Released* (1962), J. B. Priestley suggests that 'the First War cut deeper and played more tricks with time because it *was* first . . . a great jagged crack in the looking-glass'. In his war novel *Death of a Hero* (1929), Richard Aldington likewise describes how it 'made a cut in . . . life and personality', adding that 'adult lives were cut sharply into three sections – pre-war, war, and post-war'.[30] A similar sense of rupture figures more covertly in Joseph Conrad's *The Shadow-Line* (1917). In describing a mysterious navigational line, evidently uncrossable by mortal men, Conrad may be mingling awareness of the deadly boundaries of contemporary trench warfare – and concerns for the novella's dedicatee, his son Borys, who was serving in France – with memories of early struggles during his own career at sea.[31]

Cuts, cracks and shadows running across recent history help explain why long accounts of lives developing through time seem scarcer in fiction after the Great War. Forms of extreme truncation began to appear more frequently instead – novels such as James Joyce's *Ulysses* (1922) or Woolf's *Mrs Dalloway* (1925), compressed into single days, or, like William Faulkner's *The Sound and the Fury* (1929), concerned with only a few. Woolf offers the most telling example in *To the Lighthouse* (1927), concentrated on single days around ten years apart, divided by a short, sharp, middle section, 'Time Passes', describing the troubled, intervening years of the war. 'Time Passes' also shows the war and its losses extinguishing the kind of vestigial hopes of restoration or redemption in a natural world which Lawrence struggles to maintain in *The Rainbow*. 'Did Nature supplement what man advanced?', *To the Lighthouse* directly asks. Dark traces of naval conflict, soiling and staining the sea, help suggest only that 'with equal complacence she saw his misery, condoned his meanness, and acquiesced in his torture'.[32] Nature, in the novel's middle section, has largely ceased to be affirmative, figuring instead as an aspect of the immense darkness and emptiness surrounding the fragile domain of human affairs.

---

[30] Woolf, 'The Leaning Tower' (1940), *Essays*, VI, 264; Thomas Mann, *The Magic Mountain*, trans. H. T. Lowe-Porter (1928; London: Vintage, 1999), 1; Ford Madox Ford, *Parade's End* (1924–8; Harmondsworth: Penguin, 1982), 510; Priestley, *Margin Released*, 88; Richard Aldington, *Death of a Hero* (1929; London: Hogarth Press, 1984), 323, 199.

[31] See Larabee, *Front Lines of Modernism*, 134–60.

[32] Virginia Woolf, *To the Lighthouse* (1927; Harmondsworth: Penguin, 1973), 153.

Descriptions of cuts, cracks, and historical chasms also suggest symmetries between 1840 and 1914. A first cut, made by railways, canals and industrialisation, displaced older, cyclical temporalities in favour of a strong sense of change and forward movement in history, consolidating what Hugh Kenner describes as 'the most pervasive idea' of the nineteenth century – 'the idea of continuity'.[33] This idea contributes not only to a chronotype in fiction, in those sagas and *Bildungsromane*. For Kenner, it also shapes – and is reinforced by – underlying assumptions in the work of influential thinkers including Charles Darwin and Karl Marx, based in each case on belief in necessary or inevitable progress through time and history. As Henry James swiftly realised, any general idea of continuity or progress was decisively curtailed by a second cut across landscape and history made by the trenches extending across Europe in the autumn of 1914. Comparisons of *Women in Love* and *The Rainbow* are directly useful in highlighting this diminished faith in progress, following the Great War, along with its implications for the structuring of this period's fiction. They also introduce in this way a further mode of understanding literary form in relation to time and history. As Chapter 1 suggested, narrative structures and relations between *fabula* and *sjuzet* can be seen to respond to the exigency of the clock's control over contemporary daily life. They also, obviously, engage with perceptions of contemporary history, internalising or redrawing shadow-lines which recent events have extended across memory and the past. New precisions of railway timetabling cut a 'groove, a mysterious mark' across Marcel's afternoon in *À la recherche du temps perdu* (I, 419). Memories of the trenches, of the 'abyss of blood and darkness' of the Great War, inevitably also cut across literary imagination in later years, contributing to the shaping of narrative forms considered in Chapters 4 and 5.

War Time

The war also added in its own ways to the clock's control over contemporary life. More urgently even than systematised modern industry, military organisation required a tightened grip over time – one which soldiers often experienced quite literally. Peacetime allowed the kind of leisure enjoyed by old Captain Giles in *The Shadow-Line*, patiently

---

[33] Kenner, *Joyce's Voices*, 49.

prepared to 'haul at his gorgeous gold chain till at last the watch came up from the deep pocket like solid truth from a well'. In wartime, many soldiers shared instead the discovery Willa Cather's hero makes in her Great War novel *One of Ours* (1922) – that 'the wrist watch, which he had hitherto despised as effeminate and had carried in his pocket, might be a very useful article'.[34] Fob- or pocket-watches of the kind Captain Giles favours, still very widely in use at the start of the twentieth century, were often displaced during the Great War by timepieces firmly bound to a wrist, allowing time in the trenches to be instantly accessed. It also had to be reliably coordinated, on a large scale. Troop movements had to be synchronised and mapped out still more exactly than the shifts of workers whose motions and timings Taylor had sought to regiment. Edmund Blunden is one of many Great War writers who recall how 'watches were synchronized and reconsigned to the officers' before an attack – often by runners who took them to and from headquarters.[35] Reinventing tactics employed by railway companies to synchronise station clocks in the 1840s, the strategy ensured that attacks could be initiated simultaneously even over very wide areas. The start of the Somme campaign demonstrated the results. On the sunny summer morning of 1 July 1916, a huge barrage was punctually halted at 7.20am, and at exactly 7.30am, British troops began an attack on a front of more than fifteen miles. By 11am, nearly 60,000 of them had been killed or wounded. By 1916, death – like life and work generally – was ever more firmly in the hands of the clock.

Wartime measures had recently consolidated its rule over the home population. Following a report in April 1915 about bad timekeeping in key industries, and intoxication among munitions workers, legislation introduced under the Defence of the Realm Act curtailed pub closing times in areas of the country deemed to be closely involved in the war effort.[36] Sobriety would be ensured, it was hoped, by shorter pub hours. Stricter closing times further dispelled the fears of alcohol-fuelled disorder which had added, during the Victorian Age, to the influence of the railways in encouraging national standardisation of time. The new licensing laws were consequently considered worth extending nationwide in 1921. The call punctuating the second

---

[34] Joseph Conrad, *The Shadow-Line: A Confession* (1917; Oxford: Oxford University Press, 2003), 22; Willa Cather, *One of Ours* (1922; New York; Alfred A. Knopf, 1975) 297–8.
[35] Blunden, *Undertones of War*, 91.
[36] See Stevenson, *British Society 1914–45*, 71 et seq.

section of T. S. Eliot's *The Waste Land* – 'HURRY UP PLEASE IT'S TIME' – is often read as suggesting more than pub closing, introducing into the poem a sombre note of *memento mori*, or *carpe diem*. It would at any rate have sounded a particularly topical, newly familiar note when the poem was first published in 1922. The disparaging metaphor employed by a psychoanalyst in Rebecca West's wartime novel *The Return of the Soldier*, published in 1918 – of self-control as 'a sort of barmaid of the soul that says, "Time's up, gentlemen . . . you've had enough"' – would likewise have had an immediate contemporary resonance.[37]

Another new measure introduced in 1916 forced even teetotallers – indeed, the whole British population, including those serving abroad – towards sharper awareness of the clock's rule over their lives, and of the government's rule over the clock. Daylight Saving – 'Summer Time' – had first been recommended by William Willett in a pamphlet published in 1907, and later advocated unsuccessfully in Parliament by Winston Churchill, as Home Secretary, in 1911. Wartime needs to save energy and maximise production encouraged the eventual adoption of the measure a few weeks before the Somme campaign began. The Summer Time Act was passed by Parliament in May 1916, decreeing that all clocks in Britain should be moved an hour forward at 2am on the 21st of that month. A similar measure had been implemented three weeks earlier by Germany, and was soon adopted by its ally Austro-Hungary, and by other countries including France, Italy and Holland. Within Britain, Summer Time was much discussed in the newspapers. *The Times* compared the measure to the calendrical reforms which excised eleven days from the month of September, 1752, in accordance with Parliamentary legislation adopted the previous year. It also reported particular objections raised by farmers and rural communities. Their preference for 'real time as shown by the sun' extended the arguments described in Chapter 1, regularly made when 'Railway Time' and Greenwich Mean Time were first introduced in the mid-nineteenth century.[38]

---

[37] Rebecca West, *The Return of the Soldier* (1918; London: Virago, 2004), 163.

[38] 'Summer Time: Tonight's Change of Hour: Official Notices', *The Times*, 20 May 1916, 7; 'The Extra Hours: First Summer Time Day: Success of the Innovation: Farmers' Protest', *The Times*, 22 May 1916, 9. 'Summer Time' also reported that 'a battalion of professional clock-winders, many of them dug out of a peaceful retirement', would soon be 'feverishly at work'. The Office of Works had responsibility for over 4,000 public clocks.

'Wheels within Wheels' 69

IMPORTANT.
ALTERATION OF TIME

In the night of Saturday-Sunday, May 20th-21st, at 2 a.m., the time on all railways, at all Post Offices and other Government establishments, will be put forward one hour to 3 a.m.

The altered time will be used for all ordinary purposes during the Summer. For instance, licensed houses, factories and workshops, and other establishments where hours are regulated by law will be required to observe the altered time.

The Government requests the public to put forward all clocks and watches by one hour during the night of Saturday, May 20th.

Normal time will be restored at 2 a.m. on the night of Saturday-Sunday, September 30th-October 1st.

The chief object of this measure at the present time is to reduce the number of hours during which artificial lighting is used in the evenings, and so save to the nation part of the fuel and oil for lighting and release large quantities of coal which are urgently needed for other purposes arising from the War.

By Order of the Home Secretary.

Fig. 3.3 A Home Office poster informing the public of the introduction of Summer Time in May 1916. Imperial War Museum.

Yet advocacy of 'God's time', the sun's time, or natural time fell on deafer ears in 1916, in a society now more resigned to government regulation, particularly during the war. One letter to *The Times*, from Devon, even remarked that people in that area – one especially resistant to the original imposition of GMT – had grown so 'accustomed to differences between clock-time and sun-time' that further interference would pass almost unnoticed.[39] When finally introduced, the added hour seemed as much an intriguing novelty as a break in any natural order. According to *The Times* of 22 May,

---

[39] Alfred Croft, letter to the Editor, *The Times*, 12 May 1916, 9.

children even asked to be allowed to stay up until 2am to witness the new measure being implemented on household clocks. Some contemporary authors were also favourably impressed, attracted by a new light cast over Britain's cities, possibly even restoring appreciation of the natural world beyond or above them. Consequences of 'the ingenious process of lengthening the summer days by altering clocks' figure in Arnold Bennett's *The Pretty Lady* (1918), set in London in 1916. 'Long after ten o'clock', the novel remarks, 'an exquisite faint light lingering in the sky still revealed the features of the people in the streets'. Several years later, this new light and 'prolonged evening' still seemed intriguing enough to Virginia Woolf to mention in *Mrs Dalloway*, set in 1923. Like Bennett, Woolf records how slowly the summer sky 'paled and faded' above the city streets, an 'inspiriting' result of 'the great revolution of Mr Willett's summer time'. Though often adversaries in their literary priorities in the 1920s, Woolf and Bennett could at least agree about Willet's improvement of their city's summer skies. In *Between the Acts* (1941), set in 1939, Woolf's characters continue to recall, more than two decades later, 'one good the war brought us – longer days'.[40]

For other authors, the war cast a peculiar new light over temporality generally – a strangeness also suggested by Home Office posters publicising the introduction of Daylight Saving (Fig. 3.3). Widely displayed in police stations, post offices and railway stations in mid-May 2016, these advertised an 'Alteration of Time' rather than of the hour, or the clock – an odd wording which might on occasion have seemed only too appropriate. For J. B. Priestley, who served as an infantryman throughout, the war did seem somehow to have altered time itself. He wonders in his autobiography whether 'the very hours began shrinking during the murderous imbecility of the First World War. I will swear that afternoons were never the same again'.[41] Siegfried Sassoon was also a combatant throughout the war, figuring its reductive influences in relation to clocks carefully characterised in his autobiography *Siegfried's Journey: 1916–1920* (1945) in a passage set around 'midnight on the last day of 1918', a few weeks after the Armistice. Sassoon describes 'the leisurely tick of the grandfather

---

[40] Arnold Bennett, *The Pretty Lady* (1918; Leek, Staffordshire: Churnet Valley Books, 2009), 277; Virginia Woolf, *Mrs Dalloway* (1925; Harmondsworth: Penguin, 1975), 178–9; Virginia Woolf, *Between the Acts* (1941; London: Granada, 1978), 90.

[41] Priestley, *Margin Released*, 29. A fuller account of the war's effects on perceptions of time and its measurement, among combatants and on the Home Front, appears in Stevenson, *Literature and the Great War*, 69–74.

clock in the front hall . . . presiding over the quietude of the house without concerning itself about my future', recalling instead bygone 'summer days of childhood . . . sunlight and garden freedom'. This 'old friend . . . unconscious and impercipient' is sharply contrasted with a new clock, purchased in 1914, which seems to be 'alert and inquisitive', associated with 'progress' and 'political economy', and determined to 'tick . . . on to achievements'.[42] As in *Women in Love* and *The Secret Agent*, these personified descriptions ascribe a strange animacy to clocks, evidently ever ready to appropriate human qualities and powers. Contrasts between Sassoon's two timepieces highlight how this readiness had recently increased, evidenced by new 'inquisitiveness' – a new, enhanced empowerment to intrude into human affairs – which the second clock has confidently assumed by the end of the war.

Fullest demonstration of the clock's ever-expanding powers nevertheless occurred neither during the war, nor at its end, but a year later, on the first anniversary of the Armistice. A message from the King, reported in *The Times* of 7 November 1919, outlined arrangements for 'universal expression' of public feeling on this first Remembrance Day. The King wished that 'for the brief space of two minutes', at 11am on 11 November, 'all work, all sound, and all locomotion should cease, so that, in perfect stillness, the thoughts of every one may be concentrated on reverent remembrance of the Glorious Dead'.[43] The article gives details of some of the arrangements required for this two minutes' silence, including the synchronisation of clocks in fire stations, charged with setting off maroon signals at exactly 11am. The Board of Trade arranged for trains to be halted throughout the country at 11am, and for the police to stop traffic in the streets of every town and city. All pedestrians were invited to stand still, and men to remove their hats. Ships were to be stopped at sea, and activity of any kind brought to a standstill in colonies abroad – as far as possible, by 'everybody in every part of the Empire'.[44] Never before had a King or a government organised so many people – many millions, throughout Britain – into doing the same thing at so exactly the same time. Experience of that 'brief space of two minutes' was more widely

---

[42] Siegfried Sassoon, *Siegfried's Journey: 1916–1920* (London: Faber and Faber, 1945), 118, 120–1.
[43] 'The Glorious Dead: King's Call to his People: Armistice Day Observance: Two Minutes' Pause from Work', *The Times,* 7 November 1919, 12.
[44] 'The Glorious Dead: Tuesday's Two-Minute Silence: Maroon Signals: The Churches' Appeal', *Times*, 8 November 1919, 12. In the colonies, and at sea, the two minutes' silence was observed at 11am local time.

shared, on 11 November 1919, and more exactly, universally, clock-controlled, than any previously in British history – perhaps rivalled only by general awareness, at 11pm on 4 August 1914, that the country had probably just declared war.[45]

Chronological controls of this kind exemplify the 'monumental time' Paul Ricoeur defines in *Time and Narrative* (*Temps et récit*, 1983–5) as a growing influence on the twentieth century. Society in this period, in his view, finds itself enthralled as never before to an 'official time', empowered not only by the 'time of clocks but all that is in complicity with it'. The clock, for Ricoeur, had become by the 1920s inextricably complicit with affairs of state – with the work of 'figures of authority and power' who rule 'the imperial capital' and the world beyond, directing the whole history of the age.[46] Ricoeur emphasises in this way, like Lukács, how completely the clock had ceased to function merely as a neutral or objective time-measurer. For Lukács, its measures were comprehensively complicit with industrial economics and wage slavery, and consequently with commodifying pressures threatening to make humanity and machinery interchangeable. For Ricoeur, the clock colluded just as comprehensively in a 'monumental history' of military organisation and empire, and in the general regulatory work of government and state – from hours of pub opening or Daylight Saving to declarations of war or the timing of remembrance of its dead. By the beginning of the 1920s, *l'heure définitive* – the 'definitive hour', established by the Bureau International de l'Heure a few weeks after Remembrance Day – could just as appropriately have been named *l'heure définant*, the defining hour.[47] Shifts of workers, waves of troops, railway passengers, ships on the seas, once-leisured drinkers – even passing pedestrians – were now moved or arrested, more firmly than ever, by 'twitching . . . clock fingers'. As Gudrun fears, in other words, 'all life, all life' might have seemed by this period to turn around the wheels within wheels of the clock – a bondage threatening 'no escape . . . no escape'. Alternatives to this bondage, or means of escaping or reshaping its threats, nevertheless began to figure widely, in literature and culture, at almost exactly the same historical moment. These are considered in the next chapter.

---

[45] Britain's ultimatum to Germany expired at midnight, Berlin time. But as C. E. Montague's novel *Rough Justice* (1924) records, there was some confusion at home about whether Britain was at war at 11pm or midnight, GMT.
[46] Ricoeur, *Time and Narrative*, II, 106.
[47] See also Chapter 1. The Bureau began its international role on 1 January 1920.

Chapter 4

Times in the Mind: Modernism in the 1920s

Paul Ricoeur introduces his term 'monumental time' specifically, and appropriately, in discussing *Mrs Dalloway* (1925). Virginia Woolf's novel addresses many of the issues summed up at the end of the previous chapter, extending in doing so several features of her writing which emerged distinctively during the period following the Great War. One of these is the growing prominence her fiction accords to clocks and their unsettling influences. *Night and Day* (1919) describes 'mellow strokes ... of the hour ... a message from the great clock at Westminster' falling fairly benignly across London, offering a reminder only of 'the just and inexorable nature of time ... the unhasting and unresting march of that divinity'. In *Jacob's Room* (1922), 'the worn voices of clocks' are heard rather more regularly and insistently, dividing 'time into quarters' or asserting 'the fact of the hour'. The 'large white clock of Westminster' also makes a significant reappearance, its chimes described as resonating throughout the institutions of government, adding to the 'inexorable gravity' of authorities who 'decreed ... the course of history'.[1]

Clocks – the 'clock of Westminster' particularly – proclaim their iron measures still more intrusively in *Mrs Dalloway*, and at every stage of the day the novel describes. An opening salvo from Big Ben resounds as early as its second page: 'out it boomed. First a warning, musical; then the hour, irrevocable. The leaden circles dissolved in the air'.[2] This 'great booming voice' returns repeatedly thereafter, its 'extraordinary vigour' even figured on one occasion 'as if a young

---

[1] Virginia Woolf, *Night and Day* (1919; Oxford: Oxford University Press, 2009), 46, 345; *Jacob's Room* (1922; London: Triad, 1976), 96, 129, 168.
[2] Virginia Woolf, *Mrs Dalloway* (1925; Harmondsworth: Penguin, 1976), 6. Subsequent references are to this edition.

man, strong, indifferent, inconsiderate, were swinging dumb-bells this way and that' (55, 54). Big Ben's vigorous influence is regularly supplemented through being 'blent with that of other clocks' – ones which, echoing its magisterial divisions of the day, likewise 'counselled submission, upheld authority' (104, 113). Those in Harley Street have a particularly invidious role. The passage quoted in Chapter 1 goes on to explain how their 'shredding and slicing, dividing and subdividing' of the June day is reinforced by

> a commercial clock, suspended above a shop in Oxford Street, [which] announced, genially and fraternally, as if it were a pleasure to Messrs Rigby and Lowndes to give the information gratis, that it was half-past one.
>
> Looking up, it appeared that each letter of their names stood for one of the hours; subconsciously one was grateful to Rigby and Lowndes for giving one time ratified by Greenwich; and this gratitude ... naturally took the form later of buying off Rigby and Lowndes socks or shoes. (113–14)

While this Oxford Street clock associates 'time ratified by Greenwich' with commercial interests, other sections of the novel show the powers of 'the great clock at Westminster' chiming, in every sense – as in *Jacob's Room* – with wider powers of government and officialdom. Set in 1923, *Mrs Dalloway* shows a whole society barely recovering from the Great War, still a source in 'all men and women, [of] a well of tears' (12). 'Everyone has friends who were killed in the War', the novel reflects, its losses recently re-emphasised by Westminster Abbey's inauguration of a 'tomb of the Unknown Warrior', memorial to 'thousands of poor chaps, with all their lives before them, shovelled together' (74, 148, 128). Woolf shows the institutions which presided over the war nevertheless continuing to exercise undiminished authority over contemporary life and 'the course of history' – their influences empowered and defined by the measures of the clock and the 'monumental time' Ricoeur describes. Big Ben's 'majesty laying down the law, so solemn, so just' resonates throughout *Mrs Dalloway* with references to imperial power and state authority, and to a militarism apparently almost unsullied, in popular apprehension, by the 'well of tears' of the war (141). Clarissa Dalloway's admirer Peter Walsh still encounters 'strict in step ... boys in uniform, carrying guns ... on their faces an expression like the letters of a legend written round the base of a statue praising duty, gratitude, fidelity, love of England'. Marching up Whitehall under the 'marble stare' of 'all the exalted statues', the cadets' mechanical movements and stony expressions suggest to Peter that 'life, with its varieties, its irreticences, had been laid under a pavement of monuments and wreaths and drugged into a stiff yet staring corpse by discipline' (57–8). Similarly engrained allegiances to monuments, discipline and authority figure in descriptions of 'veneration whether for Queen, Prince, or Prime Minister . . . greatness . . . majesty', and for 'the flag . . . Empire . . . the House of Windsor' (19, 21). The most disturbing allegiance is Sir William Bradshaw's unswerving faith in 'divine proportion', described as his 'goddess' (110). Characterised by association with railway timetabling, as Chapter 1 described, as well as by the 'chorus' of clocks around Bradshaw's Harley Street surgery, this 'sense of proportion' is deployed with near-homicidal rigour in Bradshaw's disastrous treatment of the shell-shocked war victim, Septimus Smith (110, 113).

Remembrance and Time Regained

While representing in this way many of the pressures that Chapter 3 concluded by describing, Woolf also demonstrates a range of new fictional strategies for resisting 'monumental time', based on the alternative 'time in the mind' that Chapter 1 outlined. As *Mrs Dalloway* indicates, tactics involved had developed strongly by the mid-1920s, sometimes extending the example of authors earlier in the century, or priorities expressed in critical writing shortly after the Great War, notably by Woolf herself. Commentators at the time were quick to emphasise that an uncertain life following the war – fractured by shadow-lines, cuts and chasms it had stretched across the history of the age – required new strategies of narrative representation. The formlessness and anarchy that T. S. Eliot identified in contemporary history in 1923 – in his essay '"Ulysses", Order and Myth' – led him to consider conventional fictional forms redundant, or incommensurate with the needs of a troubled new age. In 'Modern Novels' – an essay first published a few months after the Armistice, in April 1919 – Woolf likewise stressed a need to depart from literary custom and convention. Like Eliot, she uses as an example of properly 'modern' fiction James Joyce's *Ulysses* (1922) – some of whose chapters had recently appeared in literary journals – particularly praising its innovative representation of 'the flickerings of that innermost flame which flashes its myriad messages through the brain'.[3]

---

[3] Woolf, 'Modern Novels', *Essays,* III, 34. *The Little Review* published thirteen sections of *Ulysses* between 1918 and 1920. Five parts also appeared in *The Egoist* in 1919.

Her essay's emphasis on mental messages and 'innermost flame' is usually considered an early recommendation of modernist stream of consciousness and interior monologue styles. These were preferable, Woolf considered, to the excessive concentration on an external, material world she attributes to authors successful before the war, Arnold Bennett particularly. Yet in demanding that novelists record the innermost movements of consciousness, 'Modern Novels' also has obvious implications for the temporality and structure of fiction. These are highlighted in Woolf's suggestion that – in examining consciousness 'exposed to the ordinary course of life' – novelists should 'record the atoms as they fall upon the mind in the order in which they fall', however 'disconnected and incoherent' this may appear (33–4). Since 'atoms' of thought may originate as readily in memory as in immediate impression, Woolf's recommendation of a new, inward focalisation for modern novels inevitably implies departure from narrative's 'ordinary course' or conventional linear order. Perhaps assured by the development of her own writing in the intervening years, Woolf further emphasised this implication when she republished her essay as 'Modern Fiction' in 1925.

'Life is not a series of gig lamps symmetrically arranged', this revised version of the essay adds: 'life is a luminous halo, a semi-transparent envelope surrounding us from the beginning of consciousness to the end'.[4] Evoking the days of horse-drawn carriages, reference to gig lamps seems incongruous, or deliberately antiquated, in an essay on modern fiction. Woolf's series of lamps nevertheless aptly recalls the vision of authors – T. S. Eliot and Joseph Conrad – whose work earlier in the century anticipated the modernist idioms she recommends. Her exactly arranged gig lamps obviously resemble the sequence of horometrical street lamps in T. S. Eliot's 'Rhapsody on a Windy Night' – written around 1910, and similarly indicating inner reaches of mind and memory as alternatives to the bright, artificial precisions of the material world. Eliot's dissolving 'lunar synthesis' and Woolf's 'luminous halo' or 'semi-transparent envelope' likewise suggest a wholeness which survives, within consciousness, despite the fragmented temporalities of 'Rhapsody on a Windy Night', or the 'dividing and subdividing' clocks Woolf represents in *Mrs Dalloway*. Her series of gig lamps also recalls Joseph Conrad's description in *The Secret Agent* (1907) of nocturnal footsteps resounding regularly

---

[4] Woolf, 'Modern Fiction', *Essays*, IV, 160.

'in the quiet, narrow street ... as if the passer-by had started to pace out all eternity, from gas-lamp to gas-lamp in a night without end'. Extending the novel's concerns with temporality, and with relations between measured time and eternity, these disturbingly regular footsteps both resemble and accentuate 'the ticking of the old clock' within the Verloc's household.[5]

Both 1919 and 1925 versions of Woolf's essay record 'unconditional gratitude' for Conrad's work.[6] These feelings were naturally shared by Ford Madox Ford, recalling in the early 1920s, in *Joseph Conrad: A Personal Remembrance* (1924), his collaboration with Conrad in the opening years of the century. Along with *Ulysses* and, naturally enough, *Mrs Dalloway* – each discussed below – Ford's Great War tetralogy, *Parade's End* (1924–8), probably offers the best illustration of how priorities of the kind Woolf outlined in her essays came to be developed in fiction after the Great War. For Ford, this involved extending idioms adopted more tentatively in earlier years. *Parade's End* moves 'backwards and forwards over [the] past' much in the manner he recalled devising with Conrad, and had previously deployed in *The Good Soldier* (1914), but more sustained concentration on the flickerings of inner consciousness allows still more decisive departure from life as a series.[7] The tetralogy's central figure, Tietjens, provides what is almost a theoretical description of narrative strategies involved when he asks his eventual lover, Valentine, to ignore conventionally measured time and instead

> cut out from this afternoon, just before 4.58 it was when I said that to you and you consented ... I heard the Horse Guards clock. ... To now. ... Cut it out; and join time up. ... It *can* be done. ... You know they do it surgically; for some illness; cut out a great length of the bowel and join the tube up.[8]

The temporal surgery Tietjens describes is ingeniously undertaken by the chapter in which his suggestion appears. It begins and ends with his return home around 3.30am, and his subsequent departure

---

[5] Joseph Conrad, *The Secret Agent: A Simple Tale* (1907; Harmondsworth: Penguin, 1967), 55. Subsequent references are to this edition.
[6] Woolf, 'Modern Novels', *Essays*, III, 31; 'Modern Fiction', *Essays*, IV, 158.
[7] Ford, *Joseph Conrad*, 130.
[8] Ford Madox Ford, *Parade's End* (1924–8; Harmondsworth: Penguin, 1982), 285. Subsequent references are to this edition. In this passage and others quoted from *Parade's End*, the ellipses appear in the original.

for the Western Front. Between, the narrative moves back through his recollections of events earlier in the day, including those around 4.58pm. As in much of the novel, recollections of this kind and the thoughts they provoke are mediated through the voice of both character and author, in a version of Free Indirect Style which offers very full, fluent entry into individual minds and memories, Tietjens's predominantly. The method allows Ford to cut substantial sections from the slack bowel of time and reshape them, repeatedly, into recursive loops. Each of these delves back into memories of earlier incidents and then proceeds forward to join up again with the moment at which the character's retrospection began.

Mixing recollections into present thought and experience in this way reshapes conventions not only of narrative order, but of duration – shrinking and expanding beyond even the pliant limits shaping Conrad's writing twenty years or so earlier, or those Mann describes in *The Magic Mountain*. Reflections of the kind that occur to Inspector Heat in *The Secret Agent* – about 'ages' of experience somehow contained 'between two successive winks of an eye' – are expressed more frequently in *Parade's End*, and the 'ages' concerned are still more extensive, even extravagant, in length. Occasionally, the scale of this chronological compression and mental expansion surprises even the characters involved, perhaps incidentally suggesting an element of authorial self-congratulation regarding the brilliantly anachronous narrative tactics required. 'Good God!', Tietjens's wife remarks to herself after one set of reflections, 'only one minute. . . . I've thought all that in only a minute'. After another expanse of introspection, stretching over several pages, Valentine likewise reflects on the strangeness of 'what thought was', prompted by realising what 'a hell of a lot' could be 'thought of in ten minutes' (417, 519).

For Tietjens, intrusions of memory into present consciousness not only happen 'a hell of a lot', but bring him a lot closer to hell, of a kind – to infernally intense memories of life and death in the trenches. Between two lines of conversation, for example – a General's infuriating question, and a more-or-less immediate response – pages of text represent current thoughts overtaken by Tietjens's chaotic recollection of recent experiences, including the death of one of his soldiers, Morgan. Inexpugnable memories ensure that

> Panic came over Tietjens. He knew it would be his last panic of that interview. No brain could stand more. Fragments of scenes of fighting, voices, names, went before his eyes and ears. Elaborate problems. . . . The whole map of the embattled world ran out in front of him – as

large as a field. An embossed map in greenish *papier mâché* – a ten-acre field of embossed *papier mâché*, with the blood of O Nine Morgan blurring luminously over it. Years before . . . How many months? . . . Nineteen, to be exact, he had sat on some tobacco plants on the Mont de Kats. . . . No, the Montagne Noire. In Belgium. . . . What had he been doing? Trying to get the lie of the land. . . . No. . . . Waiting to point out positions. (492–3)

Tangled memories of this kind make positions as hard to establish temporally as topographically, regularly leaving Tietjens feeling he has 'lost all sense of chronology' (486). Like Richard Aldington's central character in *Death of a Hero* (1929), he finds of his most disturbing war experiences that 'he did not know how many days and nights [they] lasted, lost completely the sequence of events, found great gaps in his conscious memory'. While struggling to sort out memories of dates and sequences of events on the Home Front, during the Great War, Valentine likewise concludes that 'when you thought of Time in those days your mind wavered impotently like eyes tired by reading too small print' (517). Ford's anachronous tactics ensure that his readers 'waver' in the same way, encountering wartime experience as the kind of 'timeless confusion' Aldington describes, and which medical science later recognised as characteristic of trauma.[9] *Parade's End* forcefully communicates, in this way, the nature of 'Time in those days', using strategies of the kind Woolf recommends to represent a society struggling to understand its position within the chaotic, blood-blurred map the Great War had made of recent history.

The same might be said of *Mrs Dalloway*, though only to a limited extent. Like Ford, Woolf traces the effects of shell-shock on an individual soldier – Bradshaw's unfortunate patient, Septimus Smith. Less able even than Tietjens to separate immediate experience from obsessive memory, Septimus even finds the war dead somehow still lurking around the park where he sits on a June morning. Like *Parade's End*, too, *Mrs Dalloway* concentrates not only on individual trauma, but on a 'well of tears' discernible throughout a whole society. Yet Woolf works towards different ends to Ford's, reaching back more affirmatively, through memory, into the years preceding the Great War, and developing, in doing so, potentials offered by different literary models and antecedents. While Ford owed his tactics

---

[9] Richard Aldington, *Death of a Hero* (1929; London: Hogarth Press, 1984), 323. Subsequent references are to this edition.

of going 'backwards and forwards' to Conrad, Woolf's suggests that whatever her 'gratitude' to this example, she may have found Marcel Proust – 'far the greatest modern novelist', in her view – more suggestive of directions she sought to follow herself.[10] Consistently with her distaste for life as a series, Woolf complains in a diary entry of 1928 about the 'appalling narrative business of the realist: getting on from lunch to dinner', resolving instead to 'read Proust . . . go backwards and forwards'.[11] She might more accurately have mentioned reading *more* Proust, having probably already covered three volumes of *À la recherche du temps perdu* (1913–27) by the time she wrote *Mrs Dalloway*. As early as 1922 – in a letter to Roger Fry, who first interested her in *À la rechereche* late in 1919 – she was already expressing a wish to write like Proust, and a belief that, occasionally at least, she could.[12]

Enthusiasm of this kind was not unusual among Anglophone writers and readers in the 1920s. Proust's work had been early introduced across the Channel by a *Times Literary Supplement* review of the first volume of *À la recherche du temps perdu* – *Swann's Way* (*Du côté de chez Swann*) – in the year it appeared, 1913. Proust's fiction became more readily accessible after C. K. Scott Moncrieff's translations began to appear in 1922, as *Remembrance of Things Past*. Scott Moncrieff's choice of title is significant – like Ford's, for his 1924 memoir of Conrad – suggesting how extensively 'Remembrance' figured as a general concern in the years after the Great War. A straightforward version of the title, often preferred by later translators – 'In Search of Lost Time', or 'In Search of Lost Times' – would have reflected more accurately Proust's wishes for the English version, as well as his immediate interests throughout much of his novel-sequence. These are not much centred, explicitly, on remembrance of the war: obviously not at all in *Du côté de chez Swann*, published before its outbreak, and scarcely in the other opening volumes that Scott Moncrieff was translating in the early 1920s. During the process of writing *À la recherche du temps perdu*, Proust relocated its early stages

---

[10] See Woolf, letter to Vanessa Bell, 21 April 1927, *Letters*, III, 365.
[11] Woolf, diary entry for 28 November 1928, *A Writer's Diary*, 138.
[12] Woolf mentions having read three volumes of *À la recherche du temps perdu* in a letter to Margaret Llewelyn Davies, 9 February 1925, *Letters*, III, 166; letter to Roger Fry, 2 November 1919, *Letters*, II, 396; 'Oh if I could write like that! . . . I feel I *can* write like that, and seize my pen and then I *can't* write like that. Scarcely anyone so stimulates the nerves of language in me', Woolf remarks in another letter to Fry, 6 May 1922, *Letters*, II, 525.

to areas devastated by the war, ensuring that times and places the narrator Marcel recalls are accessible *only* in memory. But it is only in the last volume, *Time Regained* (*Le temps retrouvé*, 1927), that he describes a letter informing Marcel that landscapes remembered since his childhood have become 'a ravaged countryside, where vast battles are fought to gain possession of some path, some slope which [he] once loved'.[13] The same volume describes Marcel returning to Paris in 1916 and finding that effects of war have in other ways left it, too, a ravaged city, its once-glittering salons and social circles now weary, frayed and ageing.

Time Regained suggests a remedy for these losses when Marcel pronounces himself ready to undertake an artistic struggle, dedicated towards reintegrating lost time into a narrative shaped by memory and the paths it offers into his beloved past. The end of *Time Regained* thus shows him discovering, or re-emphasising, the narrative potentials that Chapter 1 discussed – opportunities to reconfigure life through imagination and desire; times in the mind rather than times only of loss and decay. These potentials have of course been deployed throughout *À la recherche du temps perdu* in showing Marcel successfully chasing his own tale. Naturally, the novel itself is the kind of narrative he eventually pronounces himself ready to write, and the ambitions he eventually expresses have already been fulfilled by the sophisticated, complex strategies it deploys. Paths followed into memory often involve not only a single analepsis, but several embedded within each other. These excursions into the past often hugely stretch norms of duration, as well as of order, flooding voluminous memories into supposedly brief moments of recall, and occasionally leaving the story flowing on at a stage well beyond the point at which retrospection began. Such devices sometimes suspend conventional chronology almost completely, as Gérard Genette emphasises in *Narrative Discourse* (*Discours du récit*, 1972) – a study of narrative strategies largely based on analyses of Proust's tactics. *À la recherche du temps perdu*, in Genette's view, is 'undoubtedly, as it proclaims, a novel of Time lost and found again, but it is also . . . a novel of Time ruled, captured, bewitched, surreptitiously subverted'.[14]

---

[13] Marcel Proust, *Remembrance of Things Past*, trans. C. K. Scott Moncrieff and Terence Kilmartin (Harmondsworth: Penguin, 1983), III, 778. Subsequent references are to this edition, though Proust's original title, *À la recherche du temps perdu*, is retained.

[14] Genette, *Narrative Discourse*, 160.

Though evolving in complexity throughout, Proust's means of subverting time and recovering the past would have been clear enough, to early readers, almost from the beginning of his first volume. Its opening section ranges particularly freely over intermingled recollections of both childhood and adulthood – summed up as 'shifting and confused gusts of memory' (I, 7). The section concludes with Proust's most celebrated instance of near-total recall – of 'reality mysteriously recovered from the back of . . . consciousness', as that early *Times Literary Supplement* reviewer suggested.[15] This occurs when Marcel eats a tea-soaked madeleine cake and finds that from it 'sprang into being'

> all the flowers in our garden and in M. Swann's park, and the water-lilies on the Vivonne and the good folk of the village and their little dwellings and the parish church and the whole of Combray and its surroundings, taking shape and solidity . . . town and gardens alike, from my cup of tea. (I, 51)

This early episode illustrates the possibility that Marcel goes on to celebrate near the end of *Time Regained*: that memory, 'when it introduces the past, unmodified, into the present – the past just as it was at the moment when it was itself the present – suppresses the mighty dimension of Time' (III, 1087). Proust recovers in this way a huge range of 'unmodified' pictures of society during France's pre-war *belle époque,* suppressing the time that has intervened, resisting the 'insolent indifference' of the clock, and drawing attention away, for much of the novel, from the disasters of the Great War (I, 8).

Woolf achieves a comparable recovery in *Mrs Dalloway*, employing memory to depart regularly, as her essays recommend, from life in serial sequence. In *Orlando* (1928), she sums up – along with contrasts between 'time in the mind' and 'time on the clock' – views of memory echoing Proust's conviction that 'the simplest act or gesture remains immured as within a thousand sealed vessels . . . disposed over the whole range of our years' (III, 903). Memory, for Woolf, is a 'seamstress',

> and a capricious one at that. Memory runs her needle in and out, up and down, hither and thither . . . the most ordinary movement in the world, such as sitting down at a table and pulling the inkstand

---

[15] 'Art or Life? "A Small Boy and Others"', *Times Literary Supplement*, 4 December 1913, 585.

towards one, may agitate a thousand odd, disconnected fragments . . . our commonest deeds are set about with a fluttering and flickering of wings, a rising and falling of lights.[16]

Extending the views of 'Modern Novels' and 'Modern Fiction', her comments offer a theoretical version of narrative strategies she had already employed in *Mrs Dalloway*, relying extensively, like Proust, on memory's capacity to stitch into flickering present consciousness distant and often more congenial periods in the past. Throughout the novel, memories open promising portals, apparently spontaneously, into characters' earlier experiences – most often not in the recent years of the Great War, but in earlier ones, belonging to a *belle époque* comparable to Proust's.

Entries to this remembered period open on the novel's first page, even before the chimes of Big Ben are first heard booming across London. Woolf's third paragraph begins by connecting Clarissa's pleasures on a fine summer morning in 1923 with ones experienced much earlier, in the country house of her youth, thirty years or so previously, long before the Great War:

> What a lark! What a plunge! For so it had always seemed to her when, with a little squeak of the hinges, which she could hear now, she had burst open the French windows and plunged at Bourton into the open air. (5)

That 'little squeak of the hinges' could almost be read as Woolf's comment on her own textual practices. Though a sentence in the previous paragraph – 'the doors would be taken off their hinges' – refers to arrangements for Clarissa's evening party, it could likewise be taken to describe freedoms of temporal movement throughout the novel. Flickerings of her characters' consciousnesses – represented in forms of Free Indirect Style, or of indirect speech and thought – allow Woolf to stitch together current perceptions and memories almost seamlessly, opening doors between present and past with minimal grating of hinges, or none. Between single sentences of bright chat at Clarissa's party, for example, long reflections on past experience flow almost unimpeded through characters' minds – available, intriguingly and poignantly, to readers, though not to both conversants. Like Septimus, registering while sitting in the park 'there was his

---

[16] Virginia Woolf, *Orlando* (1928; Harmondsworth: Penguin, 1975), 55, 69. Subsequent references are to this edition.

hand', yet, somehow simultaneously, 'there the dead', Peter Walsh sometimes comes close to conflating past and present completely (28). Sitting on Clarissa's sofa in June 1923, he is convinced she is somehow making the moon 'rise at Bourton on the terrace in the summer sky', as it had during his unsuccessful courtship of her there, decades earlier (53). 'There above them it hung, that moon', Peter thinks, holding out his hand like Septimus, yet picturing it as if the terrace at Bourton were still its backdrop (47–8). Clarissa herself feels of Peter that, regardless of their years of separation, 'some days, some sights' would continue to return him to her – through involuntary yet inescapable memories – with almost complete immediacy. She reflects that this 'perhaps was the reward of having cared for people; they came back in the middle of St James's Park on a fine morning – indeed they did' (9).

Finding figures from the past reappearing in the park, on this fine June morning, is one of several experiences establishing covert connections between Clarissa and Septimus, though they never meet or interact directly. Clarissa learns of him only at the end of the novel, from Bradshaw, whose arrival at her party has been delayed by Septimus's suicide. She acknowledges that she feels 'somehow very like him – the young man who had killed himself' (206). Comparisons between them nevertheless also highlight distinctions – principally in the intensity, or even just sanity – with which each allows the past to re-enter present experience. For Septimus, genuinely unhinged, the doors of perception really have come off, leaving the war dead still walking among London's living, and existence intolerable as a result. For Clarissa, past and present alternate or coalesce through less disturbed forms of memory and imagination, contributing some sense of continuity to her personal life, despite dislocations in the once-steady progression of days and years enforced by the chasm of the war. Unlike the 'young man who had killed himself – had . . . plunged' (204), Clarissa plunges into earlier times in ways that transcend recent experiences of loss, evading the clock-centred 'monumental time' comprehensively controlling post-war society.

Grief and loss are eventually transcended more decisively in Woolf's next novel, *To the Lighthouse* (1927), though for much of its length it extends strategies – flickerings of memory, particularly – similar to those Woolf deploys in *Mrs Dalloway*. Like Clarissa, characters in the later novel find memory opening doors into the past unpredictably, though compellingly. While painting her picture, in the novel's third part, Lily Briscoe feels that 'as she dipped into the blue paint, she dipped too into the past', finding herself 'thinking again of Mrs Ramsay on the beach ... as if a door had opened, and one went in and stood gazing silently about'.[17] For Lily herself, openings of this kind provide little consolation. Instead, 'the pain increased' as she vainly cries out to Mrs Ramsay, whose earlier death, during the war years, figures briefly in the novel's second section (205). In 'tunnelling her way into her picture, into the past', Lily nevertheless highlights the movement of To the Lighthouse itself towards another form of consolation, through the formal containment and closure offered by art (197).

Like Proust, regularly describing the work of artists, musicians and writers in À la recherche du temps perdu, Woolf ensures in To the Lighthouse that references to art's potentials – focused around Lily's painting – extend self-reflexively towards the form and strategy of her own fiction. The 'cut' made by the war is reduplicated by the decisive line, drawn 'there, in the centre', which concludes both Lily's painting and the novel itself. This central line also makes her 'vision' formally correlative, as well as co-terminous, with the fiction in which she appears (237). The tripartite structure of Lily's completed painting is reduplicated both by a novel one of the characters reads – somehow seeming like a 'trident' – and by To the Lighthouse itself, divided in the middle by the short, sharp section, entitled 'Time Passes', describing loss and destruction in the war years (236). By the end of the novel, time passing during that period has faded into time past, its pain no longer so immediate. Despite its losses, members of the Ramsay family finally fulfil – or even move beyond – the ambition to reach the lighthouse that had so preoccupied them during the pre-war summer's day the first section describes. Watching their journey towards the island on which the lighthouse stands, Lily finds that she is 'losing consciousness of outer things', and that the sea around Skye 'had melted away into a blue haze'– the colour she dips into when painting the past (181, 236). The lighthouse itself fades towards invisibility, perhaps discernible only as the kind of line Lily uses to complete her picture. 'Outer things', this conclusion suggests – events in the world, and the shadow-line of the war – may be dissolved and resolved, contained or transcended, within the semi-transparent envelope of consciousness, and through the settling of memories, much as Proust affirmed, into the consoling patterns offered by art and literature themselves.

---

[17] Virginia Woolf, To the Lighthouse (1927; Harmondsworth: Penguin, 1973), 195. Subsequent references are to this edition.

A comparable vision – encompassing memory, blue distances, and the open sea and sky – concludes the work Eliot and Woolf identified as pioneering new possibilities for fiction in the early 1920s: *Ulysses*, first published as a single volume in 1922. Like Woolf and Ford, Joyce deploys extravagantly the reshapings of duration and order offered by 'time in the mind'. *Ulysses* repeatedly departs from life as a series, often demonstrating – still further than *Parade's End* – what 'a hell of a lot' can be thought in minutes. A single day of thought, *Ulysses* shows, may provide enough material, or more than enough, to fill an entire thousand-page novel. Joyce's tactics also show how comprehensively past experience can be represented, through repeated analepses, within a narrative of consciousness, 'exposed to the ordinary course of life' even of a single day. Though *Ulysses* moves forward, chapter by chapter, through eighteen hours of 16/17 June 1904, repeated recursions into Leopold Bloom's memories ensure that his life is represented as fully as any in a *Bildungsroman* – though readers' knowledge of the past is obviously acquired in a much less chronologically orderly way.[18] In the 'Hades' section, for example, set at Paddy Dignam's funeral, Bloom's memories move far beyond recent death and loss, turning back to his father's suicide, long ago, and the burial of his infant son Rudy, ten years previously. Typically, Bloom's thoughts also stray further and more freely – over his marriage to Molly, their earlier life in Lombard Street West, and the childhood of their daughter.

Flowing thoughts figure most freely in the final section of *Ulysses*, in following Molly's mingling of memories and perceptions on the dreamy threshold of sleep. In the novel's closing pages, these move far beyond the present moment – in the early hours of 17 June 1904 – not through a single memory, but Molly's conflation of several. The first of these returns to the day Bloom proposed to her, '16 years ago my God' – i.e. in 1888 – on the vantage point of Howth Head, poised above the sea near Dublin. Molly recalls that she chose not to answer immediately, but instead 'only looked out over the sea and the sky ... thinking of so many things he didnt know'.[19] Her seaward gaze

---

[18] In *About Time*, Mark Currie suggests that characters' memories of this kind – like those in *Mrs Dalloway* – are not strictly analeptic, since in terms of the time of their *occurrence* they do not depart from the chronological order of the story. As he also acknowledges, though, such memories wrench readers back into the past just as decisively, and anachronously, as 'truer' forms of analepsis (36).

[19] James Joyce, *Ulysses* (1922; Harmondsworth: Penguin, 1992), 931, 932.

follows much the same direction as Stephen Dedalus's, in Joyce's *A Portrait of the Artist as a Young Man* (1916). Idling in a 'waste of wild air and brackish waters' on the shores of Dublin Bay, Stephen is enthralled, half-erotically, by a girl standing nearby, barelegged, in a rivulet in the sand. 'Alone and still, gazing out to sea', she draws his vision outward over an empty expanse of sky and water, as if towards 'the strange light of some new world'.[20] Molly's remembered gaze turns out to be still more erotic, though in looking seaward not only towards a new world, but one familiar from another, earlier part of her past, during her youth in Gibraltar.

References to this location hugely expand the temporal, spatial and imaginative scale of Joyce's concluding vision in *Ulysses*. Versions of the story of Odysseus – followed parodically throughout the novel – describe a final voyage beyond the rock of Gibraltar, one of the mythic Pillars of Hercules which marked in the Classical period the point where the known world opened out into uncharted infinity. Moving in this way towards a location on the edge of knowable space, Joyce also stretches as far as possible the limits of specific or measurable time. Molly's memories of accepting Bloom in 1888 interfuse with recollections of saying 'yes' to another, remembered lover in Gibraltar. Yet in looking back from 1904 to 1888, and thence earlier – moving from Howth to Gibraltar, and toward open seas beyond each – Molly's mind mingles memory, recollection and remembered recollection fluently enough to create a conclusion unlimited by any particular place, time, episode or individual. Extending the spirit of parody which directs his whole novel, Joyce follows literary conventions of comedic closure – generally in marriage or sexual union – but ingeniously stretches and subverts them. Molly's final 'yes' could be delivered to any or all of unknowable numbers of lovers. *Ulysses* thus ends in a kind of mega-marriage, or comprehensively consummate relationship – ultimately, not only between individuals, but between vision or desire and life itself. The infinite reach of this ending is confirmed in the plans and schemas Joyce used to explain his tactics in *Ulysses*, stipulating a particular hour of the day for all its chapters except the last.[21] In one plan, no specific time is suggested for this chapter. In another, Joyce uses the symbol ∞ to indicate infinity instead of a numbered hour – even to

---

[20] James Joyce, *A Portrait of the Artist as a Young Man* (1916; Harmondsworth: Penguin, 1992), 185–7.
[21] These plans have been widely reproduced, including by Richard Ellmann in *Ulysses on the Liffey*, 188 et seq.

suggest that one of those '8s' in 1888 might have fallen sideways, as if the calendar and the counting of time had somehow collapsed or been cast aside.

This concluding vision of oceanic infinity is highlighted by the contrasting constraints on space and time which figure in the previous chapter. In this 'Ithaca' section, Joyce invents the FAQ, anticipating requests for information – Frequently Asked Questions – about his own text. Concentrated on objective fact and calculative accuracy, 'Ithaca' was described by Joyce himself as 'mathematical catechism', intended to offer readers the opportunity to 'know everything and know it in the baldest, coldest way'.[22] The narrative of 'Ithaca' consequently claims that it is absolutely 'unaltered by modifications', and many of its exchanges carry the apparent authority of scientific language, unadorned and coldly precise (868). Even the intimate details of Bloom's habitual sleeping arrangements – head to toe with Molly, as usual, while she listens to the narrative of his day – are delivered in the form of navigational coordinates, precisely defining global positioning:

> In what directions did listener and narrator lie?
> Listener, S.E. by E.; Narrator, N.W. by W.: on the 53rd parallel of latitude, N. and 6th meridian of longitude, W.: at an angle of 45° to the terrestrial equator. (870)

Like many apparently objective or 'unaltered' details in 'Ithaca', the coordinates offered are nevertheless more parodic, or even deliberately inaccurate, than viable. As careful readers of *Ulysses* can hardly fail to notice, 'Ithaca' regularly undermines the scientific certitudes its generally bald, coldly technical language seems so confidently to provide.[23]

For readers of modern fiction generally, there is also a wider resonance in the 'catechetical interrogation' directed around Bloom's bed (868). Exactly specified meridians of latitude and longitude recall the challenges that Joseph Conrad endured in his 1880s nautical examinations – described in Chapter 2, and recalled in his essay 'Outside Literature', published in the same year as *Ulysses*.

---

[22] Joyce's comments were made when he was writing the 'Ithaca' section in February 1921, and are quoted in Budgen, *James Joyce and the Making of Ulysses*, 263.

[23] Even 'the cold of interstellar space', for example, cannot be 'thousands of degrees below ... absolute zero' (827). Bloom's and Molly's angle to the equator, in Dublin at 53°N, is likely to be 37°, and not 45°, though depending on how this angle is configured.

In moving on from 'Ithaca' to Molly's stream of thoughts, ending in erotic, oceanic infinitudes of recollection, Joyce offers the most comprehensive alternative imaginable to the constraints of calculation and chronology that Conrad encountered so demandingly, and, among modernist authors, so early. Molly's vision of sea and sky restores the unlimited expanse of ocean dreamed of in Conrad's first romantic imaginings of seagoing adventure. Fathomless streams of consciousness and memory flow towards the infinity and eternity Stevie's endless drawing of circles seeks, in *The Secret Agent*, beyond Greenwich-ratified longitudes and exact temporalities.

The end of *Ulysses* thus confirms that between the 1880s – or the 1890s, when Conrad began publishing – and the early 1920s, fiction found new ways of flying by nets imposed by meridians, mean times and the rationalisations of technology, commerce and industry generally. Crucially, too, at the end of a novel written largely during the years of the Great War, between 1914 and 1922 – one in which history is defined as 'a nightmare' (42) – Molly eventually finds means, through blissful memory, of imaginatively escaping history altogether. Moving in this way towards 'the light of some new world' – freer of the ravages of history and the rationalisations of the clock – *Ulysses* and the novels considered above resisted 'monumental time' at just the historical moment, following the Great War, when such resistance had become more than ever desirable. The 'fault line' in the evolution of literary modernism, identified by Fredric Jameson in Joseph Conrad's writing, developed in the 1920s into a whole tectonic shift. The investigation of conflict between 'time on the clock' and 'time in the mind' that *Orlando* recommends was already quite complete by the end of the decade – contributing to a flexible, memorious modernist chronotype, moving freely beyond constraints of 'monumental time' and of literary representation of life as a series.

Time and Space Obliterated: Physics and Philosophy

Even as the decade began, the general public – not only novel readers – might have been growing more aware of alternatives to the clock's constraints. Some of these were strongly in evidence even at that most chronologically controlled moment, at 11am on the first Remembrance Day, 11 November 1919. The day's ceremonies generally followed plans that the King had outlined, but with results sometimes stranger than might have been anticipated. Newspapers the following day reported that the two minutes' silence had been thoroughly maintained, interrupted only by a few random sounds – the sneeze of a horse, the distant bark of a dog, human cries or sobs that could not be suppressed. Deeper and more unbroken than ever before, and occurring in the middle of an otherwise ordinary morning, this deathly hush on Britain's streets inevitably seemed odd, even uncanny. 'Secure mental environment', *The Times* remarked, was unsettled by a 'calm in which recognizable things became strange and the ordinary limitations of the human imagination were extended'. An aspect of this extension, *The Times* added, was that

> one hardly knew whether the two minutes appeared short or long. Time and space were obliterated. In an interval of seconds, men must have revisited the torn and blasted fields of France, the ridges of Flanders, the beaches of Gallipoli, and many a cemetery where long rows of wooden crosses mark the resting place of those who fell.[24]

The moment at which 'monumental time' enforced its firmest constraint on public life thus turned out to be one in which – also on a new scale – time was 'obliterated' by memory and imagination. Though the clock obviously did control absolutely the public's physical presence and actions from 11.00 to 11.02am, the silence and stasis it imposed left 'mental environment' unusually free. No doubt the majority of those standing in silence did use those minutes of freedom to concentrate, as the King wished, on 'reverent remembrance'. Yet this remembrance must have been very various and wide-ranging. Memories need not have been confined to the battlefields of France, Flanders and Gallipoli, but might have extended much more widely over the lives of those who died there. While the war might have remained in the foreground, there would have been every reason to think further back, too – over happier days and years preceding 1914 – or to imagine how lives lost might have developed if they had been allowed to continue into the future. All sorts of memory and desire, in other words, might have unfolded during that brief silence on Remembrance Day. Public experience of it – general or almost universal throughout the country – strongly accentuated remembrance within the outlook of the early 1920s, also demonstrating potentials soon extended in the modernist novel. Emphasising what 'a hell of a lot' could be thought in minutes, or even 'an interval of seconds', the experience showed how the mind's freedoms – perennially available,

---

[24] 'At St Paul's: Silence of Remembrance'; 'The Abbey Service: A Real Communion', *The Times*, 12 November 1919, 16.

but especially desirable in an age of 'monumental time' – might reorient the clock's controls, and how far remembrance might evade its constraints.

Other influences developing around Remembrance Day contributed to suggestions of this kind, and to movements towards 'the strange light of some new world', independent of strict chronological control. Noting that 'time and space were obliterated' during the previous day's ceremonies, readers of *The Times* on 12 November 1919 might have reflected that this was not the first time, in the past week, that their newspaper had offered comments of this kind. In referring to time and space, the report on Remembrance Day might itself have been influenced by sensational news appearing in *The Times* five days previously, almost alongside plans for the memorial ceremonies. The King's wishes were reported on 7 November, at the far left of page 12. Opposite, on the right, appeared the headline 'Revolution in Science: New Theory of the Universe: Newtonian Ideas Overthrown' (Fig. 4.1). The column it headed described a joint session of the Royal Society and the Royal Astronomical Society, convened the previous evening to receive reports of an eclipse of the sun that had occurred six months earlier, on 29 May 1919. Teams of observers, one led by Arthur Eddington, had been despatched to photograph this eclipse, and their observations confirmed, or seemed to confirm, that the sun's gravitational field deflected light passing through it – or bent spacetime itself – much as Albert Einstein had predicted.[25] This deflection could not be fully explained by Newtonian physics. Fundamental, longstanding, Newtonian principles – including conceptions of the universe as temporally and spatially homogeneous – therefore seemed likely to be untrustworthy, requiring new understanding in terms of the non-homogeneous time and space proposed by Einstein's Theories of Relativity.

The immense implications of this eclipse report led the President of the Royal Society to describe it, as *The Times* noted, as 'one of the most momentous, if not the most momentous, pronouncements of human thought'.[26] There were good reasons for it to seem particularly momentous on 7 November 1919. On the same day – even on the same page – the public learned of the unusually absolute civic order

---

[25] The observations were not of ideal quality. Scientists questioned their accuracy, and Eddington's interpretation of them. Later observations confirmed that there were flaws in those made in 1919, though substantiating nevertheless the conclusions reached at the time. See Hawking, *A Brief History of Time*, 32.

[26] 'Revolution in Science: New Theory of the Universe: Newtonian Ideas Overthrown', *The Times*, 7 November 1919, 12.

Fig. 4.1 *The Times*, 7 November 1919.

imposed by the King's 'monumental time', it also received the momentous pronouncement that time, if it existed at all, might operate in ways much less than absolutely orderly. By 12 November, emotionally charged experiences of Remembrance Day, along with intellectually challenging news of Relativity – the former requiring exact timing, but each apparently tending to obliterate time and space – could hardly avoid combining into a substantial challenge to 'human thought'. To borrow the kind of generalisation Woolf used in one of her essays on modern fiction – remarking that 'on or about December 1910 human character changed' – there is good reason to consider that in or about the second week of November 1919 human experience of time was decisively changed.[27]

Change, of course, generally evolves more gradually, however suddenly its results may seem to appear. Einstein's Relativity theories immediately became sensational world news, but their complex mathematics mostly thwarted immediate understanding of their implications. In a long letter to *The Times*, three weeks after the Royal Society meeting, Einstein did what he could to clarify his work. His 'special relativity theory', he confirmed, did demand 'a change . . . in the doctrine of the physical laws of space and time'. Rather than relying on a single frame of reference, applicable throughout the universe, Relativity required individual events to be understood in relation to 'a system of co-ordinates' specifically associated with each. 'The mass of bodies and the rate of movement of clocks', his letter explained, 'must depend on their state of motion with regard to the co-ordinates'.[28] Einstein's attempts at clarification were soon extended by other commentators. Edwin E. Slosson published his engagingly entitled *Easy Lessons in Einstein: A Discussion of the More Intelligible Features of the Theory of Relativity* in 1920, with some input from Einstein himself. Many other popular expositions followed during the next decade.[29] One of the best of them, Bertrand Russell's *The ABC of Relativity* (1925), explained further the areas that Einstein had briefly outlined in his letter. 'The universal cosmic time which used to be taken for granted

---

[27] Woolf, 'Character in Fiction' (1924), *Essays*, III, 421.
[28] Dr Albert Einstein, 'Einstein on His Theory: Time, Space, and Gravitation: The Newtonian System', *The Times*, 28 November 1919, 13.
[29] Within a few years, expository studies had appeared by authors including H. L. Brose, J. H. Thirring, W. H. V. Reade, Charles Nordmann, James Rice and Thomas P. Nunn.

is ... no longer admissible', Russell remarks, since 'watches and clocks are affected by motion' and 'the time-order of events is in part dependent upon the observer'.[30] Wyndham Lewis probably exaggerated in estimating, in 1927, that 'within a few years of the arrival of Einstein upon the european scene the layman ... knows more about Relativity physics than any layman has ever known about the newtonian cosmology'.[31] Commentaries such as Russell's nevertheless did ensure that by the mid-1920s the immense popular excitement generated by Einstein's ideas had developed into some measure of general understanding.

As Lewis also notes, Einstein's influence – even much public knowledge of his theories – had in other ways been deferred for some time before his 'arrival' in 1919. As Einstein mentioned in his letter to *The Times*, proposals about 'the rate of movement of clocks' belonged originally to the Special Theory of Relativity he had published in 1905. Interest this had attracted – mostly among mathematicians, scientists and astronomers – was extended by the General Theory of Relativity he completed in 1915, developing his earlier conclusions to incorporate the influences of gravity and of acceleration. Several factors had continued to delay the full impact of this theory. The only empirical evidence initially supporting it was offered by the anomalous orbit of Mercury, the planet closest to the sun and therefore most substantially influenced by its gravity. Fuller proof required study of a total solar eclipse – ideally, as Arthur Eddington pointed out, one occurring on 29 May, when the bright stars of the Hyades appear in convenient proximity to the occluded disk of the sun, facilitating minute measurement of possible deflections of starlight. The occurrence of just such an eclipse in 1919 offered cosmic encouragement, or at any rate a perfect opportunity, for empirical confirmation of Einstein's theories.

Cosmic coincidence or convenience was consolidated by earthly developments, later in 1919, including a transition towards more restrained remembrance of the Great War, rather than belligerence regarding all things German. As a Quaker, pacifist and conscientious objector, Eddington had long advocated Einstein's ideas, along with international scientific cooperation generally. He had received little support during the war, and even after its conclusion, residual

---

[30] Russell, *The ABC of Relativity*, 50, 39, 44.
[31] Lewis, *Time and Western Man*, 11.

hostilities to German culture threatened to retard the reception of Relativity. On 8 November 1919, the day after reporting the 'momentous pronouncement' at the Royal Society meeting, *The Times* evidently found it advisable to include a short column outlining Einstein's character and allegiances. This emphasised that he was 'a Swiss Jew ... of liberal tendencies' who had protested against the war and undertaken no official duties while working in Berlin.[32] In his letter of 28 November, Einstein offered a wry, relativistic joke about this careful positioning. He notes that 'by an application of the theory of relativity to the taste of readers, to-day in Germany I am called a German man of science, and in England I am represented as a Swiss Jew' (13).

Whether earthly or celestial in their causes, delays in verifying Einstein's ideas focused attention all the more strongly, at the start of the 1920s, on issues which had perplexed scientists for some time even before the appearance of the Special Theory of Relativity. This early phase of Einstein's work resolved problems which had been troubling scientists for nearly a quarter of a century, following analyses of the velocity of light undertaken by Albert Michelson and Edward Morley in 1881. Challenges to conventional physics were extended a few years later through the work of Ernst Mach. In a study that Einstein admired, *The Science of Mechanics* (*Die Mechanik*, 1883), Mach dismissed the Newtonian idea of 'absolute, true, and mathematical time' as 'an idle metaphysical conception'.[33] While the clock, during the 1880s, was steadily strengthening its hold on the world – through the Prime Meridian Conference in Washington, and legislation in London – science was showing a growing disposition to challenge any absolute trust in the measurement or even existence of time. This inclination can be seen extending more widely through contemporary thinking, in philosophy as much as physics, and particularly in the work during the 1880s of a figure sometimes later compared with Einstein, or even seen as an influence on his ideas – Henri Bergson.

Connections between Bergson and Einstein are emphasised in Wyndham Lewis's compendious study of 1920s culture, art and writing, *Time and Western Man* (1927). Lewis insists that the work of 'Einstein, the later space-timeist' is 'identical with the old ... bergsonian philosophy' – probably because, he suggests, Einstein had 'at least read the work of Bergson'. In this and other areas,

---

[32] 'Dr Albert Einstein', *The Times*, 8 November 1919, 12.
[33] Mach, *The Science of Mechanics*, 272, 273.

Lewis's judgements were often coloured by the strong personal preference he declared – as an artist, as well as a writer – for 'definition and logical integrity', rather than 'flowing ... succession in time'.[34] Resulting concerns about the directions that 1920s culture seemed to be following sometimes led him to construe in terms of causation or even conspiracy what might only have been coincidence. Yet in this case, his views receive some support from a particularly well-informed 1920s commentator – Bergson himself. In a study of Einstein's work, *Duration and Simultaneity* (*Durée et Simultanéité: À propos de la théorie d'Einstein*, 1922), Bergson explained that he hoped to show that 'the salient features of time and its role in the physicist's calculations ... turned out to complete, not just confirm, what we had of old said about duration'.[35] His demonstration of this 'completion' was only partially convincing, though. Bergson had come close to following a career in mathematics himself, before embracing philosophy, but acknowledged that his expertise allowed him to consider only Einstein's Special Theory of Relativity, not its later development into the General Theory. Scientists and mathematicians in the 1920s often questioned his treatment even of the Special Theory, challenging in particular his interpretation of the Lorentz equations defining motion. Faced with what seemed at best partial understanding of his views, and his own perhaps limited grasp of Einstein's, Bergson discontinued publication of *Duration and Simultaneity* after 1931.[36]

Einstein and Bergson nevertheless had enough in common – superficially at least, in challenging conventional understanding of 'the salient features of time' – to make contemporary connections between their work understandable. As Lewis emphasises in *Time and Western Man*, '*the clock* is the central object of Bergson's time-philosophy, naturally, as it is the central object in einsteinian physics' (439). The clock does figure substantially – and as unreliably as it did for Einstein – in views that Bergson developed during the 1880s, published at the end of the decade in his *Essai sur les données immédiates de la conscience* (1889).

---

[34] Lewis, *Time and Western Man*, 102, 14, 129, 148.
[35] Bergson, 'Preface' to *Duration and Simultaneity*, xxviii.
[36] See *Duration and Simultaneity*, 151–2. From their beginning – a brief exchange of views in April 1922 – discussions between Bergson and Einstein suffered from a kind of *différend*: a lack of agreed terms and bases of debate, rather than differences only about the issues involved. Perhaps as result, in the later 1920s and thereafter, the two thinkers sometimes came to be considered as adversaries, contrary to Lewis's assessment. For an account of this and other developments in debates about their work, see Canales, *The Physicist and the Philosopher*.

'The dial of a clock' and 'the movement of the hand which corresponds to the oscillations of the pendulum', Bergson concludes, offer no true version of time.[37] They express no more than a set of speciously separated segments – 'lifeless mathematical intervals', in Lewis's summary – which correspond only to the spatial demarcations geometrically inscribed on the clock face (439). For Bergson, as for Woolf, life should therefore not be conceived as a series – a succession of clock-dissected discrete instants – nor in terms of quantifiable, divisible, or 'measureable . . . magnitude' of any kind. Instead, temporality should be experienced not only intellectually, but intuitively: within the self, as 'a process of organisation or interpenetration of conscious states . . . which constitutes true duration' (*durée*).[38] In this durational view of time, memories play a key role – constantly associated with present consciousness, and seamlessly incorporated into its evolving continuity. Bergson went on to analyse this role further in his work around the turn of the century, remarking in 'Dreams' ('Le Rêve', 1901), in terms similar to those later used by Proust and Woolf, that

> Behind the memories which crowd in upon our present occupation and are revealed by means of it, there are others, thousands on thousands of others, below and beneath the scene illuminated by consciousness . . . our past life is there, preserved even to the minutest details; nothing is forgotten; all we have perceived, thought, willed, from the first awakening of our consciousness, persists indefinitely.[39]

Bergson's thinking attracted a growing audience in France by the turn of the century, and a still wider one after translations into English began to appear, with *Essai sur les données immédiates de la conscience* published as *Time and Free Will* in 1910. By that date, interests in temporality among philosophers paralleled or outstripped those of physicists, figuring widely in the work of otherwise-disparate thinkers. As the philosopher Samuel Alexander remarked in 1916, 'Time has recently come into its full rights, in science through the mathematical physicists, in philosophy also through Prof. Bergson'.[40] John McTaggart had first published his arguments about the unreality of time in the journal *Mind* in 1908, later developing them further in *The Nature of Existence* (1927). Alexander's 1916 Gifford

---

[37] Bergson, *Time and Free Will*, 107–8.
[38] Ibid., 107, 108.
[39] Bergson, 'Dreams', *Mind-Energy*, 94.
[40] Alexander, *Space, Time, and Deity*, I, 36.

Lectures, published as *Space, Time, and Deity* (1920), considered on the other hand that empirical reality itself was the manifestation of interrelated dimensions of space and time. In *The Principles of Psychology* (1890) and earlier work, William James remained closer to Bergson's view of the essentially separate existence of space and time. Like Bergson, too, James considered that memories move into present consciousness without any 'time-gap', and that this consciousness 'flows', and 'does not appear to itself chopped up in bits'. It should therefore be seen, he remarks – coining the term later much used in literary criticism – as a *'stream of thought, of consciousness, or of subjective life'*. Edmund Husserl admired James's work, and his own thinking in the 1890s and later also had affinities with Bergson's – particularly in its concerns with memory, with internal rather than 'objective' time, and with 'the absolute time-constituting flow of consciousness'.[41] Bergson's ideas could also be compared with some of Friedrich Nietzsche's thinking during the 1870s and 1880s. Nietzsche was sometimes as critical as Bergson of 'divisible time spans' and of imposing 'arbitrary division and dismemberment' on the 'continuum' or 'flux' of experience. Nietzsche might even be seen as anticipating Einstein in his scepticism of 'space, time, and causality as absolutely and universally valid laws'.[42] Like all such 'laws', for Nietzsche, space and time were merely constructs of human consciousness, lacking valid or verifiable connection with the external, physical universe, yet imposed on it, arbitrarily, nevertheless.

Another thinker gaining prominence in the English-speaking world around 1910 – Sigmund Freud – sometimes shared in contemporary reconsiderations of temporality. Freud envisages the unconscious, the key determinant of human behaviour, as essentially timeless – its contents neither ordered, nor altered, in relation to the passage of time. Events from the distant past can therefore continue to exert powerful, unresolved pressures on the present. In early, foundational explanations of psychoanalysis, Freud consequently stresses the influential role of *'reminiscences . . .* and mnemic symbols' in patients' pathologies. For the analyst, it is therefore essential 'to reproduce the whole chain of pathogenic memories in chronological order, or rather in reversed order, the latest ones first and the earliest

---

[41] James, *Principles of Psychology*, I, 239 – James's italics; Husserl, *Phenomenology of the Consciousness of Internal Time*, 77.

[42] Nietzsche, *The Gay Science*, 172, 173 and *The Birth of Tragedy*, 111. Contrary views appear elsewhere in Nietzsche's writings. His notebooks of 1888, for example, suggest that 'every successive phenomenon in consciousness is completely atomistic'. Nietzsche, *The Will to Power*, 265.

ones last'.⁴³ Recommending in his own way going 'backwards and forwards over the past', Freud shares some of Bergson's conviction that 'nothing is forgotten', and that continuity in identity, between past and present selves, is maintained in reservoirs of memory 'below and beneath the scene illuminated by consciousness'.

The Culture of Time and Space

These extensive interests in temporality suggest that Freud, Nietzsche, James and others might be considered belonging, with Bergson, to a turn-of-the-century chronotype in philosophy – or at any rate clearly sharing in the 'Culture of Time and Space: 1880–1918' that Stephen Kern describes in his historical study of that name. Kern provides an admirably comprehensive account both of factors consolidating the clock's influence during the period, and of others which resisted it. Yet his 1918 terminus precludes full attention to key questions that his study raises, or emphasises, for literary critics. How far were the innovative temporalities of 1920s fiction influenced by recent thinking from other areas? Were modernist authors responding primarily to historical, social and technologic pressures, outlined in this chapter and in Chapters 2 and 3, or, on the other hand, to physics, philosophy and abstract thought developing during the previous two or three decades?⁴⁴

In dealing with such questions, critics often seem to have shared the views that Wyndham Lewis expressed in 1927 when he suggested that 'no outstanding exponent in literature or art of einsteinian physics' had appeared, 'for necessarily there is a certain interval, as things are, between the idea and the representation'.⁴⁵ Though Freud's significance for modernism has been widely discussed, it has less often been considered in terms of narrative structure and temporality. Where Bergson is concerned, on the other hand, criticism has often been confidently affirmative. Tim Armstrong, for example, concludes that 'Bergson . . . had such a marked impact on modernism'. In defining 'Time-consciousness as an inescapable topos of Modernism', Michael Levenson likewise suggests that, for Proust's

---

⁴³ Freud, *Five Lectures*, 12–13, 10. Freud's italics.
⁴⁴ Kern's later study, *The Modernist Novel*, goes further in answering these questions, but without looking fully at the range of factors he describes in *The Culture of Time and Space*.
⁴⁵ *Time and Western Man*, 105.

fiction and later developments in Britain, 'the way had been prepared by the philosophy of Henri Bergson'.[46]

Views of this kind are as long-established as modernism itself. That 1913 *Times Literary Supplement* review of *Du côté de chez Swann* traced Bergson's likely influence on 'the fluid moving flood of life' that Proust presents, as well as on contemporary French culture generally.[47] More vehement and still more wide-ranging views appear throughout *Time and Western Man*. Lewis concludes not only that 'Bergson and his time-philosophy exactly corresponds to Proust, the abstract for the other's concrete', but also that

> without all the uniform pervasive growth of the time-philosophy starting from the little seed planted by Bergson, discredited, and now spreading more vigorously than ever, there would be no *Ulysses*... Mr. Joyce is very strictly of the school of Bergson-Einstein... he is of the great time-school they represent. His book is a *time-book*. (105–6)

Lewis goes even further, finding Bergson 'more than any other single figure ... responsible for the main intellectual characteristics of the world we live in' (166), with Einstein merely occupying a secondary role, in consolidating, or reviving, hostilities to the clock in contemporary culture at the start of the 1920s.

Modernist literature does offer some evidence which might support these claims. Its concentration on streams of inner consciousness – not 'chopped up in bits', but a 'fluid moving flood' – bears obvious comparison with the views of Bergson and William James. Remembrance and recollection of past life, powerfully initiated by present thought and activity – as in *Mrs Dalloway*, or Proust's writing – can likewise be compared with Bergson's description of memories which 'crowd in upon our present occupation and are revealed by means of it'. Modernist views of the clock also seem to correspond to Bergson's antipathy towards its divisive influences. Distinctions between its incisive exactness and the durational continuities of consciousness reappear, for example, in Marcel's reflections in *À la recherche du temps perdu* on the railway timetable and on the 'cut, at a precise point in every afternoon', made by 'the 1.22 train'.[48] In 'Rhapsody on a Windy Night', Eliot similarly contrasts the precise divisions of

---

[46] Armstrong, *Modernism*, 13; Levenson, 'The time-mind of the twenties', in Marcus and Nicholls, eds, *Cambridge History of Twentieth-Century Literature*, 207.
[47] 'Art or Life?', 4 December 1913, 585.
[48] I, 419. See Chapter 1.

the street lamps, exactly recording the hour, with darker, dissolving effects of memory in the spaces between them. Contrasts of this kind appear throughout Virginia Woolf's writing. They are evident in the preferences 'Modern Fiction' expresses for 'a luminous halo', rather than a 'series . . . symmetrically arranged', and are extended in *Mrs Dalloway* in the favouring of a 'mound of time' – unified and whole – over the 'shredding and slicing, dividing and subdividing' effect of clocks (113). Comparable antinomies reappear in *To the Lighthouse* when Lily Briscoe considers 'how life, from being made up of little separate incidents which one lived one by one, became curled and whole like a wave' (55).

Conflicting experiences of time, fragmented or fluid, also figure in D. H. Lawrence's descriptions, in *The Rainbow* (1915) and *Women in Love* (1921), of the disintegral effects of industrialisation and of intensities of inner life and emotion which sometimes resist them. Sharper contrasts appear in *The Trespasser* (1912), Lawrence's account of a love affair intense enough to move characters beyond experience 'made up of sections of time' or 'parcelled up into mornings and evenings and nights'. Whereas their 'days used to walk in procession like seven marionettes', Lawrence describes them as now 'smeared into one piece, as if the clock-hand only went round once in a lifetime'.[49] In *The Plumed Serpent* (1926), too, intense relationships and preferences for a life that 'dissolves and resolves' encourage characters to 'turn . . . from the clock to the sun', and even to rename the hours in terms of natural phenomena rather than number. Determined that 'she would not be timed', Lawrence's heroine refuses to look at her watch, and seeks instead mystic states in which 'the clock didn't go. Time . . . fell off, the days walked naked and timeless, in the old, uncounted manner of the past. The strange, old, uncounted, unregistered, unreckoning days of the ancient heathen world'.[50]

For several modernist writers, responsiveness to Bergson's ideas might have been encouraged by direct contact with the philosopher, or recent reading of his work. Proust was acquainted with Bergson personally, as well as through his writings and attendance at his lectures. In 1892, he undertook an honorary role at the wedding of his distant cousin, Louise Neuburger, to Bergson. In *À la recherche du temps perdu*, the minor character Bergotte is sometimes said to be modelled on Bergson, whose theories are discussed at some length in the course

---

[49] D. H. Lawrence, *The Trespasser* (1912; London: Heinemann, 1976), 55–6.
[50] D. H. Lawrence, *The Plumed Serpent* (1926; Harmondsworth: Penguin, 1995), 361, 132, 288.

of one of the novel's many commentaries on the nature of memory.[51] Views of time and memory in 'Rhapsody on a Windy Night' might likewise have been directly indebted to Bergson, whose lectures at the Collège de France Eliot attended around the period he was writing the poem. Among 1920s US writers, William Faulkner recommended reading Bergson, remarking that he agreed with 'Bergson's theory of the fluidity of time'.[52] Evidence of this agreement is suggested by *The Sound and the Fury* (1929). Fluid streams of thought run through the first two sections of Faulkner's novel, thoroughly intermingling diverse times and experiences. Appropriately, too, the central figure in the second section, Quentin Compson, begins his last day at Harvard by breaking the glass face of his watch and twisting off its hands. Throughout the rest of the day, he avoids measured time as completely as possible, sharing his father's view that 'clocks slay time' and that 'time is dead as long as it is being clicked off by little wheels', or when represented by 'mechanical hands on an arbitrary dial'.[53]

Like Faulkner, Lawrence knew of Bergson's work, though Woolf denied having read any of it.[54] Any encounter she might have had with his ideas was probably indirect, through intermediaries, or her readings of Proust. Yet even direct contact obviously did not guarantee thorough acquiescence in Bergson's thinking. Proust acknowledges resemblances between his writing and Bergson's, but was disinclined to consider that these similarities were a consequence of his influence. Bergson was sceptical himself about the influence of his work, particularly regarding the extent to which philosophy could affect other cultural forms.[55] In any case, significant differences appear – alongside similarities – in views of time and memory each writer offers. *À la recherche du temps perdu* does elide present consciousness and remembered past, fluently and frequently, but there

---

[51] II, 1016–17. For the significance of Bergotte, see Painter, *Marcel Proust*, I, 68, and for Proust's acquaintanceship with Bergson, Soulez and Worms, *Bergson*, 90, etc.

[52] Quoted in Blotner, *Faulkner*, 563.

[53] William Faulkner, *The Sound and the Fury* (1929; Harmondsworth: Penguin, 1971), 81, 74. Subsequent references are to this edition.

[54] See Worthen, *D. H. Lawrence*, 346, and Woolf's letter to Harmon H. Goldstone, 16 August 1932, *Letters*, V, 91. Woolf had promised to settle 'questions of fact' for Goldstone, who was considering writing a study of her work (*Letters*, V, 79).

[55] See Soulez and Worms, *Bergson*, which considers that Bergson and Proust would have attributed any similarities between their work only to 'the spirit of the times' ('l'esprit du temps' (200)).

are also moments when individual experiences are envisaged as discrete and atomistic – shaped by the 'distinctness of different events', or convictions that 'the life of the mind' is 'most episodic' (III, 903; I, 200). Marcel finds himself recalling his lover Albertine in this way – as 'a succession of momentary flashes' – and concludes that 'it was not Albertine alone who was a succession of moments, it was also myself . . . I was not one man only, but as it were the march-past of a composite army' (III, 487, 499). Proust also diverges from Bergson in the role he accords to memories in their more involuntary forms – ones not necessarily dissolved into intermingling conscious states. Remembered scenes can instead return separately and specifically, when triggered by external stimuli – not only by the taste of a madeleine, but by a 'blatter of rain . . . the smell of an unaired room' or much besides (I, 692). Rather than steady immersion in streams of recollections and impressions, in recovering these scenes Proust seeks to build bridges to particular, colourful islands in the past – ones standing out in memory, whole and unique, high and dry, above the 'fluid moving flood of life'.

Overly insistent in conflating Bergson with Proust, and with Einstein, Wyndham Lewis is similarly unconvincing when he suggests that without his supposedly seminal influence 'there would be no *Ulysses*', or no modernist culture more generally. Reductive or scarcely logical elements figure in his explanation in *Time and Western Man* that

> point for point what I had observed on the literary, social and artistic plane was reproduced upon the philosophic and theoretic . . .
> It resolved itself in both instances into *a cult of Time*. There seemed no doubt, after a little examination of the facts, that the more august of these two regions had influenced the lower and more popular one. (219)

Doubts about this judgement are unavoidable at just the point where Lewis suggests there seem to be none. Even if philosophy is assumed to be somehow more 'august' than literature, novelists do not necessarily depend on it solely, uncritically – or even at all – for the views informing their writing. Proust gives evidence of this, and Lewis himself still more. Like Eliot, he attended Bergson's lectures while domiciled in Paris early in the century, and traces of the theory of comedy Bergson developed in *Laughter* (*Le Rire*, 1900) reappear in some of Lewis's ideas in *The Wild Body* (1927). Yet as *Time and Western Man* demonstrates, far from passively accepting Bergson's philosophy, Lewis eventually rejected most of it with manifest distaste.[56] So too – more mildly – did T. S. Eliot, after the period in which 'Rhapsody on a Windy Night' was written.

If, moreover, literature is reckoned to be as permeable to outside influences as Lewis suggests, philosophy or even physics might need to be similarly assessed – in terms of their own susceptibility to external or historical pressures. The work of several of the thinkers mentioned above can be revealingly considered in this way – as itself responding, like the literature it is supposed to have influenced, to new temporalities shaping or disturbing the daily life of the late nineteenth and early twentieth centuries. Influences of this kind can be traced even in the work of Einstein, despite its concern with realms of gravity and starlight apparently remote from everyday life on Earth. *Ulysses* shows Leopold Bloom pondering in 1904 the Dublin time-signal that he believes 'falls at Greenwich time. It's the clock is worked by an electric wire from Dunsink' (211). Einstein's interests may have been similarly oriented, around that date, by daily work in the Swiss Patent Office in Bern, where he had been employed as a 'technical expert third class' since 1902. As Peter Galison explains in *Einstein's Clocks, Poincaré's Maps* (2003), between 1902 and 1905, when the Special Theory of Relativity was published, the Patent Office evaluated thirty proposals for new electrochronometric devices. One of these, for an 'Installation with Central Clock for Indicating the Time Simultaneously in Several Places Separated from One Another', sums up in its title the kind of interests involved. By the later nineteenth century, the spread of railways, and more exact timing in public life generally, made it increasingly necessary to coordinate clocks situated at a distance from each other, by means of an 'electric wire' or otherwise.[57] In Britain, the operation of Big Ben's clock had been monitored by means of an electronic time-signal from Greenwich Observatory almost ever since its installation in 1859. 'Time ratified by Greenwich', described in *Mrs Dalloway*, had become steadily more available throughout the country, carried by wire-borne electric impulses to shops, Post Offices, public buildings, and often – in response to the requirements of new licensing laws – to pubs. Assessment of proposals for improving electrochronometric technology, Galison suggests, may have introduced to Einstein interests

---

[56] For Lewis's early acceptance of Bergson's ideas, and continuing use of some of them, see Campbell, 'Equal Opposites'.

[57] Demands for the synchronisation of public clocks within cities, and some of the problems involved – in Paris particularly – are described by Ogle, *The Global Transformation of Time*, 29–30 etc.

in time and its measurement which were scarcely evident in his thinking before 1902. Relativity's concern with separate, diverse, temporal coordinate systems – and with the possibility of defining simultaneity in contexts remote from one another – may therefore have originated not only in the inspiration of a 'wholly abstracted "Einstein philosopher-scientist"'. The 'underlying metaphysics' of the Special Theory of Relativity, Galison concludes, may also have had more mundane origins: in growing demands, often commercially driven, during the first years of the twentieth century, for ever-more-exact means of living by the clock.[58] A decade later, the Great War substantially delayed verification and acceptance of Einstein's theories. Their origins, too, require to be assessed in relation to social, economic and political factors shaping the life of the times.

Bergson and other philosophers can be considered in similar ways. Views that Bergson published at the end of the 1880s – in his *Essai sur les données immédiates de la conscience* – originated in his thinking about the paradoxes of Zeno of Elea, while he was teaching in Clermont-Ferrand earlier in the decade. These paradoxes include the claim that a flying arrow cannot be supposed to traverse space, since if it is imagined at any precise individual instant it must be supposed static, frozen in mid-flight. Such claims offer particular inspiration, or provocation, for Bergson's thinking. The Eleatic paradoxes depend, he explains, on the misunderstanding he is most committed to eliminating: the concept of time not as seamlessly durational, but as 'numerical multiplicity', infinitely divisible into discrete instants. 'Confusion' regarding the nature of motion and change, Bergson stresses, is the inevitable result, with consequences he considered crucial throughout the history of metaphysics.[59] It was certainly a problem or confusion examined widely, along with discussion of the Eleatic paradoxes, in late nineteenth- and early twentieth-century philosophy. Zeno's paradoxes figure in the work of Bertrand Russell, Samuel Alexander, William James, Nietzsche and others, providing a natural context for reflection in a period when the increasing pace of transport and communication enforced profound changes in perceptions of motion and distance – and, consequently, time.

---

[58] Galison, *Einstein's Clocks*, 246, 248, 255.
[59] *Time and Free Will*, 113, 124. Commenting on astronomers' difficulties, during transits of Venus in the 1870s and 1880s, in determining the exact instant at which the planet's disc appeared to contact the orb of the sun, Bergson likewise suggested that this resulted from the misconception that an 'exact instant' had any basis in reality. See also Bergson, *La Perception du Changement*, 16–17 and 20–3.

These consequences are summed up by Joyce's friend Frank Budgen, in his epigrammatic conclusion that 'spacetime came in with the taximeter', or – less enigmatically – by Marcel, reflecting in *À la recherche du temps perdu* that 'distances are only the relation of space to time and vary with it'.[60] He reflects further on distances 'habitually shortened by speed' when describing his own admiration for the 'instantaneous speed' of the telephone, and Albertine's astonishment when visiting by car, in a single afternoon, villages previously separated by journeys of a day or more (II, 1029; III, 413, 96). The new speeds of motor transport also greatly excited the Italian Futurists. 'Time and Space died yesterday . . . because we have created eternal, omnipresent speed', F. T. Marinetti exclaimed in 'The Founding and Manifesto of Futurism' in 1909.[61] Time and space, more soberly, might be considered not to have died, but to have become more than ever alive in the imagination of an age disturbed or enthralled by accelerations achievable through new forms of travel and technology. New experience of this kind – in Bergson's case, as he travelled from Paris to teach in Angers, Carcasonne, and Clermont-Ferrand during the 1880s – naturally encouraged philosophers, as it did modernist authors, towards new interests in time, space and their mutual interrelation. Philosophy developed such interests in common with literature, and was not necessarily, as Lewis assumed, the cause of their appearance in modernist fiction.

Contemporary thinkers' close engagement with the new pressures and potentials of their age is in some cases confirmed by the unusual popularity of their work. The success of lectures that Bergson delivered at the Collège de France, from around 1903 until the Great War, was on a scale which sometimes embarrassed the lecturer himself. Even standing room was often exhausted, leaving excluded admirers struggling at the doors, or trying to watch or listen from outside, through the windows. There were occasions when enthusiastic audiences smothered Bergson's lecture podium with flowers, and suggestions about moving to a larger venue – even to the Opéra. Bergson worried that he might have become a kind of popular entertainer.[62] Vivid and often poetic in expression, his lectures *were* entertaining. Even Wyndham Lewis found them excellent. Yet the key to their

---

[60] Budgen, *James Joyce and the Making of Ulysses*, 132.
[61] F. T. Marinetti, 'The Founding and Manifesto of Futurism 1909', in Apollonio, *Futurist Manifestos*, 22.
[62] 'Je ne suis pas une danseuse!' was Bergson's comment on the flowers (Soulez and Worms, *Bergson*, 100).

popularity lay more in what they offered the public's imagination, or even its self-esteem. In an age more than ever subject to the shredding and slicing of the clock, Bergson's emphases on profound, creative interconnectedness within experience and the self – on duration, freely flowing beyond measure, counting or division – were inevitably widely welcomed.

Georg Lukács recognised the nature both of this appeal and of the wider context which occasioned it. In the early 1920s, in the essay discussed in Chapter 3, 'Reification and the Consciousness of the Proletariat', Lukács highlighted the effect of capitalist industry on working life, ensuring that 'time sheds its qualitative, variable, flowing nature; it freezes . . . time is transformed into abstract, exactly measurable, physical space'. In a later essay, 'The Ideology of Modernism' (1957), he goes on to suggest what an ideal antidote to this temporal shedding and shredding, slicing and freezing, Bergson offers in emphasising 'subjective time'. Lukács nevertheless disapproved of the modernist literary tactics he considered to have developed from such emphases. 'The Ideology of Modernism' assesses 'subjective time' as part of what it describes as a wider 'surrender to subjectivity' – an evasive 'denial of history', in Lukács's view, rather than a responsible attempt to confront and criticise its negative forces.[63] Other commentators viewed more affirmatively Bergson's relevance, or the nature of his appeal, in relation to these forces. Walter Benjamin notes the role of an 'inhospitable, blinding age of big-scale industrialism' in establishing the conditions from which Bergson's philosophy 'evolved or, rather, in reaction to which it arose' – though about which it remains silent. In tracing ways that modern industry had made time 'a commodity in the sense that money had become a commodity', Lewis Mumford likewise values Bergson's views as an attractive alternative to 'time accounting' and to 'mechanical time . . . strung out in a succession of mathematically isolated instants'.[64]

Einstein's denial of time's absolute, measurable existence obviously shared in the kind of popular appeal surrounding Bergson's work – or

---

[63] Lukács, 'Reification and the Consciousness of the Proletariat', in *History and Class Consciousness*, 90; Lukács, 'The Ideology of Modernism', *Marxist Literary Theory*, 156, 147, 154. For comparisons of Bergson with Lukács, and the evolution of the latter's thought between the 1920s and the 1950s, see Colletti, *Marxism and Hegel*, 184 et seq.

[64] Benjamin, 'On Some Motifs in Baudelaire' (1939), in *Illuminations*, 157; Mumford, *Technics and Civilization*, 14, 16.

revived it, according to Lewis – at any rate once his theories were more generally understood. Strategies used to explain them highlight the nature of their appeal. Typically of popularising, explanatory accounts, Bertrand Russell's *The ABC of Relativity* relies on many metaphors drawn from travel – rail travel especially. *The ABC of Relativity* begins with a surreal train journey from London King's Cross to Edinburgh Waverley, and its pages remain infested with trains throughout, with journeys by road or air mentioned only very occasionally. This concentration is in one way natural enough: railways remained the principal public transport system in the 1920s. Yet trains figure not only frequently, but in very odd and undignified roles – struck by lightning; attacked simultaneously at front and rear by separate groups of bandits; obliged to travel, sometimes at astounding velocities, on tracks which change shape 'like avalanches'.[65] Greenwich Observatory figures almost as frequently, and nearly as strangely. Like the references to trains, regular mention of its role – as the celebrated centre of global time-keeping – is in one way natural enough. Yet Russell's accounts of the Observatory, as of railways, seem almost to relish their emphases on its unreliable, diminished status – including the conclusion that Greenwich time-keeping depends merely on 'accidental circumstances of the earth', which may not 'deserve to be taken so seriously' in an age of Relativity (112).

At these points, *The ABC of Relativity* seems to be taking covert or perhaps inadvertent revenge for the regulation and rationalisation railways and Greenwich had established by the early 1880s and further extended throughout public life thereafter. There are even sections – noting variations in the dimensions of degrees of longitude, relative to the distance north or south of the equator at which they are measured – which might have particularly appealed to Conrad during his preparation for nautical examinations during that decade. Published in the same year as *Mrs Dalloway*, *The ABC of Relativity* at any rate offers appealing, even zany, alternatives to the public temporalities Woolf describes – 'monumental' or 'ratified by Greenwich' – and to the 'proportion' made so redolent of railway timetables by the naming of its chief proponent, Bradshaw. Russell concludes that 'in Einstein's world there is more individualism and less government than in Newton's' (196). Like Bergson's, Einstein's thinking offers in this way the kind of 'Utopian compensation' Fredric Jameson

---

[65] Russell, *ABC of Relativity*, 6. Einstein referred to railways in some of his own explanations, but only in later writings. See Mook and Vargish, *Inside Relativity*, 57.

outlines: alternative or ameliorative means of envisaging the historical stresses of the age. Like the ending of *Ulysses*, Relativity offered the 1920s what seemed unconstrained freedoms of individual vision and of temporal and spatial imagination. These freedoms were all the more attractive because they evidently derived, in Einstein's theories, from the kind of mathematical and rational calculation which had once seemed so responsible for their loss.

D. H. Lawrence summed up this appeal in 1923, in *Fantasia of the Unconscious*. 'The latest craze is Mr. Einstein's Relativity Theory', he remarks, adding that 'everybody catches fire at the word Relativity. There must be something in the mere suggestion, which we have been waiting for'.[66] Along with views later expressed by Dorothy Richardson, Lawrence's comment offers more convincing answers to the question Kern's work raises than most of those suggested by Wyndham Lewis. Author of the modernist novel-sequence *Pilgrimage* (1915–67), and an admirer of Proust, Richardson explained she was unaware of 'any specific influence' exercised on her writing by Bergson's philosophy. Instead, she suggested that 'no doubt Bergson influenced many minds, if only by putting into words something then dawning within the human consciousness: an increased sense of the inadequacy of the clock as a time-measurer'.[67] In this role, the work of Bergson or other thinkers can be revealingly related to modernist writing – as expression, not origin, of some of its concerns; 'putting into words' some of the ideas informing its practices. Philosophy may not cause, but it can clarify – even offer, in Lewis's terms, an abstract version of what fiction makes concrete. Bergson remains in this way worth reading in parallel even with authors such as Woolf, who may have had no direct contact with his ideas, and yet share to an extent some of the priorities his philosophy emphasises.

Considering the period's literary and philosophical writing collectively, in this way, consolidates and extends the concepts of chronotype, or of 'culture of time and space', mentioned earlier. It confirms that between 1880 and the 1920s, responses to new temporalities and the dominance of the clock were by no means confined to literature, but appeared in cognate forms in philosophy and science, and in many other areas of contemporary culture. Comparable responses can also be recognised in the period's literary criticism. Several

---

[66] Lawrence, *Fantasia of the Unconscious*, 163.
[67] Quoted in Kumar, *Bergson and the Stream of Consciousness Novel*, 36–7.

figures mentioned in Chapter 1's discussion of narrative temporality began their work in the 1920s, or a little earlier – Viktor Shklovsky and other Russian Formalists largely before modernism's principal innovations appeared; E. M. Forster, in *Aspects of the Novel* (1927), partly in response to their recent development. Though the idea of 'chronotope' appeared slightly later, Mikhail Bakhtin acknowledges its indebtedness to Einstein's work. The terminology of space-time, he explains, 'is employed in mathematics, and was introduced as part of Einstein's Theory of Relativity . . . we are borrowing it for literary criticism almost as a metaphor'.[68]

Enthusiasm for Relativity also spread very rapidly through newspapers, magazines and popular culture during the 1920s.[69] Though *Time and Western Man* suggests that by 1927 Einstein had found 'no outstanding exponent in literature', several brief expositions did appear in popular writing during the decade. Naturally, these figured frequently in fantasy and early science fiction, such as E. V. Odle's account in *The Clockwork Man* (1923) of a future 'world of many dimensions', of time as 'a relative thing', and of 'really important questions in life [that] came under the heading of Time and Space'.[70] Rose Macaulay's *Potterism* (1920) offers a still earlier example, and in a novel set in an otherwise ordinary, recognisable social milieu. Describing newspaper headlines announcing confirmation of Einstein's theories, *Potterism* notes that 'space and light would be discussed . . . in many a cottage, many a club, many a train . . . people were interested . . . in light and space, undulations and gravitation'.[71] Similar discussions figure at the end of the decade in Dorothy L. Sayers's detective novel *The Documents in the Case* (1930). Some of Sayers's characters read Eddington, and several worry about 'things like Einstein, which are so very modern and difficult', or about whether 'Heraclitus and Bergson and Einstein are correct in stating that everything is more or less flowing about'.[72]

---

[68] Bakhtin, 'Forms of Time and of the Chronotope in the Novel', in *The Dialogic Imagination*, 84.
[69] See Price, *Loving Faster than Light*.
[70] E. V. Odle, *The Clockwork Man* (1923; Boston, MA: HiLoBooks, 2013), 48, 59, 102. Odle's novel and 1920s science fiction are further discussed in Chapter 6.
[71] Rose Macaulay, *Potterism: A Tragi-Farcical Tract* (1920; London: Collins, 1950), 230.
[72] Dorothy L. Sayers, *The Documents in the Case* (1930; London: Hodder and Stoughton, 1989), 14, 57.

In their choice of narrative tactics, Sayers and Macaulay may illustrate a further – formal – level of response to Relativity. *Potterism* and *The Documents in the Case* each shift perspectives between several different characters – in Sayers's case, through the use of an epistolary form. Each novel offers as a result a set of divergent, highly subjective interpretations of events. As Bertrand Russell pointed out, Einstein's theories were not strictly an endorsement of this kind of subjective relativity in perception.[73] Yet his ideas were often interpreted in this way – even on occasion by Einstein himself, as he suggests when joking in *The Times* about the relativity of national identities established for him in Germany and in Britain. For many contemporary readers – of newspapers, rather than careful expositions by Eddington or Russell – Einstein was likely to be understood much as Wyndham Lewis half-facetiously suggests in *Time and Western Man*. Lewis anticipates casual conversations conveniently concluding that '"It appears that there is no such thing as time"', or '"Everything is relative", Einstein says. "I always thought it was"' (105).

D. H. Lawrence offers further evidence of looseness in apprehending Einstein's work when he describes popular imagination 'catching fire' at the idea of Relativity. Part of its inflammatory appeal, *Fantasia of the Unconscious* explains, lay in its supposed suggestion that 'each individual living creature is absolute: in its own being. And that all things in the universe are just relative to the individual living creature' (164). This appeal may have encouraged a development in modernist fiction as distinctive as its new treatment of time – its movement, in the direction Woolf proposed in 1919, and Lukács later criticised, towards subjective streams of consciousness, rather than supposedly objective accounts of experience. At its most radical in the modernist writing of Ford, Joyce and Woolf herself, this development is also discernible in the more conventional fiction of Aldous Huxley. Characters in *Antic Hay* (1923) ponder 'the laws of gravidy [sic], first formulated by Newton, now recodified by the immortal Einstein'.[74] Huxley goes on in *Point Counter Point* (1928) to use multiple subjective perspectives to establish diverse characters – some of them well aware of 'Einstein and Eddington ... Mach' – as centres of gravity, or specific frames of reference, within the novel's complex interplay of outlooks and ideas.[75]

---

[73] See Russell, *ABC of Relativity*, 14–15.
[74] Aldous Huxley, *Antic Hay* (1923; Harmondsworth: Penguin, 1976), 66.
[75] Aldous Huxley, *Point Counter Point* (1928; Harmondsworth: Penguin, 1975), 158.

Other novelists popular late in the 1920s found in Relativity a sanction for different kinds of narrative experiment. 'Juggling with time', T. F. Powys's remarks in *Mr Weston's Good Wine* (1927), 'can happen, so say our modern mathematicians ... in any place on the surface of our known world, or, indeed, throughout the whole universe, if God so wills it'. Powys's fantasy is located both within and beyond our known world. The remote rural village he describes already engages in rather relativistic understanding of time, known to pass – regrettably – much faster during pub opening hours. This idiosyncrasy is agreeably modified when God appears, in the guise of an itinerant wine salesman, halting all the clocks one early evening to ensure that 'time be stopped ... and eternity ... begun'. *Mr Weston's Good Wine* offers in this way a strange 1920s wish-fulfilment – describing a world in which 'time and the stars might stop when they chose', allowing desire and imagination to be wholly freed of clocks, restrictive licensing hours, or indeed any of the constraints of ordinary reality.[76]

The clock's constraints, and its interference with desire, also figure in lighter 1920s fiction, remote from direct interest in Relativity. The hero of P. G. Wodehouse's *The Small Bachelor* (1927), wildly impatient for the return of his girlfriend, concludes that 'something must have happened to the sidereal moon and that time was standing still'. His fears are extended by reflections on 'many ways of measuring time ... through the ages'. As if in a nightmare version of Conrad's examination papers, these include Tycho Brahe's use of 'altitudes, quadrants, azimuths, cross-staves, armillary spheres and parallactic rules' – though Brahe's habit of 'winding up the azimuth and putting the cat out for the night' perhaps makes the list less threatening.[77] Along with work by Macaulay, Sayers and Powys, Wodehouse's novel is one of the 'typical productions of to-day' which Cyril Connolly suggested showed a 'common philosophic outlook' extending, by the end of the 1920s, through and beyond 'Proust, *Ulysses*, and the novels of Mrs Woolf'. Referring to *Time and Western Man*, Connolly adds that the 'obsession with the passage of Time that Mr Lewis would remove is really the nearest approach to a unity of conception that we have'.[78]

---

[76] T. F. Powys, *Mr Weston's Good Wine* (1927; Harmondsworth: Penguin, 1937), 183, 128, 231.

[77] P. G. Wodehouse, *The Small Bachelor* (1927; London: Methuen, 1933), 114–15.

[78] Cyril Connolly, 'Chang' [Review of Wyndham Lewis's *The Childermass*], *New Statesman*, 31, 7 July 1928, 426.

Bolts of Iron and Dances of the Hours

The wide range of Wyndham Lewis's attention in *Time and Western Man* suggests how far this 'common philosophic outlook' might be traced in contemporary culture. His unswervingly adversarial attitudes – in literary as well as critical writing – also help to make Lewis a suggestive witness regarding its manifestations. In the 1920s and earlier, his fiction exhibits an outlook so contrary to those of other modernist authors that it highlights very effectively, in antithesis, the new directions followed by their work. Particularly sharp contrasts appear in the attitude to time maintained by the artist-hero of Lewis's first serious novel, *Tarr* (1918). Rather than expressing hostility to the clock, along with so many characters in modernist novels, Tarr controls his life and emotions in rigorous accord with its orderly measures, agreeing to see his girlfriend Bertha – eventually his wife – only between four and seven o'clock daily. Against her proclivity for vagueness and disorder, Tarr uses his 'heavy watch' almost as a weapon, presenting 'its face to her ironically' and reflecting that 'she had asked for the watch; he would use it'. Preferences for order and exactitude likewise dispose Tarr against the novel's oddest character – Kreisler, who 'lived an hour as easily and carelessly as he would have lived a second'. An eccentric bohemian, Kreisler seems to drift in 'a fog of Time and Space' – expressing with relish, after pawning his watch, a Proustian conviction that he has 'lost all sense of time . . . perdu le temps'.[79]

Tarr's attitudes to art and literary form are also revealingly contrary to those expressed by Lewis's modernist contemporaries. In contrast to Woolf's stress on the flickering, innermost flame of consciousness, Tarr considers art should exclude 'restless, quick, flame-like ego . . . imagined for the *inside* of it' – also eliminating, more generally, 'anything living, quick and changing' (299–300). These preferences for stasis and external perspective extend into the style of the novel itself, in ways immediately evident in its striking first paragraph:

> Paris hints of sacrifice.= But here we deal with that large dusty facet known to indulgent and congruous kind . . .
>
> Inconceivably generous and naïve faces haunt the Knackfus Quarter.= We are not however in a Selim or Vitagraph camp (though

---

[79] Wyndham Lewis, *Tarr* (1918), as *Tarr: The 1918 Version*, ed. Paul O'Keeffe (Santa Rosa, CA: Black Sparrow Press, 1990), 63, 80, 185, 96. Subsequent references are to this edition.

'guns' tap rhythmically the buttocks).= Art is being studied.= Art is the smell of oil paint, Henri Murger's 'Vie de Bohème,' corduroy trousers, the operatic Italian model.[80]

Along with Tarr's views, writing of this kind reflects the preferences for 'the distinct, the geometric' which Lewis explains in *Time and Western Man* were essential for his own work as a graphic artist (443). It also emphatically opposes any Bergsonian ideas of life and time as flowing or continuous. Lewis's invention of the '.=' punctuation mark ensures instead that sentences are separated as sharply as possible, each of them conveying a discrete, autonomous observation. In contrast to Joyce's unpunctuated stream of consciousness in the final section of *Ulysses*, Lewis offers a frame of consciousness, or rather a series of frames, encapsulating both impressions and external scenes. At some points, the effect is comparable to looking at the frames of a film, one by one, rather than smoothly run through the apparatus of a projector – a means of perception that Bergson specifically criticises in *Creative Evolution* (*L'Évolution créatrice*, 1907).[81] Mention of 'Selim or Vitagraph' in the opening paragraphs of *Tarr* – and of 'a kind of living cinematograph', later in the novel – suggest that Lewis might have deliberately set out to establish an effect of this kind (123). Selig and Vitagraph were pioneering film companies, each founded in the late 1890s and influential in the first decade of the twentieth century. When Lewis revised the novel for republication in 1928, their names were replaced with a straightforward reference to 'Hollywood', ensuring that the relevance of film would still be recognised by contemporary readers.

Tarr was first published as a serial in *The Egoist* in 1916–17, immediately following Joyce's *A Portrait of the Artist as a Young Man*, though Lewis had begun the novel years before the Great War, as early as 1907, completing it by 1915. As the dates indicate, Lewis's style, ideas, and concepts of temporality had been worked out independently – though possibly in part-reaction to Bergson's lectures – well before

---

[80] The '.=' form of punctuation in this passage and throughout the novel appears only in the first US edition of *Tarr* (New York: Knopf, 1918). The edition published in Britain, nearly simultaneously, by the Egoist Press, and the earlier serialisation in *The Egoist,* use the more modest, though still unusual, form '.–'. Lewis's letters make clear that the '.=' form appeared in his original typescript, and that he wished it to be retained in the published text. Both forms are omitted from the revised, 1928 edition. See Wyndham Lewis, *Tarr: the 1918 Version*, 372. The text of this edition is based on the US 1918 edition.

[81] See Chapter 6.

Fig. 4.2 Wyndham Lewis, *Portrait of the Artist as the Painter Raphael* (1921). Canvas, clock and artist combine in geometric stasis. © Manchester Art Gallery, UK/Bridgeman Images.

other modernists' contrasting aesthetics began to appear strongly in the 1920s. This independence and originality is less in evidence in Lewis's late-1920s novel, *The Childermass* (1928), shaped instead by his hostile reaction to those new modernist aesthetics, and by extensions into satiric fiction of criticisms already developed in *Time and Western Man*, published the previous year. Several clues indicate that one of the central characters, Pullman, is in part a caricature of Joyce. Another, the Bailiff, loosely resembles Bergson, or at any rate functions as a composite figure, representative of the range of philosophies Lewis disliked. The latter part of *The Childermass* is taken up with debates – between this figure and others often representing Lewis's own views – concerning issues such as 'the difference ... between Space-Time and Space and Time'.[82]

---

[82] Wyndham Lewis, *The Childermass* (London: Chatto and Windus, 1928), 148. Subsequent references are to this edition.

In earlier sections, satire extends even into Lewis's description of the novel's landscape. Its setting resembles one Rudyard Kipling employed in a story published two years previously – 'On the Gate', describing harassed angels trying to control entry to heaven, while almost overwhelmed by huge crowds of souls, parted from their bodies on the battlefields of the Great War. Lewis employs a similarly purgatorial setting to express a concern he notes in *Time and Western Man* – that as a result of the 'Time doctrine' initiated by Bergson, 'dead, physical nature comes to life. Chairs and tables, mountains and stars, are animated into a magnetic restlessness and sensitiveness . . . all is alive' (449). Lacking what *The Childermass* describes as 'admirable fixity in the time-system . . . encountered on earth', the 'Time flats' around the gates of heaven are disturbingly unsettled and amorphous, dominated by 'dynamical flux', 'durational depth', and 'sensational chaos' (161, 95, 153, 96, 152). 'Problematical spaces – *and* times' make '*near* and *far* . . . very relative' (162, 95). Characters seeking a 'Time-track' through 'Time spaces' are distracted by 'time-hallucination', sometimes deprived of sufficient 'Time-air', and occasionally even obliged to avoid 'Time-shrubbery' (91, 96, 82, 100).

After 123 pages of detailed description of this 'Time-trek', a watch is consulted and characters find that it is 'just a little over an hour since we started' (97, 123). At such moments, the novel clearly satirises tactics Lewis so deplored in modernist writing – in particular, its readiness to expand, textually, representation of thoughts and experiences far beyond their likely temporal duration. His elastic hour implicitly mocks suggestions of the kind Woolf makes in *Orlando*, about 'time in the mind' stretching to 'fifty or a hundred times its clock length' (69) – or Ford, in *Parade's End*, about what 'a hell of a lot' could be 'thought in ten minutes' (417, 519). The amorphous landscape of *The Childermass* also functions occasionally as a more specific satire – or parody – of the 'Work in Progress' which Joyce began publishing in the 1920s, after *Ulysses* appeared, and eventually issued as *Finnegans Wake* in 1939. Beginning and ending with 'rivverrun' into the sea, around 'Howth Castle and Environs', *Finnegans Wake* expands still further the unconstrained, seaward vision through which Molly concludes *Ulysses*.[83] Circular in structure, and based around Giambattista Vico's ideas of 'cyclewheeling history', Joyce's representations of Anna Livia – of the River Liffey,

---

[83] James Joyce, *Finnegans Wake* (1939; London: Faber, 1975), 3. Subsequent references are to this edition.

the stream of life – move through nocturnal desires and dreams as free of temporality as Freud considered the unconscious (186). Dissolving the usual boundaries of thought and language, Joyce's 'waters of babalong' make *Finnegans Wake* the most fluid and timeless of all modernist novels (103).

As *The Childermass* indicates – particularly when the Bailiff ponders '"Neggs-in-progress" and "wirk-on-the-way" … with Vico the mechanical for guide' (173) – Lewis was well aware, at an early stage, of the directions Joyce's 'Work in Progress' was taking.[84] As Joyce chose to publish this work in Paris-based literary magazines of fairly limited circulation, the first readers of *The Childermass* – and many later ones – would not necessarily have shared this awareness. Nor would they necessarily have recognised in Lewis's novel – apart from moments such as his mention of a 123-page hour – a clear representation, satiric or otherwise, of modernist fiction they might have read earlier in the 1920s. Rather than a readily recognisable caricature of modernist fiction, *The Childermass* offers a strange, sometimes esoteric representation of what Lewis feared this fiction might become, or might indicate about the wider culture of the 1920s. Fluidity and timelessness obviously do figure in Molly's stream of consciousness, in Clarissa Dalloway's ever-unfolding layers of memory, or in Tietjens's traumatic mental meandering through jumbled months and days. Yet the fiction concerned is less comprehensively amorphous than Lewis suggests – either in his satiric landscapes in *The Childermass*, or in some of the analyses of *Time and Western Man*. One reason for this is that modernist novels treat the clock as a less thoroughgoing 'enemy' than he assumes.[85]

In several of them, the clock might even be considered to play an unusually prominent or vociferous role – one unusually essential, whatever hostilities may also be involved, for the vision and structure of the novel concerned. This is clearly the case in *Mrs Dalloway*, originally entitled *The Hours*, and as clock-conscious as any novel

---

[84] Joyce was also well aware of Lewis's riposte, incorporating into 'Work in Progress' references to 'windy Nous' and to '*Spice and Westend Woman*' (56, 292). Wider interests in 'convolvuli of times lost or strayed' also appear in references to 'the sopohology of Bitchson' and 'theorics of Winestain', and in the fable of the Mookse and the Gripes (*Finnegans Wake*, 292, 149, 152 et seq.).

[85] In *The Childermass*, the Bailiff enquires 'How's the enemy?' as a way of asking the time – one quite often employed in everyday parlance in the 1920s (264). 'The Enemy' was also an authorial persona Lewis adopted for his satirical and critical work during the decade.

in English. However fluently Woolf's narrative enters inner thoughts and memories, it is rarely long before these are interrupted by the chimes of Big Ben, first resounding across the novel almost as soon as Clarissa's 'door' into memory is opened. Time on the clock is never decisively banished from *Mrs Dalloway*, but combines with time in the mind in subtly various ways, distinguishing characters from each other – or even from themselves at other stages of the day – and contributing overall to the unusually diverse, complex visions of temporality the novel presents. Joyce likewise gives clocks a resonant, insistent voice in *Ulysses*, describing in its early pages how

> the bells of George's church . . . tolled the hour: loud dark iron.
> *Heigho! Heigho!*
> *Heigho! Heigho!*
> *Heigho! Heigho!*

This tolling re-echoes towards the end of the novel, in 'the sound of the peal of the hour of the night by the chime of the bells in the church of Saint George' (85, 826). Across the 'flowing . . . stream of life' represented in the intervening pages, the iron voice of the clock – or some equally sharp indication of the time of day, such as Bloom's reflection on the Dublin time-signal – regularly intrudes (193). However fluent and wide-ranging her thoughts in the closing pages, even Molly remains sleepily aware of the 'unearthly hour', and of the imminence of 'the alarmclock next door at cockshout clattering the brains out of itself' (930). 'Morning hours, noon, then evening coming on, then night hours' are discernible as an ordering basis for all the streams of life and thought flowing through the Dublin day. A 'dance of the hours' firmly patterns *Ulysses*, as Joyce's various schemas for the novel confirm, indicating an hour of the day for each chapter except the last (84).

In some ways, patterning of this kind in the work of Joyce and other modernist writers was made unusually necessary – reciprocally – by the extent of their commitments to fluidity and the stream of life. The possibility that 'the fluid moving flood of life . . . exceeds the strict limits of a perfect art' immediately concerned that early *Times Literary Supplement* review of *Du côté de chez Swann* in 1913.[86] Similar reservations were soon being expressed about the work of Dorothy Richardson, as fluid in some ways as Proust's

---

[86] 4 December 1913, 585.

in following inner thought in *Pilgrimage*. Virginia Woolf naturally welcomed a novel so determined to 'look within' and 'examine . . . the mind', though when reviewing its early stages in 1919 she also worried about an absence of 'shapeliness' and 'accepted forms'.[87] Firmer commitment to 'accepted' form and order, including horological order, ensures that Woolf's writing, and Joyce's, shares instead aesthetic priorities of the kind Lily Briscoe expresses in *To the Lighthouse* when she suggests that a work of art should be

> beautiful and bright . . . on the surface, feathery and evanescent, one colour melting into another like the colours on a butterfly's wing; but beneath the fabric must be clamped together with bolts of iron . . . a thing you could ruffle with your breath; and a thing you could not dislodge with a team of horses. (194)

For writers including Joyce and Woolf, the clock's 'dark iron' and its tolling of the hours provides some of the 'bolts of iron' required for structures sufficient to contain the 'fluid moving flood of life' their fiction seeks to represent.

Modernist fiction indicates the importance of this kind of stability not only for structuring literature, but as an antidote to crisis and uncertainty in its characters' lives. In *Mrs Dalloway*, Rezia hears 'the clock . . . striking – one two three' and thinks 'how sensible the sound was', compared with the chaos surrounding her husband Septimus's suicide (166). At the critical moment when Clarissa learns of his death, feeling 'somehow very like him', she nevertheless experiences a commitment to life 'going on', reflecting that 'with the clock striking the hour, one, two, three, she did not pity him' (206). Complete rejection even of this tentative regard for the clock's orderly measures is often presented in modernist fiction as a kind of mental debility – however understandable, or admirable, it might seem in more moderate forms. In *The Secret Agent*, Stevie's habitual drawing of 'circles, circles' suggests an engaging vision of 'eternity', but also the fragility and 'chaos' of his mentality. In Rebecca West's *The Return of the Soldier* (1918), the hero's mental regression from 1916 into the idyllic summer of 1901 is in one way an understandable response to experience of the Great War – symptomatic of modernist fiction's disposition towards remembrance of happier Edwardian years. Yet it is also

---

[87] Virginia Woolf, 'The Tunnel', *Essays*, III, 12.

a symptom of severe shell-shock: of traumatised responses to the war similar to those leading Tietjens to conflate past and present occasionally in *Parade's End*, or Septimus to do so more continuously in *Mrs Dalloway*. Personal, familial and historical trauma also imperils Quentin's sanity in the second section of *The Sound and the Fury*. Destruction of his watch and his pathological shunning of clocks free him from 'time . . . clicked off by little wheels'. Yet his actions are also both symptom and consequence of his family's disabling apprehension of historical loss – of vanishing eminence in their own situation, exacerbated by wider decline in the southern states of the USA. In the novel's first section, comprehensive inability to distinguish past from present detaches Quentin's brother Benjy still more completely from the control of clock and calendar, and from almost all social structures, leaving him one of the most thoroughly deranged characters in modernist fiction.

Even for figures secure in their mental equilibrium, the fullest engagement with memories and temporal freedoms occurs significantly often – and naturally enough – at moments least constrained by rational waking consciousness. Sleep and dream offer a natural, daily pathway, regularly followed in modernist fiction, into the timelessness Freud ascribes to the unconscious. In *Women in Love*, Gerald sleeps 'as if time were one moment, unchanging and unmoving'.[88] In *The Secret Agent*, it is 'dreams dreamed in the instant of waking' which suggest to Inspector Heat the possibility of rising 'above the vulgar conception of time' (78). In *À la recherche du temps perdu*, Marcel likewise describes sleep as 'outside the range of time and its measurements' (II, 1015). Some of his most free-ranging engagements with memory occur in the novel's opening pages, which recall the early bedtimes of his childhood and the half-wakeful, half-dreaming hours which succeeded them. Molly's hovering on the edge of sleep and dream, at the end of *Ulysses*, similarly facilitates her mind's movement towards infinitudes beyond measurable time and space. Dreams and streams of *un*consciousness continue this movement throughout the night language of *Finnegans Wake*. In this area, as in many others, Bergson offers a succinct expression of modernism's interests when he emphasises that during sleep or dream 'we no longer measure duration, but we feel it'. Where time is concerned, he adds, this ensures that 'mathematical estimate gives place to a confused instinct'.[89] This 'instinct' also appealed to J. W. Dunne, whose study *An Experiment*

---

[88] D. H. Lawrence, *Women in Love* (1921; Harmondsworth: Penguin, 1971), 391.
[89] Bergson, *Time and Free Will*, 126.

with Time (1927) – popular at the end of the 1920s and later – bases its views of alternative temporal dimensions around the mind's supposed ability to move beyond the present through sleep, dream or visionary states.[90]

These interests in 'confused instinct', unconsciousness, dream, even madness – and in the alternatives they offer to deductive, rational intelligence – demonstrate modernism's extension of priorities shaping the Romantic movement a hundred years or so earlier. Commitments of this kind – to what Conrad might have called 'unreasonable process of thought' – are often directly emphasised in the period's fiction. One of Richard Aldington's characters in *Death of a Hero* resembles Bergson in suggesting that it is 'so much better to trust to the deeper instincts than to talk about things with "the inferior intelligence"' (25). In *À la recherche du temps perdu*, Marcel is likewise sceptical of the intellect – particularly of its interference with the spontaneity of memory. In the first volume of *The Man Without Qualities (Der Mann ohne Eigenschaften*, 1930, 1932), Robert Musil criticises the 'wicked intellect that, while making man the lord of the earth, also makes him the slave of the machine' – leaving his soul 'ruined by mathematics' and by 'calculations . . . materialism . . . bleak rationalism'. D. H. Lawrence's characters complain in *Lady Chatterley's Lover* (1928) that 'the mind can only analyse and rationalize', at the expense of spontaneity and 'the intuitive side'.[91] One of Mrs Ramsay's virtues, in *To the Lighthouse*, is that 'her simplicity fathomed what clever people falsified' (34). Her capacities contrast favourably with the stringent, deductive intelligence of her husband, committed to 'facts uncompromising' and ready to separate thought itself into an alphabet of categories, each as distinct as the keys of a piano (6).

Resistance to measured time, in modernist writing, thus shares in wider scepticisms of 'the whole hostile reasonable world', as Rebecca West expresses it in *The Return of the Soldier*, though with much less than complete rejection of faculties concerned, or of the forms and orders they support.[92] Modernist fiction does not suggest unreserved approval for the kind of society Samuel Butler describes in *Erewhon* (1872) – its leading thinkers educated in 'Colleges of Unreason'; its

---

[90] Dunne's theories are considered in Chapter 5.
[91] Robert Musil, *The Man Without Qualities*, trans. Eithne Wilkins and Ernst Kaiser (1954; London: Picador, 1979), I, 40, 125; D. H. Lawrence, *Lady Chatterley's Lover* (1928; Harmondsworth: Penguin, 1982), 39, 159.
[92] Rebecca West, *The Return of the Soldier* (1918; London: Virago, 2004), 178.

machines long ago banished; its clocks and watches viewed with 'hatred' and custodially confined to museums.[93] By 1920, the authority of the clock – strengthened for more than half a century by industry, transport, technology, war and statecraft – often seemed thoroughly oppressive. Yet outright rejection of its orders was ultimately unthinkable: as the characters mentioned above illustrate, that way madness lies, or, just as unappealingly, the tedious time-flats of Wyndham Lewis's purgatorial fantasy. Modernist literature therefore interests itself extensively in the mentalities of figures inhabiting timeless or clock-free worlds, but without supporting unreservedly the evasions or alternatives their conditions offer.

Conventional orders of time and space, in other words, were not wholly 'obliterated' in late 1919, nor in modernist literature during the decade that followed – not at any rate to the extent Lewis suggests in *The Childermass*. In the terms Theodore Ziolkowski employs, quoted in Chapter 1, the modernist clock was more often 'deformed or improved upon' than shattered, dropped or entirely ignored. Modernist interests were principally in reconfiguration: in adding greater fluidity and anachrony to established narrative tactics – particularly those of order and duration – while continuing to provide plausible 'fictive models of the temporal world' of the kind Frank Kermode describes in *The Sense of an Ending* (1967). As he emphasises, respect for 'what we think of as "real" time, the chronicity of the waking moment' remains at some level essential to fiction. 'A modern novel', Kermode adds, therefore 'has to hold some kind of balance' between '"realism" about time' and various contrary impulses.[94] Without ignoring this requirement for realism, modernist fiction simply shifted the balance, in its treatment of time, in favour of desire, vision and fluidities freed of constraints increasingly influential within the contemporary 'temporal world'. Rather than abandoning 'time on the clock' in favour of the 'time in the mind' described in *Orlando*, novelists shifted their priorities – towards mind rather than machine – along a spectrum of possibilities stretching between the two. 'Time on the clock', after all, inevitably remains a 'time in the mind' itself, as *Mrs Dalloway* shows – impossible to expunge completely from consciousness, at least during waking hours, or in conditions of ordinary sanity within the world modernity has shaped.

---

[93] Samuel Butler, *Erewhon* (1872; Harmondsworth: Penguin, 1983), 82, 96.
[94] Kermode, *Sense of an Ending*, 54–5.

Any spectrum of modernist temporalities may also need to include potentials beyond mind altogether. As Proust suggests, 'the mighty dimension of Time' may not be suppressed or reshaped through acts of will, imagination, or consciousness alone. Memories which are chemically or physically sedimented within the body, within 'involuntary memory of the limbs', may also be involved, or ones somehow 'hidden . . . in some material object' – latent in a blatter of rain, uneven paving stones, half-forgotten tastes and odours, or the echoings of a bell across the years (III, 716; I, 47–8). In expressing the full extent of temporal possibilities and pressures affecting the 1920s, a later passage in *Orlando* may provide an apter summary than its straightforward distinction of times on the clock and in the mind. Confirming the newly disorienting, confusing effects of 'omnipresent speed', Woolf's heroine finds that 'twenty minutes . . . motoring fast out of London' leaves 'body and mind . . . like scraps of torn paper' and 'seventy-six different times all ticking in the mind at once' (217).

Division of time into seventy-six categories might seem to reinstate the kind of 'numerical multiplicity' Bergson dismissed. Yet it does aptly suggest the challenging diversities of the age, confronted with times physical, mental, monumental or memorious; industrial and military; clockwork or dreamlike; shaped by Remembrance and Relativity, Bergson and Big Ben; dissolved into streams of consciousness or framed into sharply separate images. It might simply be supposed fortunate that writers emerging in the 1920s proved themselves so flexible and inventive in dealing with such diverse temporalities. Yet the logic of this supposition might also be usefully inverted. New temporalities and the pressures they exerted might themselves be seen as responsible in significant measure for the success of authors concerned – challenging established narrative practices profoundly enough to make essential the new strategies which so distinguish the writing of the decade. Accumulating for three-quarters of a century, and devastatingly concentrated by the Great War, 'obsession' with the passage of time and the measures of the clock stressed life at the start of the 1920s probably more acutely than in any years before or since. A uniquely innovative decade in fiction followed, with the imaginative reshaping of temporality a key component of its success.

Chapter 5

Not Like Old Times: the 1930s to Mid-Century

Cyril Connolly and Wyndham Lewis outline a late 1920s 'obsession with the passage of Time' quite strong enough simply to have continued into the next decade. Any such continuity was nevertheless marked by new emphases and by significant mutations within established ones. Some of these can be traced in Virginia Woolf's writing, discussed in this chapter's second section. Even before the end of the 1920s, they were apparent in other ways in J. W. Dunne's popular *An Experiment with Time,* published in 1927 and reissued in several further editions by the mid-1930s.[1] Though Dunne's views often seem odd or implausible, the widespread interest they aroused in the late 1920s and 1930s makes them worth considering further, as an intriguing symptom of some of the concerns of his times.

Future Present

J. W. Dunne had been a pilot and aircraft engineer during the pioneering days of aviation, designing the first British military aircraft in 1906, three years after the Wright brothers had first achieved powered flight. He later took his friend H. G. Wells flying, around 1912. He describes his first flights – 'the sensation was most extraordinary' – in *An Experiment*

---

[1] Concerns with time can also be seen continuing – and mutating – in contemporary philosophy, particularly in Martin Heidegger's *Being and Time* (*Sein und Zeit,* 1927). Heidegger's views sometimes resemble – though also criticise and move beyond – Henri Bergson's emphases on lived, subjective time. As *Sein und Zeit* was not translated into English until 1962, it had a limited impact among Anglophone readers and writers at the time of its publication.

with Time, and discusses temporal dimensions in terms which might be considered to resemble the aloof vision of spatial landscapes afforded by his earlier work as a pilot.[2] Experience of precognitive dreams persuaded Dunne that the sleeping mind could rise above the 'first-term world, where time appears as a succession of simple three-dimensional scenes, with the future entirely hidden'. Dreams, Dunne believed, could allow access to a 'second-term world . . . brilliant and real', in which 'your past and your future lie stretched out before you like an unrolled scroll'.[3] Like another thinker seeking to divide time into various series, John McTaggart – whose study, *The Nature of Existence*, also appeared in 1927 – Dunne's interest in a 'second-term world' led him on towards further, timeless, ontological planes, and ultimately towards asserting the eternal existence of the soul. Though arcane diagrams and semi-algebraic formulations make sections of *An Experiment with Time* difficult reading, affirmative accounts of vision and the soul carry an obvious appeal. This is enhanced by the lucid, cajoling style and adroit metaphors Dunne employs in the opening section. As that image of the unrolled scroll suggests, his ideas seemed engagingly to diminish life's uncertainties by suggesting that past, present and future are all as safely controlled and predetermined as experiences described in the pages of a book. Accounts of fascinating dreams, and invitations to readers to try glimpsing the future for themselves, further ensured Dunne's popularity at the end of the 1920s, and during the next decade, when he was a regular contributor to *The Listener* magazine, even appearing in an early television broadcast, in 1937.

Dunne's work also attracted the interest of philosophers, and of a range of contemporary authors. H. G. Wells incorporated precognitive dreams into some of his 1930s stories. James Joyce is said to have 'regarded highly' Dunne's ideas. Critics have compared them to T. S. Eliot's views of times present, past and future in *Four Quartets* (1936–42), noting that further editions of *An Experiment with Time* were published in the 1930s by Faber and Faber, for whom Eliot was currently working as a director.[4] Similar comparisons could be made

---

[2] Dunne, *Experiment with Time*, 111.
[3] Dunne, 'Serialism', 483.
[4] The philosopher A. J. Ayer, for example, invited Dunne to lecture in Oxford; Eugène Jolas, 'Memoir of Joyce' (1941), in Deming, *James Joyce*, I, 385; see T. S. Eliot, *The Poems of T. S. Eliot,* vol.1, *Collected and Uncollected Poems*, ed. Christopher Ricks and Jim McCue (London: Faber and Faber, 2015), esp. 864 and 904–5. The editors note that Eliot was well aware of Dunne's ideas by the time he wrote *Burnt Norton* (1936), the first of *Four Quartets*.

with ideas expressed in William Gerhardie's *Of Mortal Love* (1936), some of whose characters consider that 'time was an illusion' and that 'in the real and timeless world, everything which is to be has been'. Intrigued by 'another side to what we call dreams', Graham Greene professed himself 'convinced that Dunne was right' and referred to *An Experiment with Time* as an explanation for some of his vision in *The Confidential Agent* (1939) and *The End of the Affair* (1951).[5] In a way, Wyndham Lewis responded still more directly to Dunne, although with customary hostility. Lewis considered *An Experiment with Time* simply to provide further, relatively minor evidence of the huge contemporary 'time-cult' – originating with Bergson, and reinforced by Einstein – which he was so determined to expose in *Time and Western Man* (1927). He describes Dunne in that volume as merely 'one of the most amusing of the time-romancers', extending his criticism in a satiric short story, 'You Broke My Dream, or An Experiment with Time' (1927). This features a character convinced he finds proof of the theory, attributed to 'R. Dunne', that 'in our dreams the future is available for the least of us'.[6]

John Buchan is not much more supportive in *The Gap in the Curtain* (1932), though claiming his novel was inspired by *An Experiment with Time*. *The Gap in the Curtain* describes a mysterious professor who bases some of his convictions, like Dunne, around ideas Henri Bergson discusses in *Creative Evolution* (*L'Évolution créatrice*, 1907). These ideas and others contribute to the professor's 'new theory of Time', which explains that the immediate world is 'contained within a world one dimension larger'. Like Dunne, he considers that 'the Future is here with us now, if we only knew how to look for it', and that an ideal vantage point is provided by 'the anticipating power of the dreamer', freed from 'petty reason' and 'the bonds of ratiocination'.[7] Demonstration of these ideas requires characters to concentrate intensely on reading *The Times*, in its current issues, in order to look into the future and record what the newspaper will be reporting in a

---

[5] William Gerhardie, *Of Mortal Love* (1936; Harmondsworth: Penguin, 1982), 192, 30; Greene, *World of My Own*, xxi, which records a prescient childhood dream about the sinking of the *Titanic*. See also Greene, *Ways of Escape*, 92, 137.

[6] Lewis, *Time and Western Man*, 204; Lewis, *The Wild Body* (London: Chatto and Windus, 1927), 295. Lewis's story was first published in 1927 as 'You Broke my Dream: An Experiment with Time'. Dunne's volume had appeared in March of that year.

[7] John Buchan, *The Gap in the Curtain* (1932; Edinburgh: Polygon, 2012), 18, 24, 37, 39. Subsequent references are to this edition.

year's time.[8] Predictions generally prove accurate, though with consequences perplexing or disastrous for nearly all concerned – readers of Buchan's novel probably included. Suggesting how disturbing life can be when the future is anticipated, *The Gap in the Curtain* also demonstrates the dreariness of fiction – especially set in Buchan's vapid upper-class milieu – when it is based so fully around conclusions foregone and foreknown.

Dunne's ideas are employed more adroitly by J. B. Priestley in 1930s plays including *Dangerous Corner* (1932), *Time and the Conways* (1937) and *I Have Been Here Before* (1937). Characters' visionary freedoms allow each play to move backwards and forwards in time, highlighting Priestley's habitual concern with the decline of the middle classes – moral and financial – during the decades following the Great War. *Time and the Conways* begins with a cheerful family party, shortly after the Armistice, but follows in its second act a troubled urge to 'see round the corner – into the future'. This reveals how far, by 1937, problems which were scarcely visible in 1919 have expanded – towards personal and financial ruin – under the unfolding influence of the 'great devil in the universe . . . Time'. A devilishly difficult future is also outlined in broader terms. In the play's first act, younger characters hopefully believe that there will be 'no more wars', and that in twenty years' time they will be 'staggered at the progress that's been made'. Such remarks carried a painful irony for Priestley's audiences in 1937, only too aware – and reminded anyway by a character in the second act – that 'this isn't just after the War. It's just before the next War'.[9] Along with other plays mentioned, *Time and the Conways* indicates in this way how effectively Dunne's ideas could be adopted in literature, if Buchan's limitations could be avoided – largely in sanctioning extended prolepses, casting a revealing if sinister light back from the future across action in the present.

In a later study, *Man and Time* (1964), Priestley describes himself as a 'Time-haunted man' – one owing 'an enormous debt' to Dunne, whom he assesses as 'so far the most important figure in the campaign against the conventional idea of Time'.[10] Priestley's remarks – and the context in which they appear in *Man and Time* – help to define the particular nature of Dunne's appeal during the 1930s, and how

---

[8] *An Experiment with Time* also describes precognitive dreams about newspaper headlines, though ones appearing in the *Daily Telegraph*.
[9] J. B. Priestley, *Time and the Conways* (1948); in *Time and the Conways and Other Plays* (Harmondsworth: Penguin, 1981), 18, 60, 73, 50.
[10] Priestley, *Man and Time*, viii, 265.

far it extended or amended the 1920s 'obsession' that Connolly and Lewis identified.[11] Priestley's chapter on Dunne appears between his accounts of dreams and of esoteric thinkers about time and eternal recurrence, including George Gurdjieff and P. D. Ouspensky. Interest in such figures suggests how far, by the 1930s, elements of mysticism or spirituality had begun to figure in popular views of temporality, even when these were based, like Dunne's, on apparently scientific or mathematical reasoning. As Buchan suggests in *The Gap in the Curtain*, divergent fields of thinking were sometimes readily conflated during the 1930s, in 'dim regions where physics, metaphysics and mathematics jostle' (20). T. F. Powys explored a 'region' of this kind towards the end of the 1920s, in *Mr Weston's Good Wine* (1927), and an even more esoteric one figures at the beginning of a novel by his brother John Cowper Powys, *A Glastonbury Romance* (1933). Powys's opening describes something defined as 'a wave, a motion, a vibration, too tenuous to be called magnetic, too subliminal to be called spiritual' which somehow operates around a rural railway station 'and yet beyond the deepest pools of emptiness between the uttermost stellar systems'.[12]

Such interests in mysterious waves and motions, undulating between earthly life and the furthest stars, extend into new regions the impact of Relativity – 'the Relativist landslide', as Dunne calls it – and the scarcely credible views of the universe it had popularised during the previous decade (224).[13] Dunne begins *An Experiment with Time* by emphasising that 'this is not a book about "occultism"' (11), but he relies on popular awareness of Einstein's ideas – and to an extent those of Bergson – to help support what are often near-mystic conclusions.[14] Later editions of his study include an apparently supportive note from the Relativity expert Sir Arthur Eddington, adding credibility to Dunne's claim that 'Relativity admits of "seeing ahead" in Time'

---

[11] Dunne continued to interest writers in later decades: Jorge Luis Borges assesses his work in an essay, 'Time and J. W. Dunne' (1964), and Vladimir Nabokov invokes his ideas of dream-based precognition in *Ada* (1969; see Chapter 6). Along with Priestley's *Man and Time*, *An Experiment with Time* figures as reading material for Richard Matheson's protagonists in his popular romance, *Somewhere in Time* (1980). Dunne's continuing popular appeal is indicated by *An Experiment with Time* remaining in print three-quarters of a century after its first publication.

[12] John Cowper Powys, *A Glastonbury Romance* (London: John Lane, 1933), 1.

[13] This impact was still more clearly evident in the rise of science fiction, discussed in Chapter 6.

[14] In *'Intrusions?'* (1955), published posthumously, Dunne did acknowledge a mystic or spiritualist aspect in his experience and thinking.

(128). Much as Dunne considered, 'modern science' had put 'the classical theory of Time ... in the melting-pot', with popular belief in scientifically substantiated fourth or further dimensions facilitating acceptance of the 'second-order' world favoured in his writing (87). A 'craze' by 1923, according to D. H. Lawrence, Relativity on this evidence retained or extended its hold on popular imagination a decade later. The kind of loose combination of ideas Lewis defined in 1927 – of Einstein's thinking, residues of Bergson's, and some more recent esoteric influences – seemed to have coalesced, by the early 1930s, into a 'campaign against time' more wide-ranging, if rather more loosely defined and mystical, than ever. The popularity of Dunne's strange ideas was symptomatic of the influence exerted by this 'campaign' during the period.

From the Hours to the Years: the 1920s to the 1930s

Fiction which modernist novelists published in the decade or so after 1930 also, naturally enough, extended some of the 'obsession with time' shaping their 1920s fiction, though on occasion towards new interests. In one way, *The Waves* (1931), *The Years* (1937), and *Between the Acts* (1941) simply extend Virginia Woolf's long-standing concerns with temporality, including her hostility towards the mechanical, divisive aspects of clockwork criticised in *Mrs Dalloway* (1925) and *Orlando* (1928). 'The great clock, all the clocks of the city' are still found to be 'gathering their forces' in a section of *The Years* set in 1914.[15] Characters in *The Waves* remain troubled both by 'the stare of clocks' and by the susceptibility of 'the unlimited time of the mind' to painful interruption whenever 'one hears a clock tick' – much the same 'shock to the nervous system' experienced in *Orlando*.[16] The sound of ticking proves equally ominous – 'maddening' – in *Between the Acts*, though in this case produced by the repeated clicking of a gramophone, left unattended after its needle has reached the end of a record.[17] 'Tick, tick, tick the machine continued', irritatingly 'marking time' during interludes

---

[15] Virginia Woolf, *The Years* (1937; Oxford: Oxford University Press, 1992), 216.
[16] Virginia Woolf, *The Waves* (1931; Harmondsworth: Penguin, 1973), 25, 235. Subsequent references are to this edition.
[17] Virginia Woolf, *Between the Acts* (1941; London: Panther, 1980), 128. Subsequent references are to this edition.

between various acts in the historical pageant Miss La Trobe stages throughout much of the day the novel describes (64). Emblematically, the two pageant characters who most successfully escape the constraints of their historical period do so through crafty maltreatment of a clock. Removing 'the entrails of a time-piece' that had previously 'never missed a second since King Charles's day', they use the eviscerated clock-case as a convenient hiding-place, before romantically eloping into a freer new life (105, 106).

Yet in other ways, both *The Waves* and *Between the Acts* move towards more relaxed, natural encounters with time and its passage, diminishing or evading concerns about clocks and their mechanical measures. Shakespearean advice Clarissa repeats inwardly in *Mrs Dalloway* – 'fear no more the heat o' the sun' – seems to have been followed by Woolf herself in writing *The Waves*.[18] The sun's daily passage through the skies is described in lyric interludes throughout, along with the growth and fading of daylight and the rhythmic fall of waves upon the shore. These interludes intrude upon the novel's interior monologues – following characters as they grow and age through various stages of life – much more benignly than the vigorous striking of Big Ben and the 'shredding and slicing' of clocks in *Mrs Dalloway*. Woolf's lyric sections still measure out the passage of time in *The Waves*, but suggest affirmation rather than interruption of the 'sweep of [the] mind' (235), indicating the absorption of characters and their desires within the temporal rhythms of the natural world. Evidently freer, after writing *To the Lighthouse* (1927), from memories of the Great War and its blight on life and nature, Woolf re-establishes the kind of pre-industrial temporality the railway age had displaced – one measured by 'natural time, the time dictated by the sun's progress through the heavens'. As a result, though timepieces in *The Waves* remain as enervating as in Woolf's earlier fiction, her characters have more scope simply to ignore them, or to contemplate how to 'abolish the ticking of time's clock' (155). 'Time passes, yes. And we grow old', one of them acknowledges. Yet he also suggests that this might offer less reason, and not more, to 'look . . . at the clock ticking on the mantelpiece' (152).

Between the Acts also emphasises a need to look at longer reaches of time's passage in the natural world – a demand which had grown much more pressing since the middle years of the nineteenth century. The novel reflects some of the longest temporal reaches

---

[18] Virginia Woolf, *Mrs Dalloway* (1925; Harmondsworth: Penguin, 1976), 34.

imaginable. The 'Outline of History' Mrs Swithin reads in its opening pages describes a barely formed, primeval European continent, inhabited by 'barking monsters; the iguanodon, the mammoth, and the mastodon, from whom presumably ... we descend' (10, 11). By the mid-nineteenth century, as this 'Outline of History' reflects, studies in geology by James Hutton and Charles Lyell had immensely extended estimates of the age of the Earth. Noting that Lyell's 'grand work' had already shown 'how vast have been the past periods of time', Charles Darwin's *On the Origin of Species* (1859) likewise hugely expanded estimates of the period during which the Earth's life-forms had evolved.[19] Effects of these scientific views on literary imagination are widely apparent in Victorian fiction – in the hero's encounter with a fossil in Thomas Hardy's *A Pair of Blue Eyes* (1873), for example. This leads him to consider – even at a moment of extreme personal crisis – the 'immense lapses of time ... between this creature's epoch and his own', and to ponder a range of prehistoric beasts similar to those described in Mrs Swithin's 'History'.[20] Similar concerns continued to figure among the wide range of temporal pressures, outlined in Chapter 4, at work on modernist imagination by the 1920s. They appear in the vision of an 'age of tusk and mammoth' lurking beneath London pavements in *Mrs Dalloway*, and in Mrs Ramsay's view in *To the Lighthouse*, of a 'moon country, uninhabited of men', shaped by geologic aeons too vast and aloof ever to 'supplement what man advanced'.[21] Woolf's interest in a landscape of this kind, far beyond human scales of time, may even have been a motive for setting the novel, slightly implausibly, on the Isle of Skye. Beautiful but bleak, and formed from some of the oldest rocks in the world, the island's landscape – typically of much Scottish topography – is less easily configured within conventional pastoral idioms than rural areas elsewhere in Britain, usually reshaped extensively by agriculture and human activity.

There may even be a vague pun in this Skye setting, hinting at 'abysses of infinite space ... abysses of time' of a kind also mentioned in *The Waves* (193). Comparable infinitudes, in deep reaches of the sky, preoccupy Woolf's heroine in *Night and Day* (1919), fascinated by ways 'the stars ... work upon the mind [and] froze to

---

[19] Darwin, *Origin of Species*, 415–16.
[20] Thomas Hardy, *A Pair of Blue Eyes* (1873; London: Macmillan, 1975), 240.
[21] *Mrs Dalloway*, 90; Virginia Woolf, *To the Lighthouse* (1927; Harmondsworth: Penguin, 1973), 16, 153. Subsequent references are to this edition.

cinders the whole of our short human history'. Similar concerns had been evident in literature at least since – once again – the fiction of Thomas Hardy, concerned in *Two on a Tower* (1882) with the 'immensities' of 'the stars and their interspaces', described as 'deep wells for the human mind to let itself down into' (57).[22] New interests in 'uttermost stellar systems' added in the 1920s to the 'work upon the mind' Woolf mentions, and to its implications for 'human history'. Alongside Relativity's challenges, Edwin Hubble's research into galaxies during the decade identified new immensities of spatial and temporal remoteness, stretching far further into the depths of the sky than had hitherto been imagined. Popular accounts of astronomy soon helped to publicise these new views of the cosmos. Authors such as Sir James Jeans, mentioned in *Between the Acts*, emphasised that 'the universe consists in the main . . . of desolate emptiness – inconceivably vast stretches of desert space': ones thoroughly 'indifferent to life like our own' and perhaps even 'totally unintelligible to us'.[23] By the 1920s, in other words, or probably at any time from the later nineteenth century, understanding of time and its nature might have been troubled as much by agoraphobia as confinement. Alongside the new requirement Marcel Proust emphasises – the need 'to take account of minutes', in a railway age – the period also had to take new account, in a scientific age, of almost immeasurable aeons. A double demand of this kind is highlighted by Mrs Swithin's reading in *Between the Acts*, when she finds that returning her attention from 'the green steaming undergrowth of the primeval forest' to the present moment 'took her five seconds in actual time, in mind time ever so much longer' (11).

Woolf's own 'outline of history', in Miss La Trobe's pageant, covers a much more recent period, though with implications deeply troubling for the novel's present day in 1939. In one way, the pageant offers its spectators picturesque distractions from the immediate threat of war – from their 'vision of Europe, bristling with guns, poised with planes' (43). Yet even in visiting periods more peaceful or promising than the present, the pageant progresses inexorably towards the moment of its own presentation, demonstrating the inevitability of history's onward sweep towards 'the doom of

---

[22] Virginia Woolf, *Night and Day* (1919; Oxford: Oxford University Press, 2009), 202–3; Thomas Hardy, *Two on a Tower* (1882; London: Macmillan, 1975), 57. Woolf read *Two on a Tower* in 1908.

[23] Jeans, *Universe Around Us*, 87; *Mysterious Universe*, 3, 112.

sudden death' in 1939, and the powerlessness of art to resist this disastrous movement (86). For Miss La Trobe's audience, 'all caught and caged' in the present moment, 'no retreating and advancing' is possible, either in reality, or, ultimately, in imagination (128, 86). As well as focusing residual resentment of the clock's mechanical measures, the gramophone's 'maddening' ticking functions in this way as a *memento mori*, emphasising the inexorable movement of time and history towards the moment when another war will confirm the period's sense of doomed existence 'between the acts'.

These broader interests in history suggest that *Between the Acts*, like *The Waves*, remains 'time-haunted', but less thoroughly clock-harried than some of Woolf's 1920s writing. The nature of the change might be summed up through the titles of two of her novels: as a partial shift of interest from 'the hours', the original title of *Mrs Dalloway*, to 'the years'. In an essay analysing 'The time-mind of the twenties', Michael Levenson suggests that a change of this kind was more generally apparent in contemporary writing. After the 1920s, he suggests, 'altered circumstances changed the literary enactment of time . . . time lost its aura . . . it was absorbed back into history'.[24] Though Levenson does not define the circumstances or causes involved, these appear clearly enough in the doomed feelings described in *Between the Acts*. Woolf also indicates their nature in looking back over the 1930s in an essay she published a year earlier, 'The Leaning Tower' (1940). Like many commentators, Woolf considered the decade much more urgently politicised than its predecessor. 'In 1930 it was impossible', she suggests – particularly for younger writers – 'not to be interested in politics; not to find public causes of much more pressing interest than philosophy'. In the same essay, she records that when 'we turn on the wireless . . . we hear Hitler's voice as we sit at home of an evening'. No domestic space, no 'room of one's own', no private memory or 'time in the mind' could remain impervious, by the 1930s, to voices prophesying war, or, more generally, to the 'crumpling flood' – as W. H. Auden called it – of the decade's politics and public events.[25] A shift of interest from hours to years, in other words, might not have resulted only from post-Relativist relaxation in resentment of 'the terrible clock, with its eternal tick-tack', so troubling to Gudrun in *Women in Love* (1921).

---

[24] Marcus and Nicholls, eds, *Cambridge History of Twentieth-Century Literature*, 217.
[25] *Essays*, VI, 268–9, 261; W. H. Auden 'A Summer Night', *Collected Shorter Poems: 1927–1957* (1966; London: Faber and Faber, 1971), 70.

In a decade increasingly aware of its existence 'between the acts', writers were inevitably 'absorbed back into history' – engrossed by 'public causes', and by the need to scrutinise the spread of years through which their urgent stresses had evolved.

Summer Days and Sunset Songs: the 1930s

Writers emerging in the 1930s – including Christopher Isherwood, George Orwell, Aldous Huxley and Lewis Grassic Gibbon – regularly retrace these stresses to the initiatory 'act' of the Great War, cutting across history, in ways that Chapter 3 described, and destroying the supposedly placid period before 1914. Warm recollection of this period, attractive to modernist memory in the 1920s, reappeared strongly at the beginning of the next decade in Somerset Maugham's *Cakes and Ale* (1930). For Maugham, memory is as much a seductress as the 'seamstress' it seemed to Woolf, drawing characters into a past shaped less by reliable recall than by their desire for consoling or convenient versions of earlier events. In one way, this creative, consolatory aspect in memory allows distant lives – those of a writer resembling Thomas Hardy, and his charming wife – to fade still more irretrievably into the past, beyond any sure or accurate recollection. Yet it also demonstrates how far nostalgia in recollecting old times may satisfy the needs of life in the present, compensating for some of its stresses and disappointments. Maugham's 'saunter down the road of memory' – towards rural childhood and 'sunny days . . . in an unbroken line' – was soon followed by a range of 1930s novels, often extolling sunnier times enjoyed during the Edwardian period, before the Great War.[26]

One of these is Christopher Isherwood's *The Memorial* (1932). Like Maugham, Isherwood is concerned with the nature of memory, but principally with effects on it, and on the life of the period generally, resulting from the Great War. *The Memorial* concludes with a character remarking 'that War . . . it ought never to have happened': comparable regrets shape Isherwood's whole narrative, particularly its second part, '1920'.[27] Centred on the inauguration

---

[26] Somerset Maugham, *Cakes and Ale* (1930; London: Vintage, 2009), 32, 64. Subsequent references are to this edition. Edward VII became king in 1901 and died in 1910, but the whole period between 1900 and 1914 often bears his name.
[27] Christopher Isherwood, *The Memorial: Portrait of a Family* (1932; St Albans: Panther, 1978), 189. Subsequent references are to this edition.

of a war memorial, this section describes difficulties often encountered in the years immediately following the Great War, when the nationwide urge for remembrance Chapter 4 described was made concrete – often literally – in commemorative monuments installed in towns and villages throughout the country. Isherwood reflects debates often involved in their design when one of his central characters, Lily, gratefully concludes that a 'Memorial Cross' being inaugurated locally shows 'very good taste compared with the granite atrocities they were putting up in the neighbouring villages' (65, 66). But Isherwood's principal interest is less in public memorials than in contrasting the 'monumental time' they represent with the poignancy of inward, private remembrance. Like the free-ranging recollections Chapter 4 suggested might accompany any Remembrance Day ceremony, throughout the inauguration Lily's memories return not only to the war itself, but to idyllic times shared with those whom it later destroyed. Typically, too, Lily recalls these Edwardian times in terms of unbroken lines of sunny days – of

> summer, in the hot garden . . . a world where nothing will ever happen . . . a beautiful, happy world, in which next summer would be the same, and the next and the next – the County gossip, the Balls, engagements being announced, girls 'coming out' . . . plates of cress and cucumber sandwiches. The old safe, happy, beautiful world. (58)

Memories of this kind, regularly breaking into characters' thoughts, extend anachronies which also shape the overall structure of *The Memorial*. Isherwood later recorded his determination that his novel should 'start in the middle and go backwards, then forwards again', ensuring that 'time is circular, which sounds Einstein-ish and brilliantly modern'.[28] *The Memorial* is Einstein-ish only in the loose sense – described earlier, and widely current by the early 1930s – of assuming that 'the conventional idea of time' might be conveniently ignored. Isherwood is nevertheless justified in claiming that 'modern', or modernist, tactics shape his novel's form. His strategies obviously extend preferences for going 'backwards and forwards over the past' expressed in the 1920s by Virginia Woolf and Ford Madox Ford. Like William Faulkner in *The Sound and the Fury*, first published in Britain a year before *The Memorial*, Isherwood adds another dimension to such backward and forward movements by dividing his novel

---

[28] Isherwood, *Lions and Shadows*, 182.

into four sections, dated 1928, 1920, 1925 and 1929.[29] This radically anachronous structure answers, in a way, a question raised within the novel – 'what did the War mean to you?' (70). It also reflects a wish Isherwood later recalled – that *The Memorial* should 'be about war: not the War itself, but the effect of the idea of "War" on my generation'.[30] *The Memorial* suggests that the effects of the war could be reflected not only by inserting memories of happier Edwardian years into interior monologues representing characters' current thoughts. Its consequences might also be emphasised through radical fracturings of conventional literary form, representing structurally the cracks, chasms and shadow-lines the war had imposed on recent history. Isherwood admired Woolf's work: *The Memorial* shows him extending into the form of his novel the example of *To the Lighthouse*, along with some of the emphases on memory and 'time in the mind' shaping *Mrs Dalloway*.

Tactics comparable to Isherwood's appear in some of Aldous Huxley's 1930s fiction, which moves away, like Woolf's during the decade, from direct concerns with the clock. These still figure strongly in *Brave New World* (1932), but in *Eyeless in Gaza* (1935) Huxley suggests that resentment of chronometers and 'time for its own sake' – measured out 'imperiously . . . categorically' – had a more significant role in the earlier years of the twentieth century.[31] His concerns with chronology focus instead on the wider passage of history – or rather on its interruption, represented through a structure still more splintered than Isherwood's. *Eyeless in Gaza* reduplicates in its form one of its characters' descriptions of the operation of memory – envisaged as sometimes exhibiting 'no chronology . . . no distinction between before and after', as if 'a lunatic shuffled a pack of snapshots and dealt them out at random' (18). 'Particles of time' in *Eyeless in Gaza* – fragmentary sections or snapshots, headed by various datelines between 1902 and 1935 – sometimes do seem assembled at random (19). They nevertheless accumulate towards a terrible, concluding betrayal, set in the weeks before the Great War began. Though only its date links this episode directly with the war, *Eyeless in Gaza* inevitably emphasises, through its form, lost historical coherence and the destruction of a more decent, innocent, comprehensible world in the summer of 1914.

---

[29] Faulkner's sections are dated 'April Seventh, 1928'; 'June Second, 1910'; 'April Sixth, 1928'; 'April Eighth, 1928'.
[30] *Lions and Shadows*, 182.
[31] Aldous Huxley, *Eyeless in Gaza* (1936; London: Vintage, 2004), 24. Subsequent references are to this edition.

Like Isherwood and Huxley, in his trilogy *A Scots Quair* (*Sunset Song*, 1932; *Cloud Howe*, 1933; *Grey Granite*, 1934) Lewis Grassic Gibbon uses a complexly anachronous narrative to highlight the losses of the Great War, their memorialisation, and wider historical developments from the Edwardian years towards the politicised 1930s. As in Isherwood's novel, war memorials are a repeated interest. Lily's disgust with 'granite atrocities' is echoed in judgements of 'the War Memorial of Segget toun' in *Cloud Howe*. The town's ornate memorial angel is described as a 'trumpery flummery' in 'a stone nightgown . . . like a constipated calf'.[32] This flummery is further criticised, implicitly, by comparison with another memorial, described in the elegiac ending of *Sunset Song* in terms as austere as a wartime casualty list. The names of the dead from the highland village of Kinraddie are simply carved into the ancient Standing Stones which dominate the landscape on the edge of the moors nearby. The service inaugurating this modest community memorial describes the dead as 'the Last of the Peasants, the last of the Old Scots folk' and their loss as marking 'the sunset of an age and an epoch' (255–6). Despite descriptions of this farming community's perennially harsh struggles for a livelihood, like other 1930s authors Grassic Gibbon looks back on the age before the 'sunset' of the Great War as a brighter, surer one than any succeeding it.

The brooding presence of the Standing Stones also contributes to the novel's broader sense of time and history, emphasising, in a bleak landscape, the kind of deeper, geologic or near-eternal sense of the past figuring occasionally in Woolf's fiction. 'Nothing endured at all', Grassic Gibbon's central figure Chris Guthrie reflects in *Sunset Song*, 'nothing but the land she passed across, tossed and turned and perpetually changed below the hands of the crofter folk since the oldest of them had set the Standing Stones by the loch' (119). Yet while the stones, like 'gnomons of a giant dial', indicate dimensions of time almost beyond human history, they also emphasise particular needs and courses of action operating within it (63). Reflecting Grassic Gibbon's interest in Diffusionism, the Standing Stones function as liminal markers, in time rather than space, of the disappearance of a distant Golden Age of nomadic hunters, free of the constraints of class, religion and social hierarchy whose first appearance in the ancient world the stones

---

[32] Lewis Grassic Gibbon (James Leslie Mitchell), *A Scots Quair: Sunset Song, Cloud Howe, Grey Granite* (1932–4; Edinburgh: Canongate, 1995), 44–5. Subsequent references are to this edition.

memorialise.[33] In its later volumes, the trilogy increasingly converts regret for the distant loss of this idyllic past age into utopian 1930s hopes for the political future, suggesting that 'if there was once a time without gods and classes couldn't there be that time again?' (*Grey Granite*, 43–4). This is the possibility pursued by Chris's son Ewan, his hardening commitment to progressive politics and historical action contrasting sharply with his mother's faith in the eternal, cyclic recurrences of the natural world.

This contrast is further emphasised by the trilogy's narrative form. In tracing the impact of modernity on an agrarian community, *A Scots Quair* often resembles *The Rainbow* (1915), and Grassic Gibbon, like D. H. Lawrence, structures into his novel a sense of time in both linear and cyclic forms. Individual chapters throughout *A Scots Quair* are circular, much in the manner of Ford Madox Ford's *Parade's End* (1924–8). In *Sunset Song*, each begins with Chris escaping the demands of farm labour to enjoy brief leisured moments near the Standing Stones, 'the only place where ever she could come and stand back a little from the clamour of the days' (108). Through Chris's reminiscent interior monologue, the chapter then goes back to describe recent events, ending with the story advanced once again to the leisured present moment from which it began. The effect throughout is of a narrative drawn back strongly towards the past – like so much fiction after the Great War – and consequently reluctant to commit itself completely to the progress of time and history in conventionally linear forms. Instead, the use of looping, recursive individual chapters – within the forward movement of the novel as a whole – both engages readers with immediate events, yet also encourages them to 'stand back a little from the clamour of the days', allowing a wider, even utopian, view of past or future.

Along with his highly inventive use of Free Indirect Discourse and interior monologue, such carefully directed anachronies suggest that Grassic Gibbon was one of few novelists to redeploy 1920s modernist strategies effectively in dealing with the political stresses of the next decade. While adding to modernist initiatives an element

---

[33] The 'new school of thought' of Diffusionism is explored more fully in Grassic Gibbon's time-travel novel *Three Go Back* (1932; Edinburgh: Polygon, 1995). This describes characters, fleeing traumatic memories of the Great War, who find themselves 'in the dawn of time' and among 'the earliest true men on earth', living in a society 'absolutely without superstitious fears, cruelties or class-divisions' (105, 90–1).

of political responsibility they have sometimes been considered to lack, *A Scots Quair* loses none of their imaginative and emotional power. This is particularly apparent in the nostalgic conclusion of *Sunset Song*. In juxtaposing immediate history and time immemorial – regrets for pre-war years, for lives lost after 1914, and for the disappearance of an ancient Golden Age – Grassic Gibbon creates a sedimentation of times and memories as complex as James Joyce's at the end of *Ulysses* (1922). Unlike Joyce, moreover, he is not concerned only to reconfigure the 'nightmare' of history imaginatively, but also to indicate political means through which some of its disasters and abuses might be eradicated.

A Scots Quair, and *Sunset Song* especially, also share in longer-established patterns in literary history, re-emerging strongly in the later 1920s and 1930s. Nostalgia in the period's fiction frequently focuses on remembered scenes of rural life and the natural world – on landscapes extending visions of 'summer, in the hot garden' appearing in *The Memorial*, or of the 'airy sunny garden' recalled, also from before the Great War, in *To the Lighthouse* (211). This pattern is at its clearest in the most sustained 1930s engagement with nostalgia and Edwardian memories – George Orwell's *Coming up for Air* (1939). Exasperated by dreary urban domesticity and his tedious job, and by late-1930s commercialism, bureaucracy and fears of war, Orwell's narrator George Bowling has good reason to look back longingly on his tranquil rural childhood in the Thames valley, around the village of 'Lower Binfield'. Yet when he seeks escape, returning to the village in the novel's fourth part, it is only to discover that the landscape he so fondly remembered has long since succumbed to the forces he fears – destroyed almost completely by sprawling urbanisation, industrial expansion and commercial exploitation.

His disappointing return to the actual Lower Binfield is nevertheless preceded by an idyllic return in memory. This is recorded in an analepsis – more extended even than those in *The Memorial* – which occupies the whole of the novel's second part, around half its overall length. It is introduced through a semi-Proustian moment of recall. Late-1930s headlines about King Zog of Romania reconnect Bowling – 'How it came back to me!', he remarks – with childhood Sunday-morning psalm-singing about Og the king of Bashan.[34] Interrupted only briefly by recollection of 'the unspeakable idiotic mess' of the Great War, there

---

[34] George Orwell, *Coming up for Air* (1939; Harmondsworth: Penguin, 1962), 33. Subsequent references are to this edition.

follows a thoroughgoing and thoroughly affirmative re-engagement with the Edwardian period and the years preceding it:

> Before the war, and especially before the Boer War, it was summer all the year round ... 1911, 1912, 1913. I tell you it was a good time to be alive ... the white dusty road stretching out between the chestnut trees, the smell of night-stocks, the green pools under the willows, the splash of Burford Weir – that's what I see when I shut my eyes and think of 'before the war' ... the feeling inside you, the feeling of not being in a hurry and not being frightened ... A settled period, a period when civilization seems to stand on its four legs like an elephant. (37, 102–4, 107–8)

Bowling's rosy memories display most of the components – endless summer, solidly reliable faiths and values, unspoiled life and landscape – attributed to the years before 1914 by novelists in the 1930s, and indeed by fiction, fairly regularly, ever since the Great War. Green pools, splashing weirs and pungent night flowers figure equally prominently in Rebecca West's vision of the past in *The Return of the Soldier*, published in the last year of the Great War, and much concerned with its traumas. Severely shell-shocked in 1916, West's hero has still more compelling cause than Bowling to retreat into memories – returning completely, in his mind, to a romance enjoyed on an idyllic Thames island in 1901. Steeped in seductive summer twilight, or drenched in romantic moonlight, this island idyll is described – also much in the manner of *Coming up for Air* – in an extended analepsis occupying the whole of the novel's third part. Such symmetries of sentiment and structure between *The Return of the Soldier*, appearing in 1918, and *Coming up for Air*, published in 1939, confirm how compelling the Edwardian years appeared throughout a period caught 'between the acts'. Memories of war, along with hardening certainties of its recurrence, inevitably heightened the appeal of a time apparently so much freer of historical stress – a period seeming, in retrospect, safely *before* 'the acts'.

This appeal is confirmed explicitly by several novelists, and by other forms of contemporary commentary. During the Great War, in 1917, Virginia Woolf's brother-in-law Clive Bell was already looking back warmly on 'society before the war ... curious, gay, tolerant, reckless'. In *Disenchantment* (1922), C. E. Montague suggests of the Edwardian period 'surely there never was any time in the life of the world when it was so good ... to be alive'. In the first volume of *Parade's End* (1924), Ford Madox Ford regrets the loss of the 'perfectly appointed ... luxuriant, regulated ... admirable' characteristics of this period. Richard Aldington describes in *Death of a Hero* (1929) 'the feeling of tranquil security which existed, the almost smug optimism of our lives' during the 'golden calm' before the Great War. A few years later, in *A Letter to Mrs Virginia Woolf* (1932), Peter Quennell continues to wonder forlornly 'was the pound really worth twenty shillings, and were there parties every night and hansom cabs?' 'How tranquil and olympian it must have been', he reflects, in this 'placid pre-war universe', before the outbreak of 'the War to End Wars and so good-bye'.[35]

Shadows in Eden: the 1940s and later

George Bowling finds memories of this placid past disturbingly interrupted by reminders of the present day, similar to those Priestley includes in *Time and the Conways*. 'Before the war!', Bowling remarks, 'How long shall we go on saying that, I wonder? How long before the answer will be "Which war?"' (35). When the Second World War did break out – a few weeks after Bowling's question appeared in *Coming up for Air*, published in June 1939 – it might have been expected radically to reshape literary constructions of time, the past and contemporary history. Instead, existing patterns and continuities were not generally eliminated by its impact, but continued in amended form, rather as at the beginning of the 1930s – perhaps naturally enough, as in one way the war merely confirmed fears which were already familiar and well established. Yet its outbreak obviously heightened convictions of impending 'doom of death' already in place by 1939, challenging established apprehensions of temporality. Military hazards in the previous war, Max Plowman recalled, had invaded even the temporal structures of language: soldiers serving in the trenches had 'to forget "I shall"' and accept that '"if" stands before every prospect', confining them to an immediate, potentially futureless existence in present or conditional tenses.[36] During the blitzes of 1940–1, the same fearful provisionality extended to much of the civilian population in Britain's cities, in London especially. Recalling the 'heady

---

[35] See Hynes, *A War Imagined*, 252; Montague, *Disenchantment*, 218; Ford Madox Ford, *Parade's End* (1924–8; Harmondsworth: Penguin, 1982), 3; Richard Aldington, *Death of a Hero* (1929; London: Hogarth Press, 1984), 199, 200 – subsequent references to this edition; Quennell, *Letter to Mrs. Virginia Woolf*, 17.

[36] Mark VII (Max Plowman), *A Subaltern on the Somme: in 1916* (1927; New York: E. P. Dutton, 1928), 54.

autumn of the first London air raids', Elizabeth Bowen's characters in *The Heat of the Day* (1949) conclude that the '"time being" ... war had made the very being of time. War time, with its makeshifts, shelvings, deferrings ... tideless, hypnotic, futureless day-to-day'. Emblematically, the novel's heroine finds that 'her wrist watch seemed to belie time', and that efforts to correct it are frustrated by many of London's public clocks having been 'shock-stopped' during the raids. The clock's measures appear as ruined as the city whose affairs they once ordered – existence in the blitz often figuring as 'hourless'; taking place 'in no given hour of time'.[37]

Rather than terminating 1930s nostalgias, this 'makeshift', futureless war time often strengthened incentives to look back over an idealised or more orderly past. Authors were inevitably disposed to share views Evelyn Waugh's narrator, Charles Ryder, sums up in *Brideshead Revisited* (1945) when he remarks that 'we possess nothing certainly except the past'.[38] Surveying fiction in 1946, Rosamond Lehmann likewise indicates that a threatening present and an uncertain future ensured that 'most novelists are likely to turn back to the time when, the place where they knew where they were ... where their imaginations can expand and construct among remembered scenes'.[39] In a novel published in the same year, *Back*, Henry Green's central figure sums up this urge when he returns from the war and reflects, while thinking about the hands of a clock, that 'all that he was after was to turn them back'. His wish is almost too fully realised, leaving him long trapped in the past, like Rebecca West's shell-shocked hero in *The Return of the Soldier* – rosy memories having 'grown between the minutes and the hours, and so entwined that the hands were stuck'.[40] The steady forward movement of clocks could be arrested, Green suggests, just as much by emotional shock – metaphorically, at any rate – as by the seismic effects of bombing raids.

Recollection of the past, moreover, as 1930s fiction had sometimes demonstrated, could offer not only a refuge from the present, but some explanation, in surveying recent history, of how its stresses might have originated and developed. Several 1940s novelists returned in this way to the circumstances of the First World War in order to reflect on the outbreak of the Second, or on wider historical pressures underlying

---

[37] Elizabeth Bowen, *The Heat of the Day* (1949; Harmondsworth: Penguin, 1983), 100, 97, 99, 8, 21.
[38] Evelyn Waugh, *Brideshead Revisited* (1945; Harmondsworth: Penguin, 1972), 215. Subsequent references are to this edition.
[39] Lehmann, 'Future of the Novel', 7.
[40] Henry Green, *Back* (1946; London: Hogarth Press, 1951), 9.

the current conflict. James Hilton's *Random Harvest* (1941) begins with a Remembrance-Day conversation about J. W. Dunne, then uses a character's recovery from amnesia as a means of intermingling experience of the First World War directly with circumstances just before the Second.[41] In the second volume of his wartime 'Triptych', *To be a Pilgrim* (1942), Joyce Cary's narrator Tom Wilcher finds that 'new war fever' in 1939 has left him 'more agitated . . . than any time since before the last war'.[42] *To be a Pilgrim* shows his concerns with history extending further into a complicated past. Frail and fading towards death – in the decaying country house, Tolbrook, he has spent a lifetime trying to maintain – Wilcher lets his memory wander beyond the Great War, or even the Boer War, resuming public and family events since the latter part of the nineteenth century. These are recalled through analepses almost as extended as Orwell's in *Coming up for Air*. Initially, Wilcher's memories distract him only momentarily from his uneasiness on the brink of the Second World War. As the novel progresses, they take over his narrative more completely, leaving an impression – for reader as well as narrator – that 'reality had actually disappeared out of the world', overtaken by 'appearance from the past' (245).

A related impression concerns the disturbing complexity of the past's influence on the present, making it difficult to maintain nostalgic or affirmative views of earlier times, unalloyed by darker recollections. In his 'old house . . . charged with history', and in the countryside around it, Wilcher sometimes experiences an enjoyment of remembered moments profound enough – like George Bowling's – to suffuse the present with 'a sense of peculiar happiness' (193). Yet the promise of the past as an escape from stressful present experience is vitiated – as in *Between the Acts* – by the sense either of its close resemblance to later events, or sometimes its direct responsibility for them. Commenting on the strategies of his 'Triptych', Joyce Cary suggests that his narrators 'recall . . . the history of the times, as part of [their] own history.'[43] In Wilcher's case, a largely loveless, sometimes perverse private life is both analogue and consequence of the tangled historical events he recalls, while those events themselves regularly suggest sources, or anticipations, of the impending doom of the Second World War.

---

[41] Vera Brittain uses a character's amnesia to comparable effect in *Account Rendered* (1945).

[42] Joyce Cary, *To be a Pilgrim* (1942), in *Triptych: Herself Surprised, To be a Pilgrim, The Horse's Mouth* (Harmondsworth: Penguin, 1985), 383. See also Chapter 6. Subsequent references are to this edition.

[43] Joyce Cary, 'Prefatory Essay' to *Herself Surprised* (1941; London: Michael Joseph, 1958), 7.

Waugh's *Brideshead Revisited* offers a still clearer instance of nostalgia amended by a second war, its pressures attenuating the kind of affirmations 1930s novelists found in recalling earlier times. Like Orwell, Waugh develops his narrator's memories through an extended analepsis, though one reaching back less far than the Edwardian years, and towards an idyll much more uncertain. The novel begins with Charles Ryder returning to an aristocratic family's country manor, Brideshead – representative, like Tolbrook in *To be a Pilgrim*, of longstanding values which are more and more imperilled, along with the building itself, by change and decay. Commandeered by the army during the war, Brideshead has become 'a great barrack of a place', evoking for Ryder the painful recollection that

> I had been there before; first with Sebastian more than twenty years ago on a cloudless day in June, when the ditches were creamy with meadowsweet and the air heavy with all the scents of summer . . . it was to that first visit that my heart returned on this, my latest. (22–3)

'My theme is memory', Ryder remarks, and much in the manner of *The Return of the Soldier*, or *Coming up for Air*, the cloudless summer days of the past are recalled at length throughout Book One of *Brideshead Revisited* (215).

These sunny, Arcadian Oxford days are nevertheless heavily clouded by anticipations of the drunkenness and dissipation which will eventually destroy Sebastian. Emblematically, during the times he recalls, Ryder kept in his Oxford rooms 'a human skull . . . resting in a bowl of roses . . . it bore the motto "*Et in Arcadia Ego*" inscribed on its forehead' (43). Indicating that death, too, was in paradise, this gloomy inscription also provides the title for Book One. It both confirms and extends a judgement that Henry Reed offers in his study *The Novel since 1939*, published in 1946. Discussing writers' recent interests in childhood and the past, Reed suggests – like Rosamond Lehmann, writing in the same year – that 'in a world of darkness . . . it is natural to turn and attempt to recapture and understand and detail that lost possibility of Eden'.[44] Full understanding of the Edenic past, *Brideshead Revisited* demonstrates, requires recognition of its role not only as an alternative to the darkness of the present, but as its source. Experience of a second world war inevitably made it more difficult to recall any paradise free of the seeds of its own destruction, complicating as a result, though not eradicating, forms

---

[44] Reed, *The Novel since 1939*, 23.

of nostalgia and memoriousness which had been so evident in writing between 1918 and 1939. In 1940s fiction, sunny remembered landscapes often show shadows lengthening towards later years, and Edenic analepses regularly feature proleptic snakes.

Other 1940s novels confirm this change, approximating more closely even than *Brideshead Revisited* to myths of paradise, the Garden of Eden, and their loss. Rosamond Lehmann's *The Ballad and the Source* (1944) hints even in its title at the kind of modified nostalgia *Brideshead Revisited* practises. This is extended through various narratives which recall a sometimes happier past, or the innocence of childhood, yet also emphasise that 'far back and in [a] dark tangle of monstrous roots lies the undying worm' and that 'poisons from . . . far-back brews' have been 'corroding' throughout intervening years.[45] The principal 'poison', or primal error, is located in personal choices made long before the Great War – ones whose consequences leave succeeding generations on a 'road, forward and back, far back . . . cratered with disastrous pits of guilt' (82). At their worst, these disasters not only coincide closely with the outbreak of the Great War – occurring, like crises in Huxley's *Eyeless in Gaza*, in July 1914 – but even seem to outdo it in ferocity. A central character recalls her family's 'midsummer madness' in terms of 'roaring armies marching against one another and land mines bursting under everybody. When the real war started and every one else was in a state of chaos, it seemed to me a mere rumble on the horizon' (257–8). By this time, recent experience has persuaded her permanently to renounce love and relationship. For other characters, life in general, by 1916, has taken on a similarly 'fixed melancholy' (219).

Likewise employing a recursive structure, along with clear allusions to the myth of Eden, Malcolm Lowry's *Under the Volcano* (1947) is still less idyllic in its retrospection. Lowry's novel is in a way analeptic nearly throughout. It opens on Mexico's Day of the Dead in 1939, returning in the following eleven chapters to describe disastrous events which unfolded around this November festival a year previously. Foreknowledge of the outcome of these 1938 events contributes to a sense of tragic inevitability steadily accumulating throughout the novel. Each of its chapters corresponds to an hour in Geoffrey Firmin's last day on earth, with effects compared by Lowry to hearing 'a clock slowly striking midnight for Faust'.[46]

---

[45] Rosamond Lehmann, *The Ballad and the Source* (1944; London: Virago, 1982), 42, 211. Subsequent references are to this edition.

[46] Lowry, letter to Jonathan Cape, 2 January 1946, *Selected Letters*, 66. See also Chapter 6.

This single-day structure also corresponds to tactics established by modernist literature – *Ulysses* and *Mrs Dalloway* in particular. Along with Lewis Grassic Gibbon, Lowry is one of fairly few novelists successfully extending 1920s modernist strategies into the next decades. Protracted interior monologues, interspersed with 'blown fragments of . . . memories', vividly communicate the 'whirling cerebral chaos' of Firmin's habitually drunken mind.[47] *Under the Volcano* also resumes some of modernism's hostilities to the clock and its measures. In various states of drunkenness, Firmin finds that his 'swimming-pool ticked like a clock', and mishears an answer to his question about the time as 'half past sick by the cock' – inadvertently equating measured temporality with venereal disease (75, 353). A disastrous Ferris-wheel ride, literally turning his life upside down, recalls related modernist anxieties about infernal machines – in this case, one which turns inexorably through a full circle, like a clock, or like the doomed hours of the novel itself.

Typically, though, of fiction in the 1930s and 1940s, *Under the Volcano* remains less concerned with clockwork divisions in time's daily passage than with the broader, threatening movements of contemporary history. At the novel's opening, these are strongly represented in recollections of the outbreak of the Second World War, continuing to figure in later chapters through repeated hints and references, including to a terrible crime probably committed during the Great War years. They are also highlighted in Firmin's prolonged arguments with his half-brother about history's 'worthless stupid course' (311), and by the latter's profound concerns about the Spanish Civil War. A still deeper sense of loss and uncertainty is emphasised through a fragment of Spanish recurrently crossing Firmin's mind during his last day. In response to the use of nuclear weapons at the end of the Second World War, Lowry also includes this fragment on a separate last page of the novel. Firmin translates the Spanish as 'You like this garden? Why is it yours? We evict those who destroy!' – wondering to himself if 'there isn't more in the old legend of the Garden of Eden, and so on, than meets the eye' (132, 137). Lowry emphasises the full significance of this 'old legend' in a letter to his publishers in 1946. This explains that in *Under the Volcano* 'the allegory is that of the Garden of Eden, the Garden representing the world, from which we ourselves run

---

[47] Malcolm Lowry, *Under the Volcano* (1947; Harmondsworth: Penguin, 1983), 72, 309. Subsequent references are to this edition.

perhaps slightly more danger of being ejected than when I wrote the book'.⁴⁸

Edenic visions of this kind – of idyll and error, paradise and loss, and of the vanished glories of the Edwardian age – extend well beyond the end of the Second World War, continuing to appear in the work of novelists in the 1950s and even later. L. P. Hartley is one of these. He begins one of his early novels, *The Shrimp and the Anemone*, by describing life-defining events disrupting an otherwise innocent Edwardian childhood, tracing their later implications throughout further volumes of his *Eustace and Hilda* trilogy (1944–7). Similar implications are explored in *The Go-Between* (1953), though Hartley focuses them more concisely, by means of an analeptic structure resembling those often employed in 1930s and 1940s fiction. Discovery of an old diary at the novel's opening leads the narrator to look back, throughout the chapters that follow, on life-changing events experienced fifty years earlier. Much in the manner of Charles Ryder in *Brideshead Revisited*, he recalls enjoying a distant, brilliant summer in an affluent family's country manor and its grounds, visited, as his rediscovered diary records, in 1900. Typically, his 'dreams for the year 1900, and for the twentieth century' – and for himself – are soon destroyed by the devastating revelation of a family secret.⁴⁹ Its implications cast a shadow deep enough to make the rest of his life permanently loveless and unhappy. Returning to the manor at the end of the novel, he finds that no better fate has awaited the figures he considered in 1900 to be 'larger than life . . . the substance of [his] dreams . . . the incarnated glory of the twentieth century' (19). Some have been killed in the Great War, others in the Second World War. One lives on embittered in the present. As in other novels discussed above, recollection of Edwardian dreams and disillusions provides in this way an apt metaphor for the experience of the twentieth century generally, ensuring that Hartley's characters encapsulate 'the history of the times, as part of [their] own history'. Like P. H. Newby in his Second World War novel *The Retreat* (1953), authors concerned employ 'thinking of Eve and the Garden of Eden' as a means of representing a general sense of loss, during the first half of the twentieth century, of what seemed a 'state of grace before . . . the present'.⁵⁰

---

⁴⁸ Letter to Jonathan Cape, 2 January 1946, 66. Lowry began work on the novel during the 1930s, completing a first version by 1940. See also Chapter 6.
⁴⁹ L. P. Hartley, *The Go-Between* (1953; Harmondsworth: Penguin, 1981), 28. Subsequent references are to this edition.
⁵⁰ P. H. Newby, *The Retreat* (London: Cape, 1953), 172, 171.

Comparable retrospection continues to figure in Angus Wilson's novels in the 1950s, and later, and in some of Henry Williamson's. In *Anglo-Saxon Attitudes* (1956), Wilson describes lives confused and darkened for decades by an act of fraud committed in 1912. *No Laughing Matter* (1967) looks back across six decades of the twentieth century to the formative years of Edwardian childhood. These are considered again in *Late Call* (1964), which recalls with intense nostalgia the hot summer of 1911, described at length in the novel's Prologue. Recollections of the same brilliant summer figure in Henry Williamson's *The Golden Virgin* (1957), sixth of the fifteen volumes of *A Chronicle of Ancient Sunlight* (1951–67), and one of several describing the experiences of his central character, Phillip Maddison, during the Great War. His response to 'fugacious' wartime life includes at one point

> trying to re-enter the past, to drag it out of memory, to make live again in his mind the dappled sunlight under the trees and see himself, his sisters and friends and all who were there on that hot summer day of 1911, when in the shade the temperature was a hundred degrees, according to Negretti and Zambra, the instrument makers who were always mentioned in the newspapers before the war. Come back, he cried wildly in his mind, come back, O summer day of my childhood, let me re-enter just one crystal moment; but he could see nothing, all was beyond invisibility, far away in ancient sunlight, life lost for evermore ... layer on layer of ghosts, perhaps helping to suspend sunlight in the air.[51]

A quarter of a century after Lily's recollections of the Edwardian period in *The Memorial*, and more than a decade after a second world war, Williamson continues to emphasise vivid, painful regret for the sunny years before 1914. Retrospection of this kind throughout the fiction discussed above – determination 'to re-enter the past, to drag it out of memory' – suggests another chronotype that might be recognised in twentieth-century writing. Characterised by analeptic forms, nostalgic sentiments, and the use of Edenic myth in exploring the losses of recent history, this recurrent pattern might be discerned shaping fiction strongly throughout the period between 1930 and the 1950s, and sometimes beyond.[52]

---

[51] Henry Williamson, *The Golden Virgin* (London: MacDonald, 1957), 418, 419–20. Subsequent references are to this edition.

[52] Novels extending this pattern into later decades include J. L. Carr's *A Month in the Country* (1980), Paul Bailey's *Old Soldiers* (1981), or even Thomas Pynchon's *Against the Day* (2006) – see Chapter 6.

Look Backward Angel Now

This suggestion nevertheless raises several questions: about the authenticity, or justification, of fiction's rosy views of the Edwardian years; also, more generally, about how far strongly nostalgic sentiments can be considered unique to the decades following the Great War. Assessment of the latter issue might acknowledge that something close to nostalgia – some inclination to retain hold of the past – may be fundamental to all narrative, or at any rate to most fictional narrative. One of the novel's powers and pleasures is its potential for what Orwell calls in *Coming up for Air* 'looking at two worlds at once' – at 'the thing that used to be, with the thing that actually existed shining through it' (178). Narrative generally structures earlier experiences into meaningful relations with those that have followed, making fictional temporality inherently bifocal: keeping in view, in the novel's present, another world of influences and antecedents through which current circumstances can be seen to have developed. This past world need not, of course, be viewed nostalgically, but it requires nonetheless to retain a strong hold on awareness in order to provide 'that concordance of beginning, middle, and end which is the essence of our explanatory fictions', according to Frank Kermode.[53]

Whether or not narrative depends inherently on nostalgia and retrospection, there are innumerable examples throughout the history of literature – certainly not only in the decades after the Great War – of novelists using their fiction to revisit more alluring earlier periods.[54] When not directly criticising recent developments of stations and steam engines – as in *Dombey and Son* (1848) – Charles Dickens often chooses to set his novels decades earlier, in an era of journeys by coach and horse, before travel and the countryside were transformed by the advance of the railways. Early stages of this advance are described by George Eliot in *Middlemarch* (1871–2), set several decades in the past, in the 1830s, like much of Dickens's fiction. 'Five-and-thirty years ago the glory had not yet departed from the old coach roads', Eliot likewise reflects in *Felix Holt: the Radical* (1866), describing a time just after 'the recent initiation of Railways'.[55] In *The Mayor of Casterbridge*

---

[53] Kermode, *Sense of an Ending*, 35–6.
[54] Though the term 'nostalgia' itself, in its modern sense of regret for an engaging period in the past, may be unique to the twentieth century – its first use dated by the *Oxford English Dictionary* to 1900.
[55] George Eliot, *Felix Holt: the Radical* (1866; Harmondsworth. Penguin, 1995), 3, 8.

(1886), also set in the 1830s, Thomas Hardy describes how 'the railway had stretched out an arm towards Casterbridge at this time, but not yet reached it'. This leaves intact numerous 'old-fashioned features' whose 'rugged picturesqueness' – but imminent obliteration by 'time and progress' – Hardy emphasises even through the use of footnotes to this text, directing readers' particular attention to the extent of historical change and loss.[56] Neither Dickens's descriptions of earlier nineteenth-century landscapes and cityscapes, nor Hardy's or Eliot's of life in country towns at the time, altogether share the idyllic, high-summer vision often projected onto the Edwardian age by authors in the next century. There is nevertheless a comparable sense of looking back at a world still innocent in comparison to the present – still at least relatively unscathed by modernity and the industrial revolution, compared to life at the time these authors were writing.

Still clearer comparisons might be drawn between the temporal patterning or chronotype described above and the literary tactics of earlier centuries. Twentieth-century retrospections on lost Edens and Golden Ages invite obvious comparison with the great English epic of idyll, error, and everlasting consequence – *Paradise Lost* (1667) – and with the historical circumstances underlying Milton's vision. Though the central concerns of *Paradise Lost* are religious and moral, they are also shaped by covert connections with the Civil War – probably the most traumatic event in British history until 1914, and one whose consequences particularly oppressed Milton's imagination at the time he composed his epic. That pressure is never wholly explicit in *Paradise Lost*, though its existence is confirmed by Milton's friend and assistant Andrew Marvell. In 'Upon Appleton House' (1651), Marvell describes pre-Civil-War Britain as 'the garden of the world ere while' and a 'paradise . . . /Which heaven planted us to please', but goes on to wonder 'What luckless apple did we taste,/To make us mortal, and thee waste?'[57]

Given transhistoric or even archetypal aspects of nostalgic narrative, how particular should nostalgia in the decades after 1930 be considered? An answer can be offered by first examining the other issue mentioned above, regarding the legitimacy or persuasiveness of nostalgic feelings centred on the years before 1914. This question of authenticity is one which writers recalling the Edwardian age often raise themselves. John Osborne does so in *Look Back in Anger* (1956),

---

[56] Thomas Hardy, *The Life and Death of the Mayor of Casterbridge: A Study of a Man of Character* (1886; London: Macmillan, 1971), 265, 93, 65.

[57] Andrew Marvell, *The Complete Poems*, ed. Elizabeth Story Donno (Harmondsworth: Penguin, 1972), 85.

a play considered to mark a thorough break from convention and the past when it was first performed, though it offers nevertheless another example of Edwardian nostalgia surviving into the 1950s. Affirmative views of 'the old Edwardian brigade' and 'their brief little world', expressed by Osborne's otherwise iconoclastic hero, Jimmy Porter, conform quite thoroughly to convention, offering a familiar account of 'high summer, the long days in the sun'. In another way, Porter is also conventional enough in acknowledging that this is a 'romantic picture', and 'phoney too, of course. It must have rained sometimes'.[58] His scepticism resumes doubts – notably about the supposedly flawless weather – often sensibly expressed even by those earlier authors most enthusiastic about the virtues of the Edwardian age, or earlier ones. Maugham's narrator in *Cakes and Ale* admits that his memories of an 'unbroken line' of sunny summer days – and his recollections that in general 'the English climate was better' – may have resulted merely from 'an illusion of youth' (64). In *Coming up for Air,* George Bowling likewise acknowledges that the idea that 'before the war it was always summer' is 'sentimental' and 'a delusion'. 'If you look back on any special period of time', he explains, 'you tend to remember the pleasant bits' (103, 106).

Other novelists confirm a wider need for selective memory of this kind, indicating that freedoms from historical stress, so often ascribed to the period before 1914, may have been as much imaginary as real. Writing just after the Great War, in *Potterism* (1920), Rose Macaulay remarks that 'those of us who are old enough will remember that in June and July, 1914, the conversation turned largely and tediously on militant suffragists, Irish rebels, and strikers'.[59] In *To be a Pilgrim*, Tom Wilcher similarly recalls what he sees as a lack of 'decency and reason' around 1912: a time when 'the Irish threatened civil war; the suffragettes were burning letters and beating policemen; and the air was filled from all sides with ... threat'. As he suggests, the years between 1900 and 1914 were frequently ones of 'bitterness and fury' in their political struggles (375, 363). This was often a consequence, after 1906, of Liberal governments' vigorous commitment to reform, though also, more generally, of the enormous inequities in the distribution of wealth which made their initiatives so urgent. As little as 1 per cent of the population is estimated to have owned nearly 70 per cent of the

---

[58] John Osborne, *Look Back in Anger* (1957; London: Faber and Faber, 1978), 17. Subsequent references are to this edition.

[59] Rose Macaulay, *Potterism: A Tragi-Farcical Tract* (1920; London: Collins, 1950), 16. Subsequent references are to this edition.

nation's wealth at the time.[60] A straightforward 'no' might thus be the most appropriate answer to the question Peter Quennell raises in his *Letter to Mrs Virginia Woolf*, about whether parties and hansom cabs were constantly and copiously available in the years before the Great War. If they were, it was only for an affluent minority who lived, like Isherwood's characters in *The Memorial*, in a 'safe, happy, beautiful world' of 'County gossip . . . Balls, engagements being announced, girls "coming out"'. Part of the disenchantment recorded by C. E. Montague, in his 1922 study of that name, was that the pre-eminent time in the life of the world he recalled was accessible only to the 'fairly well-to-do'. 'Elysian years', he adds, were only 'Elysian for anyone who was not poor' (217–18).

If the Edwardian period was a twentieth-century Eden, in other words, it may have been one of limited, exclusive access – also requiring selective deafness, or later a selective memory, in order to shut out the clamour of struggles troubling the supposedly 'golden calm' prevailing before 1914. Yet the authors most affirmative of the period's appeal do not generally show themselves either deaf, blind or amnesiac about its darker aspects – even apart from their readiness to allow that rain must have fallen, or that primal 'poisons' were covertly distilling themselves during its sunny days. In *Coming up for Air*, George Bowling recognises that

> It isn't that life was softer then than now. Actually it was harsher. People on the whole worked harder, lived less comfortably, and died more painfully. The farm hands worked frightful hours for fourteen shillings a week and ended up as worn-out cripples with a five-shilling old-age pension and an occasional half-crown from the parish. And what was called 'respectable' poverty was even worse. (106)

Acknowledging elements of sentimentality in his recollections of what may have been a 'harsher' period, Bowling nevertheless still insists that

> it's also true that people then had something that we haven't got now. What? It was simply that they didn't think of the future as something to be terrified of . . . a feeling of security, even when they weren't secure. More exactly, it was a feeling of continuity . . . whatever might happen to themselves, things would go on as they'd known them . . . The old English order of life couldn't change. (106–8)

---

[60] See Thompson, *The Edwardians*, 3.

Bowling's views recall Hugh Kenner's characterisation of the nineteenth century as one dominated by a 'pervasive ... idea of continuity'– one which could scarcely outlast the Great War, but had survived strongly, Orwell and others suggest, into the Edwardian years.[61] Even in recalling the period's troubled, conflictual aspects, Rose Macaulay acknowledged in 1920 that 'it was a curious age, so near and yet so far, when the ordered frame of things was still unbroken' (16). C. E. Montague also stressed that he and his contemporaries could recall in 1914 'a century of almost unbroken European peace – unbroken, that is, by wars hugely destructive' (90). Veterans of the Crimean, Boer or Franco-Prussian wars might have dissented, though perhaps not from Richard Aldington's broader conclusion, in *Death of a Hero*, that until the Great War 'a wholesale shattering of values had certainly not occurred since 1789' (199).

Unknown in Europe since 1789, or in Britain perhaps since the Civil War in the 1640s, such wholesale shattering accounts for twentieth-century nostalgias, after the Great War, unusual and intense enough to justify identification of the chronotype mentioned earlier. Fractured fictional forms appearing in the years that followed – so often departing from the conventional sequences of beginning, middle and end Kermode considers fundamental to 'explanatory fictions' – further confirm this identification. As Kermode explains, '"making sense" of the world' through such sequences can be more difficult in certain historical periods (35). The 'explanatory' strategies followed by many novelists between 1930 and the 1950s – trying to make sense of recent history by starting in the middle, as Isherwood recommended, then working backwards and forwards – suggest that this was such a period. These anachronies can even be seen as evidence of an underlying, general change in understanding of the onward passage of time and history themselves – also particular to the period – of the kind Orwell suggests and Chapter 3 discussed. Confidence that the old order of life couldn't change, or that 'next summer would be the same, and the next and the next', could scarcely have been shared universally in the early years of the twentieth century. Yet even those most sceptical of everlasting continuity would have found stronger reasons in June 1914 than in December 1918 for assuming that change would generally take the form of improvement. This was just the reassuring, longstanding faith in 'gradual bettering', which Henry James recognised had been destroyed immediately in August 1914 – a loss of any 'smooth road into the future', which D. H. Lawrence was still lamenting a decade after the war's end.[62]

---

[61] See Chapter 3.
[62] See Chapter 3.

Part of the uniqueness of nostalgia in the years after the Great War can therefore be recognised not only in the scale of regret about 'a wholesale shattering of values', but also, in looking back, about the wholesale loss of affirmative ways of looking forward. A still more comprehensive loss might be defined through Paul Fussell's judgement, in surveying the literature of 1914–18, that 'the Great War was perhaps the last to be conceived as taking place within a seamless, purposeful "history", involving a coherent stream of time running from past through present to future'.[63] Like Lawrence's views of the loss of a 'smooth road into the future', Fussell's assessment helps further explain the appeal of J. W. Dunne at the end of the 1920s and thereafter. Strange and esoteric though Dunne's ideas may have seemed, the vision in *An Experiment with Time* of past and future 'stretched out . . . like an unrolled scroll' offered exact, reassuring compensation for the loss of 'a coherent stream of time' Fussell records as a legacy of the Great War. J. B. Priestley emphasises the continuing strength of this appeal in a survey of Dunne's theories he published early in the Second World War, in 1940, suggesting their potential importance among 'wartime recreations' and in offering 'welcome relief' from the current conflict.[64]

Losses of the kind Orwell, Lawrence and Fussell identify can also be summed up through Walter Benjamin's celebrated image of 'the angel of history'. In his 'Theses on the Philosophy of History', Benjamin describes this angel with

> his face . . . turned toward the past . . . a storm is blowing from Paradise . . . This storm irresistibly propels him into the future to which his back is turned, while the pile of debris before him grows skyward. This storm is what we call progress.[65]

Writing a few months after the outbreak of the Second World War, early in 1940, Benjamin had more reason than ever to view 'what we call progress' in this way, though his image is also summary of the movement of history, more generally, during previous decades of the twentieth century. As Henry James and many other commentators suggest, particular crises or reversals of faith in progress inevitably accompanied the outbreak of war in 1914. The change of view involved, and its timing, can be confirmed through another angelic image, drawn from a legend originating in the first full

---

[63] Fussell, *Great War and Modern Memory*, 21.
[64] Priestley, 'The Time Problem', 55.
[65] Benjamin, *Illuminations*, 257–8.

engagement of the Great War between the British army and the advancing Germans. On 23 August 1914, at the battle of Mons, angels bristled in the sky above the British Expeditionary Force, glaring at the Germans, shooting arrows at them, and forcing them into a temporary retreat, unusual at that early stage of the war. So it was said at the time. The supposed 'miracle' at Mons resulted more plausibly from the hardened competence of the British Regular Army, experienced in directing rifle fire with a rapidity the Germans mistakenly attributed to machine guns. Probably through the intervention of British propagandists, the episode was conveniently conflated with Arthur Machen's short story, 'The Bowmen', published the following month. Legends of the Angel of Mons at any rate suggest August 1914 as the last moment in the twentieth century – however imaginary – when an angel engaged in historic action could be envisaged purposefully facing forward and looking in the right direction.

Thereafter, forward-looking or progressive views of history seemed at least partially outmoded – never as innocent or plausible again, even if they could still be conceived at all. A change of this kind is often recognised by authors who lived and fought through the war, and by later commentators, though they sometimes differ about its exact date. The historian John Keegan saw 'an age of vital optimism in British life' ending with the slaughter of 'an army of innocents' – including the first volunteers of August 1914 – at the Battle of the Somme in July 1916.[66] In *The Golden Virgin*, Henry Williamson considers that 'the watershed of the Somme' marked the end not only of an age, but of 'ideas that had endured a thousand years' (340). Whatever initial date is suggested for the change – August 1914, or July 1916 – by the end of the war, outlooks on history and 'progress' had begun to rotate 180 degrees, leaving affirmative urges to look forward unavoidably warped by the gravity of the past and the need to look back. In terms F. Scott Fitzgerald employs in *The Great Gatsby* (1925), after the Great War anyone still dreaming of a utopian or 'orgiastic future' was likely to be 'borne back ceaselessly into the past' – drawn back towards some period when days ahead still seemed pristine and promising.[67] The radical nature of this change, and in fictional forms reflecting it, confirm an element of uniqueness in nostalgias after the Great War, and in the chronotype earlier described.

---

[66] Keegan, *First World War*, 321.
[67] F. Scott Fitzgerald, *The Great Gatsby* (1925; Harmondsworth: Penguin, 1968), 188.

Mid-Century

Angelic images also help to suggest why nostalgia's hold on literary imagination might have faltered after mid-century. Straightforward reasons for this slackening are once again indicated by Jimmy Porter, when he ascribes the 'phoney' aspect of 'long days in the sun' partly to the dwindling likelihood of anyone being able to recall them from personal experience. 'If you've no world of your own', he suggests, 'it's rather pleasant to regret the passing of someone else's' (17). As he indicates, by the mid-1950s the brief Edwardian world had inevitably begun to seem 'someone else's'. Grassic Gibbon, Hartley, Huxley, Isherwood, Orwell, Lehmann, Waugh and Williamson were all near-coevals of the century itself, able to recall its early, Edwardian years from their childhoods. The period's coincidence with a relatively innocent, uncomplicated part of their personal pasts no doubt contributed to their views of its appeal – also encouraging the analogies developed in their fiction between individual experience and the wider life of the century. Authors such as Angus Wilson, on the other hand, born in 1913 – or still more clearly, John Osborne, born in 1929 – could engage only in forms of second-hand recollection, continuing to endow the Edwardian years with values established by older authors before mid-century. Nostalgia for the period, in other words, might naturally have been at its most influential in the 1930s and 1940s, when it could be directly remembered, with novels by Hartley and Williamson in the 1950s a late extension of feelings concerned. Williamson's use of a largely straightforward chronicle form, emphasised in his sequence's title – rather than the analeptic tactics often used earlier, casting remembered events into the midst of present experience – may further indicate a diminishing urgency in memory's hold over imagination by this time.

Benjamin's angel, and the growing piles of debris he contemplates, suggest further reasons for this diminution. For two or three decades, novelists could look back relatively straightforwardly on sunlit Edwardian landscapes, still more or less visible beyond the detritus of the Great War. By the 1940s, piles of historical debris, growing further skywards, left longer shadows across any recollected Eden, Edwardian or otherwise. After the Second World War, it grew harder still to look back – within living memory, or even in imagination – on anything *other* than debris. The 1920s, the crisis-ridden 1930s, and the war years scarcely offered as promising a location as the Edwardian period for affirmative visions of the past. Yet the appetite for idealised recollection evidently remained. This appetite and the difficulties of its fulfilment are demonstrated in H. E. Bates's popular

1950s novels, often recalling the 1920s or set during the decade. One of the most popular of them, *Love for Lydia* (1952) contrasts revealingly with a recent novel also concerned with the long history of a family and its home – Rumer Godden's *A Fugue in Time* (1945). This shares 'the sense of the past' that Henry James explored in his unfinished novel of that name, describing a hero who seeks 'the very tick of the old stopped clocks' within an ancestral London mansion.[68] An admirer of J. W. Dunne, Godden traverses periods as fluently as James, describes conversations between characters living and dead, and affirms continuities immune even to the destructiveness of the Second World War. These are maintained as much by the durability of the building itself – 'in the house the past is present' – as by connections between the successive generations inhabiting it.[69]

In *Love for Lydia*, Bates shares instead the tactics of several mid-century novels discussed above – *To be a Pilgrim, Random Harvest, Brideshead Revisited, The Go-Between* – in using an ancestral home as an emblem not so much of continuity as of change and decay in the lives of characters and their societies generally. Like Waugh in *Brideshead Revisited*, Bates describes an aristocratic family whose country mansion, first visited in the 1920s, fades steadily in grandeur, its initially 'beautiful and comforting and inviolable' aspects destined eventually to be eradicated during the Second World War.[70] Though engagingly described throughout, even the surrounding countryside seems as precarious as the family's splendid mansion – regular prolepses indicating how idyllic landscapes will eventually be despoiled, like the house itself, by military requirements during the war. Not surprisingly, as inhabitants of such a precarious idyll, Bates's characters often seem uneasy with their time and place. Even the new 1920s diversions of partying and motoring seem merely to add to their attraction towards a more distant past. Part of the charm of the garage that hires them their motor cars is that it remains cluttered by 'horse cabs, station flies, a landau, a number of black horse-hearses, and two old yellow wagonettes' – all somehow surviving from a bygone, Dickensian, horse-drawn age (80). *Love for Lydia* is nostalgic in these ways not only for the period its characters inhabit, but also for some still more alluring, inviolate or imaginary past age, vanished long before the novel begins. The same kind of

---

[68] Henry James, *The Sense of the Past* (London: Collins, 1917), 48. James tried unsuccessfully to complete the novel during the Great War.
[69] Rumer Godden, *A Fugue in Time* (1945; London: Virago Press, 2013), 4.
[70] H. E. Bates, *Love for Lydia* (1952: London: Methuen, 2007), 191. Subsequent references are to this edition.

dislocated or redoubled nostalgia continues to appear in Bates's *The Sleepless Moon* (1956), along with a landscape and plot – concerning the mayor of a country town and his wife – which seem closer to Thomas Hardy's times than the mid-twentieth century. The novel opens with the heroine longingly recalling that 'it was still possible, in the year 1922, to hire carriages . . . carriages with white horses', and ends with her husband's regret – emblematic of his constrained, unemotional disposition – for the town clock's greater accuracy in his father's times.[71]

Evidence of such unstable, frustrated nostalgia helps answer a question that Elizabeth Bowen raises in her essay 'The Bend Back', published in 1951: 'does our century fail us, or we it?' In one way, her essay simply confirms how, and why, nostalgia continued to figure strongly in imagination around mid-century – not only as a literary preference, but also, Bowen suggests, as an aspect of the general outlook of the times. Reluctance to 'acclimatise ourselves to our own time', in her view – augmented by awareness, in a new atomic age, of a future that 'in a split second, could become nothing' – explains why 'contemporary writing retreats from the present-day'. She adds that 'in making the past their subject',

> writers respond instinctively to a general wish – they react to, voice, what is in the air around them. Nostalgia is not a literary concoction, it is a prevailing mood . . . novels set back in time . . . books about old homes . . . are now in universal demand.

Yet Bowen also acknowledges how hard this demand is to satisfy, except possibly through narratives remaining confined within personal life and 'direct memory' of childhood. Recollection on a wider scale, of whole historical ages, she describes as more problematic, requiring 'factitious memory', able to ensure that 'harsh, alien, formidable or shocking . . . elements' can be appropriately 'toned down'. Only the first decade of the twentieth century, she suggests – like most authors discussed in this chapter – can be much exempted from this requirement. Faith that '"better days" were . . . the future' was 'broken by 1914', she concludes – the century lacking, after that date, 'zest for its progress . . . its delights, its ameliorations and its discoveries'.[72]

---

[71] H. E. Bates, *The Sleepless Moon* (1956; London: Companion Book Club, 1957), 9.
[72] Bowen, 'The Bend Back', 221, 222, 224, 226.

Bowen's question might therefore be answered, in terms she suggests herself, by accepting that by the 1950s the century *had* 'failed us', or at any rate ceased to allow the imagination any straightforwardly affirmative engagement with its history. The impossibility of 'retreating and advancing' that Woolf described in 1941 might be seen in this way as a lasting condition of the times. Experiencing 'decline of love for the present', according to Bowen, and lacking 'zest' for the future, writers also lacked access to any part of the past – uncluttered by historical debris, and directly available to living memory – in which consolatory visions could be constructed (221). This lack contributed in the latter half of the century to the kind of 'memory crisis' which commentators such as Anne Whitehead considered profoundly exacerbated by the legacies of the Second World War, and of the Holocaust especially. While confidence in the future continued to be undermined by the proliferation of the atomic weapons first used at the end of the war – as Bowen notes, and Lowry emphasises in *Under the Volcano* – discovery in 1945 of the massacres in the concentration camps thoroughly blackened memories of the recent past. As the century went on, recollection of this past imposed deeper senses of trauma even than those registered by Bowen at mid-century, extending into private as well as public life, as Whitehead notes, and leaving 'concerns about the very possibility of representation and remembrance'.[73] In this atmosphere, the nostalgic chronotype of the 1930s, 1940s and early 1950s inevitably faded or expired. After mid-century, memory seemed more likely to offer pathways towards deeper stresses, historical and often personal, rather than much prospect of escape from them. These and other challenges to late twentieth-century narrative and its temporalities are considered in the next chapter.

---

[73] Whitehead, *Memory*, 89, 84.

Chapter 6

'Time is Over': Postmodern Times

'Have you not done tormenting me with your accursed time! It's abominable!' Pozzo's exclamation – in Samuel Beckett's play *Waiting for Godot* (*En attendant Godot*, 1953) – might be considered simply to extend into the latter half of the twentieth century attitudes to 'accursed time' familiar from literature in its opening decades. Beckett might be supposed a natural inheritor of these attitudes, acquired through his thorough acquaintance with modernist writing at the end of the 1920s. His earliest work includes an essay published in 1929 on James Joyce, whom he knew personally as well as through his fiction; a critical study, *Proust*, which appeared in 1931; and 'Whoroscope', the winner of a prize offered the previous year for the best poem on the subject of time.

Yet Pozzos's outburst, and *Waiting for Godot* generally – while exhibiting some continuities with modernist writing – also reflect new and graver stresses following the Second World War. 'When! When!', Pozzo continues:

> One day, is that not enough for you, one day like any other day ... one day we were born, one day we shall die, the same day, the same second ... They give birth astride of a grave, the light gleams an instant, then it's night once more.[1]

Temporality, for Pozzo, threatens not on account of the exacting clockwork that troubled the modernists. Struggling to find his chronometer, a much-prized heirloom, he protests instead, regretfully, that 'surely one should hear the tick-tick', remarking 'damnation' when only his heartbeat proves audible (46). Temporality, in this view, is troubling

---

[1] Samuel Beckett, *Waiting for Godot* (1956; London: Faber, 1971), 89. Subsequent references are to this edition.

not because of its mechanical measurement, but because it scarcely seems meaningfully measurable at all – existing instead only in isolated fragments; days or seconds 'like any other', lacking distinction, extension or mutual relation. Life continues, in *Waiting for Godot,* and changes do occur – the heart beats on, the tree grows leaves, Pozzo becomes blind, and Lucky dumb – but independently of conventional, coherent continuity. In a setting as empty and featureless temporally as it is topographically – stage directions specifying only 'A country road. A tree. Evening' – words such as 'yesterday' or 'tomorrow' almost lose their meaning (7). Not surprisingly, Vladimir suggests it may not only be Pozzo's watch that has been lost, or ceased to tick, but rather that 'time has stopped' in general (36). 'The hours are long, under these conditions', he adds, 'and constrain us to beguile them with proceedings . . . to prevent our reason from foundering' (80). Much of the play follows his attempts with Estragon to fabricate pastimes and expectations, patterns and prospects – such as the hopes of Godot's arrival – which might free existence from its stasis and make time seem to progress purposefully and reasonably once again. At best, these 'proceedings' persuade the characters that 'it's already tomorrow . . . Time flows again . . . The sun will set, the moon will rise' (77). For the most part, though, they provide only fleeting distractions from being 'alone, waiting for the night' (77).

Time for Nothing

The Great War, according to Ford Madox Ford in *Parade's End* (1924–8), often left servicemen – when not in periods of violent action – enduring 'eternal hours when Time itself stayed still'.[2] Experience of the Second World War seemed to many writers and commentators to have had the same effect. Describing pastimes – 'proceedings' – invented during tedious, seemingly interminable days of war service, Henry Green's hero in *Back* (1946) recalls that 'the idea had been to make the clock's hands go round', suppressing feelings, accentuated in the post-war years, that 'the hands were stuck'. In an essay published in 1941, 'Time, Violence and Macbeth', Stephen Spender describes a similar 'sense of endless waiting and of time standing still in the midst of the most violent happenings', leading ultimately to a 'loss of the sense of the continuity of time'. The loss of 'time and measure and place' he describes could also be compared to feelings

---

[2] Ford Madox Ford, *Parade's End* (1924–8; Harmondsworth: Penguin, 1982), 569.

of 'hourless', 'futureless' or 'shock-stopped' stasis Elizabeth Bowen envisages in wartime in *The Heat of the Day* (1949), and ascribes to mid-century life generally in her essay 'The Bend Back' (1951).³ Early audiences of *Waiting for Godot*, in other words, might have found in Beckett's vision of restless, purposeless, indefinite waiting a loss of 'time and measure' – even a sense of time stopped altogether – already familiar from some of their own experience in recent years. Yet in omitting explicit reference to recent history, or indeed much reflection of ordinary life of any kind, *Waiting for Godot* left its first, puzzled 1950s audiences struggling to find connections with their own experience. Understanding of Beckett's work in relation to its times – and to the period's views of time itself – advanced only gradually, helped by his next play, *Endgame* (*Fin de partie*, 1957), and by some of the critical commentary it provoked.

Stasis in *Endgame* seems almost more complete than in *Waiting for Godot*. 'What time is it? . . . the same as usual', characters remark in *Endgame*, also wondering, like Vladimir and Estragon, what 'yesterday' can mean, and even whether 'time was never and time is over'. Yet in declaring that 'the whole place stinks of corpses . . . the whole universe', characters offer readier means of contextualising, historically, this and other puzzling features of the play.⁴ One of Beckett's most influential early critics, Theodor Adorno, indicates an obvious origin for the play's deathly atmosphere when he remarks that the concentration camps were among 'the catastrophies that inspire *Endgame*'. In his essay 'Trying to Understand *Endgame*' (1961), he emphasises that 'a historical moment is revealed' in the play: one in which

> after the Second World War, everything is destroyed, even resurrected culture, without knowing it; humanity vegetates along, crawling, after events which even the survivors cannot really survive, on a pile of ruins which even renders futile self-reflection of one's own battered state.⁵

For Adorno, it is as if Walter Benjamin's angel of history no longer looked only backward towards piles of debris. Debris now surrounds him on every side, and it is within this 'pile of ruins' that survival must somehow, implausibly, be maintained – within a shattered present, almost excluded from wider vision of history. Experience of time,

---

³ Henry Green, *Back* (1946; London: Hogarth Press, 1951), 8–9; Spender, 'Books and the War II', 126.
⁴ Samuel Beckett, *Endgame* (London: Faber, 1958), 13, 32, 52, 33. Subsequent references are to this edition.
⁵ Adorno, 'Trying to Understand *Endgame*', 126, 122.

Adorno remarks, could once 'still imply hope', but now 'the temporal itself is damaged; saying that it no longer exists would already be too comforting. It is and it is not' (124). As he notes, time does still exist for characters in *Endgame*. Like Vladimir and Estragon, they register change, albeit in very limited forms in the deadened world around them. Yet as in *Waiting for Godot*, time fails to figure in ways that offer progress or meaning: a coherent sense of temporality is among casualties the war's ruins seem to have buried. Time still is, but is not – any longer – reliably significant. Like Macbeth, whose experience in Shakespeare's play is invoked by Stephen Spender as a paradigm of wartime temporality, Beckett's characters experience all their days and yesterdays as 'signifying nothing' – lights gleaming for aimless instants, 'brief candles' flickering momentarily between phases of the dark.

Tomorrows, in *Endgame*, seem as empty and threatening as yesterdays. The stink of corpses, in the play's denatured domain, and its references to a 'nearly finished' existence, hint at future apocalypse as much as the Holocaust in the recent past (12). As Adorno suggests, the discovery of the concentration camps in 1945 was only one of the 'catastrophies that inspire *Endgame*' – also in his view a 'drama of the atomic age' (123) which followed the first use of nuclear weapons at Hiroshima in the same year. Rapid development of this weaponry after 1945, along with the increasing chill of the Cold War, made an encounter with the 'last syllable of recorded time' envisaged in *Macbeth* seem a genuine or even imminent possibility. As Elizabeth Bowen explains in 'The Bend Back', by 1951 it seemed more and more likely that the world 'in a split second, could become nothing', confirming the impossibility of 'retreating or advancing' Chapter 5 discussed.[6] With anticipation of the future as troubling as recollection of the past, mid-century historical vision – much as Adorno describes – could scarcely reach beyond a shattered, arrested present, sharing with Beckett's characters a feeling of aimlessly 'waiting for the night'.

Feelings of this kind received a further, much-publicised emphasis through the inauguration in June 1947 of the most disturbing of all twentieth-century timepieces, the 'Doomsday Clock'. Its image continued to appear monthly on the cover of the *Bulletin of the Atomic Scientists*, and widely in the world's press, representing the views of experts – many of whom had worked on the 'Manhattan Project' developing the first atomic bomb – about humanity's proximity to the midnight of nuclear annihilation. By the early 1950s, the hands of this Doomsday Clock, originally positioned at 11.53pm, had been reset

---

[6] William Shakespeare, *Macbeth*, V, v.

at only two minutes to midnight.[7] Warnings about a world so 'nearly finished' might have made Vladimir's conclusion – 'time has stopped' – seem almost welcome when *Waiting for Godot* was first performed in 1953. Any forward movement in time, during the late 1940s and 1950s, might have appeared only as it did to Faust – as a tormenting ticking towards imminent, perhaps inevitable, destruction.

This sense was directly represented in two novels – Malcolm Lowry's *Under the Volcano* and Thomas Mann's *Doctor Faustus* – published in 1947 and closely comparable in their views, though coming from opposing sides in the recent war. Lowry's protagonist in *Under the Volcano*, Geoffrey Firmin, struggles like Faust with 'spirits' of a kind (albeit mostly alcoholic) and suffers tormenting guilt about a crime he may have committed during the Great War – though one whose details strongly recall the recently discovered concentration camps. Repeated references to artistic and legendary versions of the Faust story – one of Firmin's friends even considers directing a film adaptation – make analogies between the two doomed figures inevitable. In his explanatory letter to his publishers, Lowry nevertheless further stresses the parallels, describing his novel as a kind of Doomsday Clock in itself. 'I have to have my 12', he remarks of his chapter divisions, in order to 'hear a clock slowly striking midnight for Faust'. His letter goes on to explain that Firmin's drunkenness and Faustian fate 'should be seen also in its universal relationship to the ultimate fate of mankind', as this had begun to appear around the time of the Second World War.[8] Any doubts regarding for whom the bell tolls, or the clock strikes, were further dispelled, as Chapter 5 described, by Lowry's addition on the novel's final page, after news of the atom bomb reached him, of a final warning about humanity's new potential to destroy itself.

A similarly representative central figure in *Doctor Faustus* allows Mann to juxtapose events around the time of the Great War with experience of the Second, and to explore impulses towards darkness and self-destruction informing each phase of this history. This figure, Adrian Leverkühn, believes that he has invoked Satanic powers to enhance his musical genius and ensure success as a composer. His personal Faustian pact, Mann's narrator stresses, should also be seen

---

[7] Even after the relaxation of Cold War tensions at the end of the 1980s, the hands have never been further than seventeen minutes from midnight. By the end of the century, they stood at around nine minutes to, and, in response to new concerns about climate change, at less than three minutes to midnight by 2017.

[8] Lowry, letter to Jonathan Cape, 2 January 1946, *Selected Letters*, 65–6.

as representative of 'historical conditions . . . shattering events of the time' affecting the German people generally, both in their experience of the Great War and in their willing complicities with Hitler and Nazism in succeeding years.⁹ These connections with dark historical forces are made especially disquieting, as in *Under the Volcano*, by the cultured character of the protagonist concerned. Each novel suggests that even if civilisation and art are not wilfully complicit with the darker forces of history, they are at any rate impotent to resist the destruction they threaten. Firmin's tragedy, like Faust's and Leverkühn's, is that he embraces darkness and his own destruction while in unusually full knowledge of the light – sustained focalisation within his troubled mind highlighting his awareness of centuries of art, literature and culture.

Doubts about art and its ordering potentials are still more explicit in *Doctor Faustus*, one character reflecting that 'daemonic powers stand beside the order-making qualities in any vital movement' (122). For Leverkühn himself, even these dark powers are unable to maintain a viable role for contemporary art, his own included, in the face of a disastrous history. Instead, he considers that 'all the methods and conventions of art today *are good for parody only*' (131–2). His conclusion directs upon art itself the kind of sceptical, bifocal view of a damaged temporality which Adorno expresses in 'Trying to Understand *Endgame*'. Art's capacities for ordered vision and representation still exist, but voided of much of their conventional promise, offering instead only parodic, self-reflexive scrutiny of their own strategies and limitations.¹⁰ Like the patterns and pastimes invented by Vladimir and Estragon, art's orders seemed more than ever essential in negotiating chaotic, desolate experience following the Second World War. Yet these orders also appeared – more self-evidently than ever – artificial, groundless, inadequate, or even distracting in the imaginary consolation and coherence they might offer.

Views in *Doctor Faustus* of 'historical conditions . . . shattering events' and their consequences are markedly more pessimistic, in this way and others, than those Mann expressed in *The Magic*

---

⁹ Thomas Mann, *Doctor Faustus: The Life of the German Composer Adrian Leverkühn as Told by a Friend*, trans. H. T. Lowe Porter (1949; Harmondsworth: Penguin, 1971), 168. Subsequent references are to this edition.

¹⁰ Mann's italics. Adorno extends views of this kind when discussing the role of poetry after Auschwitz in an essay published the year after 'Trying to Understand *Endgame*' – 'Commitment' (1962).

Mountain (*Der Zauberberg*, 1924) around a quarter of a century earlier. Comparison of the two novels helps identify wider scepticisms developing across the intervening period, particularly decisively during and after the Second World War. These extend well beyond issues of art and temporality considered above. Writing in the wake of the Great War, Mann naturally raises troubled questions about the darker forces of history and how they might be resisted. Yet some residual credibility, alongside extensive irony, still surrounds the figure most committed to alternative, ameliorative powers – Settembrini, who continues to believe, at any rate before the outbreak of the Great War, that

> reason and enlightenment have banished the darkest ... shadows that tenanted the soul of man ... the powers of reason and enlightenment will in the end set humanity wholly free and lead it in the path of progress and civilization toward an even brighter, milder, and purer light.[11]

Powers of the kind Settembrini favours were inevitably subject to more sceptical appraisal after 1939, particularly influentially in Adorno's writing. His connection of Beckett's drama with the 'catastrophies' of recent history extends views expressed in 'The Concept of Enlightenment', written with Max Horkheimer in 1944. Their essay looks back sceptically at a longstanding 'general sense of progressive thought', sustaining faiths in reason, science and technology – in improvement generally – originally promoted by Enlightenment thinkers in the later eighteenth century.[12] Finding late in the war that 'the fully enlightened earth radiates disaster triumphant', Adorno and Horkheimer question how far faith in a 'project of modernity' – in ever-evolving progress and development – had survived, or deserved to survive, into the twentieth century (3). Doubts of this kind had been accumulating for at least thirty years. For Henry James – or for Mann, in *The Magic Mountain* – the outbreak of the Great War in August 1914 questioned how much 'gradual bettering' had achieved, or could be expected to achieve. For Walter Benjamin, in 1940, 'progress' no longer seemed by any means an uncomplicatedly benign movement, but rather a violent, tempestuous force, piling up debris behind history's ostensibly

---

[11] Thomas Mann, *The Magic Mountain*, trans. H. T. Lowe-Porter (1928; London: Vintage, 1999), 98.
[12] Adorno and Horkheimer, *Dialectic of Enlightenment*, 3.

forward movement. Adorno and Horkheimer go further still, questioning not only the results of progress and modernity, but even the principles around which its supposedly ameliorative drive towards the future had been based. In their view, these principles had always been overly reliant on materialist 'computation and utility', at the expense of other values (6). This urge to 'reduce to numbers', Adorno and Horkheimer suggest, 'confounds thought and mathematics' and establishes a narrowly 'mathematized world' (7, 25). Imperious confidence in the rational organisation of society and the domination of nature, moreover, display a potentially totalitarian aspect, embracing the kind of 'daemonic powers' that *Doctor Faustus* warns against. Rather than resisting Hitler's practices, 'The Concept of Enlightenment' notes, supposedly enlightened 'order-making' sometimes seemed to resemble them, or to be readily employed in extending their abuses.

Later commentators often develop criticisms of this kind, further emphasising how questionable Enlightenment faiths in reason and technology appeared after 1945.[13] Though the Great War had already demonstrated the destructive powers of technology and modern industry, these were developed on a hitherto unimaginable scale by the atom bomb. Yet if considered only in itself, purely as a piece of machinery, the bomb was a triumph of scientific progress and inventiveness. The Nazi concentration camps, in this view, likewise extended homicidal destruction on an almost unimaginable, industrial scale, yet could be considered not – or not only – as utter contradictions of Enlightenment initiative. Instead, they could be envisaged as monstrous forms of social engineering, suppressing humane or moral thinking in favour of abstract, efficient, 'computation and utility' – requiring sophisticated logistics dependent, as Martin Amis records in *Time's Arrow* (1991), on a railway station, at Auschwitz, which 'served all Europe, direct'.[14] For Jean-François Lyotard, the implications of Auschwitz contributed to 'a sort of grief in the *Zeitgeist*', leaving it 'no longer possible to call development progress'. This lost faith in progress marked for Lyotard a decisive departure from the 'project of modernity', and the initiation in the later twentieth century of a *post-modern age* – one which could no longer maintain 'grand narratives' such as the longstanding Enlightenment commitment to progress and

---

[13] See, for example, the introduction to Docherty, ed., *Postmodernism*, which discusses Zygmunt Baumann's *Modernity and the Holocaust* (1989).

[14] Martin Amis, *Time's Arrow: or the Nature of the Offence* (1991; Harmondsworth: Penguin, 1992), 146-7.

modernisation.¹⁵ In this postmodern age, deprived of foundational, securing assumptions about progress towards the future, there was good reason to consider 'the temporal itself ... damaged', or even that 'time is over' or 'is not'. Time, obviously, continued to pass in daily life, but not, any longer, in ways readily conceivable as progressive, coherent, or meaningful.

Postmodern Times

This postmodern scepticism or sense of 'damage' figures widely in fiction after mid-century, evident both in challenges to narrative conventions of temporality and representation, and in more general questions about the powers of reason to comprehend and control the world. Questions and challenges of this kind shape the theory and practice of fiction emerging in France in the early 1950s, often under Beckett's influence, and soon designated as the '*nouveau roman*' or 'new novel'– occasionally, as '*anti-roman*'. Priorities of this innovative fiction were summarised by one of its principle practitioners, Alain Robbe-Grillet, whose critical commentary made him almost as influential as a narrative theorist as he was as a novelist. Discussing contemporary literature in essays in the 1950s and early 1960s, Robbe-Grillet notes a 'general change in the relations man sustains with the world in which he lives', suggesting that

> we had thought to control [this world] by assigning it a meaning, and the entire art of the novel, in particular, seemed dedicated to this enterprise. But this was merely an illusory simplification ... we no longer consider the world as our own, our private property, designed according to our needs and readily domesticated.¹⁶

Narrative and art generally should therefore cease functioning, Robbe-Grillet considers, as 'a testimony offered in evidence concerning an external reality' (153–4). The novel, instead, can offer 'no possible order outside of that of the book', reflecting only – much as Adrian Leverkühn suggests – on its own orders and practices (154). These include its departures from what Robbe-Grillet describes as

---

[15] Lyotard, 'A Note on the Meaning of "Post-"' (1985), in Docherty, ed., *Postmodernism*, 48–9. See also Lyotard, *The Postmodern Condition*.
[16] Robbe-Grillet, *For a New Novel*, 32, 23–4.

'external chronology' – the temporality of ordinary lived experience (154). His essay 'Time and Description in Fiction Today' (1963) explains that contemporary films and novels engage in 'the construction of moments, of intervals, and of sequences which no longer have anything to do with those of clocks or calendars' (151). By following 'birth, growth . . . decline and fall', conventional fiction ensured that 'time played a role . . . but in the modern narrative, time seems to be cut off from its temporality. It no longer passes . . . space destroys time . . . moment denies continuity' (154–5).

Forms of 'cut off . . . temporality', independent of external chronology, figure in the early work of other authors of the *nouveau roman* – such as Michel Butor and Natalie Sarraute – though particularly clearly in Robbe-Grillet's own *Jealousy* (*La Jalousie*, 1957). Time 'is and . . . is not', in *Jealousy*, in the terms Adorno suggests. Time passes and change occurs within its individual episodes, yet these often appear both to precede *and* succeed each other. Events such as the squashing of a centipede apparently occur both before and after others, including a potentially momentous journey to a nearby town. The novel's French title offers a key to this peculiar temporal construction – 'jalousie' signifying not only jealousy, but a venetian blind. The landscape of *Jealousy*, temporal and sometimes topographic, is presented as if seen through venetian blinds – light gleams for an instant in separated, semi-autonomous sections, connected only by contiguity rather than through continuity, causality or coherent chronology. Roland Barthes offers a further key to this practice in his essay on Robbe-Grillet, 'Objective Literature' ('Littérature Objective', 1954). This suggests that after employing 'a circular sense of time which somehow cancels itself out' in his first novel, *The Erasers* (*Les Gommes*, 1953), Robbe-Grillet offers in *Jealousy* 'a series of slices . . . an unwonted sort of time, a time *for nothing*'. 'Unwonted' resistance to conventional causality and continuity, Barthes concludes, contributes to 'a mirror time – specular time', focusing attention self-reflexively on the fiction's own representational strategies, rather than 'external reality' or 'external chronology' beyond these textual 'blinds'.[17]

In some of Robbe-Grillet's other essays about the *nouveau roman*, its self-reflexive tactics are emphasised less strongly and exclusively than they are in 'Time and Description' or in Barthes's 'Objective Literature'. In 'The Case for the New Novel' (1961), Robbe-Grillet seeks to justify 'unwonted' temporality by asking why it should be

---

[17] Barthes, 'Littérature Objective', *Œuvres complètes*, II, 300–1. My translation.

necessary 'to reconstruct chronological time when our story is concerned only with human time? Isn't it wiser to think in terms of our own memory, which is never chronological?' This emphasis on 'human' rather than chronological time, and on memory, suggests that the strategies of the *nouveau roman* might be understood partly as extensions of modernist priorities. 'The Case for the New Novel' stresses what Robbe-Grillet describes as an 'evolution' of this kind, mentioning among other influences Marcel Proust, Franz Kafka, James Joyce and William Faulkner, as well as Beckett. 'We certainly don't attempt to blot out this past', he explains of the *nouveaux romanciers*, 'in fact, it is in admiration of our predecessors that we are most united; our ambition is only to move on from there ... to follow in their trail, in our own way, in our own time'.[18] As the *nouveau roman* developed in the later 1950s and 1960s, it often moved on towards more thoroughgoing self-reflexiveness and 'specular time'. Yet as 'The Case for the New Novel' suggests, at least in its early stages – in a watch-salesman's obsessive counting of clock time in Robbe-Grillet's *The Voyeur (Le Voyeur,* 1955), as well as in *Jealousy* – it could be seen still to follow fairly closely 'in the trail' of modernism. In prolonging this trail, its innovations can be understood not only in terms of postmodern scepticism of the project of modernity. They can also be considered, like Beckett's work, as contributions to a post*modernist* writing, extending and modifying – for a troubled age following the Second World War – modernist literary practices established earlier in the twentieth century.

Writing of this kind also developed across the Channel after mid-century, often under the influence of the *nouveau roman,* or of Beckett's work. The translator of Robbe-Grillet's *Dans le labyrinthe* (1959), Christine Brooke-Rose, modelled *Out* (1964) partly around *Jealousy,* its conclusion – that 'time is nothing, nothing' – also echoing Barthes's views. Her later fiction continues to challenge conventional narrative forms radically: in the chaotic vision of 'spinning meridians, latitudes and spirals' in *Such* (1966), and in the inventive typography and other evasions of 'the linearity of the text' in *Thru* (1972).[19] Similar challenges figure in the work of another admirer of French literature, and of the *nouveau roman* in particular, Rayner Heppenstall. In *The Connecting Door* (1962), he describes characters who seem simultaneously to inhabit alternate, irreconcilable planes of

---

[18] Robbe-Grillet, 'The Case for the New Novel', 261.
[19] Christine Brooke-Rose, *The Christine Brooke-Rose Omnibus: Four Novels: Out, Such, Between, Thru* (Manchester: Carcanet, 1986), 198, 302, 620.

time and reality, and in *Two Moons* (1977) sustains stories set in two different months, one recorded on the left-hand pages of the novel, the other on the right-hand ones. In any conventional, page-by-page reading, *Two Moons* might seem to offer as decisive a challenge to the conventional linearity of the text as could be imagined.

Heppenstall is nevertheless matched by B. S. Johnson, who invites readers to look into the future of his narrative in *Albert Angelo* (1964) by means of holes cut through several pages of his text. He offers further challenges in one of the most celebrated fictional experiments of the 1960, his novel-in-a-box, *The Unfortunates* (1969). Fractured more decisively even than Robbe-Grillet's 'slices', *The Unfortunates* is made up of individual loose-leaf sections, intended to be shuffled and read in whatever order the reader chooses. Radical though this unravelling of conventional order seems, at least one critic judged *The Unfortunates* – much as Robbe-Grillet considered the *nouveau roman* – as in part an extension of modernist innovations. In *Chronoschisms: Time, Narrative, and Postmodernism* (1997), Ursula Heise describes Johnson using 'the loose-leaf novel to represent physically the arbitrariness of associations as they occur in the human mind'. By concentrating on associations and recollections during a single afternoon, Heise suggests, *The Unfortunates* undertakes 'an exploration of human memory not in principle unlike Proust's'.[20] Like the *nouveau roman,* in this view, Johnson's work – which he acknowledged was indebted to Beckett and Joyce – can be seen sharing in postmodernist development of earlier innovative literary idioms, as well as in post-war, postmodern scepticism of reason and 'order-making' more generally.

John Fowles's narrator in *The Magus* (1966) offers another version of this scepticism when reflecting on the demise of 'adherence to reason' in recent decades and suggesting that

> in mid-century ... words had lost their power, either for good or for evil; still hung, like a mist, over the reality of action, distorting, misleading, castrating; but at least since Hitler and Hiroshima they were seen to be a mist, a flimsy superstructure.[21]

Like Robbe-Grillet, Fowles emphasises the elusiveness of 'order outside of that of the book' at a time after the war when language itself sometimes seemed no more than another 'blind', a mist potentially

---

[20] Heise, *Chronoschisms*, 52–3.
[21] John Fowles, *The Magus* (1966/1977; London: Triad/Panther, 1983), 189–90.

obscuring 'the reality of action'. In his next novel, *The French Lieutenant's Woman* (1969), Fowles offers further evidence of fiction's consequent turn towards reflection on its own orders and tactics. Fowles shared with several of the British authors mentioned above an admiration for French literature – a source of inspiration figured in the novel's iconic opening description of a character looking longingly across the Channel. It is also emphasised explicitly in Fowles's acknowledgement – or his narrator's – that he is writing 'in the age of Alain Robbe-Grillet and Roland Barthes', and under the influence of these 'theoreticians of the *nouveau roman*'. This influence appears throughout *The French Lieutenant's Woman* in often-ironic commentary on the novel's own practices, extending into a final, playful flourish in Fowles's provision of two alternative endings for his novel. These are managed by a further narrator-figure: an appropriately 'Frenchified' one, who 'takes out his watch – a Breguet – and selects a small key' in order to make 'a small adjustment to the time'.[22] His gesture sets the story back by fifteen minutes, allowing events just described to evolve towards a different conclusion. Fowles deploys in this way a 'specular time' of the kind Roland Barthes describes in theorising the *nouveau roman*: a chronotype for the postmodern age, focusing attention on narrative's manipulation of temporal order, and not on 'reality of action' or any singular, plausible, 'external chronology' it might represent. Rather than undertaking uncomplicatedly the 'organization that humanizes time by giving it form', in Frank Kermode's terms, fiction of this kind redirects attention – sceptically and self-consciously – on the nature of that organisation itself, and on the means through which it might be conducted.[23]

Fowles's doubled endings exemplify another reconfiguration of temporality appearing in fiction around mid-century. A time which 'no longer passes', in Robbe-Grillet's view, along with a history apparently no longer flowing purposively forward, inclined narrative – as if dammed in its usual onward course – to divide itself out laterally into multiple channels, diverse versions of the same period in characters' lives. Examples appear in three novels, or novel-sequences, set around wartime, each illustrative of the 'repeating narrative' forms – covering and re-covering much the same set of events – which Gérard Genette discusses in *Narrative Discourse*.[24] Joyce Cary's 'Triptych' – *Herself*

---

[22] John Fowles, *The French Lieutenant's Woman* (1969; London: Triad/Panther, 1977), 85, 348, 394, 395.
[23] Kermode, *Sense of an Ending*, 45. See Chapter 1.
[24] Genette, *Narrative Discourse*, 116.

Surprised (1941), *To be a Pilgrim* (1942) and *The Horse's Mouth* (1944) – follows in each of its volumes the idiosyncratic outlook of one of Cary's three central figures. Contrasts between their divergent visions ensure the trilogy provides the 'three-dimensional depth and force' Cary explained he was seeking – extended not only through characters' conflicts with each other, but in their conflicting responses to 'the character of their times' in the years around the war.[25]

Graham Greene's narrator, Bendrix, experiences equally disturbing relations with his times in *The End of the Affair* (1951). Recalling a relationship begun in 'one of those bright condemned pre-war summers' and apparently ended, painfully and puzzlingly, during the Blitz, Bendrix naturally reflects that 'if I could have turned back time I think I would have done so'. His narrative enacts this wish. Greene recorded that *The End of the Affair* was 'ingeniously constructed to avoid . . . the time sequence', drawing on modernist tactics employed by Ford Madox Ford in *The Good Soldier* (1914).[26] Each chapter in the opening section begins with an account of dreary days immediately after the war, then resumes part of the ended affair through its association, in Bendrix's memory, with this drab present experience. 'Turned back time' also shapes the novel's third section, which shows Bendrix encountering a radically different account of the affair, recorded in his former lover's diary. The novel's poignancy develops in this way not only from recollections of bright summer days before 1945, and of their irreparable loss – along with a sense of coherent 'time sequence' generally – during the war. It also derives from the painful disparities Greene's repeating narratives demonstrate in interpretations of the same set of events – even by individuals supposedly experiencing them mutually and intimately.

Comparable effects figure in *The Alexandria Quartet* (1957–60). Like 'Triptych' and *The End of the Affair*, Lawrence Durrell's tetralogy develops what one of its characters calls a story 'told . . . in layers . . . [a] palimpsest where different sorts of truth are thrown down one upon the other'.[27] This demands constant reappraisal of events and their significance, both by readers and by the characters themselves – ones often divided, like Greene's and Cary's, by very

---

[25] Joyce Cary, 'Prefatory Essay' to *Herself Surprised* (1941; London: Michael Joseph, 1958), 7.

[26] Greene, *The End of the Affair* (1951; Harmondsworth: Penguin, 1976), 25, 66; Greene, *Ways of Escape*, 136.

[27] Lawrence Durrell, *The Alexandria Quartet* (1957–60; London: Faber, 1983), 338. Subsequent references are to this edition.

different personal perspectives on their romantic liaisons. Durrell explains in his Preface that in employing these tactics he sought to go beyond merely 'three-dimensional depth and force', and that in 'trying to work out [his] form' he had 'adopted, as a rough analogy, the relativity proposition'. This involved attempting to shape the first three parts of his tetralogy around dimensions of space, then moving on to a fourth, of time, in its concluding volume. The first three novels therefore function as

> 'siblings' of each other and not 'sequels': only the last novel was intended to be a true sequel and to unleash the time dimension. The whole was intended as a challenge to the serial form of the conventional novel: the time-saturated novel of the day.

As this Preface suggests, it is only Durrell's final volume, *Clea* (1960), that moves decisively forward towards new events and resolutions. Each of the first three – *Justine* (1957), *Balthazar* (1958), and *Mountolive* (1958) – resumes an earlier phase of the story largely through the distinctive perspective of the character named in its title, though with further contributions from several subsidiary narrators and commentators. One of these, a novelist himself, aptly sums up the resulting impression – of 'a book which is not travelling from a to b but standing above time and turning slowly on its own axis ... things do not all lead forward to other things: some lead backwards' (198). Along with the novel's unusual construction, self-reflexive commentary of this kind ensures that *The Alexandria Quartet* emphasises 'its own axis' throughout, drawing attention away from external chronology in favour of the 'specular time' established by its own narrative strategies and perspectives.

The scale of these self-reflexive interests confirms that, as Durrell acknowledged, *The Alexandria Quartet* is in general 'only half secretly about art'. He was also disposed to agree, in an interview in 1963, that this was 'the great subject of modern artists'.[28] This may have been an exaggerated assessment, at any rate regarding contemporary writing. Literature and art in the early 1960s, as at most other stages of the century, continued in Britain and elsewhere mostly to favour tradition. Much fictional narrative remained in conventional, 'time-saturated' serial form, largely unaffected by the innovative modes appearing in work discussed above. The range of that work,

---

[28] Cowley, *Writers at Work*, 231.

and the number of authors involved, nevertheless suggest that postmodern idioms did figure distinctively, in Britain and elsewhere in Europe, in the decades following the Second World War – probably more clearly than in later ones, when postmodernist fiction developed more strongly in the USA.

The timing of these developments, on opposite sides of the Atlantic, may have contributed to some limiting or overly negative judgements of postmodernism, especially among critics in the United States. The most influential and wide-ranging of these judgements appears in Fredric Jameson's *Postmodernism, or, the Cultural Logic of Late Capitalism* (1991). For Jameson, literature or art dominated by postmodern parody and textual self-scrutiny could 'no longer gaze directly on some putative real world', consequently neglecting the political, economic and other forces which continued to shape its affairs.[29] Robbe-Grillet's 'blinds', in this view, had been altogether too fully drawn down, leaving readers looking primarily at textual devices rather than the putative realities they had once been used to represent. Jameson records consequences especially regrettable where historical understanding is concerned, suggesting that the novel 'can no longer set out to represent the historical past; it can only "represent" our ideas and stereotypes about that past' (25). This 'disappearance of the historical referent', for Jameson, extends the general short-sightedness, or amnesia, of 'an age that has forgotten how to think historically' (25, ix).

'Forgetting' of this kind had concerned critics earlier in the twentieth century. As Chapter 4 described, in the 1950s Georg Lukács criticised – as a 'denial of history' – some of the ways modernism responded to the mechanical, reifying forces he had identified himself, three decades earlier, troubling the industrialised life of the 1920s. In *The Political Unconscious* (1981), Jameson is readier to appreciate these responses, criticising Lukács for underestimating modernist strategies which offer – by emphasising freedoms of inner consciousness and memory – 'a whole Utopian compensation for increasing dehumanization on the level of daily life' and 'for everything reification brings with it'.[30] Alert in this way to modernism's response to early twentieth-century conditions, Jameson might have been expected to offer similarly acute analyses of postmodernism's reaction to forces shaping life and imagination in later decades.

---

[29] Jameson, *Postmodernism*, 25.
[30] Jameson, *The Political Unconscious*, 42, 236.

To an extent, this is what *Postmodernism, or, the Cultural Logic of Late Capitalism* duly provides. As his title promises, Jameson explains that the innovations of postmodernist literature and culture are determined by the demands of a late twentieth-century globalised economy. 'Aesthetic production today', in this view,

> has become integrated into commodity production generally: the frantic economic urgency of producing fresh waves of ever more novel-seeming goods (from clothing to airplanes), at ever greater rates of turnover, now assigns an increasingly essential structural function and position to aesthetic innovation and experimentation (4–5).

Postmodernist literary imagination should therefore be seen, Jameson argues, as essentially modish and commercially driven, and its self-referentiality as an evasion – anodyne but all the more conveniently marketable – of any troubling engagement with history, contemporary society, or 'some putative real world'.

In the context in which they were delivered, in the early 1990s, there was some justice in such judgements, though the next section will suggest that even in that decade, and in the 1980s, there were forms of self-reflexive postmodern writing which addressed history unusually responsibly and effectively. The limitation in Jameson's analysis is that it considers 'social and historical impotence', genuinely evident in some late twentieth-century writing, to have been permanently present throughout postmodernism's evolution – endemic in developments ranging from the 'autoreferential... "new novel"' to 'the end of "master narratives"' (369, 367). This does scant justice to the originary phase of postmodernist literature considered in this section and the previous one. This phase of writing can be better understood as demonstrative of historical shock, rather than historical impotence, though some of the symptoms of the two ailments – including self-conscious questioning of art's potentials – might appear the same.

Georg Lukács offers a better way of appraising this early phase of postmodernism when he remarks – though in looking back to the modernists – that 'there can be no literature without at least the appearance of change or development'.[31] For writers in the years following the Second World War, any such appearance was hard to discover in the life of the times, and problematic in its lineaments

---

[31] Lukács, 'The Ideology of Modernism', 155.

even if it could be discerned. In this 'time for nothing' – one in which it seemed time 'no longer passes', and that the coherent flow of history had been arrested – terms such as 'change', 'progress' and 'development' offered only uncertain significances, awkward mutual relations, even negative implications. Innovative forms in the work of Beckett, the French new novelists, and writers who followed them were shaped not by modishness, but by attempts to find strategies sufficient to deal with challenges of this kind, ensuring that literature could somehow still exist; still shed some light on history's debris. Looking back in this way at writing in the post-war years helps to identify in postmodernist literature the kind of social and historical responsibility Jameson and other commentators have often considered it to lack. Recognising the period as a 'time for nothing' – one in which 'time is . . . and is not' – contributes substantially to this more affirmative understanding.

Black Holes and History's Gravity

Fiction in the latter half of the twentieth century also offers straightforward answers to questions about historical responsibility. Some of these are suggested by three long novel-sequences begun, or expanded, around mid-century. C. P. Snow's *The Light and the Dark* (1947) extends an earlier novel towards an eleven-volume sequence, *Strangers and Brothers,* completed in 1970. The fifteen volumes of Henry Williamson's *A Chronicle of Ancient Sunlight* began to appear in 1951, continuing over the next two decades. The first of twelve volumes in Anthony Powell's *A Dance to the Music of Time* series, completed in 1975, appeared in the same year. Each of these sequences attempts to look back beyond 'a veil, a thick curtain' which one of Powell's characters records 'had fallen between "now" and "before the war"'.[32] As well as the Second World War, Powell and Williamson extensively recall the Great War – early volumes of *A Chronicle of Ancient Sunlight* returning still further, to the years around the turn of the century. Patterns of recurrence or analogy between widely separated periods provide for each sequence what Powell – an admirer of Marcel Proust – describes as 'deep fissure[s] through variegated seams of Time'.[33] These interconnections and

---

[32] Anthony Powell, *The Soldier's Art* (1966; London: Heinemann, 1975), 123.
[33] Anthony Powell, *Books Do Furnish a Room* (1971; London: Heinemann, 1972), 5.

patterns in characters' lives help resolve a problem each sequence confronts, and confirms in the scale and complexity of its narrative: the difficulties of maintaining some sense of the individual's significance within a history whose violence repeatedly threatened to eradicate it. In their scale and extent, the sequences also restore some of the consoling sense of past and future 'stretched out . . . like an unrolled scroll', in J. W. Dunne's terms, which the century's wars had done so much to interrupt or destroy.

By the time the sequences were completed, experience of the Second World War was being reconsidered in other forms of historical fiction, gradually moving beyond the 'shock-stopped' phase described in previous sections. Events in the early 1960s – the trial of the Nazi war criminal Adolf Eichmann in 1961, and the Cuban Missile Crisis the following year – in one way simply extended shadows cast over the post-war years by the Holocaust and Hiroshima. Yet in other ways each functioned as a form of recovered memory, indicating that events which had seemed unspeakable or unthinkable in the immediately post-war years must, eventually, be confronted and discussed. Experiences described in Muriel Spark's *The Mandelbaum Gate* (1965) give evidence of this recognition, and of a corresponding readiness to move beyond a first phase of literary responses to the war. *The Mandelbaum Gate* refers to *Waiting for Godot* to characterise its heroine's experience of Eichmann's trial, which she attends while visiting Jerusalem. She finds the defendant himself comparable to 'a character from the pages of a long *anti-roman*', and that the deadening, vacuous language of the proceedings reminds her of 'the novels and plays of the new French writers . . . repetition, boredom, despair, going nowhere for nothing . . . a tight, unbreakable statement of the times at hand'.[34] Her responses confirm the aptness of Beckett and the *nouveau roman* in representing 'the times at hand' at levels of form and language, even while making almost no direct reference to the war and its disasters. Direct description of the Eichmann trial and the crimes of Nazism in *The Mandelbaum Gate* also suggests possibilities of moving on, by the mid-1960s, towards considering the war, the concentration camps, and their consequences explicitly – as potential subjects, however challenging, for literary treatment.

Throughout the rest of the century, much imagination was directed towards finding viable means of developing this treatment – strategies for encompassing potentially unspeakable historical events within the

---

[34] Muriel Spark, *The Mandelbaum Gate* (1965; Harmondsworth: Penguin, 1967), 180, 179, 177.

form of the novel. Among British writers, Olivia Manning, in the *Balkan Trilogy* (1960–5), Richard Hughes, in *The Fox in the Attic* (1961), and Gabriel Fielding, in *The Birthday King* (1962), began from the early 1960s to examine Nazism through German perspectives, or others located in continental Europe. Describing consequences of the war continuing to reverberate within individual lives, long afterwards, Elizabeth Jane Howard's *After Julius* (1965) illustrates a strategy more often followed by later novelists. Graham Swift's *Waterland* (1983) offers a paradigm of forms of writing widely employed in this way during the last two or three decades of the century. Accounts in *Waterland* of a history teacher's life in Greenwich in the present day occupy much less of the novel than the classroom monologues in which he analyses – garrulously, on the eve of his retirement – a range of defining past experiences, private and public. Concentrating on his 'vision of the world in ruins' in 1946 – and on emotional entanglements leading back to a life-changing personal crisis in 1943 – these reminiscences also encompass the consequences of the Great War, and of family misfortunes still further in the past.[35]

Late twentieth-century novels by Penelope Lively, Ian McEwan, Zadie Smith, Lawrence Norfolk and Martin Amis employ comparable strategies. Like Swift's, Lively's central figure in *Moon Tiger* (1987) is a historian, similarly working back, through diaries and recollections, towards defining events – principally the death of her lover in the desert war in 1942 – which 'align [her] own life with the history of the world'.[36] The narrator in Ian McEwan's *Black Dogs* (1992) is a recent visitor to the sites of concentration camps, reconsidering at length the events immediately after the war – when the camps were 'still a news story' – which provided the 'defining moment' in the lives of his parents-in-law. Opening with a description of these lives as they have evolved by the late 1980s, the novel concentrates in later chapters on the couple's troubled honeymoon in France in 1946. This was marked, in various ways for each of them, by the war's legacy of 'more sadness than anyone could ever begin to comprehend', and by the thoroughgoing evil symbolised by the dogs of the title, recently used by the Nazis to terrorise the locals.[37] The opening section of Zadie Smith's *White Teeth* (2000), headed '1974, 1945', resumes a similarly defining incident at the end of the war: an

---

[35] Graham Swift, *Waterland* (1983; London: Picador, 1984), 207. Subsequent references are to this edition.
[36] Penelope Lively, *Moon Tiger* (1987; Harmondsworth: Penguin, 1988), 2.
[37] Ian McEwan, *Black Dogs* (1992; London: Vintage, 1998) 37, 50, 165. Subsequent references are to this edition.

encounter with a Nazi doctor which has consequences still shaping events described at the novel's conclusion, in the 1990s. Lawrence Norfolk's *In the Shape of a Boar* (2000) presents even more complexly interrelated recollections. Its second section moves repeatedly between the 1970s production of a film adaptation of a celebrated poem, and the events which its author, Sol Memel, described in his original work – flight from the Nazis, and encounters with Greek partisans who fought against them in the mountains of Aetolia.

Martin Amis offers a revealing version of recursive strategies shaping all these novels. In *Time's Arrow*, he adopts the tactics that Kurt Vonnegut suggests in *Slaughterhouse-Five* (1969) when his hero watches – or imagines – a film of wartime military action shown in reverse. Naturally, shown in inverse order, even the film's most disturbing incidents appear affirmative or restorative rather than violent and destructive. *Time's Arrow* likewise envisages a Nazi war criminal living time backwards, starting from death and old age, then returning to wartime work in Auschwitz, and eventually beyond, to his birth in Adolf Eichmann's home town. In one of the novels of his *Strangers and Brothers* sequence, C. P. Snow describes the concentration camps as 'a primal, an original, an Adamic fact'.[38] Along with Amis's example, and the others mentioned, his remark indicates the historical gravity of the war's influence, continuing late in the century to draw narrative imagination back towards events initiating loss and destruction still darkening the present. As Snow's reference to Adam suggests, recursive structures involved might in some ways be compared with forms of Edenic retrospection discussed in Chapter 5. Yet no golden age – of the kind earlier writers had envisaged in the Edwardian years – remained readily available to memory or imagination by the century's end. Arcadian or even just affirmative views of its history could be established only through flagrant reversal of the directions it had actually followed – through the kind of 'specular time' employed in *Time's Arrow* or *Slaughterhouse-Five*, entirely and self-evidently artificial. 'Adamic facts', in the novels mentioned, refer not to paradise but only historical loss, shown continuing to shape individual lives long after 'primal . . . original' disasters occurred.

Another comparison with authors discussed in the previous chapter highlights a common problem – though ultimately an opportunity – for those considered in this section. By the middle years of the twentieth century, as Chapter 5 remarked, authors could recall the Edwardian

---

[38] C. P. Snow, *The Sleep of Reason* (London: Macmillan, 1968), 276.

age only at second hand, through borrowed memories. Most of the writers mentioned above were likewise too young for the Second World War to have figured directly in their own adult experience. They were therefore obliged to rely on an older generation's recollections – a difficulty often explored in their fiction. In *Black Dogs*, McEwan's narrator acknowledges that he has had to work out his own version of events on the basis of widely differing accounts of them. These have been shaped by the radically contrastive temperaments of his parents-in-law, who are described, respectively, as 'rationalist and mystic . . . scientist and intuitionist' (19). Problems of this kind figure still more acutely in Graham Swift's *Shuttlecock* (1981). 'Born in August 1945 . . . a product of those times', the novel's narrator is prevented from recovering a reliable version of wartime events by uncertainties surrounding his father's memoirs – also entitled 'Shuttlecock', and included as part of Swift's text. Suspicions that his father might have glamorised this account of his military career prove impossible either to verify or refute, as the war has become literally, for him, an unspeakable experience, following a breakdown which has left him in 'a kind of language-coma', unable or indisposed to talk.[39]

No such difficulties restrain Swift's history teacher in *Waterland*, loquacious and articulate throughout. Yet his narrative repeatedly raises others. Like Lively's historian-heroine in *Moon Tiger* – perplexed by conflicting perspectives in the records she considers – he is forced continually to question the validity of the discipline he teaches, the motives of authors who serve it, and the capacities of their writing to document authentically the events they describe. History, in his view, is never wholly objective, nor free of 'old swamps of myth', nor independent of needs – shared by its authors and audiences – for coherence and a consoling sense of order (74). Instead, like all 'made-up stories, true stories; soothing stories, warning stories . . . believable stories and unbelievable stories', history may offer only another of the 'meanings, myths, manias . . . imbibe[d] in order to convince ourselves that reality is not an empty vessel' (1, 35).

'Swamps of myth' trouble Sol Memel equally profoundly – almost literally, as his celebrated poem uses ancient myths and legends, included in one version at the opening of Norfolk's *In the Shape of a Boar*, as analogies for the activities of the Aetolian partisans he describes. Despite having witnessed these activities personally, and

---

[39] Graham Swift, *Shuttlecock: A Psychological Thriller* (1981; Harmondsworth: Penguin, 1982), 151, 40.

recorded them – contrary to his critics – as faithfully as he could, Memel acknowledges 'the core of irreducible doubt which resided within even the most careful recollection'. He is eventually obliged to accept the views of his childhood friends, and the 1970s film-maker: that narrative and history idealise, reshape and may ultimately obscure experience in the very act of communicating it, much as Swift's teacher suggests. Recognising that he never knew, truly and fully, the nature and intent of some of the actions he described, Memel admits that

> our memories never tell us the stories we need. Our heroes never live the lives we require. Such lives leave no trace for those who follow. Their true acts take place in darkness and silence, and their untellable stories rest with them.

Appropriately, the novel concludes by making 'true acts' literally invisible, ending stories of the mythical boar-hunt – and of the partisans' pursuit of a Nazi officer – in the utter darkness of a cave, profound enough to leave 'no trail to follow now and nothing more to know'.[40]

Cognitive problems that Norfolk and Swift examine are relevant to all narrative and history, and were regularly highlighted in late twentieth-century historiography.[41] Yet as several of the novels mentioned suggest, the enormity of events in the Second World War imposed problems particularly forcefully on later imagination. As McEwan's narrator in *Black Dogs* records of his visit to a preserved concentration camp, 'the extravagant numerical scale, the easy-to-say numbers – tens and hundreds of thousands, millions – denied the imagination its proper sympathies, its rightful grasp of the suffering' (110). William Golding emphasises problems of the same kind, remarking that the experience of

> Belsen, Hiroshima and Dachau cannot be imagined... Those experiences are like black holes in space. Nothing can get out to let us know what it was like inside. It was like what it was like and on the other hand it was like nothing whatsoever. We stand before a gap in history... a limit to literature.[42]

---

[40] Lawrence Norfolk, *In the Shape of a Boar* (2000; London: Phoenix, 2001), 136, 345, 350.
[41] See, for example, White, *Metahistory*.
[42] William Golding, *A Moving Target* (London: Faber, 1982), 102.

Golding's image of the black hole emphasises the implacable gravity that drew late twentieth-century imagination back towards the Second World War, but also recalls the annihilating darkness and invisibility of the cave *In the Shape of a Boar* describes. As his description of this 'limit to literature' suggests, recent historical events most urgently demanding literary treatment were also those most vigorously resisting its vision and capacities to express – even, in John Fowles's view, annulling the power of words, deadened into 'a kind of language-coma'.

Novels discussed above partly circumvent these problems by choosing to address and explore them directly, through forms of self-reflexive commentary. Highlighting difficulties in speaking of the experiences concerned potentially offered the best opportunity of communicating the unspeakable nature of these experiences themselves. Self-referential, specular elements in the novels discussed – commentaries on the limits of imagination, narrative and written history – offer in this way further evidence for the defence of postmodern idioms outlined in the previous section. Threatened by a 'gap' in literature or history, and by language's potential for 'distorting, misleading, castrating . . . since Hitler and Hiroshima', narrative could be construed as seeking greater historical responsibility through scrutinising its own means of expression, rather than merely exhibiting 'historical impotence'. In a century in which totalitarian governments – and others – had all too regularly proclaimed their constructions of events as the absolute truth, novels' self-conscious scrutiny of their own strategies had the further advantage of alerting readers to potentials for prejudice and manipulation inherent in any narrative, even in language itself. In emphasising potentials of this kind in *A Poetics of Postmodernism: History, Theory, Fiction* (1988), Linda Hutcheon generally provides a more affirmative analysis of late twentieth-century writing than Fredric Jameson offers in *Postmodernism, or, the Cultural Logic of Late Capitalism*. For Hutcheon, 'autoreferential' texts are motivated neither by modishness, nor reluctance regarding 'thinking historically', nor despair about their own capacities to represent 'the reality of action'. She coins instead the term 'historiographic metafiction' to describe novels – such as Graham Swift's – 'whose self-reflexivity works in conjunction with [its] seeming opposite (historical reference) in order to reveal both the limits and the powers of historical knowledge'.[43]

---

[43] Hutcheon, *Poetics of Postmodernism*, 5, 223.

In identifying this synthesis between attention to textual devices and to historical events, Hutcheon offers more than a defence of postmodernism. Her views also highlight relations between the two phases of post-war writing which met at Spark's *Mandelbaum Gate*. Shocked scepticism of all rational constructs, textuality and temporality included, was followed later by a determination to approach shocking events themselves, though in full recognition of the difficulties of expression they present. Fiction, in this analysis, had managed by the end of the century to incorporate some of the self-conscious formal and linguistic innovations of the 1940s, 1950s and 1960s within a more direct confrontation with the historical pressures that had occasioned them. A further paradigm of this development appeared in the year following the publication of *White Teeth* and *In the Shape of a Boar* – in Ian McEwan's *Atonement* (2001). Within a single novel, McEwan provides an apparently truthful narrative of the British army's retreat to Dunkirk, alongside warnings about the ineradicable mendacity of all narrative imagination, and a conclusion nevertheless hinting that *only* literary imagination can offer consolation – atonement – for the disastrous history of the century just completed.

Time Unwound

Throughout the latter half of the twentieth century, as the previous sections have shown, the novel remained thoroughly responsive to history – to the nature and pace of its movement, or, sometimes, apparent stasis. Yet readers of the period's fiction were less likely to 'hear the tick-tick' of the clock in the menacing ways it had often resounded in literature in earlier decades. Clock-centred stresses so evident in modernist novels, already fading in the 1930s and 1940s, seem to vanish still further from fiction later in the century. Comparable antipathies do still appear, but usually in the form only of occasional or incidental commentary. 'Calendars and clocks are our inadequate inventions', John Berger remarks in *G.* (1972), explaining that 'time is measured not by numerals on a clock face but by the incidence of our apprehended possibilities'.[44] Angela Carter's heroine in *Nights at the Circus* (1984), Fevvers, likewise disdains

---

[44] John Berger, *G.* (1972; London: Chatto and Windus, 1985), 148, 50. Subsequent references are to this edition.

time measured by 'clumsy cogs and springs', preferring the symmetry of a stopped clock whose 'hands stood always at either midnight or noon, the minute hand and the hour hand folded perpetually together as if in prayer'. This preference for stasis – for 'the shadowless hour, the hour of vision and revelation, the still hour in the centre of the storm of time' – even seems to extend its sway over the wider world around her.[45] A listener gripped by Fevvers's epic account of her life is convinced he hears Big Ben striking midnight, in the distance, not once but twice in succession.

Lawrence Durrell's characters in *The Alexandria Quartet* seem similarly ready to discard, or discount, 'the key to a watch which is Time' (701). Yet references to this key – like the 'small key' employed by Fowles's narrator-figure at the end of *The French Lieutenant's Woman* – focus attention primarily on the novel's own practices, rather than on any general criticism of the clock or its constraints. Durrell's narrator acknowledges that his attitudes to temporality are driven mostly by artistic priorities – by a wish to ensure that 'the writer I was becoming was learning ... to inhabit those deserted spaces which time misses – beginning to live between the ticks of the clock' (659). In *G.*, Berger likewise explains that 'intimations about ... aspects of time' the novel records are concerned with 'the way my imagination forces me to write this story' (148) – one whose fragmentary, obliquely related paragraphs require readers to reconstruct a view of European history largely for themselves. In the first chapters of *Nights at the Circus*, Fevvers's apparently miraculous influence over Big Ben helps introduce her semi-magical powers – and the novel's own ready movements between realism and fantasy – rather than any sustained disdain for clockwork chronology. In each case, references to the clock exemplify the self-reflexive, postmodern 'specular time' discussed in the previous sections, rather than the direct hostility to measured chronology distinguishing modernist writing earlier in the century.

Disappearance or diminution of this hostility might be attributed to the same cause identified in Chapter 5 – to a wider history overwhelming enough to suppress novelists' specific concerns with the clock. Additional influences are suggested in Fredric Jameson's essay 'The End of Temporality' (2003). This explores further what Jameson describes in *Postmodernism, or, the Cultural Logic of Late Capitalism* as 'the waning of the great high modernist thematics of time and temporality, the elegiac mysteries of *durée* and memory' (16). Novelists and poets later

---

[45] Angela Carter, *Nights at the Circus* (1984; London: Vintage, 1994), 31, 29.

in the century, 'The End of Temporality' speculates, may simply have given up interest in time 'under the entirely plausible assumption that it had been largely covered by Proust, Mann, Virginia Woolf, and T. S. Eliot and offered few further chances of literary advancement'.[46] More persuasively, the essay goes on to envisage authors driven not only by literary ambition, or anxieties of influence, but by the exigencies of the period they inhabit. Jameson suggests that for modernist writers – unlike their successors – this had entailed 'comparatist perception of the two socioeconomic temporalities which [they] had to negotiate in their own lived experience' (699). As Chapter 2 outlined, Joseph Conrad's encounter with a particular 'socioeconomic temporality' – with tightening, Greenwich-centred constraints in an industrialising, commercial age – helps account for his fiction's concerns with measured time, and for its early development of alternative, anachronic modernist idioms. Though many of the other leading modernist writers were born a quarter of a century after Conrad, in the 1880s, they too grew up in a world in which memories of earlier, more leisurely temporalities still strongly survived – displaced only gradually, as the clock tightened its grip on everyday life. The 'sensitivity to deep time' Jameson notes in their writing partly results, as he suggests, from their living 'in two distinct worlds simultaneously' – their recollection of older, alternate outlooks accentuated by enforced negotiation with the new (699). For later generations, on the other hand, 'the very sense of an alternate temporality disappears' – the clock's ubiquitous control over daily life seeming instead simply an established, almost unquestionable condition of the modern industrialised world (699).

Later generations encountered other factors which reduced incentives to question the clock, or made its controls seem less insistent and constraining. These included changes in the technologies and practices of industry itself. Lewis Mumford's claim that 'the key-machine of the modern industrial age' was 'the clock, not the steam-engine' inevitably seemed startling when he published *Technics and Civilization* in 1934, given the extent of transport and industry's reliance on steam power for more than a century previously. But as the twentieth century went on, his claim began to appear relevant only to an earlier age. In later decades, steam engines came to seem picturesque objects of nostalgia, long overtaken by technologies both more powerful and yet sometimes less exigent in the demands they made on the time and life of workforces. Some of the changes involved might already have been underway in the 1930s. As Mumford explains, industry's

---

[46] Jameson, 'End of Temporality', 695.

displacement of older, agrarian forms of life and employment during the nineteenth and early twentieth centuries – traced by D. H. Lawrence in *The Rainbow* (1915), along with more recent, Taylorist developments described in *Women in Love* (1921) – often shocked and alienated workers, and their societies generally. By the 1930s, Mumford perceived counter-movements, away from the 'gross use of power and machinery', and 'beyond Taylor's original mechanical motion study'. He even suggests that 'the next step toward the genuine rationalization of industry lies in widening the interests and increasing the social incentives to production'.[47] Incentives of this kind, towards establishing a less alienated labour force, developed only gradually in later decades, and never very completely. Yet more flexible working hours, and the export of heavy industry to countries offering cheaper labour, ensured that – in the privileged West, at any rate – clocks, clocking-in, and Taylorist methods came to rule working life less oppressively, towards the end of the twentieth century, than during its earlier decades.[48]

The clock's constraints were certainly further diminished by the 1930s – and still more so in later decades – by the emergence of a technology which *Technics and Civilization* describes as 'directed toward the service of life' and distinguished 'from the cruder forms that preceded it'. 'Some of our most characteristic mechanical instruments – the telephone, the phonograph, the motion picture', Mumford explains, ensured that 'the organic has become visible again even within the mechanical complex' (6). As he suggests, new technologies available in the 1930s, or even by the 1920s, were as often an enhancement as a threat to individuals' enjoyment of their life and times – offering new possibilities of transcending the constraints of chronology and the boundaries of memory or even mortality. In Joyce's *Ulysses* (1922), Bloom suggests one form of this potential when wondering

> How could you remember everybody? ... Have a gramophone in every grave or keep it in the house. After dinner on a Sunday. Put on poor old greatgrandfather Kraahraark! Hellohellohello ... Remind you of the voice like the photograph reminds you of the face.[49]

---

[47] Mumford, *Technics and Civilization*, 14, 387, 386, 385. See also Chapter 3.
[48] Though this movement was often reversed in the opening decades of the twenty-first century, when the prevalence of 'zero-hours' contracts – contrary to their name – made time and the hours seem more than ever exigent and commodified.
[49] James Joyce, *Ulysses* (1922; Harmondsworth: Penguin, 1992), 144.

As Bloom remarks, the gramophone added to powers of recall already strengthened during the latter half of the nineteenth century by the popularity of daguerreotype and photography. These powers naturally provided convenient resources for literature – characters' encounters with photographs, or descriptions of them, offering obvious, straightforward ways of introducing analepses, or otherwise reshaping literary temporality. 'Time is not before and after, but all at once, present and future and all the periods of the past', T. S. Eliot remarked when reflecting in 1917 on a family photograph album, suggesting that the temporality of *Four Quartets* (1936–42) had sources long predating any influence from J. W. Dunne.[50] Within fiction, it is in a way surprising that so few novels go beyond descriptions of photographs towards incorporation of actual pictures – at any rate until W. G. Sebald took this step in his early twenty-first-century novel of memory, *Austerlitz* (2001, see Chapter 7).

By the end of the nineteenth century, photography's time-warping potentials were being greatly extended by cinematography, popularised by the Lumière brothers and patented by them in 1895. Its invention, operation and machinery might in themselves be seen as synthesising or resolving contemporary temporal stresses. Creating an impression of continuous motion out of separate static images, the cinematograph produced the kind of fluid vision that Henri Bergson advocated as an alternative to the clock's divisive intrusion into life and thought. Bergson was well aware of this potential, though he remained sceptical of the use of static images in producing a mechanically fabricated impression of movement. Stressing the illusory quality of this impression, in *Creative Evolution* (*L'Évolution créatrice*, 1907) he criticises the resemblance of the cinematograph to 'the mechanism of our ordinary knowledge' – more fragmentary and less trustworthy than intuition. Similarly critical views of the mechanics of cinematography – of 'a movie projector being built like a clock' – were recorded in a novel published a hundred years later, though set around the end of the nineteenth century: Thomas Pynchon's *Against the Day* (2006).[51] For early cinema pioneers, such as the influential director Sergei Eisenstein, film and its processes of montage and editing nevertheless offered many opportunities – sometimes apparently more flexible

---

[50] See Chapter 5. T. S. Eliot, letter of 30 December 1917 to his mother, Charlotte Champe Stearns Eliot, *Letters*, 243.

[51] Bergson, *Creative Evolution*, 322–3; Thomas Pynchon, *Against the Day* (London: Jonathan Cape, 2006), 451, 456. See Chapter 7.

than those of written narrative – to depart from or even abandon the continuous forward experience of lived time.[52] The Lumière brothers made a very early discovery of one form of this potential, finding audiences entertained as much, or more, when their new invention was used in reverse.[53] Such reversals continued to amuse audiences as far as the 1960s and beyond – films rewound after amateur or schoolroom screenings offering the inverted but engaging vision of the world, moving from disarray to order, which Kurt Vonnegut incorporates into *Slaughterhouse-Five*.

Technologies developing later in the century extended these opportunities to reshape or turn back time. Though soon obsolete, the tape recorder offered further scope to recover the past in ways Bloom envisages in *Ulysses*. One provides a convenient plot device in Ann Quin's novel, *Three* (1966). Another is used in a more structural role in Beckett's *Krapp's Last Tape* (1958), requiring the play's solitary protagonist to 'be again, be again' through repeatedly re-encountering the 'old misery' of recorded fragments of his earlier life.[54] Further, more vivid opportunities to 'be again', reliving scenes exhumed from the past, were made widely available in the 1980s and 1990s by video and later DVD recording. As Thomas Pynchon remarked in 1993, as a result of 'the timely invention . . . of the remote control and the VCR':

> television time is no longer the linear and uniform commodity it once was. Not when you have instant channel selection, fast-forward, rewind and so forth. Video time can be reshaped at will . . . we may for now at least have found the illusion, the effect, of controlling, reversing, slowing, speeding and repeating time – even imagining that we can escape it.[55]

By the end of the century, as Pynchon suggests, these rewindings and reshapings of time seemed familiar, unremarkable parts of everyday life. Almost any spectacle or action – in sports events especially – could be replayed, slowed down or accelerated at will, freed from the measured ordering of the clock. Reconfigured temporality of this kind was occasionally highlighted in early twenty-first-century fiction. Descriptions of video installations in Ben Lerner's

---

[52] 'Through editing, he found, he could destroy real time altogether', Arthur Knight records of Eisenstein in *The Liveliest Art*, 78.
[53] See Canales, *Physicist and the Philosopher*, 289–90.
[54] Samuel Beckett, *Krapp's Last Tape* and *Embers* (1959; London: Faber, 1979), 19.
[55] Pynchon, 'The Deadly Sins: Sloth', 57.

10:04 (2014) are used to question how 'fictional time synchronized with nonfictional duration', and similar issues are raised in Don DeLillo's *Point Omega* (2010), discussed in Chapter 7.[56] Even independently of their more radical powers to resist or reshape time, cinema and video technology continued – throughout the twentieth century and beyond – to exercise incisive influences on novelistic techniques and temporalities. They particularly encouraged abbreviation of individual scenes and the acceleration of interchanges between them, adapted to the preferences of potentially impatient readers, accustomed to the rapid, sensational pace of cinematic action and exposition.

By the end of the century, a globalised economy and the lifestyles it fostered had further diminished the clock's constraints – though in ways not much foreseen, understandably, around mid-century and in the 1960s. Analysts at the time – less optimistic or forward-looking than Mumford – sometimes saw economic conditions still extending those assessed by Georg Lukács at the start of the 1920s. In *The Society of the Spectacle* (*La société du spectacle*, 1967) Guy Debord argued, like Lukács, that the development of capitalism had established a quantified, commodified, 'time of economic production', abstract and arbitrary in its workings, and therefore 'not general in character, but *particular*'. Despite its particularity, this construction of temporality had continued to advance, '*on a world scale*', becoming, Debord emphasises, 'the time officially promoted all round the world as the *general time of society*'.[57] As the twentieth century went on, Debord's conclusions seemed in some ways simply to be confirmed by the strengthening hold over contemporary life exercised by institutionalised forms of global or 'general time'. Though still based closely on GMT, these were increasingly redesignated, after the 1960s, not as merely general, or even global, but as universal – as Co-ordinated Universal Time, or Universel Temps Coordonné. This relied on atomic clocks – the kind of 'cesium devices that measure the life and death of the smallest silvery trillionth of a second' mentioned in Don DeLillo's *Underworld* (1997) – to provide levels of accuracy essential not only for astronomers, but for globalised business, communications and aviation.[58]

---

[56] Ben Lerner, *10:04: A Novel* (New York: Faber and Faber, 2014), 57. Lerner's title alludes to a key moment in the film *Back to the Future* (1985), discussed in the following section. See Figure 6.1.
[57] Debord, *Society of the Spectacle*, 107.
[58] Don DeLillo, *Underworld* (1997; London: Picador, 1998), 235. For an explanation of relations between Universal Time, Atomic Time, and other world standards, see West-Pavlov, *Temporalities*, 24 et seq.

Yet the interests demanding this ever-more-stringent globalised temporality were also indirectly responsible, in later years, for re-emphasising contrasting senses of the local or particular, or of the arbitrariness of measured time generally. As Chapter 1 described, a new age of railway travel in the mid-nineteenth century steadily eliminated local idiosyncrasies and ensured the mutual agreement of public clocks throughout the country. In the latter half of the twentieth century, air travel and international communications often reinstated the significance of individual time-zones, local or national. Hotels, airports, banks and businesses began to display – alongside Greenwich Mean Time, or British Summer Time – clocks recording the hour in cities such as Tokyo, Paris, or New York. Flatteringly, this implied that customers' globe-trotting lives or business commitments required constant attention to different times of day in fashionable destinations elsewhere. Yet as tourism and international travel grew more routine, some measure of this attentiveness did become more necessary, occasionally at least. Even within Europe, travellers often found themselves landing in different time-zones, while those undertaking longer journeys were reminded by the ensuing jet-lag of awkward gaps between natural or bodily cycles and the contrary temporalities imposed by clocks around the world.

Tourism and travel expanded awareness of time-zones of another kind, introducing Westerners to regions of the world distant enough from their own industrialised societies to have allowed the survival of more relaxed attitudes to temporality. In some cases, these attitudes could be identified as deeply structured into the languages and cultures of the peoples concerned. Jeanette Winterson is one of several late-twentieth-century writers and commentators – often referring to the work of the linguistic ethnologist Benjamin Lee Whorf – to describe tribes or races that have 'no tenses for past, present and future'. 'What does this say about time?', Winterson asks at the beginning of her novel *Sexing the Cherry* (1989).[59] Anthropologists and linguisticians sometimes seemed doubtful of the validity of this question. Experts including Stephen Pinker and Alfred Gell challenged the reliability of Whorf's analyses of Native American languages – Gell arguing instead for 'cognitive universality' in apprehensions of time.[60] Most commentators towards the end of the century – including Gell, in acknowledging

---

[59] Jeanette Winterson, *Sexing the Cherry* (1989; London: Vintage, 1990), [8]. Subsequent references are to this edition. Jay Griffiths offers a conspectus of cultural or linguistic alternatives to Western temporality in *Pip Pip*, ch. 1.

[60] See Pinker, *Stuff of Thought*, ch. 3, and Gell, *Anthropology of Time*, 118 et seq.

substantial cultural and linguistic diversities – nevertheless recognised the need for some form of 'geography of time', attentive to divergent attitudes, around the world, towards the pace and progress of life and the means of their measurement.[61] As postcolonial criticism emphasised, this attention obviously required a political and historical component, identifying when and how a 'time of economic production' had impacted upon temporalities in non-industrial societies remote from the West. In the view of this postcolonial analysis, it was far from coincidental that the Prime Meridian Conference in Washington in 1884 was so nearly contemporaneous with the empire-ratifying conference in Berlin in 1884–5. As well as helping to determine boundaries between colonies, Greenwich-centred demarcations of global time and space contributed a key strategy in Western nations' consolidation and control of their empires – the imposition of clocks and calendars on the native societies they subjugated.

In *Gulliver's Travels* (1726), Jonathan Swift provides an early representation of resulting perplexities – and an implicit critique of the West's allegiance to mechanical forms of time – when the Lilliputians examine their gigantic visitor's watch. As Gulliver consults this 'wonderful kind of engine' so devotedly, and so conspicuously allows it to control 'every action of his life', they naturally conclude that it must be some form of personal oracle or deity.[62] In *Arrow of God* (1964), Chinua Achebe explores deeper perplexities typically encountered in a much later and more vigorous phase of colonialism, as the British Empire expanded across Africa. Its early administrators readily assume, in Achebe's description, that colonised societies have 'no idea of years' – puzzling and alienating local populations by ignoring longstanding, indigenous practices of measuring time and the seasons, crucial to agriculture and religious observance.[63] As postcolonial critics such as Giordano Nanni have pointed out, perplexed responses to Western temporalities and their conflicts with local custom were not entirely exclusive to the colonised populations involved. Like later visitors to the regions concerned, some administrators during the colonial period found that reciprocal questions were raised – as in *Gulliver's Travels* – regarding the West's stolid, almost religious allegiance to mechanical time.[64]

The arbitrary, particular nature of a supposedly universal temporality was challenged in another area of late twentieth-century critical thinking. In one of the foundational essays of feminist criticism,

---

[61] See, for example, Levine, *Geography of Time*, or May and Thrift, *Timespace*.
[62] Jonathan Swift, *Gulliver's Travels* (1726; Harmondsworth: Penguin, 1973), 70–1.
[63] Chinua Achebe, *Arrow of God* (London: Heinemann, 1964), 42.
[64] Nanni, *Colonisation of Time*, esp. 229 et seq. See also Aveni, *Empires of Time*.

'Women's Time' ('Le temps des femmes', 1979), Julia Kristeva condemns the 'conception of linear temporality' as merely part of 'father's time' and 'readily labelled masculine'. 'Both civilizational and obsessional', in her view, this temporality had become an accepted social structure despite manifestly constituting a form of enslavement. In its stead, Kristeva proposes a form of what Angela Carter describes in *The Passion of New Eve* (1977) as 'the feminisation of Father Time'.[65] Through 'female subjectivity' and 'the maternal body', Kristeva argues in another early essay, women can escape the 'temporality of day-to-day social obligations', shaping their lives around 'a specific measure that essentially retains *repetition* and *eternity* from among the multiple modalities of time known through the history of civilizations'.[66]

Later feminist criticism sometimes challenged or qualified the principles on which conclusions of this kind could be based. In *Doing Time* (2000), Rita Felski questions the idea of essential, fundamental divisions between 'men's time and women's time', also proposing that multiple modalities of time might be recognised existing not only through the history of civilizations, but at work 'at the same historical moment'.[67] Most feminist critics concerned with the issue – Felski included – nevertheless share some of Kristeva's disdain for conceptions of linear temporality, also identifying differences between men's and women's time which may not be inherent or essential, but constructed instead by longstanding social conventions and expectations. These often forced women to undertake an unequal share of domestic responsibilities, compounding temporal pressures imposed by conditions of paid employment. Even if free of the latter, everyday household work and domestic or familial responsibilities exerted stresses of their own, imposing on women's lives – as Betty Friedan suggests in another foundational study, *The Feminine Mystique* (1963) – rhythms partly exempt from the strict measures of the clock, but unsettling and unfulfilling nonetheless.[68]

Feminist critical judgements opened up in this way many opportunities for analysing not only social pressures and assumptions, but also the structures and temporalities of women's writing. Virginia Woolf's

---

[65] Angela Carter, *The Passion of New Eve* (1977; London: Virago, 1992), 67.
[66] Kristeva, 'Women's Time' and 'About Chinese Women' (1974), in *Kristeva Reader*, 193, 190, 192, 154, 191.
[67] Felski, *Doing Time*, 1, 3.
[68] 'I began to see that there was something peculiar about the *time* housework takes', Friedan remarks in *The Feminine Mystique*, 193. For analysis of 'the special relationship between women and the everyday' (5), and its effects on apprehensions of time in working life and in literature, see Randall, *Modernism, Daily Time and Everyday Life*.

dislike of the 'appalling narrative business of the realist: getting on from lunch to dinner' bears obvious comparison with later feminist scepticisms of linearity and the demands of quotidian social obligations. Woolf's mistrust of 'time on the clock', favouring of memory, and sensitivities to 'deep time' – unusually acute even among modernist writers – might likewise be understood as intensified by factors of gender. Similarly gendered influences might be recognised later in the century – in the 'hourless' London that Elizabeth Bowen envisages in *The Heat of the Day* (1949), Jeanette Winterson's resistance to time as 'a straight line', or Penelope Lively's contrasts of official records with personal memories in *Moon Tiger*, for example.[69]

Lively is equally sensitive to multiple modalities of time in *City of the Mind* (1991). Her novel indicates in several ways how far 'the general time of society' Debord defined in the 1960s had come to be questioned, modified, diffused or ignored in the decades that followed. The profession of the central figure – Matthew Halland, an architect – makes him unusually aware of sedimentations of multiple layers of time, manifest in the historically diverse styles of London's buildings. His experience also confirms how compellingly, by the 1990s, global media and communications had opened up alternatives to straightforwardly clock-defined time. For Halland, 'servitude to passing hours' has been replaced as if by the 'seventy-six different times all ticking in the mind at once' which Woolf's Orlando experiences while driving through London. Stuck in a traffic jam, Halland finds at first that 'time dissolved' simply as his memory 'flitted to a moment . . . as a boy'. It soon dissolves much further:

> driving through the city, he is both here and now, there and then. He carries yesterday with him, but pushes forward into today, and tomorrow, skipping as he will from one to the other. He is in London, on a May morning of the late twentieth century, but is also in many other places, and at other times. He twitches the knob of his radio: New York speaks to him, five hours ago, is superseded by Australia tomorrow and presently by India this evening . . . For him, the world no longer turns; there is no day or night, everything and everywhere are instantaneous . . . he coasts through the city, his body in one world and his head in many.[70]

---

[69] Woolf, *A Writer's Diary*, 138; Winterson, *Sexing the Cherry*, 83. Winterson's views are discussed in the following section.

[70] Virginia Woolf, *Orlando* (1928; Harmondsworth: Penguin, 1973), 217; Penelope Lively, *City of the Mind* (1991; Harmondsworth, Penguin, 1992), 96, 2–3.

Halland's multiple worlds and dissolving times and spaces arise out of nothing more sophisticated than personal thoughts and a car radio. As the 1990s went on, potentials of this kind were enormously expanded, not only by the 'video time' Thomas Pynchon described early in the decade. Influences of linear, clock-based chronology were also much diminished by the new technologies of email, mobile telephones and the internet which were firmly establishing themselves by the end of the century.

Some of the effects of these technologies had been foreseen in William Gibson's *Neuromancer* (1984), often credited with anticipating the developments in computer technology which led to the establishment of the internet. Gibson's novel views these new technologies with some scepticism, suggesting elements of threat as well as promise in the globalised systems and commercial interests supporting them. As Chapter 1 described, *Neuromancer* shows new devices expanding into a future world some of the exacting influences extended by the Prime Meridian Conference in the late nineteenth century. Molly's neurosurgically inserted digital clock installs what she calls 'Greenwich fucking Mean' permanently in a corner of her eyes – or almost behind them, as an inescapable imprint on her brain. Her partner, Case, experiences similarly sophisticated technologies inserting a much wider range of influences, equally directly, into his inner consciousness. Virtual-reality versions of 'cyberspace' install 'in the bloodlit dark behind his eyes' what Gibson describes as 'a graphic representation of data abstracted from the banks of every computer in the human system'. This appropriation of personal mental space seems in one way a nightmarish confirmation of the powers of global capitalism, indicating that, as the novel remarks, 'the multinationals that shaped the course of human history' had now entirely 'transcended old barriers'.[71] For the modernists, depths of consciousness and memory had provided some refuge from the industrialisation, mechanisation and constraining temporality dominating their society. In the postmodern world that Gibson envisages, even the supposedly inviolable realm of the mind seems susceptible instead to invasion by whatever influences globalised capital wishes to place in it.

Yet in other ways incursions from cyberspace offer not so much a breach of individual cognition as an enormous expansion of its reach and potential. Technology opens up entries into a 'city of the mind' immense in scale and thrillingly diverse and colourful in the visions it offers. Understandably, like Halland, Case is content to leave 'his

---

[71] William Gibson, *Neuromancer* (1984; London: Grafton, 1986), 300, 68, 67, 242.

body in one world', more or less ignored, in favour of what he experiences in his head in illimitable others. Periods of unconsciousness in the world of actual experience – even periods of near-death – are deliriously transcended by narratives and images unfolding apparently endlessly in the virtual worlds his mind explores. *Neuromancer* suggests in conclusion that such experiences may ultimately transcend old barriers still more comprehensively, opening up realms altogether beyond earthly time and mortality. Though speculative in this suggestion, in some of its other aspects Gibson's vision already seemed realistic rather than futuristic by the end of the century – even ordinary and familiar. New forms of communication, the internet particularly – global in reach, yet almost instantaneous in operation – allowed users' imaginations to expand spatially, into numerous worlds elsewhere, while diminishing the constraints of any absolute temporality; any singular, confining here-and-now.

New possibilities of this kind contributed to views, shared by Frederic Jameson and several other commentators, of a general transition in the outlook of the twentieth century, and – correspondingly – between modernist and postmodernist phases of literary imagination. Towards the end of the century, Jameson suggests, 'we now inhabit the synchronic rather than the diachronic'.[72] 'It is at least empirically arguable', he adds in *Postmodernism, or, the Cultural Logic of Late Capitalism*, 'that our daily life, our psychic experience, our cultural languages, are today dominated by categories of space rather than by categories of time, as in the preceding period of high modernism' (16). In 'The End of Temporality', published a dozen years after *Postmodernism*, he argues more confidently that 'time was the dominant of the modern (or of modernism), and space of the postmodern' (696). This conclusion echoes – but inverts – one delivered equally decisively half a century earlier, in looking back over the previous fifty years. In discussing 'The Time-Obsession of the Twentieth Century' in his critical study *Time and the Novel*, published in 1952, A. A. Mendilow suggests that 'our age has seen the conquest of space by time'. Writing only a decade later, Alain Robbe-Grillet was already suggesting – anticipating Jameson's views – that 'space destroys time'.[73] A conveniently symmetrical literary history

---

[72] Other commentators persuaded of a transition between dominant interests in time and in space include Andreas Huyssen in *Twilight Memories*, Ursula Heise in *Chronoschisms*, and Michel Foucault, who suggests in 'Of Other Spaces' that 'the anxiety of our era has to do fundamentally with space, no doubt a great deal more than with time' (23).

[73] Mendilow, *Time and the Novel*, 10; Robbe-Grillet, *For a New Novel*, 155.

might be based around these judgements, construing imagination as dominated in the first half of the century by temporal concerns, and then in the second half principally by others of space or geography.

Though too sweeping to be entirely convincing – requiring some qualification in the two following sections – this broad view of literary history might nevertheless be useful in general terms. It allows the passage quoted from *City of the Mind* to be used as a paradigm of wider developments – as a kind of literary history in miniature. The 'period of high modernism', early in the century, was one still relatively lacking in media distractions, leaving individuals largely reliant on their own resources when seeking alternatives to the stresses of daily existence. As a result, the opportunity that Matthew Halland first chooses – to flit away into memories of more congenial places and times – is one necessarily employed regularly by characters in modernist fiction, and often a key structuring element of the novels in which they appear. Later in the century, alternative places and times could be accessed on a wide scale, and probably with readier promise of novelty and entertainment, simply by twitching a knob, as Halland eventually does, or by pressing a switch, or clicking on a computer icon. History and its pressures continued to trouble imagination as profoundly as ever, or more profoundly, and to play a central role in shaping the literature the period produced. But new technologies and new challenges to linear temporality ensured that there was more opportunity, late in the century, to find alternatives to 'time on the clock' and the 'time of society', and for their remorseless 'tick-tick' to resound less often, and less disturbingly, in the period's fiction.

Time Travel

Influences from pure science – not only technology – contributed to this change. Writing in the 1960s, in *Man and Time* (1964), J. B. Priestley suggested that 'the Time situation' might have 'eased a little' since he had first assessed it, thirty years earlier. 'Wider acceptance of the theory of relativity and its space-time continuum', he explains, had left 'the conventional view of Time' more 'disturbed and blurred' in later decades.[74] This blurring continued later in the century. As Chapter 5 described, Einstein's theories had begun to figure widely in fiction by the 1930s – sometimes further popularised by those of J. W. Dunne – encouraging the novel to move into 'dim

---

[74] Priestley, *Man and Time*, 51.

regions where physics, metaphysics and mathematics jostle'. Cosmographies which had fascinated the 1920s and 1930s advanced in the latter half of the century towards further startling conclusions about the age, size and strangeness of the universe. Incorporating challenging concepts of Quantum Theory into his popular account of the cosmos, *A Brief History of Time* (1988), Stephen Hawking thoroughly dismantled conventional assumptions about temporality, space and matter, opening up absorbing new landscapes, or skyscapes, to contemporary imagination. For Joseph Conrad, the stars and the mathematical complexities they required of navigation still belonged within a mechanical, clockwork, tidily Newtonian universe. 'The night swings over our heads as if somebody below the horizon were turning a crank ... the ordered arrangement of the stars meets my eye, unclouded, infinitely wearisome', the narrator of *The Shadow-Line* (1917) complains – albeit when exasperated at being interminably becalmed.[75] By the 1980s and 1990s, awareness of new cosmologies ensured that the night sky seemed more sublime than conventionally orderly: probably more mysterious even than it had appeared to authors such as Thomas Hardy and Virginia Woolf, and likelier to occasion wonder about the infinite, rather than infinite weariness. Cloudless nights revealed still more 'immeasurable distances of time and space', mentioned in *City of the Mind*, or the 'infinitely receding darkness' envisaged in Margaret Atwood's *Cat's Eye* (1989), in which 'the stars as we see them are echoes of events that occurred light-years distant in time and space'.[76]

New theories may have been all the more enthralling because they seemed further than ever beyond ordinary rational comprehension. Fiction in later decades at any rate followed its 1930s predecessors in employing whimsically or almost mystically some of the ideas recently emerging from the physical sciences. In *Sexing the Cherry*, Jeanette Winterson bases responses of this kind around views which – like Lively's in *City of the Mind* – in one way reflect preferences for 'time in the mind' already familiar from earlier decades of fiction. 'Thinking about time', *Sexing the Cherry* reflects,

> is to acknowledge two contradictory certainties: that our outward lives are governed by the seasons and the clock; that our inward

---

[75] Joseph Conrad, *The Shadow-Line: A Confession* (1917; Oxford: Oxford University Press, 2003), 79–80.
[76] Lively, *City of the Mind,* 144; Margaret Atwood, *Cat's Eye* (1989; London: Virago, 1990), 105, 332. Subsequent references are to this edition. A light year is of course a measure of spatial distance, not primarily of time.

lives are governed by something much less regular – an imaginative impulse cutting through the dictates of daily time, and leaving us free to ignore the boundaries of here and now (89–90).

Yet *Sexing the Cherry* extends this imaginative impulse with new freedom, scorning temporal and spatial boundaries and demonstrating a conviction that ideas of 'reality as truth', or that 'time is a straight line', are merely 'lies' (83). Some of the principles involved might have seemed familiar to readers of *A Brief History of Time*, published the previous year – in particular, Winterson's avowal that 'matter, that thing the most solid and . . . well-known' can be considered 'mostly empty space' (8). 'True art', Winterson suggests, should be 'no longer bound by matter' – a freedom celebrated in the unfettered imagination of the novel itself, moving seamlessly between centuries and between historical and fantastic modes of narration (91).

In *The Child in Time* (1987), Ian McEwan transcends normal 'boundaries of here and now' only occasionally, through visionary recursions into past events – including the courtship of his central character's parents, appropriately initiated by their mutual interest in a malfunctioning clock. Elsewhere in the novel – mostly reliant on conventional realist idioms – McEwan uses more straightforward means than Winterson's of incorporating theories developed by recent science and cosmology. One of his characters, a distinguished physicist working on 'the nature of time', conveniently explains the new concepts as directly as she can to the central figure – and by extension to the reader – discussing 'relativity and quantum theories', the wave–particle duality, and 'different kinds of time, not simply . . . linear '.[77] Margaret Atwood employs comparable tactics in *Cat's Eye*, outlining theories – that 'space-time is curved . . . time can be stretched or shrunk . . . matter is not really solid' – in the voice of her narrator's brother, an eminent scientist and cosmologist (219–20). The narrator in John Updike's futuristic *Toward the End of Time* (1997) – an avid reader of popular cosmology – likewise reports directly on recent astronomical theories, though the novel exploits only tentatively the 'quantum leaps of plot and personality' this new science might encourage.[78] Similarly straightforward strategies might have been expected of Alan Lightman – unusually well qualified, as a theoretical physicist himself, to explain recent science

---

[77] Ian McEwan, *The Child in Time* (1987; London: Picador, 1988), 32, 118, 119.
[78] John Updike, *Toward the End of Time* (1997; London: Penguin, 2006), 337.

directly in his fiction. In *Einstein's Dreams* (1993) he employs instead the kind of free imagination favoured by Winterson, offering fables and fantasies based around the work on Relativity Einstein initiated while still employed at the Patent Office, in Berne, at the start of the twentieth century. These include vignettes describing timepieces worshipped, all-powerful, or entirely ignored, along with accounts of time measured when it should not be measured, or speeded up, or flowing backwards, or discontinuously, or at different rates in different cities. Concise descriptions of these diverse temporalities make *Einstein's Dreams* a kind of fantastic encyclopaedia of the twentieth century's convoluted negotiations with time and the clock.

These negotiations contributed extensively to a genre of writing also indebted to the influence of Relativity, at a key stage of its development, and offering further evidence of the 'obsession with time' of the 1920s – science fiction. Loosening of 'the boundaries of here and now' under the influence of Einstein and his popularisers sometimes added strange new dimensions to conventional fiction in the later 1920s and 1930s. It also encouraged forms of fantastic imagination to emerge strongly enough to require – more or less for the first time – their categorisation as a separate, distinct form of writing. As Roger Luckhurst and other historians of the genre explain, sheaves of 'Amazing Stories' and 'Astounding Stories' began to be designated, towards the end of the 1920s, as 'scientifiction', or just 'science fiction'.[79] In later decades, the genre continued to expand its hold on imagination, and the scale of its production, in response as much to rapid advances in technology as to developments in pure science. By the 1950s, these advances had come to seem troubling, or thrilling – or both – in ways that made technology's impact on daily life impossible to ignore, and the visions of science fiction consequently more and more relevant to the age. Atomic weaponry deployed at Hiroshima demonstrated technology's literally earth-shattering powers, hanging a Damoclean sword over all succeeding years. Yet these powers were evidently able to transcend the earth altogether, as the launch of Sputnik I, in 1957, and the succeeding space age confirmed. Such diverse potentials – extending scepticism about the project of modernity, alongside residual faith in its powers – could be reflected particularly readily through the miraculous, shiny machinery and darkling, dystopian nightmares science

---

[79] See Luckhurst, *Science Fiction*, 15 et seq. The term 'scientific romance' was in earlier use, from the mid-nineteenth century, to describe work by writers such as Jules Verne and C. H. Hinton. *Amazing Stories* and *Astounding Stories* (later renamed *Astounding Science-Fiction*) were science fiction magazines launched in the United States respectively in 1926 and 1930.

fiction liberally deploys. This flexible, ambivalent aspect of its imagination contributed to the conclusion reached in *Trillion Year Spree* (1986) by Brian Aldiss, historian as well as practitioner of the genre: that science fiction was 'the literature most suited to our progressing and doom-threatened century'.[80]

It was also a form of literature peculiarly appropriate – throughout its history – for exploring concerns with the nature of time. 'Science fiction with its tricks with Time', J. B. Priestley considered, might have been as responsible as Relativity itself for the easing of 'the Time situation' he discerned extending from the 1930s into the 1960s (51). These 'tricks' or interests had at any rate been in evidence well before science fiction's Relativity-inspired expansion in the 1920s, playing a central role in its foundational narratives at the end of the nineteenth century – most obviously in H. G. Wells's *The Time Machine* (1895). Wells is often credited with initiating the genre still earlier, in 'The Chronic Argonauts' (1888), sometimes considered the first-ever science fiction short story. In one way, its concerns with corpses, blood, murder, religion and churchyards indicate an imagination still partly in thrall to established fantasy genres of mystery, horror and the Gothic. Yet in describing an 'Anachronic Man', and the machinery his adventures require, Wells also looks firmly forward, towards the development of a genre in which time travel, in one form or another, would continue to function as an almost ineradicable, constitutive component.[81] As well as regularly describing characters' voyages through time, as in 'The Chronic Argonauts' and *The Time Machine*, science fiction often depends fundamentally on taking readers on a comparable journey – conveying them into a future whose advanced technologies may be supposed to have established marvels such as time travel as viable possibilities.

Constitutively committed to travelling in time in this way, science fiction is particularly disposed to exploit narrative devices of anachrony – prolepsis especially, though to an extent any strategy

---

[80] Aldiss and Wingrove, *Trillion Year Spree*, 18.
[81] 'The Anachronic Man' is the title of the story's second section. Time travel also began to figure regularly in another form of freely imaginative literature: children's fiction. An 'Outlandish Watch' in ch. 23 of Lewis Carroll's *Sylvie and Bruno* (1889), for example, inverts time in ways comparable to those later used by Martin Amis and Kurt Vonnegut. E. Nesbit's characters in *The Story of the Amulet* (1906; Harmondsworth: Penguin, 1971) travel freely in time, judging that H. G. Wells is a 'great reformer' and – unusually early in the twentieth century – that 'time and space are only forms of thought' (52, 231).

that can evade or reshape the constraints of conventional chronology. This aspect of the genre places it in a revealing relationship with the study of narratology, as David Wittenberg emphasises in *Time Travel: the Popular Philosophy of Narrative* (2013). Since all narratives 'set out to modify or manipulate the order, duration, and significance of events in time', Wittenberg suggests, 'one could arguably call narrative itself a "time machine"'.[82] Reciprocally, time-machines roaming the pages of science fiction might often be considered to deliver only more vivid or literal versions of the temporal dislocations narratology analyses. There might in this way be good reason for specific comparisons commentators on science fiction have made between some of its authors – including Ray Bradbury and Philip K. Dick – and modernist writers most concerned with reshaping narrative chronology, such as Marcel Proust.

Broad comparisons can at any rate be made between impulses towards anachrony in modernist narrative, and towards time-travelling imagination in the genre of science fiction. As Wells's Time Traveller explains, his machine operates in ways comparable to the effects of 'recalling an incident very vividly', and to the abilities of 'mental existences' in 'passing along the Time-Dimensions' – analogously, in other words, with the modernists' use of memory. In 'A Sketch of the Past' (1939–40), Virginia Woolf ponders a similar interchange between mental faculties and fabulous machinery, thinking of memories of 'great intensity' and wondering if 'some device will be invented' allowing her to 'fit a plug into the wall; and listen to the past'. Whether readers prefer to be moved through time by Proust's memory-saturated 'little piece of madeleine', or by devices such as the 'glittering metallic framework . . . very delicately made' described in *The Time Machine*, might therefore be viewed as no more than – almost literally – a matter of taste.[83] Even if 1920s aficionados of astounding stories did not find the work of modernist authors to their taste, some of its features might nevertheless have seemed familiar – century-hopping in Woolf's *Orlando* (1927); unearthly landscapes in Wyndham Lewis's *The Childermass* (1928); time travelling in Lewis Grassic Gibbon's *Three Go Back* (1932). Correspondences are sometimes more particular. In his time-travel novel *The Clockwork Man* (1923), E. V. Odle extends a version of

---

[82] Wittenberg, *Time Travel*, 1.
[83] H. G. Wells, *Selected Short Stories* (1927; Harmondsworth: Penguin, 1965) 11, 10; Woolf, *Moments of Being*, 81. A century after Wells's time-fiction, psychologists and neuroscientists regularly referred to personal memory and anticipation as forms of 'mental time travel'. See, for example, Michaelian et al., *Seeing the Future*.

Gudrun's nightmare vision of Gerald in *Women in Love*, extrapolating into a future world the 'many absurdities in modern life that result from a too mechanical efficiency'. Like other members of this future society, Odle's mysterious central figure resembles 'one of those mechanical toys' – his brain replaced by an intricate clock, evidently still among the most complex, disturbing forms of technology imaginable in 1923.[84]

Analogies between these forms of time voyaging – Proustian or Wellsian, memorious or fantastic – indicate a further potential in science fiction. This is the capacity of its 'tricks with Time', like anachronies in fiction more generally, to reflect or reconfigure the pressures of contemporary history and its dominant social temporalities. Even before the twentieth century began, simultaneous intuitions of progress and doom of the kind Aldiss describes figured strongly in *The Time Machine*. Contemporary excitement about new powers of technology and transportation appears in Wells's vision alongside incipient modernist uneasiness about the temporal constraints of a machine age, and continuing Victorian concerns about the implications of Darwinian evolution through the aeons. Throughout the century following, science fiction continued to use fantasies of time travel and fabulous, temporally remote worlds to explore stresses currently troubling its authors' own earthly societies. The title story of Michael Moorcock's anthology *The Time Dweller* (1969), and J. G. Ballard's 'Chronopolis', included in *The Voices of Time* (1963), illustrate particular potentials for analysing twentieth-century concerns with the clock and its restrictions on life and working practices. In 'The Time Dweller', Moorcock describes a future in which a traveller from a zone largely free of technology is puzzled to discover a nearby area in thrall to a bizarre machine:

> set in the centre of the machine was a great round plaque, divided into twelve units with each unit of twelve divided into a further five units. From the centre arose two pointers, one shorter than the other ... facsimiles of this object were everywhere.

Like the Lilliputians, perplexed by Gulliver's watch, the traveller assumes he has encountered 'some holy object or heraldic device'. He accepts only gradually, and incredulously, that its 'twelve divisions ... called hours ... divided into sixty units' entirely regulate life in the region he visits, leaving its citizens hopelessly subjugated

---

[84] E. V. Odle, *The Clockwork Man* (1923; Boston: HiLoBooks, 2013), 74, 55.

by 'time imposed on their consciousness by their method of recording and measuring it'.⁸⁵

The future society that J. G. Ballard depicts in 'Chronopolis' has been shaped by an uprising against recording, regulation and measurement of this kind. This insurrection has resulted in the outlawing of any 'calibrated timepiece' by 'Time-Police', and the smashing of all public clocks, leaving them 'mutilated, hands and numerals torn off, the circle of minute intervals stripped away'. Suggestively named 'Conrad', Ballard's protagonist learns that this defacement was instigated – as if in imitation of the society Samuel Butler describes in *Erewhon* (1872) – by a citizenry exasperated by clockwork regimentations which 'denied . . . all freedom' and left each of them only a 'cog in the wheel'. Attracted nevertheless by 'the ordered world of the past', prior to this chronophobic revolution, Conrad rediscovers and restores a range of devices belonging to an earlier history of chronometry. These include 'calibrated candles, crude sundials, sand-glasses, an elaborate clockwork contraption . . . that drove its hands faster and faster in an unintentional parody of Conrad's obsession'.⁸⁶ Like Moorcock, Ballard offers in this way an entirely intentional parody of twentieth-century 'obsession' with time-measurement, particularly satirising the Taylorist strategies for controlling workplace practices which troubled the modernist period. In holding these strategies up for ridicule, each author employs – like Alan Lightman in his fables – methods recommended by Russian Formalist criticism. Shifts of perspective into more innocent future worlds make familiar experiences and objects, such as the clock – or 'great round plaque' – seem inexplicable, challenging and alien.⁸⁷ The effectiveness of such tactics may suggest another reason why clocks appear less often in the mainstream novel later in the twentieth century. Science fiction provided readier means of highlighting any hostilities they might still arouse, and of configuring through fantasy domains in which their influence might be entirely escaped.

---

⁸⁵ Michael Moorcock, *The Time Dweller* (1969; London: Granada, 1971), 14, 15–16, 22.

⁸⁶ J. G. Ballard, *The Voices of Time* (1963; London: Phoenix, 1992), 179, 176, 189, 195, 178. As Chapter 4 described, inhabitants of Erewhon are convinced that 'there is no security . . . against the ultimate development of mechanical consciousness', and view the narrator's watch with 'horror and dismay'. Samuel Butler, *Erewhon* (1872; Harmondsworth: Penguin, 1983), 199, 82.

⁸⁷ The kind of defamiliarisation or '*ostranenie*' – challenging dulled or habitual responses to experience – favoured by Russian Formalist critics including Viktor Shklovsky.

Science fiction's excursions into the past often illumine contemporary society as sharply as its travels into the stranger worlds of the future. Some of these excursions are motivated straightforwardly – as in Jack Finney's story 'The Third Level' (1957) – by the kind of nostalgia for supposedly golden ages and happier times discussed in Chapter 5. Seeking 'escape ... refuge from reality', Finney's hero finds himself compelled to undertake a quasi-Proustian return to the 1890s, when 'summer evenings were twice as long ... the First World War still twenty years off, and World War II, over forty years in the future'.[88] Science fiction's capacities for nostalgia and for trickiness with time operate more complicatedly in the work of one of the authors Brian Aldiss compares to Proust, Philip K. Dick. In *Time Out of Joint* (1959), Dick describes candidly the new anxieties preying upon the 1950s – including 'H-bombs and Russia and rising prices'. Yet he also demonstrates elements of comfort and complacency in these 'peaceful days', especially when viewed from later ages.[89] This retrospection is curiously complicated by its actually being anticipatory – looking forward, in a novel published in the late 1950s, on ways the decade may come to appear during those that follow. The '1950s' the novel describes, as it turns out, are in any case artificial – a simulacrum set up by a technologically sophisticated but much more troubled future society, attempting through strategic reinhabitation of the past to avoid destruction in lunatic late twentieth-century nuclear wars. *Time Out of Joint* shares in this way some of the characteristics discussed above in post-war and 1950s narratives, resorting to static, self-scrutinising, conspicuously artificial forms of 'specular time' in default of assured vision of coherent progress in contemporary history.

Similarly complex retrospection figures in Fred Hoyle's *October the First is Too Late* (1966). A celebrated astronomer and cosmologist, Hoyle brings back to earth the kind of relativistic temporalities studied in distant space, describing in his novel strange events which reconfigure adjacent areas of the world into disparate historical periods. This allows a British government in the late 1960s to consider reorienting a history of decline they believe to have damaged the country ever since the Second World War, originating in developments around the time of the First. The Prime Minister explains that

---

[88] Jack Finney, 'The Third Level' (1957), in *Time Machines: the Greatest Time Travel Stories Ever Written*, ed. Bill Adler, Jr (New York: Carroll and Graf, 1998), 16, 18.
[89] Philip K. Dick, *Time Out of Joint* (1959; London: Gollancz, 2003), 8, 204.

for the last two decades we've been drifting here in Britain in a thoroughly aimless fashion. There was nothing we could do to have any real effect on the world. After the responsibilities of the nineteenth century we'd suddenly become peripheral.[90]

Learning that the Great War is currently raging in a nearby timezone – and may perhaps be stopped – the government plots a restructuration of the past, ensuring that Britain's progress throughout the twentieth century sustains the pre-eminent position it enjoyed at the end of the nineteenth. Along with *Time Out of Joint*, Hoyle's novel indicates some of the complex influences shaping nostalgia in the later twentieth century, including the contrasting effects of historical circumstances prevailing on different sides of the Atlantic. For the USA, the 1950s seemed, despite their stresses, a period of expanding world power. In Britain, a comparable period extended from the later nineteenth century until the outbreak of the Great War, ensuring that nostalgia, in subsequent decades, was directed principally on a supposedly golden age coming to an end in 1914.

Each novel also illustrates an urge to sustain golden ages by somehow dealing with 'Adamic' facts, in the distant past, which led to their destruction. This adds a further dimension to forms of retrospection discussed in Chapter 5, and earlier in this one. Science fiction could revisit past idylls – and events occasioning their loss – not only through the memories of characters and narrators. It could return time travellers directly into these idyllic periods: as if into Eden, to ensure that the serpent remains untrusted, forbidden fruit stays uneaten on the tree, and a happier history consequently ensues. Possibilities of renegotiating the past in this way were developed particularly vividly in film. Enhanced by increasingly sophisticated special effects, as well as the time-annihilating editing possibilities that Sergei Eisenstein recognised early on, cinema added enormously to the appeal of science fiction late in the twentieth century. *The Terminator* (1984) and *Back to the Future* (1985) were among its most popular successes in the 1980s, spawning a series of sequels which extended, in the former case, well into the twenty-first century. This extension towards a successful future in a way reduplicated the theme of the first *Terminator* film itself. 'Time-displacement equipment' allows its central character, Rees, to travel back to 1984 in order to secure the birth of a figure whose destiny, in distant years to come, is to secure humanity's long-term future by overthrowing the

---

[90] Fred Hoyle, *October the First is Too Late* (1966; Harmondsworth: Penguin, 1968), 78.

tyrannical rule of machines.⁹¹ Battling against robots and machines, and returning from an age following a 2027 nuclear war – bearing on his arm a tattoo inflicted in an extermination camp – Rees both embodies major dreads preying upon the later twentieth century while also offering an imagined redemption from them.

Back to the Future and its sequels likewise follow interventions into the onward flow of time, though ones mostly motivated, in this case, by the need to secure a present day roughly contemporaneous with

Fig. 6.1 The Doc (Christopher Lloyd) hazardously sets up a way back to 1985, relying on lightning striking the town clock at 10:04pm on 12 November 1955. *Back to the Future*, Robert Zemeckis, 1985 © Universal Pictures/Photofest.

---

⁹¹ Plots of this kind were already familiar from science fiction novels and stories – from some of Robert A. Heinlein's early work, for example, or Gregory Benford's *Timescape* (1980), in which scientists in the 1990s seek to avert ecological catastrophe by sending premonitory messages back to the 1960s.

production of the films. Cheerier than *The Terminator*, *Back to the Future* opens in the house of a zany inventor – 'the Doc' – teeming with eccentric timepieces and shared with a pet dog named Einstein. It moves on through events – often centred around an imposing town clock – apparently affecting the happiness only of the central character and his friends and family. Yet in repeatedly revisiting the soda-fountains, coffee-bars and high-school proms of 1955 – while the time-machine remains parked beside advertisements idealising contemporary family life – *Back to the Future I* and its sequels exhibit a strong element of nostalgia for more innocent times in the past of the United States generally. This is extended in *Back to the Future III* – though still half-ironically – by a return to another supposedly innocent era: the pioneering times of the Wild West. Individual freedom and enterprise, in this heroic era, are shown developing reassuringly towards stability, security and an affluence confirmed by the spread of the railroads and the original construction of that monumental town clock in 1885.

For commentators such as Catherine Gallagher, these nostalgic recursions into more innocent or promising eras exhibit aspects of wish-fulfilment – almost myth – connecting 'the time-travel plot . . . with our collective ambitions to undo certain events in [the] national past'. Gallagher also offers a conveniently tidy synopsis of time-travel plots concerned, following closely the graphic explanation the Doc delivers in *Back to the Future II*. The plot of *Back to the Future*, Gallagher suggests, relies – like *The Terminator* – on 'a simple, two-track system', moving 'like a railroad train, backing up past the critical juncture and throwing a metaphorical switch that gives access to a new track while closing entry to the old one'.[92] Gallagher's retro-railroad and its alluring alternate tracks could be seen as still more widely representative of 'collective ambitions' – ones relevant not only to the national past of the USA. The huge popularity of the films concerned indicates the general appeal of looking back into the past – late in a century so shocked by wars, and so sceptical of modernity's onward progress – and imagining how its history might have been redirected along more congenial lines during the intervening years. A character in a later time-warping film, *Donnie Darko* (2001), sums up desires informing much cinematic time travelling when she wishes that 'we could go back in time and take all those hours of pain and darkness and replace them with something better'. Desires of this kind can be widely discerned in novels discussed earlier – particularly in the utopian visions in

---

[92] Gallagher, 'Undoing', in Newman et al., eds, *Time and the Literary*, 18–19.

Time's Arrow and *Slaughterhouse-Five* of history run backwards, like a reversed film. The central figure in *Slaughterhouse-Five*, Billy Pilgrim, even extrapolates his vision of the retrogressive war film to imagine 'Hitler turned into a baby', and history re-run all the way back to 'two perfect people named Adam and Eve'.[93]

Recollection of the Second World War in *Slaughterhouse-Five* further defines the appeal of utopian imagination of this kind. The novel describes the fire-bombing of Dresden as 'the greatest massacre in European history', and more destructive even than the obliteration of Hiroshima. After witnessing the bombing, Billy Pilgrim becomes permanently 'unstuck in time', frequently moving to and fro between different periods of his life (70, 23). This seems in one way a deliberately chosen tactic, realising his wish to 'ignore the awful times and concentrate on the good ones' (81). Yet it is also in part an involuntary or pathological response to trauma. Its hallucinatory nature is confirmed when Billy is helped by friendly aliens – interplanetary travellers who share a conviction, similar to J. W. Dunne's, that 'all moments, past, present and future, always have existed, always will exist' (25). Whether followed voluntarily or pathologically, Billy's flights from the trauma of recent history are shown as heavily dependent on the imagination of science fiction and its tricks with time. Overwhelmed by what they have witnessed at Dresden, Billy and his companion record that they were forced into 'trying to re-invent themselves and their universe', and that 'science fiction was a big help' (70). Their experience is paradigmatic of conclusions that can be drawn from the above survey of the genre. This can do only very partial justice to science fiction's achievements, even in the area of time travel considered.[94] It explores instead only the ways interests in this area paralleled some of those in narratives discussed earlier, matching their 'specular time' with spectacular forms of imagination and temporality. Freed from the 'external chronology' of a progressing yet doom-threatened century, this fantastic imagination facilitated Edenic dreams of travelling back onto tracks that might wholly have avoided its darkness and disasters.

---

[93] Kurt Vonnegut, *Slaughterhouse-Five, or the Children's Crusade: A Duty-dance with Death* (1969; London: Granada, 1970), 54, 55. Subsequent references are to this edition.

[94] For an account of the huge range of science fiction involving time travel, and scientific and philosophical issues involved, see Nahin, *Time Machines*. In another survey, *Time Travel*, Gleick notes how often late twentieth-century time-travel novels describe journeying into the past to eliminate Hitler and avoid the Second World War.

Time Lines and Chronologic Wounds

Set on another planet, Vladimir Nabokov's *Ada* (1969) in one way further exemplifies science fiction's concerns with time and the clock. These concerns are central to a philosophical treatise, entitled *The Texture of Time*, written by Nabokov's central character and summed up in the novel's fourth part. Warning against 'the confusion of temporal elements with spatial ones' and advocating 'Pure Time, Perceptual Time, Tangible Time' over 'numerical symbol' and 'clock-time', the treatise exhibits some close resemblances to the philosophy of Henri Bergson.[95] Shortly before completing it in July 1922 (though the date is defined according to the novel's slightly un-earthly calendar), its author gives three celebrated lectures on Bergson's work. His discussions also demonstrate familiarity with the ideas of Einstein and other contemporary thinkers including Samuel Alexander and J. W. Dunne. As this list of familiar names suggests – along with many other aspects of *Ada* – Nabokov's novel is only rather tenuously other-worldly, set on a planet which is at most a partially distorted mirror-image of Earth. *Ada* as a result has less in common with science fiction narratives than with some entirely terrestrial novels which reverse the trend discussed earlier – towards diminished antipathy to the clock in literature later in the twentieth century. Like *Ada*, though, the novels concerned do not present hostility to the clock as strictly contemporary. Instead, they look back on the earlier twentieth century, or examine periods further in the past in order to appraise the evolution of modernity and its troubling temporalities in the longer term.

These explorations of earlier periods offer ways of reconsidering and summing up several issues examined throughout this study. One of these, mentioned earlier in this chapter – and concerning geography as well as time and history – is the question of how far different paces in modernity's expansion imposed divergent temporal pressures on various regions of the world. Questions of this kind are central to Ahmet Hamdi Tanpinar's *The Time Regulation Institute* (*Saatleri Ayarlama Enstitüsü*, 1962). Tanpinar's novel examines conflicts between long-established traditions in Turkish life and more modern, secular views – ones supposedly extending from the work of 'Ahmet the Timely', an 'eminent seventeenth-century scholar' and 'the most important clock smith of his time'. Description of these

---

[95] Vladimir Nabokov, *Ada: or Ardor: A Family Chronicle* (1969; Harmondsworth: Penguin, 1980), 422, 423, 430.

conflicts contributes to a wider satire of Turkish bureaucracy, and Turkish life generally, during a period following the Great War when the country experienced social and industrial developments of a kind often affecting Western Europe decades earlier. These developments require nationwide acceptance, however reluctant, that 'progress begins with the evolution of the timepiece'; that 'work requires a certain mentality and a certain conception of time'; generally, that the measures of watches and clocks have become thoroughly 'pertinent in this day and age'.[96] Four decades after D. H. Lawrence's *The Rainbow* and *Women in Love*, Tanpinar's novel confirms how completely mechanisation and developing capitalist work practices depended on the imposition of measured, rationalised temporality – and how variously, historically, its constraints took hold of different areas around the globe.

Conflicts involved reappear in Salman Rushdie's *Midnight's Children* (1981), which illustrates a range of tensions between imperially imposed temporality and influences indigenous to countries colonialism sought to subjugate. In one way, Rushdie's narrator and his fellow 'midnight's children' are inescapably 'handcuffed to history', and to Western temporal measures, in consequence of their birth at a key moment in the demise of the British Empire – 'at the precise instant of India's arrival at independence' on 15 August 1947.[97] Marking this exactly defined moment's historical significance, 'clock-hands joined palms in respectful greeting' at the opening of *Midnight's Children* – as if folded together in prayer, like those of Fevvers's clock in *Nights at the Circus* (9). Yet neither the official time reverently defined by clock hands, nor history generally, in its official versions, prove reliable or congenial as the novel goes on. Time, instead, is inevitably 'an unsteady affair' in a country still moving towards full industrialisation (79). Fallible power supplies ensure that 'the speaking clock . . . tied to electricity, [is] usually a few hours wrong', unable to maintain 'the steady beat' of 'English-made . . . relentless accuracy' (106, 102). Rushdie's narrator magnifies and valorises unsteady, divergent temporalities of this kind, delivering an alternative history of post-Independence India enlivened by fantastic reimagining of actual events, firmly divorced from convention and 'relentless accuracy'. Straightforward or 'once upon a time' modes

---

[96] Ahmet Hamdi Tanpinar, *The Time Regulation Institute*, trans. Maureen Freely and Alexander Dawe (Harmondsworth: Penguin, 2014), 278, 259, 139, 310.

[97] Salman Rushdie, *Midnight's Children* (1981; London: Picador, 1982), 9. Subsequent references are to this edition.

of storytelling are mocked from the novel's opening line, its narrator relying instead on freewheeling anachronies based on 'memory ... saved from the corruption of the clocks' (38).

Anachronies figure just as comprehensively in the novel which first strongly developed magic realist styles of the kind Rushdie employs in *Midnight's Children* – Gabriel García Márquez's *One Hundred Years of Solitude* (*Cien Años de Soledad*, 1967). Márquez's celebrated opening sentence likewise mocks straightforward, once-upon-a-time modes – by looking not back but forward, towards the moment when, 'many years later, as he faced the firing squad, Colonel Aureliano Buendía was to remember that distant afternoon when his father took him to discover ice'.[98] Anticipated retrospection of this kind extends into elaborate temporal shifts throughout the novel, developing profusions of prolepsis, analepsis and often complex interminglings of both. Only in its last pages are these devices revealed as the work of a narrator who shares the view that time 'stumbled and had accidents and could therefore splinter and leave an eternalized fragment in a room' (322). Accordingly, he has 'not put events in the order of man's conventional time, but ... concentrated a century of daily episodes in such a way that they coexisted in one instant' (382). *One Hundred Years of Solitude* eventually indicates in this way that it shares postmodern preferences for replacing conventional forms of representation with 'specular time' – with self-evidently artificial reconstructions of otherwise-intractable chronologies and histories.

Yet Márquez's artifice in some ways does less to distract from history than to emphasise its influence. Complex, confused temporalities vividly dramatise the modern world's turbulent encroachment upon the rural community of Macondo, described at the novel's opening as almost wholly isolated and autonomous. Showing supposed progress impacting on a placid pre-modern community – much as Lawrence does in *The Rainbow*, or Lewis Grassic Gibbon in *A Scots Quair* (1932–4) – *One Hundred Years of Solitude* might have been aptly subtitled 'modernity comes to Macondo'. By presenting the changes concerned through the awed perspective of members of this community, Marquez surrounds the familiar paraphernalia of technology and the modern world – electric light, cinema, the telephone, railways, manufactured ice – with intriguing and provocative strangeness. Wonders more usually associated with myth and fantasy, meanwhile – magic

---

[98] Gabriel García Márquez, *One Hundred Years of Solitude*, trans. Gregory Rabassa (1970; Harmondsworth: Penguin, 1977), 7. Subsequent references are to this edition.

carpets, limitless clouds of butterflies, 'invisible globes on the other side of death' – are presented as altogether unremarkable and everyday (366).

These tactics – not unlike those of Michael Moorcock and J. G. Ballard in the short stories discussed earlier – open up a critical distance demanding detached, objective reassessment of modernity's values, and also of its established ordering of time. Throughout *One Hundred Years of Solitude*, the linear, forward movement of history is shown in conflict – once again, as in *The Rainbow*, or *A Scots Quair* – with Macondo's immemorially longstanding patterns of circularity; of repetition and recurrence through the generations. Despite Márquez's provision of a family tree at the beginning of the novel, in much of the narrative that follows generations of seemingly boundless Buendías – scarcely distinguished by minor variations in nomenclature – resist easy reduction to straightforward temporal succession. Modernity's linear, progressive measures subordinate lineal, familial patterns only gradually as the novel goes on. Recognising the eventual result as a 'progressive breakdown of time' – at any rate in its traditional forms – one of the older characters remarks that 'the years nowadays don't pass the way the old ones used to' (228). She notes regretfully that new imperatives mean, instead, that 'time passes . . . but not so much' (310).

Realism and 'magic', or fantasy, are also juxtaposed in Alasdair Gray's critique of modernity in *Lanark* (1981), though confined in different books of the novel, rather than freely intermingling in the manner of Márquez. Books 1 and 2 – which figure, in Gray's anachronous structure, as the novel's middle sections – offer a realistic account of life in Glasgow during the decade or so after the Second World War. Conditions at the time, in 'the sort of industrial city where most people live nowadays', remain consistent with those Georg Lukács analysed in the 1920s, or Guy Debord in the 1960s. They are summed up by the worker who explains that

> life becomes a habit. You get up, dress, eat, go tae work, clock in etcetera etcetera automatically, and think about nothing but the pay packet on Friday and the booze-up last Saturday. Life's easy when you're a robot.[99]

Forces conditioning this robotic, reified life are highlighted still more starkly in the novel's opening and closing sections, Books 3 and 4.

---

[99] Alasdair Gray, *Lanark: A Life in Four Books* (1981; London: Panther, 1984), 105, 216. Subsequent references are to this edition.

These describe futuristic, dystopian domains, 'The Institute' and 'Unthank', which are ultimately ruled – like the world William Gibson describes in *Neuromancer* – by multinational corporations, federated into 'a conspiracy which owns and manipulates everything for profit' (410).

Under their malign influence, many characters – including the 'Oracle' who ostensibly narrates the life of mid-twentieth-century Glasgow – believe only in money and numbers, as if in nightmare extension of the 'mathematization' which Adorno and Horkheimer considered a consequence of the project of modernity. Materialist, consumerist pressures are intensified by advertising campaigns in Unthank – by slogans promising that 'MONEY IS TIME. TIME IS LIFE. BUY MORE LIFE FOR YOUR FAMILY . . . THEY'LL LOVE YOU FOR IT' (454). Equations of this kind reflect a comprehensively commodified treatment of time, shaped around a 'decimal hour' and a 'decimal calendar based on the twenty-five hour day' (416, 452).[100] Attempts to resist this stringent temporality include the foundation in Unthank of a 'department of chronometry' – another 'Time Regulation Institute'. It seeks to restore the previous temporal system by refurbishing old clocks, rescued from museums, and ensuring that synchronised 'church towers with bells' disseminate their measures (452). Like George Orwell's *Nineteen Eighty-Four* (1949), which opens by describing 'clocks . . . striking thirteen', Gray's fantasy anticipates temporal controls stringent enough to encourage nostalgia, paradoxically, for 'the old duodecimal time scale', which had originally helped impose a robotic existence on the industrial city that *Lanark* depicts (372).

Gray also shows his eponymous hero seeking, understandably, to free himself completely from the constraining temporalities and profit-obsessed conspiracies he encounters, despite extraordinary difficulties involved. As in Hoyle's *October the First is Too Late*, in Gray's fantastic world 'every continent measures time by different calendars, so there is no means of measuring the time between them. A traveller . . . must cross a zone where time is a purely subjective experience' (79). Escaping from the Institute, Lanark and his partner Rima find themselves in just

---

[100] Reinstatement of decimal time-measurements of the kind introduced in post-revolutionary France – though for commercial reasons – was sometimes advocated by business interests early in the twentieth century, and again in the 1950s. See Baar, *La Réforme du Calendrier*. Its Preface sums up the view of an International Congress of Chambers of Commerce in 1910: that calendrical reform was 'a matter of gaining time, and therefore money'. See also Aveni, *Empires of Time*, 162–3.

such a zone – the 'Intercalendrical Zone'. Indeterminate in space and time, it is similar in its shifty, amorphous contours to Wyndham Lewis's landscape in *The Childermass*. Full of sand, wrecks and toadstools, it is obviously not a wholly liberating zone, though perhaps as close an approximation to pastoral values as a hyper-industrialised world can expect. It is also the location where Rima finds herself absorbed into a form of natural or 'women's time' – pregnancy – leading, later in the novel, to a new life which offers some tentative alternatives to the hyper-rationalised materialism of the Institute and Unthank.

Significantly, too, Lanark and Rima escape the Institute through a door marked 'EMERGENCY EXIT 3124' – just the order, of course, of the four books making up *Lanark* itself (376). References to time as 'a purely subjective experience' in one way recall modernist forms of resistance to the clock's stringent controls in the 1920s, developed through concentration on characters' freewheeling thoughts and memories. Yet in drawing attention to his own narrative structures – further highlighted by an author figure's explanation that *Lanark* should be 'read in one order but eventually thought of in another' – Gray offers temporal freedoms primarily available only to readers, rather than within the worlds the characters inhabit (483). *Lanark* deploys in this way another form of 'specular time', ostentatiously constructed through textual manipulations and reconfigurations. In a postmodernist fashion well established by the 1980s, the novel's many references to art and to its own devices ensure that these textual tactics are self-consciously highlighted throughout.

The increasingly robotic, automated nature of twentieth-century life is also a central concern of Thomas Pynchon's *V.* (1963). For one of its characters, Stencil – 'born in 1901 ... the century's child' – influences and agencies involved constitute not only a conspiracy of the kind Gray envisages, but no less than 'the century's master cabal'. The machinations of this cabal reach a climax – almost literally – when Mélanie l'Heuremaudit arrives in Paris to perform in a ballet featuring 'a remarkable innovation ... the use of automata'.[101] These strange clockwork creatures soon invade her dreams, which begin to include fantasises of being wound up with a key herself. They also figure in a developing relationship with the enigmatic lady V., whose treatment of Mélanie as a fetish – 'an inanimate object of desire' – extends her own 'progression toward inanimateness' (386, 385). This is described steadily advancing in the course of V.'s various

---

[101] Thomas Pynchon, *V.* (1963; New York: Bantam, 1973), 42, 210, 372. Subsequent references are to this edition. See also Chapter 1.

appearances, or conjectured appearances, in other episodes. One of the prosthetic devices progressively insinuating themselves into her body extends the implications of Melanie's second name – l'Heuremaudit, the accursed hour. V.'s 'glass eye with the iris in the shape of a clock' – containing 'delicately-wrought wheels, springs, ratchets of a watch, wound by a gold key' – is described as looking like 'the evil eye of time itself' (322, 219, 363). A precursor of Molly, in Gibson's *Neuromancer*, V. has installed measured, mechanised temporality as if within her vision itself, as a key part of her movement towards inanimacy and her fetishistic embrace of the machine.

Like Stencil, several characters emphasise that this movement is of symbolic rather than only personal significance. One of them worries in general about 'a decadence . . . a falling-away from what is human' in which 'we foist off the humanity we have lost on inanimate objects and abstract theories' (380). Another wonders if 'love for an object' might have 'been going on under the rose, maybe for longer and with more people than he would care to think about', accounting for disastrous misdirections throughout twentieth-century history, ultimately evidenced by 'corpses, stacked up like . . . car-bodies' at Auschwitz (14, 275). For Stencil, this *sub rosa* encroachment into the human sphere by objects – or by love for them – represents a 'conspiracy leveled against the animate world', threatening to establish within twentieth-century history 'a colony of the Kingdom of Death' (386). V.'s drift towards inanimacy, in this view, is both complicit with the wide range of historical crises the novel surveys, and indicative of their cause – evidence that

> sometime between 1859 and 1919, the world contracted a disease which no one ever took the trouble to diagnose because the symptoms were too subtle – blending in with the events of history, no different one by one but altogether – fatal. (433)

Obsessive or even paranoid elements in Stencil's outlook tend to diminish the credibility of this conclusion, suggesting that his views may reduplicate the shape of the novel's title – *V.* – in perversely narrowing everything down to a single point. Like the 'abstract theories' troubling another character, his convictions about a single cabal or conspiracy risk codifying too stringently the diverse history he surveys, inadvertently extending the deadening tendencies he fears. By encompassing political and colonial crises from the 1890s until the 1950s, the novel's own historical vision nevertheless demonstrates how comprehensively – if not exclusively – these deadening processes of reification and mechanisation were responsible for shaping the twentieth century, and how far an exact, measured temporality was essential for their operation.

In *Mason & Dixon* (1997), Pynchon develops an equally broad historical vision in examining the origins, during the Enlightenment period in the later eighteenth century, of many of the negative processes *V.* describes. Like several postmodern writers, Márquez included, in *Mason & Dixon* Pynchon focuses late twentieth-century scepticism of the project of modernity by examining its original emergence from a pre-modern world, along with conflicts between reason and contrary forms of thinking that this entailed. These conflicts affect the outlook even of the eponymous astronomer-surveyors themselves, diligently committed – usually – to employing 'the most modern means available' to enhance precision in celestial and cartographic measurement. This commitment is evidenced in their painstaking observations of the Transit of Venus, in 1762, and their rigorous testing of clocks developed with 'Minute-Scal'd Accuracy' to deal with the contemporary problem of determining longitudes at sea. Yet Mason and Dixon are also prepared to discuss astrology, cast horoscopes, and even flirt with belief in a talking dog and a time-travelling mechanical duck. Mason even considers that the eleven days excised from the calendar when it was corrected and updated in 1752 – a recent, painful, 'chronologick Wound' – might somehow be rediscovered and re-inhabited.[102]

Not surprisingly, the surveyors often find it necessary to remind themselves that they live in 'the Age of Reason' and work as devoted 'Men of Science' (27). These reminders become much more urgent when they seek to apply reason and science to the primal wildernesses of colonial America. Assured that 'the Behavior of the Stars' can be understood 'just as you'd read a Clock-Face', they use stellar-determined latitudes and longitudes to consolidate the disputed boundary between Maryland and Pennsylvania, marking out 'a line straight through the heart of the Wilderness' by felled trees and cleared undergrowth (342, 8). This attempt 'directed by the Stars,/To mark the Earth with geometrick Scars' places modernity into direct confrontation with immemorial beliefs and untamed nature, seeming to provoke 'something ancient, that waited for them' (257, 347). The wilderness and its scarred, outraged forests disgorge disturbing manifestations of entities reason sought to discredit – beings belonging to magic or superstition, such as the 'giant Golem, or Jewish Automaton, taller than the most ancient of the Trees', or the inexplicable, half-mythical presences looming along the native 'Warrior Path' (485, 646). This ancient, near-natural line of communication – where 'Distance is not the same... nor is Time' – intersects with mathematically exact

---

[102] Thomas Pynchon, *Mason & Dixon* (1997; London: Jonathan Cape, 1998), 182, 156, 555. Subsequent references are to this edition.

demarcations made by Mason and Dixon in ways sharply focusing the 'metaphysickal Encounter of Ancient Savagery with Modern Science' which concerns much of the novel (647, 650).

Mason & Dixon also shows modernity and science driven by worse savageries of their own. Extensive complicities link the surveyors' work with commercial, colonising factions seeking to exploit the new American territories and their inhabitants. Rapacious forces of this kind are also witnessed at work elsewhere in the world – in other colonies Mason and Dixon visit in order to observe the Transit of Venus, and in their British homeland. Dixon recalls that 'his journeyman years coincided with the rage then sweeping Durham for Enclosure' – with factions only too ready to ensure that his 'Lines of Ink . . . became Fences of Stone' (587). In these ways and others, *Mason & Dixon* illustrates how quickly, and how comprehensively, the 'most modern means' and 'Minute-Scal'd Accuracy' of the Enlightenment began to enclose, exploit and eventually commodify the natural world.

Sharing postmodern scepticisms particularly evident later in the twentieth century, this critical vision of the project of modernity also extends tensions with technology, and with reason itself, discernible in the century's literature more generally. Mason and Dixon's tormenting calculative difficulties in 'the running of a real Arc upon the not quite perfectly spherickal Earth' recall Conrad's toils with the geometry and mathematics of navigation during his early years (461). Mason's zany suggestion of determining longitude at sea by means of an 'Arrangement of Anchors and Buoys, Lenses and Lanthorns, forming a perfect Line across the Ocean' (712) recalls Conrad's enigmatic 'shadow-line', or even Stevie's wayward, meridian-parodying profusion of lines and circles in *The Secret Agent* (1907). The network of scars and boundary lines Mason and Dixon inscribe upon the earth also looks forward to conditions highlighted in *Lanark*. 'By the twentieth century', one of Gray's characters remarks, 'wealth has engrossed the whole globe, which now revolves in a tightening net of thought and transport woven round it by trade and science' (543). Much the same concern about a 'great global multinational and decentred communicational network' reappears in theoretical terms at many stages of Fredric Jameson's analysis in *Postmodernism, or, the Cultural Logic of Late Capitalism* (44).

Descriptions of scars upon the landscape in *Mason & Dixon* also anticipate France's celebrations of the millennium, three years after Pynchon's novel was published, in the *incroyable pique-nique* of July 2000, described at the start of the Introduction. France's choice of celebration may even have been influenced by a domestic Mason and Dixon story of its own, published ten years before Pynchon's novel. This appeared in Denis Guedj's *The Measure of the World* (*La Mesure du monde*,

1987), a fictionalised account of struggles experienced by the surveyors Méchain and Delambre – as challenging as those encountered by Mason and Dixon – in establishing the Paris meridian in post-revolutionary France during the turbulent 1790s. Marking the millennium by permanently inscribing this historic meridian on the landscape, France in any case returned to and re-evaluated much the same Age of Reason and revolution that Pynchon explores, and by means of just the sort of 'geometrick scar' that *Mason & Dixon* describes. Time-lines, chronologic wounds, and geometric scars beginning to trouble the late eighteenth century evidently continued to cut a swathe across imagination in the twentieth – variously intense, or painful, at different stages of the century, but still clearly influential at its end. Millennial reconsideration of the Age of Reason extended contemporary concerns with 'Adamic' facts – in this case, with ways measuring the world and the 'Clock-face' of the stars had originally begun to weave the 'net of thought and transport . . . trade and science' extending globally across postmodern times.

Fig. 6.2 The famous clock at the gates of Greenwich Observatory, with the Millennium Dome in the background, on the right. Unlike France, Britain did not place its millennial monument exactly on the Meridian, but a fraction of a degree to the east. By 2000, though, the meridian used in Global Positioning Systems had itself been relocated around a hundred metres to the east of the Observatory, compensating for minor irregularities in the distribution of mass within the Earth, influential on GPS satellite orbits.

Chapter 7

Conclusion: Millennial Times, Perennial Times

Not all the events surrounding the millennium were as celebratory as France's *incroyable pique-nique*. In one instance at least, they were thoroughly alarming. As the millennium approached, computer engineers predicted widespread problems when systems based on dates beginning in '19' had to move on to '2000'. This potential 'millennium bug' threatened a disastrous global zero hour, as the century turned, disrupting or arresting air traffic, telecommunications, banking, power supplies, the internet, satellites and military systems – any or all of the innumerable agencies dependent on computerised clocks and controls. As it turned out, amended programming eliminated problems almost entirely, suggesting the risks might have been overestimated. Concerns about the bug nevertheless highlighted how comprehensively the world and its technologies had come to depend on mechanical and electronic systems of enumerating time. Global communications, computers and the internet had begun to offer some freedom from the clock, Chapter 6 suggested, but the systems and technologies involved remained thoroughly – even dangerously – in its thrall.

Concerns about the bug contributed to wider apprehensions sometimes shadowing the last hours of 1999. 'Every New Year's Eve is impending apocalypse in miniature', Zadie Smith suggests in her end-of-the-century novel *White Teeth* (2000): the eve of a new millennium naturally occasioned particularly profound concerns about epochal change and an uncertain future.[1] Commentators often used W. B. Yeats's views of twenty centuries of the Christian era, in 'The

---

[1] Zadie Smith, *White Teeth* (London and New York: Penguin, 2000), 425.

Second Coming' (1921) – and of a contrary epoch which might succeed it – when looking nervously behind and ahead. 'Mere anarchy', increasingly evident in the twentieth century, seemed to add conviction to Yeats's apocalyptic vision of a worse period to follow, inaugurated not by some computer bug, but more grandiosely – when some 'rough beast, its hour come round at last,/Slouches towards Bethlehem to be born'.[2]

Anyone dreading a Yeatsian apocalypse nevertheless shared with computer programmers – and millions of revellers content simply to celebrate the millennium – a clear conviction that the stroke of midnight on 31 December 1999 constituted a defining moment in the world's experience. Commentators invoking Yeats seldom paused to wonder if 'mere anarchy' might not offer apocalyptic beasts a good excuse for turning up late, or early, or for not knowing the difference, or the correct place to appear. Any beast – even a rough one – could apparently be relied on to check the time before slouching off to its Bethlehem appointment, and to refer when doing so to the clock and calendar in general use, and not some alternative, beastly, ones of its own. Commentators on the millennium were also reluctant to recall James Joyce's representation, in *Ulysses* (1922), of 'the bissextile year one thousand nine hundred and four of the Christian era' as the 'jewish era five thousand six hundred and sixtyfour, mohameddan era one thousand three hundred and twentytwo'.[3] Nor was it often remembered that the millennium corresponded only to the undistinguished years 2749 in Babylonian dating, 5119 in Mayan reckoning, 6236 for the Egyptians, 208 for anyone still favouring the French revolutionary calendar – and an uncertain measure even for all those following the Christian one. As David Antin points out in *i never knew what time it was* (2004), unreliable calendrical computations – particularly regarding the date of Christ's birth – meant that 'finding the year two thousand is like painting a wave white in the middle of the sea and saying   lets gather there and celebrate'.[4]

Millennial celebrants' indifference to these uncertainties confirmed how unquestioningly life had come to be dominated – in the

---

[2] W. B. Yeats, *The Collected Poems of W.B. Yeats* (1950: London: Macmillan, 1971), 211.
[3] James Joyce, *Ulysses* (1922; Harmondsworth: Penguin, 1992), 780. Subsequent references are to this edition.
[4] David Antin, *i never knew what time it was* (Berkeley and Los Angeles: University of California Press, 2005), 91. The quotation reproduces the spelling and layout of Antin's text.

West, at any rate – by a single, defining enumeration of passing minutes, hours, days and years. Writing close to the beginning of the twentieth century, in 1912, Marcel Proust remained convinced that 'time is a numbering procedure that corresponds to nothing real'. A hundred years later, as one contemporary commentator on temporality concluded, this numbering procedure had instead become 'coextensive with the very fabric of existence itself', and – as another described – 'the clock ha[d] become one of the most taken-for-granted aspects of life in the Western World'.[5] Factors the previous chapter considered – including the West's growing recognition of alternative systems and cultures elsewhere – did allow reappraisal, relaxation, or just resignation regarding chronological controls over daily life. Yet the clock's enumerations remained so solidly and centrally the measure of this life as scarcely to be recognisable, any longer, as a system or 'numbering procedure' at all. By the millennium, the kind of distinctions Shakespeare's characters draw in *As You Like It* – between questions about the 'time o'day' and 'what is't o'clock' – had become almost unintelligible. Suggestions in *As You Like It* that would still have appealed to Proust – Rosalind's, that 'time travels in divers paces with divers persons', or Orlando's, that 'there's no clock in the forest' – might have seemed similarly irrelevant to the hectic, city-dominated life of the twenty-first century.[6]

Curing Time

After the millennium, novelists therefore continued – like their late-twentieth-century predecessors, though probably still more thoroughly – to lack easy access to the 'alternative temporality' that Fredric Jameson suggests modernist writers recalled from childhood or earlier experience, or even occasionally discerned still at work in their own period. Yet despite this lack, or perhaps in response to it, fiction

---

[5] Proust, letter to Madame Straus, October 1912, *Correspondance*, XI, 242; West-Pavlov, *Temporalities*, 5; Nanni, *Colonisation of Time*, 228.

[6] William Shakespeare, *As You Like It*, III, ii. The physics of Relativity suggests time does travel at diverse paces for different persons, and in diverse circumstances, though with very minute differentiations. Proust indicates clearer diversities in *À la recherche du temps perdu*, remarking that 'the internal time-pieces which are allotted to different human beings are by no means synchronised'. *Remembrance of Things Past*, trans. C. K. Scott Moncrieff and Terence Kilmartin (Harmondsworth: Penguin, 1983), III, 1035. Subsequent references are to this edition.

early in the twenty-first century did continue to challenge clock-based controls over life, and to explore ways they might be resisted. Some of these are assessed, later in this section, in the work of US writers who discern alternative temporalities still operating even within a highly rationalised, technologised society. Other authors, considered below, followed paths established by fiction discussed in Chapter 6, or even ones still extending from the modernist period. Julian Barnes's opening in *The Sense of an Ending* (2011) offers a kind of summary of modernist preferences. His narrator extols the 'malleability' of 'subjective time' and the ways 'some emotions speed it up, others slow it down'. He also emphasises its opposition to 'ordinary, everyday time, which clocks and watches assure us passes regularly: tick-tock'. Correspondingly, his narrative readily departs from straightforward chronology, presenting various 'shreds and patches' of memory instead. Following events apparently 'in no particular order', these memories unravel only gradually into what can be construed as a coherent version of his past.[7]

Memories unfold in comparable shreds and patches in W. G. Sebald's *Austerlitz* (2001). Its narrative follows the protracted process of self-discovery, late in the twentieth century, of a central figure, Austerlitz, tormented by 'a kind of heartache which, as [he] was beginning to sense, was caused by the vortex of past time'.[8] Gradually and tortuously, Austerlitz recognises that his life has been shaped and shadowed by suppressed recollections: of his Prague childhood; of his mother's arrest and murder by the Nazis; of his own escape, in a *kindertransport* train, towards a strange new life in Britain. Mystified yet mesmerised by this vortex in his past, Austerlitz reflects at length on the nature of time, especially as it is codified by clocks and timetables in the railway stations which seem to focus – initially inexplicably – the most disturbing of his submerged memories. The minute hand of the 'mighty clock ... resembled a sword of justice', Sebald's narrator observes when meeting Austerlitz in Antwerp station, noting the way it 'jerked forward, slicing off the next one-sixtieth of an hour from the future and coming to a halt with such a menacing quiver that one's heart almost stopped' (8–9). Reflecting on the railways' standardisation

---

[7] Julian Barnes, *The Sense of an Ending* (2011; London: Vintage, 2012), 3, 122, 105.
[8] W. G. Sebald, *Austerlitz*, trans. Anthea Bell (2001; Harmondsworth: Penguin, 2002), 182. Subsequent references are to this edition.

of time in the mid-nineteenth century, Austerlitz considers that the menacing 'hands and dial of the clock' offer a 'supreme' emblem of the priorities of 'capital accumulation' – dominating the period, yet indifferent to its 'social good' (13). Understandably, Austerlitz stresses that he has 'never owned a clock of any kind, a bedside alarm or a pocket watch, let alone a wristwatch'. Rather like Proust, he considers that the temporality these devices measure is 'by far the most artificial of all our inventions', and the clock a 'ridiculous . . . thoroughly mendacious object' (141, 143-4). During a visit to Greenwich Observatory, he extends this disdain over 'the ingenious observational instruments and measuring devices, quadrants and sextants, chronometers and regulators' on display there. He is similarly scathing about the 'imaginary, average sun' required by their use in navigation – scepticisms which Joseph Conrad might not have entirely shared, but would surely have understood (140, 142).

Austerlitz reflects equally extensively on the nature of memory, often meditating on its unsettling obscurities and powers. Recalling his interests in photography and the process of developing pictures, he remarks that

> the shadows of reality . . . emerge out of nothing on the exposed paper, as memories do in the middle of the night, darkening again if you try to cling to them, just like a photographic print left in the developing bath too long. (109)

The narrator shares his worries about 'how little we can hold in mind, how everything is constantly lapsing into oblivion with every extinguished life', and about how history likewise provides only 'images at which we keep staring while the truth lies elsewhere' (30-1, 101). Sebald's narrative strategies further emphasise the past's elusiveness. His inclusion in the novel of photographs and images the narrator and Austerlitz discuss offers, in one way, unusually direct contact with the shadowy memories their conversations seek to illumine. Yet the deferral of full understanding of remembered people and places – ultimately, of any complete explanation of past events – focuses attention principally on the fickle processes of memory itself. Its complexities are also highlighted by the sinuous, unravelling sentences – adding clause on clause, reflection on reflection, recollection on fleeting recollection – which seem habitual to the narrator and Austerlitz alike. More than 1,500 words long, in one case, such sentences suggest there may never be a period to the emotions and memories even of a single life such as Austerlitz's. Neither fiction, history, memory, nor language itself may be sufficient to hold in mind – whole and unaltered – truths always, inherently, partly fugitive; always engrained in experiences either vanished or somehow centred elsewhere. *Austerlitz* offers in this way reflections on the nature of time and memory sometimes as profound as Proust's, elaborated within a narrative structure of modernist temporal complexity. Its characters' difficulties in finding affirmative directions for memory to follow, and in confronting dark evolutions of history around the Second World War, also extend idioms of late twentieth-century fiction discussed in Chapters 5 and 6. Like Lawrence Norfolk or Graham Swift, Sebald moves towards a kind of black hole – towards invisible, irrecoverable areas of the past which it is essential, morally and historically, for the novel to examine, yet inevitably demand much self-conscious questioning of literature's powers of representation.

Austerlitz's attempts to recover an image of his mother include scrutiny of archived film from a Nazi camp, which he examines in ultra-slow motion, almost frame by frame. The episode resembles several in contemporary US novels, by authors including Ben Lerner and Don DeLillo, whose interests in film and video technology were mentioned in Chapter 6. Austerlitz's slow-motion search bears particular comparison with the interests of DeLillo's narrator in *Point Omega* (2010) – a film-maker fascinated by the 'radically altered plane of time' offered by a video installation, *24 Hour Psycho*, which stretches Alfred Hitchcock's thriller into a day-long slowed-down screening.[9] The conclusion he reaches after viewing some of it – that 'real time is meaningless' (146) – is emphasised elsewhere in *Point Omega* in terms familiar from modernism, or even from Orlando's claim in *As You Like It* that 'there's no clock in the forest'. Living in the desert, 'out beyond cities and scattered towns', the novel's central character extols a time that is 'enormous . . . that precedes and survives us' (22, 56). This time is distinct, he explains to the narrator, from 'minute-to-minute reckoning, the thing I feel in cities . . . hours and minutes, words and numbers everywhere . . . dimwit time, inferior time, people checking watches and other devices' (56–7). He concludes that 'cities were built to measure time, to remove time from nature', adding that 'this is the thing that literature was meant to cure' (57). Film, the narrator adds, should undertake the same curative function.

---

[9] Don DeLillo, *Point Omega* (London: Picador, 2010), 15. Subsequent references are to this edition.

The need for this 'cure' – for alternatives to 'dimwit time, inferior time' – is emphasised elsewhere in DeLillo's fiction. *Underworld* (1997) describes 'a kind of standoff between the time continuum and the human entity, our frail bundle of soma and psyche', concluding that the latter, 'our minds and bodies', constitute 'the only crucial clocks'.[10] In *Cosmopolis* (2003), DeLillo further examines hostilities between clock-time and nature, or 'human entity' – antipathies much extended, as Austerlitz considered, by the integral relation between measured time and 'capital accumulation'. This relation is closely analysed in a conversation between the billionaire boss of a business empire and his 'chief of theory', determined to elucidate for him the ways that 'money makes time' and that 'clock time accelerated the rise of capitalism'. Instead of 'thinking about eternity', she explains, 'people . . . began to concentrate on hours, measurable hours, man-hours, using labor more efficiently'. As a result, she concludes, 'time is a corporate asset now', and 'we need a new theory of time'.[11] Along with views in his other novels, this conclusion suggests that interests in temporality, though a minor concern of DeLillo's fiction, nevertheless add significantly to its exploration of stresses experienced within a highly technologised society, and of ways these might be avoided or transcended. The weird, almost unimaginable reliance of 'cyber-capital' on nanoseconds, or 'zeptosceonds . . . yoctoseconds', in *Cosmopolis*, or the apparently infinite malleability of cinematic temporality in *Point Omega*, might belong to some hesitant movement towards the 'new theory of time' mentioned, even towards the sublime (79). In each case, DeLillo stresses the immense impact of technological advances, yet indicates that their extraordinary powers may stimulate or enthral the very imagination they sometimes threaten to overwhelm.

Twenty-first-century fiction by another US author, Thomas Pynchon, provides a more extended scrutiny of temporal, technologic and economic pressures, and of ways these might be circumvented. *Against the Day* (2006) greatly expands Pynchon's assessment, discussed in Chapter 6, of ways these pressures affected earlier periods – mostly in the twentieth century, in *V.* (1963), and in the eighteenth, in *Mason & Dixon* (1997). The 1,000 pages of *Against the Day* examine a particularly crucial phase in the conversion of time into 'a

---

[10] Don DeLillo, *Underworld* (1997; London: Picador, 1998), 235.
[11] Don DeLillo, *Cosmopolis* (London: Picador, 2003), 77, 79, 86. Subsequent references are to this edition.

corporate asset', describing numerous instances, in the United States and elsewhere, of land and resources appropriated by 'capitalism and the Trusts' during the period from the 1890s to the 1920s.[12] Dedicated to the unswerving pursuit of productivity and profit, and wholly contemptuous of 'social good', these agencies are more than ready to convert time, through merciless management of labour and wages, into an entirely saleable or purchasable commodity. In opposing the rationalisations and oppressions involved, characters regularly offer some version of the view that

> watches and clocks are fine . . . but they are a sort of acknowledgement of failure, they're there to glorify and celebrate one particular sort of time, the tickwise passage of time in one direction only and no going back. (456–7)

As alternatives to 'no going back', and to 'the merciless clock-beat we all seek to escape', the novel explores 'many forms of time-transcendence, timelessness, counter-time, escapes and emancipations from Time' (558, 454). Some of these are mythic or spiritual, extending the interest in *Mason & Dixon* in esoteric forces, irrational and contrary, which gravitate around the surveyors' attempts to chart the wilderness. *Against the Day* develops throughout a comparable 'architecture of dream, of all that escapes the net-work of ordinary latitude and longitude', including shamanic or spiritualist visions of 'time . . . spread out not in a single dimension but over many' (250, 143).

Yet Pynchon also expands the concerns of *Mason & Dixon* into new areas, exploring not only realms beyond ordinary reason, but emancipatory potentials discoverable within rational thought and its products – particularly in the scientific theories about time and light which were developing at the end of the nineteenth century. Many of the period's leading scientists are imagined discussing ideas involved at a 'First International Conference on Time Travel', supposedly occurring in 1895, the year H. G. Wells published *The Time Machine* (412). Wells himself is among a list of conferees including – appropriately anachronistically – Niels Bohr, Ernst Mach and Albert Einstein.[13] The Cambridge philosopher John McTaggart is another delegate, resoundingly dismissing 'the *existence* of Time as really too

---

[12] Thomas Pynchon, *Against the Day* (London: Jonathan Cape, 2006), 147. Subsequent references are to this edition.
[13] Bohr would have been around ten years old at the time, and Einstein only sixteen.

ridiculous to consider, regardless of its status as a believed-in phenomenon' (412). During the conference proceedings – and the rest of the novel – the credibility of ordinary, 'believed-in' phenomena is often radically undermined, particularly by envisaging time travel as entirely viable, or as a logical development from contemporary mathematics and scientific theory.

Against the Day engages more decisively, in this way, with nearsublime potentials that Don DeLillo's fiction hints at – possibilities of somehow transcending negative forces of technology, in an increasingly rationalised world, through science and reason themselves. Pynchon's narrative strategies consolidate confidence in such possibilities. Credible scientific concepts and historical actualities are seamlessly intermingled with the 'realm of the counterfactual' (9). Excursions into diverse fields of knowledge, and freely anachronic alternation between periods and places, resist at the level of form the reductive, enclosing influences the novel describes darkening the years leading up to the Great War. The epic extent of some of Pynchon's sentences adds to such effects. Often as sinuous as Sebald's, their restless accumulation of clauses reflects the extravagant diversity of the novel's vision, along with its characters' fascination with experiences continually drawing their imaginations beyond the immediate and everyday. Such tactics offer an alternative or transcendent engagement with ordinary experience and temporality, opening depths and distances beyond its banal, 'tickwise' constraints. Even relatively insignificant episodes provide an expansive vision in this way: a sense of free flotation in life and time. Two characters merely parting at a ferry terminal, for example, nevertheless experience a 'profound opening' towards an 'entire darkened reach of what lay ahead', and therefore, poignantly, a heightened sense of all it might mean to 'never be here, never exactly here, again' (747). Through imaginative tactics of this kind – finding limitless potentials within every instant of the here-and-now – *Against the Day* thoroughly challenges twenty-first-century acceptance of clock-time as a 'believed-in phenomenon' and a 'taken-for-granted' part of everyday existence.

Winding up the Clock

Novels discussed in the previous section show antipathies to the clock's authority often extending after the millennium. They also help to identify the sources of these hostilities in the historical experience of the twentieth century, confirming their continued relation to factors outlined in previous chapters. Tracing forces rationalising life during the 1890s and the early decades of the new century, *Against the Day* highlights origins of the 'bondage' from which modernist authors sought to free their vision, innovatively and imaginatively, in the 1920s. Looking back towards the Second World War and the rise of fascism, *Austerlitz* indicates further historical pressures, troubling imagination from the 1930s onward and continuing to darken memory – or impede its functioning – in the latter decades of the century. *Cosmopolis* reintroduces the longer line of enquiry mentioned at the end of Chapter 6, retracing pressures shaping twentieth-century life and imagination towards origins involving much earlier historical stresses. This line of enquiry is worth pursuing further, as it can identify factors responsible not only for concerns with time in later fiction, but for the original development of the novel genre itself, at any rate in its modern form.

When explaining in *Cosmopolis* time's transformation into a corporate asset, DeLillo's 'chief of theory' refers to historical changes which prioritised 'measurable hours' over 'thinking about eternity'. These can hardly be identified at work exclusively in the twentieth century – from which faiths in eternity had mostly faded – and can be more plausibly attributed to the emergence of modernity during the Enlightenment 'Age of Reason' in the eighteenth. This emergence – explored in Pynchon's *Mason & Dixon* (1997) – also shared in the longer transitions from religion towards reason, and from faith in the divine towards reliance on human agency, which are traced over several centuries in Georges Poulet's *Studies in Human Time* (*Études sur le temps humain*, 1949). By the eighteenth century, Poulet suggests, God is 'no longer . . . the ruler', while in the human sphere 'continued existence is no longer continued by an act of divine creation . . . from the present moment God the creator and preserver is absent'.[14] This absence or 'retreat of God', as Poulet calls it, obviously negates any sense of comprehensive, preordained control over existence (19). It valorises individual will, instead, as the main determinant of a life now perceived as unfolding within 'human time', rather than a temporality which is eternal, unchangeable and divinely decreed. As Georg Lukács remarks in *The Theory of the Novel* (1971), time could 'become constitutive' in this way, within human experience, 'only when the bond with the transcendental home has been severed'.[15]

---

[14] Poulet, *Studies in Human Time*, 19.
[15] Lukács, *Theory of the Novel*, 122.

In one way, this increasingly secular, constitutive role for temporality offered new opportunities, including for literary imagination – expanding the sense of individuals' significance, and of their freedom to develop through personal action, will and choice. Yet these freedoms were matched in other ways by new restrictions, especially as modernity advanced and Enlightenment enthusiasm for reason, intelligence and invention extended into the technologies and productive practices facilitating the Industrial Revolution. As Chapter 3 described, 'measurable hours' quickly became an essential component of these practices, and a growing constraint on those involved in them. Large-scale manufacturing and its wage calculations inevitably demanded greater synchronisation of workers, as E. P. Thompson emphasises in his influential study of the period, 'Time, Work-Discipline, and Industrial Capitalism' (1967). As he describes, while demanding ever-greater regulation of the workforce, new factory processes also provided the means through which this control could be maintained – cheaper manufacturing of mechanical goods contributing to 'a general diffusion of clocks and watches' during the later eighteenth century. Easier availability gradually facilitated what Thompson describes as a shift 'from "luxury" to "convenience"', allowing less affluent householders, worried about new demands for punctuality, to rely not on some nearby church or town clock, but on timepieces installed in their own living-rooms, or even in their own pockets.[16]

Thompson's straightforward account of proliferating clocks and watches has been challenged or qualified by later historians. In *Shaping the Day* (2009), Paul Glennie and Nigel Thrift's wide-ranging research indicates that extensive temporal controls – based around privately owned clocks as well as public ones – were hardly altogether new in the mid-eighteenth century. On the contrary, their study suggests, these controls had permeated society fairly widely even before the period Thompson examines, though to variable extents within different working communities. There is nevertheless much evidence of a genuinely new scale and pervasiveness in the clock's influence on the period. This is apparent not only in social and economic aspects of contemporary life, but conceptual, philosophic and literary ones as well – ones in which the clock often figures as an image or symbol, as well as an agent, of new practices and changed ideas. As Poulet remarks, 'for the Newtonian materialist of the eighteenth century', persuaded of the 'retreat of God',

---

[16] Thompson, 'Time, Work-Discipline, and Industrial Capitalism', 69.

the world in general appeared 'like the clock of Strasbourg ... so ingeniously constructed that once it starts running it keeps going by sole virtue of the interaction of its works' (19). As Poulet suggests, and other commentators on the period confirm, this analogy of world and clock became widely inscribed in contemporary literature and thought.[17] Developed in late seventeenth-century philosophy – including John Locke's *Essay Concerning Human Understanding* (1689), which refers to the Strasbourg clock – it reappears in Samuel Johnson's writing, and in Henry Fielding's image, in his novel *Tom Jones* (1749), of the world 'as a vast machine', comprised of intricately interconnecting wheels.[18]

Writers by the mid-eighteenth century, Fielding included, were therefore confronted by sharply antithetical influences, following the retreat of God – by a greater sense of the individual's freedom and potential, yet also the threat of increasingly stringent, mechanistic controls constraining society and working life. Stresses concerned help to account for the emergence of the novel genre itself – at any rate in the forms which became familiar in Anglophone literature – which critics often discern occurring around this period. Tensions between freely independent self-determination and awareness of the clock's measures and constraints are ones the novel is particularly equipped to negotiate, and might indeed have been invented to resolve. As Ian Watt describes in *The Rise of the Novel* (1957), the genre is especially suited to detailed, realistic description and extended representation of action, choice and development within individual lives. Yet it also has the capacity to depart from reality in the crucial way that Chapter 1 discussed, amending the banal, measured passage of hours and days by means of imagination, vision and desire. Reshaping of this kind is obviously as much essential as desirable, allowing the realistic representation of experience within

---

[17] See, for example, Ian Donaldson, 'The Clockwork Novel', 14–22. A clock of celebrated complexity was installed in Strasbourg Cathedral in the mid-fourteenth century, replaced around 200 years later by one featuring further automata, dials, globes and displays of astronomical data. Like many early cathedral clocks, its function was as much to represent the order of the cosmos as to indicate the time of day. The Strasbourg clock also exemplifies longstanding connections between the manufacture of clocks and of automata – ones still explored in the twenty-first century in Martin Scorsese's film *Hugo* (2011), for example, and Peter Carey's novel *The Chemistry of Tears* (2012).
[18] Henry Fielding, *The History of Tom Jones* (1749; Harmondsworth: Penguin, 1973), 212. Subsequent references are to this edition.

the manageable, abbreviated form of the novel; concentrating the sprawling plenitude of characters' lives within selected significant episodes and an acceptable overall length.

Comments on this capacity for concentration and abbreviation, within eighteenth-century fiction itself, suggests that authors were well aware of its importance for the newish genre of the novel – though still hesitant about deploying its potentials, and consequently anxious to discuss them with readers. Describing himself as 'the founder of a new province of writing', Henry Fielding famously explains that the narrative of *Tom Jones* – *The History of Tom Jones*, to give it its full original title – will not 'keep even pace with time', and that

> my reader is . . . not to be surprised, if, in the course of this work, he shall find some chapters very short, and others altogether as long; some that contain only the time of a single day, and others that comprise years; in a word, if my history sometimes seems to stand still, and sometimes to fly. (87, 88)

Equally celebrated discussions of novelistic method appear in Laurence Sterne's *The Life and Opinions of Tristram Shandy* (1759–67). The novel's self-scrutinies figure extensively enough to suggest Sterne is concerned almost as much with the theory of fiction as its practice, sharing interests and even terminologies still preoccupying Gérard Genette's narratology two centuries later. Like Genette, Tristram's father discusses 'the subject of *duration and its simple modes*', while the novel's extravagant digressions repeatedly demonstrate the immense durational gulfs which can be developed between *fabula* and *sjuzet*. These are highlighted when Tristram realises, in his fourth volume, that in describing rather less than his first full day of life, his narrative has already taken a year to produce, indicating that he 'live[s] 364 times faster' than he writes. Yet this alarming reflection scarcely diminishes his narrative's digressive reliance on '*the succession of our ideas*', nor its disdain for the contrary constraints of clocks, equipped only to 'measure out their several portions to us', in units of 'minutes, hours, weeks and months'.[19]

The depths of this disdain – and some of its origins – are memorably emphasised on the first page of *Tristram Shandy*. This records that

---

[19] Laurence Sterne, *The Life and Opinions of Tristram Shandy* (1759–67; Harmondsworth: Penguin, 1974), 199, 286, 200. Sterne's italics.

Tristram's conception only narrowly avoids being fatally interrupted by his mother's reminder about winding up the clock – a monthly duty discharged by his father with exactly the same regularity as his conjugal obligations. In 'Time, Work-Discipline, and Industrial Capitalism', Thompson records that Sterne's opening scene in *Tristram Shandy* acquired such fame, or notoriety, that the phrase 'sir, will you have your clock wound up' soon became a solicitation regularly employed by prostitutes (57). Associations of clock-winding with sexual intercourse apparently became so commonplace, Thompson indicates, that prudish householders were inclined to remove all timepieces from their living-rooms, in order to eliminate guests' lewd jokes and laughter. Literary imagination, in other words, may have encouraged the removal of the clock from eighteenth-century living spaces at just the same time that economic and social factors were demanding, ever more forcibly, its installation within them.

Though in a way simply strange, sexy and hilarious, this consequence of Sterne's imagination can also be considered emblematic of potentials inherent in the novel from its inception, and extended throughout later centuries of its development. If 'winding up' is understood to include late twentieth- and twenty-first-century connotations of mockery or teasing, then 'winding up the clock' might provide a suitable definition of the novel's operations generally – or an apt subtitle for the present study. No other genre depends so comprehensively on temporality – on following extensively the evolution of lives through time. Yet as Fielding and other novelists early recognised, literary representation of this evolution also makes it more or less essential, in W. H. Auden's phrase, to 'mock/The formal logic of the clock'.[20] As a result, for centuries, as Paul Ricoeur remarks, the novel has offered 'a prodigious workshop for experiments in the domains of composition and the expression of time'.[21] Twentieth-century fiction's readiness to 'wind up the clock' significantly extends that workshop's resources, but in ways already inherent in the conditions of the novel's emergence, in its modern form, two centuries earlier. Fielding's image of the world as a 'vast machine' is echoed in Gudrun's vision of individuals as 'pure machines ... that work like clockwork ... parts of a great machine' at the end of D. H. Lawrence's *Women in Love* (1921).[22]

---

[20] W. H. Auden, 'New Year Letter' (1940), *W. H. Auden: Collected Poems*, ed. Edward Mendelson (London: Faber and Faber, 1976), 169.
[21] Ricoeur, *Time and Narrative*, II, 8.
[22] D. H. Lawrence, *Women in Love* (1921; Harmondsworth: Penguin, 1971), 524.

Tactics that Fielding and Sterne invented for escaping the machinery of clockwork temporality likewise continue to develop in the work of Lawrence's modernist contemporaries, and to an extent in fiction generally, later in the twentieth century and in the twenty-first.

Watches, Waves and the Wilderness

If twentieth-century 'experiments in . . . the expression of time' can be seen to extend from those of the eighteenth, mightn't their origins be retraced yet further, into the attitudes and literary strategies of still earlier periods? Many commentators consider that they might, often making broad comparisons with *carpe diem* themes – regretting time's devouring of youth and opportunity – familiar from the poetry of Andrew Marvell, or Edmund Spenser's 'Mutability Cantos' (1609), or Shakespeare's Sonnets, among many other examples. Jonathan Sawday's work suggests more specific resemblances, analysing literary responses to the spreading influences of clocks and watches, even in the sixteenth and seventeenth centuries, and their contribution to a 'decisive shift in the everyday rhythms of life' at the time.[23] Numerous critics have also assessed conflicting visions of temporality and the clock Shakespeare presents in *As You Like It* – or in Prince Hal's argument with Falstaff about the time of day in *Henry IV* – or have followed Stephen Spender in examining complex attitudes to chronology and history in *Macbeth*. Comparable attitudes and conflicts could even be retraced much further – beyond the two millennia of the Christian era altogether, back as far as the life and literature of ancient Rome. Sundials, according to Roman historians, were widely introduced during the third century BCE.[24] Towards its end, their influence had apparently begun to provoke resentments of a kind still eerily familiar to modern readers – on the evidence, at any rate, of the following passage from *The Boeotian Women*, a play attributed to Plautus:

> The gods confound the man who first found out
> How to distinguish hours! Confound him, too,
> Who in this place set up a sun-dial
> To cut and hack my days so wretchedly
> Into small portions! When I was a boy,
> My belly was my only sun-dial, one more sure,

---

[23] Sawday, *Engines of the Imagination*, 76.
[24] See Landes, *Revolution in Time*, 393.

> Truer, and more exact than any of them.
> This dial told me when 'twas proper time
> To go to dinner, when I had aught to eat;
> But nowadays, why even when I have,
> I can't fall to unless the sun gives leave.
> The town's so full of these confounded dials
> The greatest part of the inhabitants,
> Shrunk up with hunger, crawl along the streets.[25]

Plautus's lines recall, and refute, the opinion Proust recorded in 1922 in *À la recherche du temps perdu* – that 'the necessity of not missing trains has taught us to take account of minutes, whereas among the ancient Romans . . . the notion not only of minutes but even of fixed hours barely existed' (II, 853). At least where fixed hours were concerned, rigorous time measurement may have seemed as intrusive to the Romans as it did to inhabitants of Proust's modernist period. Plautus's conflict between belly and sundial anticipates Quentin's tangled reflections, in William Faulkner's *The Sound and the Fury* (1929), on 'space and time confused Stomach saying noon brain saying eat o'clock'. Timepieces which 'cut and hack . . . days so wretchedly' resemble just as clearly the 'shredding and slicing, dividing and subdividing' clocks Virginia Woolf describes in *Mrs Dalloway* (1925). Plautus's 'confounded dials' likewise recall the infuriated 'confound it all' Woolf's heroine exclaims when the hour strikes in *Orlando* (1928).[26]

Conflicts of the kind *Orlando* defines, between 'time on the clock and time in the mind' – or in the belly – thus extend in one form or another across a very long history (69). Corresponding to profound divisions between intuition and calculation, continuity and division – even quality and quantity – such antinomies may be inherent, or perennial, within consciousness itself, perhaps even reflecting biases within different hemispheres of the brain. In view of this fundamental or apparently perennial aspect in temporal tensions, what implications might be extended over the analyses of twentieth-century fiction offered in earlier chapters? Affirmative ones, generally. The longevity of tensions concerned confirms their centrality in human experience, and, consequently, the importance of analysing their influence

---

[25] Aulus Gellius, *Attic Nights*, III, iii, vol.1, 247.
[26] William Faulkner, *The Sound and the Fury* (1929; Harmondsworth: Penguin, 1971), 97; Virginia Woolf, *Mrs Dalloway* (1925; Harmondsworth: Penguin, 1976), 113; Virginia Woolf, *Orlando* (1928; Harmondsworth: Penguin, 1975), 216. Subsequent references are to this edition.

on literature – particularly in their fundamental, constitutive role within the novel. The perennial, constitutive nature of this literary role, moreover, need not distract from identifying the particularity of its operation in specific historical periods. The particular characteristics and nature of this operation can be readily identified through the kind of historicised analyses of twentieth-century temporalities earlier chapters offer. The potential of analysis of this kind – reciprocally illuminating history, along with imaginative, literary responses to its stresses – might also suggest scope for its further deployment within critical discussion of the novel. It seems improvident, for example, that a century of commentary on Conrad's work – though often considering the imaginative stimulus of years at sea – acknowledges so rarely the competence in navigation his maritime career demanded, or the likely effects on his writing of the calculative expertise he had to acquire.

Ways of extending critical attention to practical, material, historical conditions of this kind – and to their shaping influence on literature – have been persuasively outlined by commentators such as Fredric Jameson, discussed in Chapter 1. Steven Connor adds support to Jameson's views when he recommends the 'many advantages' to be gained by 'asking what narrative ... *does*' – a question which can 'help to restore narrative to history in a way that does not make it merely the mirror or register of historical events'.[27] Many advantages can of course also be found simply by noting attitudes to the clock – and to time's passage and the events of contemporary history – which *are* directly registered or 'mirrored' in fiction. Chapter 1 indicated this potential, also developed in those that followed. Yet as that chapter suggested, and Connor confirms, there are additional gains to be made through asking what literature *does* to resolve or contain temporal stresses – often, as Jameson suggests, by reshaping them into alternative visions and resistive narrative forms. Conrad once again offers a good illustration of processes involved. His fiction emphasises directly the worldwide influence of Greenwich-based temporalities, in 'Karain' (1897) or *The Secret Agent* (1907), but also resists their imposition covertly, through extended anachronies typical of modernist narrative form.

Emphases and resistances of this kind might be identified in the writing of any epoch, given the perennial nature of temporal stresses

---

[27] Connor, *The English Novel in History*, 4. Jameson draws a similar distinction – between asking 'the text what it *means*' and 'how it *works*' – in *The Political Unconscious*, 108.

outlined above. Their analysis is nevertheless especially relevant to fiction in the post-eighteenth-century age of modernity, and in the twentieth and twenty-first centuries especially. Technologies, industries, wars, working conditions, and the accelerating pace of life all accentuated gaps between belly, heart or mind and the measured hour, or between the 'enormous' time DeLillo identifies in the natural world, and 'cities . . . built to measure time, to remove time from nature'. Pressures concerned might have been expected eventually to remove altogether the sense of 'natural time, the time dictated by the sun's progress through the heavens' – a sense that commentators had considered steadily suppressed ever since the railway network spread across the landscape of the nineteenth century.[28] Instead, it was often through celebrating unsullied reaches of wilderness or ocean that fiction highlighted its opposition to the clock: its sense of threats to natural time – within or beyond the 'soma and psyche' of 'human entity' – as 'the thing that literature was meant to cure'.

Contrasts and oppositions involved remain evident in early twenty-first-century novels such as DeLillo's *Point Omega*. As the examples that follow suggest, they were very widely apparent in literature for more than a century previously. In William Faulkner's 'The Bear' (1942), the 'green and soaring gloom of the markless wilderness' is accessible to a hunter only after he relinquishes his watch and compass. He removes 'the linked chain of the one and the looped thong of the other from his overalls' and hangs them both on a nearby bush. His gesture recalls Captain Brierly, in Conrad's *Lord Jim* (1900), checking the compass then signalling his abandonment of orderly shipboard life by hanging his chronometer from the ship's rail, suspended over the eternal, anarchic sway of the sea. 'Ticking off steadily the seconds of Greenwich Time' in 'Karain' (1897), the ship's chronometers resist the night's turbulence, but cannot altogether suppress its romance: its 'noiseless phantoms' and 'invisible presences'. Weary anticipation of hearing 'the alarmclock next door at cockshout', at the end of *Ulysses*, is soon submerged in Molly's romantic recollections of 'nature the wild mountains then the sea and the waves rushing' – of oceanic infinitudes opening out beyond the measurable world (930–1). In *The Waves* (1931), Woolf likewise seeks in the sea's ceaseless undulation a rhythm alternative and ulterior to the measured temporality of the clock. The seaborne 'tolling bell/ . . . rung by the unhurried/Ground swell', in the third of T. S. Eliot's *Four Quartets*, *The Dry Salvages*

---

[28] Richards and Mackenzie, *The Railway Station*, 94.

(1941), represents another limitless 'time not our time', a 'time/Older than the time of chronometers'. In *Mason & Dixon*, Pynchon's profligate imagination constructs an intimate seaside conversation between two clocks – ones which

> stood side by side, set upon a level Shelf, as just outside, unceasingly, the Ocean beat . . . what they wanted to talk about, all along, was the Ocean . . . neither Clock really knows what it is, – beyond an undeniably rhythmick Being of some sort.[29]

Incomprehension, or incompatibility, alienating Pynchon's clocks from the adjacent ocean, sums up an archetypal incongruence pervading the other instances quoted above – between chronometry and natural domains beyond any network or system of measurement and calculation. In the hundred years between the publication of 'Karain' and of *Mason & Dixon* – and still in the twenty-first century – much fictional narrative can be understood in terms of what it does to register and resolve the profound antinomies involved. Though appearing only intermittently in the primal mode exemplified above, the stresses concerned deeply inform the novel's negotiation with modern life and history, and its authors' ever-urgent desires, in every sense, to wind up the clock.

---

[29] William Faulkner, 'The Bear', *Go Down, Moses and Other Stories* (1942; Harmondsworth: Penguin, 1972), 158; Joseph Conrad, 'Karain: A Memory' (1897), in *Heart of Darkness and Other Tales* (Oxford: Oxford University Press, 2002), 56; T. S. Eliot, *The Poems of T. S. Eliot*, vol. 1, *Collected and Uncollected Poems*, ed. Christopher Ricks and Jim McCue (London: Faber and Faber, 2015), 194; Thomas Pynchon, *Mason & Dixon* (1997; London: Vintage, 1998), 121, 123.

Bibliography

Critical and background material referred to in brief in the footnotes is listed in full below, along with further studies useful to this volume, or of interest in pursuing areas it examines.

Adam, Barbara, *Timewatch: The Social Analysis of Time* (Cambridge: Polity, 1995).
Adorno, Theodor, 'Commitment' (1962), *Marxist Literary Theory: A Reader*, ed. Terry Eagleton and Drew Milne (Oxford: Blackwell, 1996).
— 'Trying to Understand *Endgame*' (1961), *New German Critique*, 26, Spring/Summer 1982.
— and Max Horkheimer, *Dialectic of Enlightenment*, trans. John Cumming (1973; London: Verso, 1992).
Ainsley, Thomas L., *A Guide Book to the Local Marine Board Examination: The Ordinary Examination* (London: Simpkin, Marshall & Co., 1880).
Aldiss, Brian W., with David Wingrove, *Trillion Year Spree: The History of Science Fiction* (London: Gollancz, 1986).
Alexander, Samuel, *Space, Time, and Deity: The Gifford Lectures at Glasgow: 1916–18*, 2 vols (London: Macmillan, 1920).
Allingham, William, *Board of Trade Examinations: Shipmasters' Society Papers,* No. 67 (London: Pewtress, 1900).
Alston, Alfred Henry, *Captain Alston's Seamanship*, new edn, revised and enlarged by Commander R. H. Harris (Portsmouth: Griffin; London: Simpkin, Marshall & Co., 1871).
Apollonio, Umbro, ed., *Futurist Manifestos* (London: Thames and Hudson, 1973).
Ardoin, Paul, S. E. Gontarski and Lacy Mattison, *Understanding Bergson, Understanding Modernism* (New York: Bloomsbury, 2013).
Armstrong, Tim, *Modernism: A Cultural History* (London: Polity, 2005).
Aulus Gellius, *The Attic Nights of Aulus Gellius*, 3 vols, trans. John C. Rolfe (London: William Heinemann, 1927).
Aveni, Anthony F., *Empires of Time: Calendars, Clocks, and Cultures* (London: Tauris, 1990).

Baar, Armand, *La Réforme du Calendrier* (Liège: Charles Desoer, 1912).
Bailes, Kendall E., 'Alexei Gastev and the Soviet Controversy over Taylorism, 1918–24', *Soviet Studies*, 29 (3), 1977.
Baker, Stephen, *The Fiction of Postmodernity* (Edinburgh: Edinburgh University Press, 2000).
Bakhtin, Mikhail, *The Dialogic Imagination: Four Essays*, ed. Michael Holquist, trans. Caryl Emerson and Michael Holquist (Austin: University of Texas Press, 1981).
Bal, Mieke, *Narratology: Introduction to the Theory of Narrative*, 2nd edn (Toronto: University of Toronto Press, 1997).
Baldick, Chris, *Literature of the 1920s: Writers Among the Ruins* (Edinburgh: Edinburgh University Press, 2012).
— *The Oxford English Literary History*, vol. 10, *1910–1940: The Modern Movement* (Oxford: Oxford University Press, 2009).
Banfield, Ann, 'Time Passes: Virginia Woolf, Post-Impressionism and Cambridge Time', *Poetics Today*, 24 (3), 2003.
Barthes, Roland, *Œuvres complètes*, 2 vols, ed. Éric Marty (Paris: Éditions du Seuil, 2002).
Bender, John, and David E. Wellerby, *Chronotypes: The Construction of Time* (Stanford: Stanford University Press, 1991).
Benjamin, Walter, *Illuminations*, ed. Hannah Arendt, trans. Harry Zohn (New York: Schocken Books, 1968).
Bergson, Henri, *Creative Evolution*, trans. Arthur Mitchell (London: Macmillan, 1911).
— *Duration and Simultaneity: Bergson and the Einsteinian Universe*, ed. Robin Durie, trans. Leon Jacobson (Manchester: Clinamen Press, 1999).
— *La Perception du Changement: Conférences a l'Université d'Oxford* (Oxford: Clarendon Press, 1911).
— *Laughter (Le Rire): An Essay on the Meaning of the Comic*, trans. Cloudesley Brereton and Fred Rothwell (London: Macmillan, 1935).
— *Mind-Energy: Lectures and Essays*, trans. H. Wildon Carr (London: Macmillan, 1920).
— *Time and Free Will: An Essay on the Immediate Data of Consciousness*, trans. F. L. Pogson (1910; London: Allen and Unwin, 1971).
Blaise, Clark, *Time Lord: Sir Sandford Fleming and the Creation of Standard Time* (London: Orion, 2001).
Blotner, Joseph, *Faulkner: A Biography* (New York: Random House, 1984).
Borges, Jorge Luis, *Other Inquisitions, 1937–1952*, trans. Ruth L. C. Simms (London: Souvenir Press, 1973).
Bowen, Elizabeth, 'The Bend Back', *Cornhill Magazine*, 165, 1951.
Boxall, Peter, *Twenty-First-Century Fiction: A Critical Introduction* (Cambridge: Cambridge University Press, 2013).
Brake, Mark, and Neil Hook, 'Aliens and Time in the Machine Age', *International Journal of Astrobiology* 5 (4), 2006.

Brendon, Piers, *Thomas Cook: 150 Years of Popular Tourism* (London: Secker and Warburg, 1991).
Bridgeman, Tess, 'Time and Space', *The Cambridge Companion to Narrative*, ed. David Herman (Cambridge: Cambridge University Press, 2007).
Brooker, Joe, *Literature of the 1980s: After the Watershed* (Edinburgh: Edinburgh University Press, 2010).
Brooks, Peter, *Reading for the Plot: Design and Invention in Narrative* (Oxford: Clarendon Press, 1984).
Budgen, Frank, *James Joyce and the Making of Ulysses* (London: Grayson and Grayson, 1934).
Campbell, SueEllen, 'Equal Opposites: Wyndham Lewis, Henri Bergson, and their Philosophies of Space and Time', *Twentieth Century Literature*, 29 (3), 1983.
Canales, Jimena, *The Physicist and the Philosopher: Einstein, Bergson and the Debate that Changed Our Understanding of Time* (Princeton: Princeton University Press, 2015).
Carle, Donald de, *British Time* (London: Crosby, Lockwood and Son, 1947).
Carr, David, *Time, Narrative and History* (Bloomington: Indiana University Press, 1986).
Colletti, Lucio, *Marxism and Hegel*, trans. Lawrence Garner (London: Verso, 1979).
Connor, Steven, *The English Novel in History: 1950–1995* (London: Routledge, 1996).
— *Postmodernist Culture: An Introduction to Theories of the Contemporary* (Oxford: Blackwell, 1989).
Conrad, Joseph, *The Collected Letters of Joseph Conrad*, 9 vols, ed. Frederick R. Karl, Laurence Davies, Owen Knowles, J. H. Stape and Gene M. Moore (Cambridge: Cambridge University Press, 1993–2007).
— *Last Essays*, ed. Harold Ray Stevens and J. H. Stape (Cambridge: Cambridge University Press, 2010).
— *The Mirror of the Sea* and *A Personal Record*, ed. Zdzisław Najder (Oxford: Oxford University Press, 1988).
Cowley, Malcolm, ed., *Writers at Work: The 'Paris Review' Interviews*, second series (London: Secker and Warburg, 1963).
Crosthwaite, Paul, *Trauma, Postmodernism, and the Aftermath of World War II* (Basingstoke: Palgrave Macmillan, 2009).
Currie, Mark, *About Time: Narrative, Fiction and the Philosophy of Time* (Edinburgh: Edinburgh University Press, 2007).
— *Postmodern Narrative Theory* (London: Macmillan, 1998).
— *The Unexpected: Narrative Temporality and the Philosophy of Surprise* (Edinburgh: Edinburgh University Press, 2013).
Danius, Sara, *The Senses of Modernism: Technology, Perception, and Aesthetics* (New York: Cornell University Press, 2002).

Darwin, Charles, *On the Origin of Species: by means of Natural Selection of the Preservation of Favoured Races in the Struggle for Life* (1859; London: John Murray, 1902).
Debord, Guy, *The Society of the Spectacle*, trans. Donald Nicholson-Smith (New York: Zone, 1995).
Deming, Robert H., ed., *James Joyce: the Critical Heritage*, 2 vols (London: Routledge and Kegan Paul, 1970).
Docherty, Thomas, ed., *Postmodernism: A Reader* (Hemel Hempstead: Harvester Wheatsheaf, 1993).
Donaldson, Ian, 'The Clockwork Novel: Three Notes on an Eighteenth-Century Analogy', *Review of English Studies* (New Series), XX1, 1970.
Dunne, J. W., *An Experiment with Time* (1927; London: Faber and Faber, 1934).
— *'Intrusions?'* (London: Faber and Faber, 1955).
— 'Serialism – A New Theory of the Universe – II', *The Listener*, 24 September 1930.
— *The Serial Universe* (1934; London: Scientific Book Club, 1942).
Eagleton, Terry, and Drew Milne, eds, *Marxist Literary Theory: A Reader* (Oxford: Blackwell, 1996).
Eliot, T. S., *The Letters of T. S. Eliot*, ed. Valerie Eliot and Hugh Haughton, vol.1, 1898–1922 (London: Faber, 2009).
— *Selected Prose of T. S. Eliot*, ed. Frank Kermode (London: Faber, 1975).
Ellmann, Richard, *Ulysses on the Liffey* (London: Faber and Faber, 1974).
Engels, Frederick, *The Condition of the Working Class in England: From Personal Observation and Authentic Sources* (1845; London: Panther, 1972).
Erdinast-Vulcan, Daphna, '"Sudden Holes in Space and Time": Conrad's Anarchist Aesthetics in *The Secret Agent*', in Gene M. Moore, ed., *Conrad's Cities: Essays for Hans van Marle* (Amsterdam: Rodopi, 1992).
Evers, Liz, *It's About Time: From Calendars and Clocks to Moon Cycles and Light Years – A History* (London: Michael O'Mara, 2013).
Felski, Rita, *Doing Time: Feminist Theory and Postmodern Culture* (New York: New York University Press, 2000).
Ferguson, Trish, ed., *Victorian Time: Technologies, Standardisations, Catastrophes* (Basingstoke: Palgrave Macmillan, 2013).
Ferrebe, Alice, *Literature of the 1950s: Good, Brave Causes* (Edinburgh: Edinburgh University Press, 2012).
Ford, Ford Madox, *Joseph Conrad: A Personal Remembrance* (London: Duckworth, 1924).
Forster, E. M., *Aspects of the Novel* (1927; Harmondsworth: Penguin, 1971).
Foucault, Michel, 'Of Other Spaces' (1967), *Diacritics* 16 (1), Spring 1986.
Frank, Adam, *About Time: From Sun Dials to Quantum Clocks. How the Cosmos Shapes Our Lives – and We Shape the Cosmos* (Oxford: Oneworld, 2012).
Fraser, J. T., *The Voices of Time* (London: Allen Lane, 1968).

Freud, Sigmund, *Five Lectures on Psycho-Analysis*, trans. and ed. James Strachey (1910; New York and London: W.W. Norton, 1989).
— *The Interpretation of Dreams*, trans. A. A. Brill (London: George Allen, 1913).
Friedan, Betty, *The Feminine Mystique* (1963; London: Penguin, 2010).
Frow, John, *Time and Commodity Culture: Essays in Cultural Theory and Postmodernity* (Oxford: Clarendon Press, 1997).
Fussell, Paul, *The Great War and Modern Memory* (London: Oxford University Press, 1977).
Galison, Peter, *Einstein's Clocks, Poincaré's Maps: Empires of Time* (London: Hodder and Stoughton, 2003).
Garfield, Simon, *Timekeepers* (Edinburgh: Canongate, 2016).
Gell, Alfred, *The Anthropology of Time: Cultural Constructions of Temporal Maps and Images* (Oxford: Berg, 1992).
Genette, Gérard, *Narrative Discourse,* trans. Jane E. Lewin (Oxford: Blackwell, 1986).
— *Narrative Discourse Revisited*, trans. Jane E. Lewin (Ithaca: Cornell University Press, 1988).
Gillies, Mary Ann, *Henri Bergson and British Modernism* (Montreal: McGill-Queen's University Press, 1996).
Gleick, James, *Time Travel: A History* (New York: Pantheon, 2016).
Glennie, Paul, and Nigel Thrift, 'Reworking E. P. Thompson's "Time, Work-Discipline, and Industrial Capitalism"', *Time and Society* 5 (3), 1996.
— *Shaping the Day: A History of Timekeeping in England and Wales 1300–1800* (Oxford: Oxford University Press, 2009).
Greene, Graham, *Ways of Escape* (London: Bodley Head, 1980).
— *A World of My Own: A Dream Diary* (London: Viking/Penguin, 1994).
Griffiths, Jay, *Pip Pip: A Sideways Look at Time* (London: HarperCollins, 2000).
Hammond, Claudia, *Time Warped: Unlocking the Mysteries of Time Perception* (Edinburgh: Canongate, 2013).
Harrington, Ralph, 'The Railway Journey and the Neuroses of Modernity', in Richard Wrigley and George Revill, eds, *Pathologies of Travel* (Amsterdam: Rodopi, 2000).
Harvey, David, *The Condition of Postmodernity: An Enquiry into the Origins of Cultural Change* (Oxford: Blackwell, 1990).
Hassard, John, *The Sociology of Time* (London: Macmillan, 1990).
Hawking, Stephen W., *A Brief History of Time: From the Big Bang to Black Holes* (London: Bantam, 1988).
Hay, Eloise Knapp, *The Political Novels of Joseph Conrad: A Critical Study* (Chicago: University of Chicago Press, 1963).
Head, Dominic, *The Cambridge Introduction to Modern British Fiction, 1950–2000* (Cambridge: Cambridge University Press, 2002).
Heidegger, Martin, *Being and Time*, trans. John Macquarrie and Edward Robinson (1962; Oxford: Blackwell, 2005).

Heise, Ursula, *Chronoschisms: Time, Narrative, and Postmodernism* (Cambridge: Cambridge University Press, 1997).
Henry, Holly, *Virginia Woolf and the Discourse of Science: the Aesthetics of Astronomy* (Cambridge: Cambridge University Press, 2003).
Herman, David, Manfred Jahn and Marie-Laure Ryan, eds, *Routledge Encyclopedia of Narrative Theory* (Oxford: Routledge, 2005).
Higdon, David Leon, 'Conrad's Clocks', *The Conradian*, 16, 1971.
— *Time and English Fiction* (London: Macmillan, 1977).
Hobsbawm, E. J., *Labouring Men: Studies in the History of Labour* (London: Weidenfeld and Nicolson, 1968).
Howse, Derek, *Greenwich Time and the Longitude* (London: Philip Wilson, 1997).
Husserl, Edmund, *On the Phenomenology of the Consciousness of Internal Time* (1893–1917), trans. John Barnett Brough (Dordrecht: Kluwer Academic, 1991).
Hutcheon, Linda, *A Poetics of Postmodernism: History, Theory, Fiction* (London: Routledge, 1988).
Huyssen, Andreas, *Twilight Memories: Marking Time in a Culture of Amnesia* (London: Routledge, 1995).
Hynes, Samuel, *A War Imagined: the First World War and English Culture* (1990; London: Pimlico, 1992).
Isherwood, Christopher, *Lions and Shadows: An Education in the Twenties* (1938; London: Methuen, 1982).
Jackson, Kevin, ed., *The Book of Hours: An Anthology* (London: Duckworth, 2007).
James, David, ed., *The Legacies of Modernism: Historicising Postwar and Contemporary Fiction* (Cambridge: Cambridge University Press, 2012).
James, Henry, *Henry James: Letters*, vol. IV, *1895–1916*, ed. Leon Edel (Cambridge, MA: Belknap Press, 1984).
— *The Letters of Henry James*, 2 vols, ed. Percy Lubbock (London: Macmillan, 1920).
James, William, *Principles of Psychology*, 2 vols (London: Macmillan, 1890).
Jameson, Fredric, 'The End of Temporality', *Critical Inquiry*, 29 (4), 2003.
— *The Political Unconscious: Narrative as a Socially Symbolic Act* (1981; London: Routledge, 1983).
— *Postmodernism, or, the Cultural Logic of Late Capitalism* (London: Verso, 1991).
Jeans, Sir James, *The Mysterious Universe* (1930; Cambridge: Cambridge University Press, 1948).
— *The Universe Around Us* (Cambridge: Cambridge University Press, 1929).
Keegan, John, *The First World War* (Oxford: Oxford University Press, 1988).
Kenner, Hugh, *Joyce's Voices* (London: Faber and Faber, 1978).
Kermode, Frank, *Lawrence* (London: Fontana, 1985).

— *The Sense of an Ending: Studies in the Theory of Fiction* (1967; Oxford: Oxford University Press, 2000).
Kern, Stephen, *The Culture of Time and Space: 1880–1918* (Cambridge, MA: Harvard University Press, 1983).
— *The Modernist Novel: A Critical Introduction* (Cambridge: Cambridge University Press, 2012).
Kertzer, J. M., 'Joseph Conrad and the Metaphysics of Time', *Studies in the Novel*, 11, 1979.
Klein, Stefan, *Time: A User's Guide*, trans. Shelley Frisch (Harmondsworth: Penguin, 2007).
Knapp, James F., *Literary Modernism and the Transformation of Work* (Evanston: Northwestern University Press, 1988).
Knight, Arthur, *The Liveliest Art* (New York: Macmillan, 1959).
Kohler, Dayton, 'Time in the Modern Novel', *College English*, 10 (1), 1948.
Koselleck, Reinhardt, *Futures Past: On the Semantics of Historical Time* (New York: Columbia University Press, 2004).
Kristeva, Julia, *The Kristeva Reader*, ed. Toril Moi (1986; Oxford: Blackwell, 1995).
Kumar, Shiv K., *Bergson and the Stream of Consciousness Novel* (London: Blackie, 1962).
Landes, David S., *Revolution in Time: Clocks and the Making of the Modern World* (Cambridge, MA: Harvard University Press, 1983).
Larabee, Mark D., *Front Lines of Modernism: Remapping the Great War in British Fiction* (Basingstoke: Palgrave Macmillan, 2011).
Lawrence, D. H., *Fantasia of the Unconscious* (1923; London: Secker, 1930).
— *The Letters of D. H. Lawrence*, 8 vols, ed. James T. Boulton et al. (Cambridge: Cambridge University Press, 1979–2002).
— ['Lawrence H. Davison'], *Movements in European History* (1921; Oxford: Oxford University Press, 1971).
— *Phoenix: The Posthumous Papers of D. H. Lawrence*, ed. Edward D. McDonald (1936; London: William Heinemann, 1961).
Lefebvre, Henri, *Rhythmanalysis: Space, Time, and Everyday Life*, trans. Stuart Elden and Gerald Moore (London: Continuum, 2004).
Lehmann, Rosamond, 'The Future of the Novel', *Britain Today*, June 1946.
Lemon, Lee T., and Marion J. Reiss, *Russian Formalist Criticism* (Lincoln: University of Nebraska Press, 1965).
Levine, Robert, *A Geography of Time* (New York: Basic, 1997).
Lewis, Wyndham, *Time and Western Man* (London: Chatto and Windus, 1927).
Lightman, Alan, *The Accidental Universe* (London: Constable and Robinson, 2014).
Lowry, Malcolm, *Selected Letters of Malcolm Lowry*, ed. Harvey Breit and Margerie Bonner Lowrie (1967; Harmondsworth: Penguin, 1985).
Luckhurst, Roger, *Science Fiction* (Cambridge: Polity, 2005).

Lukács, Georg, *History and Class Consciousness: Studies in Marxist Dialectics*, trans. Rodney Livingstone (London: Merlin Press, 1990).
— 'The Ideology of Modernism', *Marxist Literary Theory: A Reader*, ed. Terry Eagleton and Drew Milne (Oxford: Blackwell, 1996).
— *The Theory of the Novel*, trans. Anna Bostock (London: Merlin, 1971).
Lyotard, Jean-François, *The Postmodern Condition: A Report on Knowledge*, trans. Geoff Bennington and Brian Massumi (Manchester: Manchester University Press, 1984).
McHale, Brian, *Postmodernist Fiction* (London: Routledge, 1987).
— and Len Platt, eds, *The Cambridge History of Postmodernism* (Cambridge: Cambridge University Press, 2016).
McTaggart, John McT. E., *The Nature of Existence* (1921–7; Cambridge: Cambridge University Press, 1988).
Mach, Ernst, *The Science of Mechanics: A Critical and Historical Account of Its Development*, trans. Thomas J. McCormack (1893; Chicago: Open Court, 1960).
Malpas, Simon, and Andrew Taylor, *Thomas Pynchon* (Manchester: Manchester University Press, 2013).
Marcus, Laura, and Peter Nicholls, eds, *The Cambridge History of Twentieth-Century Literature* (Cambridge: Cambridge University Press, 2004).
Marle, Hans van, 'Plucked and Passed on Tower Hill: Conrad's Examination Ordeals', *Conradiana*, 8, 1976.
Marx, Karl, *Capital: A Critique of Political Economy*, 2 vols, trans. Ben Fowkes (1976; Harmondsworth: Penguin, 1988).
May, Jon, and Nigel Thrift, eds, *Timespace: Geographies of Temporality* (London: Routledge, 2001).
Mendilow, A. A., *Time and the Novel* (London: Peter Nevill, 1952).
Meyerhoff, Hans, *Time in Literature* (Berkeley: University of California Press, 1955).
Meyers, Jeffrey, 'Conrad's Examinations for the British Merchant Service', *Conradiana*, 23 (2), 1991.
Michaelian, Kourken, Stanley B. Klein and Karl K. Szpunar, *Seeing the Future: Theoretical Perspectives on Future-Oriented Mental Time-Travel* (New York: Oxford University Press, 2016).
Milet, Jean, *Bergson et le calcul infinitésimal* (Paris: Presses Universitaires de France, 1974).
Montague, C. E., *Disenchantment* (1922; London: Chatto and Windus, 1924).
Mook, Delo E., and Thomas Vargish, *Inside Relativity* (Princeton: Princeton University Press, 1987).
Morris, Charles, *Answers to the Definitions, etc., at the Board of Trade Examinations in Navigation* (London: Houlston and Sons, 1898).
Mullarkey, John, ed., *The New Bergson* (Manchester: Manchester University Press, 1999).

Mumford, Lewis. *Technics and Civilization* (1934; London: George Routledge & Sons, 1947).

Nahin, Paul J., *Time Machines: Time Travel in Physics, Metaphysics, and Science Fiction*, 2nd edn (New York: Springer-Verlag, 1999).

Najder, Zdzisław, ed., *Conrad's Polish Background: Letters to and From Polish Friends*, trans. Halina Carroll (London: Oxford University Press, 1964).

— *Joseph Conrad: A Chronicle* (Cambridge: Cambridge University Press, 1983).

Nanni, Giordano, *The Colonisation of Time: Ritual, Routine and Resistance in the British Empire* (Manchester: Manchester University Press, 2012).

Nehls, Edward, ed., *D. H. Lawrence: A Composite Biography* (Madison: University of Wisconsin Press, 1957).

Newman, Karen, Jay Clayton and Marianne Hirsch, eds, *Time and the Literary* (London: Routledge, 2002).

Newton, John. *Newton's Guide to the Board of Trade Examinations of Masters and Mates of Sailing Ships and Steam Ships in Navigation and Nautical Astronomy*, 7th edn (London: John Newton, Sailors' Home, 1884).

Nietzsche, Friedrich, *The Birth of Tragedy and the Genealogy of Morals*, trans. Francis Golffing (New York: Random House, 1956).

— *The Gay Science*, trans. Walter Kaufmann (New York: Vintage Books, 1974).

— *The Will to Power*, trans. Walter Kaufmann (New York: Vintage Books, 1968).

Nordmann, Charles, *The Tyranny of Time: Einstein or Bergson?*, trans. E. E. Fournier d'Albe (London: T. Fisher Unwin, 1925).

Novikov, Igor D., *The River of Time*, trans. Vitaly Kisin (Cambridge: Cambridge University Press, 1998).

Ogle, Vanessa, *The Global Transformation of Time: 1870–1950* (Cambridge, MA: Harvard University Press, 2015).

Painter, George D., *Marcel Proust: A Biography* (London: Chatto and Windus, 1959).

Pinker, Steven, *The Stuff of Thought: Language as a Window into Human Nature* (Harmondsworth: Penguin, 2007).

Pouillon, Jean, *Temps et romain* (Paris: Gallimard, 1946).

Poulet, Georges, *Studies in Human Time*, trans. Elliott Coleman (Baltimore, MD: Johns Hopkins Press, 1956).

Prerau, David, *Saving the Daylight: Why We Put the Clocks Forward* (London: Granta, 2005).

Price, Katy, *Loving Faster than Light: Romance and Readers in Einstein's Universe* (Chicago: University of Chicago Press, 2012).

Priestley, J. B., *Man and Time* (1964; New York: Dell, 1968).

— *Margin Released: A Writer's Reminiscences and Reflections* (London: Heinemann, 1962).

— 'The Time Problem', *The Spectator*, no.5847, 19 July 1940.

Proust, Marcel, *Correspondance*, 21 vols, ed. Philip Kolb (Paris: Plon, 1970–92).

Pynchon, Thomas, 'The Deadly Sins: Sloth; Nearer, my Couch, to Thee', *New York Times Book Review*, 6 June 1993.

Quennell, Peter, *A Letter to Mrs. Virginia Woolf* (London: Hogarth Press, 1932).

Quinones, Ricardo, *Mapping Literary Modernism: Time and Development* (Princeton: Princeton University Press, 1985).

Radstone, Susannah, *The Sexual Politics of Time: Confession, Nostalgia, Memory* (London: Routledge, 2007).

Randall, Bryony, *Modernism, Daily Time and Everyday Life* (Cambridge: Cambridge University Press, 2007).

Reed, Henry, *The Novel since 1939* (London: Longmans, Green, and Co., 1946).

Richards, Jeffrey, and John M. Mackenzie, *The Railway Station: A Social History* (Oxford: Oxford University Press, 1986).

Richardson, Brian, ed., *Narrative Dynamics: Essays on Time, Plot, Closure and Frames* (Columbus: Ohio State University Press, 2002).

Ricoeur, Paul, *Time and Narrative*, 3 vols, trans. Kathleen McLaughlin, Kathleen Blaney and David Pellauer (Chicago: University of Chicago Press, 1985–1988).

Robbe-Grillet, Alain, 'The Case for the New Novel', *New Statesman*, 17 February 1961.

— *For A New Novel: Essays on Fiction*, trans. Richard Howard (1965; Evanston: Northwestern University Press, 1989).

Rooney, David, and James Nye, '"Greenwich Observatory Time for the Public Benefit": Standard Time and Victorian Networks of Regulation', *British Journal for the History of Science*, 42 (1), March 2009.

Rossington, Michael, and Anne Whitehead, *Theories of Memory: A Reader* (Edinburgh: Edinburgh University Press, 2008).

Russell, Bertrand, *The ABC of Relativity* (1925; London: Kegan Paul, Trench, Trubner and Co., 1926).

Sawday, Jonathan, *Engines of the Imagination: Renaissance Culture and the Rise of the Machine* (London: Routledge, 2007).

Schivelbusch, Wolfgang, *Disenchanted Night: The Industrialization of Light in the Nineteenth Century*, trans. Angela Davies (Berkeley: University of California Press, 1988).

— *The Railway Journey: The Industrialization of Time and Space in the 19th Century* (Berkeley: University of California Press, 1986).

Schleifer, Ronald, *Modernism and Time: The Logic of Abundance in Literature, Science, and Culture 1880–1930* (Cambridge: Cambridge University Press, 2000).

Schlör, Joachim, *Nights in the Big City: Paris Berlin London 1840–1930* (London: Reaktion, 1998).

Slosson, Edwin E., *Easy Lessons in Einstein: A Discussion of the More Intelligible Features of the Theory of Relativity* (London: Routledge and Sons, 1920).
Smethurst, Paul, *The Postmodern Chronotope: Space and Time in Contemporary Fiction* (Amsterdam: Rodopi, 2000).
Smyth, Edmund, ed., *Postmodernism and Contemporary Fiction* (London: Batsford, 1991).
Sobel, Dava, *Longitude: the True Story of a Lone Genius Who Solved the Greatest Scientific Problem of His Time* (London: Fourth Estate, 1996).
Soulez, Philippe, and Frédéric Worms, *Bergson: Biographie* (Paris: Presses Universitaire de France, 2002).
Spender, Stephen, 'Books and the War II: Time, Violence and Macbeth', *The Penguin New Writing*, February 1941.
Spengler, Osbert, *The Decline of the West*, trans. Charles Frances Atkinson (London: G. Allen and Unwin, 1934).
Stape, John, *The Several Lives of Joseph Conrad* (London: William Heinemann, 2007).
— and Owen Knowles, eds, *A Portrait in Letters: Correspondence to and about Joseph Conrad* (Amsterdam: Rodopi, 1994).
Stevenson, John, *British Society 1914–45* (London: Allen Lane, 1984).
Stevenson, Randall, 'Greenwich Meanings: Clocks and Things in Modernist and Postmodernist Fiction', *Yearbook of English Studies*, 30, 2000.
— *Literature and the Great War* (Oxford: Oxford University Press, 2013).
— *Modernist Fiction* (Hemel Hempstead: Prentice Hall, 1998).
— *The Oxford English Literary History*, vol. 12, *1960–2000: The Last of England?* (Oxford: Oxford University Press, 2004).
Stewart, Victoria, 'J. W. Dunne and Literary Culture in the 1930s and 1940s', *Literature and History*, 17 (2), 2008.
— *Narratives of Memory: British Writing of the 1940s* (Basingstoke: Palgrave Macmillan, 2006).
Stites, Richard, 'Utopias of Time, Space, and Life in the Russian Revolution', *Revue des études slaves*, 56 (1), 1984.
Taylor, Frederick Winslow, *The Principles of Scientific Management* (1911; New York: Harper and Brothers, 1919).
Thompson, E. P., 'Time, Work-Discipline, and Industrial Capitalism', *Past and Present*, 38, 1967.
Thompson, Paul, *The Edwardians: the Remaking of British Society* (London: Routledge, 1992).
Tolkien, J. R. R., *Tree and Leaf* (1964; London: Unwin, 1989).
Tomashevsky, Boris, 'Thematics' (1925), *Russian Formalist Criticism: Four Essays* (1925), trans. Lee T. Lemon and Marion J. Reis (Lincoln: University of Nebraska Press, 1965).
Trotter, David, *The English Novel in History: 1895–1920* (London: Routledge, 1983).

Tung, Charles M., 'Modernism, Time Machines, and the Defamiliarization of Time', *Configurations*, 23 (1), Winter 2015.
Villiers, Peter, *Joseph Conrad: Master Mariner* (Suffolk: Seafarer Books, 2006).
Warner, Deborah, 'The Ballast-Office Time Ball and the Subjectivity of Time and Space', *James Joyce Quarterly*, 35/36, 1998.
Watt, Ian, *The Rise of the Novel: Studies in Defoe, Richardson and Fielding* (1957; Harmondsworth: Penguin, 1972).
West-Pavlov, Russell, *Temporalities* (London: Routledge, 2013).
White, Hayden, *Metahistory: The Historical Imagination in Nineteenth-Century Europe* (London: Johns Hopkins University Press, 1975).
Whitehead, Anne, *Memory* (London: Routledge, 2009).
Whitrow, G. J., *Time in History* (Oxford: Oxford University Press, 1988).
Whitworth, Michael, *Einstein's Wake: Relativity, Metaphor, and Modernist Literature* (Oxford: Oxford University Press, 2001).
Whorf, Benjamin Lee, *Language, Thought, and Reality: Selected Writings of Benjamin Lee Whorf,* ed. John B. Carroll (1956; Cambridge, MA: The MIT Press, 1964).
Wild, Jonathan, *Literature of the 1900s: the Great Edwardian Emporium* (Edinburgh: Edinburgh University Press, 2017).
Wittenberg, David, *Time Travel: The Popular Philosophy of Narrative* (New York: Fordham University Press, 2013).
Woolf, Virginia, *The Essays of Virginia Woolf*, 6 vols, ed. Andrew McNeillie and Stuart N. Clarke (London: Hogarth Press, 1986–2011).
— *The Letters of Virginia Woolf*, 6 vols, ed. Nigel Nicolson and Joanne Trautmann (London: Hogarth, 1975–1980).
— *Moments of Being*, ed. Jeanne Schulkind (London: Pimlico, 2002).
— *A Writer's Diary: Being Extracts from the Diary of Virginia Woolf*, ed. Leonard Woolf (1953; London; Triad, 1978).
Worthen, John, *D. H. Lawrence: The Early Years* (Cambridge: Cambridge University Press, 1991).
Ziolkowski, Theodore, *Dimensions of the Modern Novel: German Texts and European Contexts* (Princeton: Princeton University Press, 1969).

Index

Achebe, Chinua, *Arrow of God*, 192
Adorno, Theodor, 169, 214
  'Commitment', 165n
  'The Concept of Enlightenment', 166–7
  'Trying to Understand *Endgame*', 162–3, 165
Aldington, Richard, *Death of a Hero*, 65, 79, 121, 141, 153
Aldiss, Brian, 201, 203, 205
  Trillion Year Spree, 201
Alexander, Samuel, 97–8, 105, 210
  Space, Time, and Deity, 98
Alston, Alfred Henry, *Captain Alston's Seamanship*, 33
Amis, Martin, 179, 180, 201n
  Time's Arrow, 167, 180, 208–9
anachrony, narrative, 19, 20, 23, 43–5, 76–81, 86, 122, 135–8, 153, 169–71, 173–4, 186, 199, 201–2, 203, 212, 213, 223, 228, 236; *see also* analepsis and prolepsis; duration (narrative)
analepsis and prolepsis, 23, 43–4, 81, 86n, 127, 129, 135–40, 143, 144–5, 147, 148, 156, 157, 188, 201, 212
Antin, David, *i never knew what time it was*, 221
Armstrong, Tim, 99
astronomy and cosmology, 3, 6, 7, 29, 30, 31–4, 36, 41, 91, 94, 104, 105n, 112, 128, 131–2, 190, 198–200, 205, 217, 219, 231n; *see also* Relativity
atomic age, the, 146–7, 158, 159, 163–4, 167, 171, 178, 182, 183, 200, 205, 207, 209; *see also* Doomsday Clock, the
Atwood, Margaret, *Cat's Eye*, 198
Auden, W. H., 133, 233
Auschwitz *see* Holocaust, the
automata, 55, 56, 57, 60, 62, 213, 214, 215, 217, 231n; *see also* reification
Aytoun, W. E., 12–13

Baar, Armand, *La Réforme du Calendrier*, 214n
Back to the Future (film), 190n, 206–8
Bailey, Paul, *Old Soldiers*, 148n
Bakhtin, Mikhail, 110
  'Forms of Time and of the Chronotope in the Novel', 24–5
Ballard, J. G., 213
  'Chronopolis', 203, 204
  The Voices of Time, 203
Barnes, Julian, *The Sense of an Ending*, 223
Barrie, J. M., *Peter Pan*, 39
Barthes, Roland, 170, 172
  'Objective Literature', 169
Bates, H. E., 156–8
  Love for Lydia, 157
  The Sleepless Moon, 157–8
Beckett, Samuel, 160–3, 166, 168, 170, 171, 177, 178
  Endgame, 162–3
  Krapp's Last Tape, 189
  Proust, 160
  Waiting for Godot, 160–2, 163, 164, 165, 178
  'Whoroscope', 160

Beerbohm, Max, *Zuleika Dobson*, 16
Bell, Clive, 140
Benford, Gregory, *Timescape*, 207n
Benjamin, Walter, 107, 156, 162, 166–7
 'Theses on the Philosophy of History', 154
Bennett, Arnold, 76
 Clayhanger, 16, 52n
 The Pretty Lady, 70
Berger, John, G., 184, 185
Bergson, Henri, 95–107, 108, 109, 110, 114, 115, 116, 117n, 120, 121, 123, 124n, 126, 128, 129, 188, 210
 Creative Evolution, 114, 126, 188
 'Dreams', 97
 Duration and Simultaneity, 96
 Laughter, 103
 Time and Free Will (*Essai sur les données immédiates de la conscience*), 96–7, 105
 see also durée
Big Ben, 58, 73–4, 83, 104, 118, 123, 130, 185
Bildungsroman, the, 63–4, 66, 86
Blunden, Edmund, 62n, 67
Bobrowski, Tadeusz, 36
Boer War, the, 140, 143, 153
Bohr, Niels, 227
Borges, Jorge Luis, 'Time and J. W. Dunne', 128n
Bowen, Elizabeth
 'The Bend Back', 158–9, 162, 163
 The Heat of the Day, 24, 141–2, 162, 194
Bradbury, Ray, 202
Bradshaw, George, 16
Bradshaw's railway guides, 16–17, 57, 75, 108
Brittain, Vera, *Account Rendered*, 143n
Brooke-Rose, Christine, 170
 Out, 170
 Such, 170
 Thru, 170
Brooks, Peter, 22, 23
 Reading for the Plot, 20–1

Buchan, John, 127
 The Gap in the Curtain, 126–7, 128
Budgen, Frank, 106
Bundy, Willard, 53n
Bureau International de l'Heure, 2, 72
Butler, Samuel, *Erewhon*, 121–2, 204
Butor, Michel, 169

calendars, 18, 21, 26, 49, 68, 88, 120, 169, 184, 192, 210, 214–15, 217, 221
calendrical reform, 2, 68, 214, 217, 221
Carey, Peter, *The Chemistry of Tears*, 231n
carpe diem, 68, 234
Carr, David, 21
Carr, J. L., *A Month in the Country*, 148n
Carroll, Lewis, *Sylvie and Bruno*, 201n
Carter, Angela
 Nights at the Circus, 184–5, 211
 The Passion of New Eve, 193
cartography, 3–4, 5, 33n, 38, 41, 55, 79, 87, 217–19, 227; see also geography; navigation
Cary, Joyce
 To Be a Pilgrim, 143, 144, 151, 157, 173
 'Triptych', 143, 172–3
Cather, Willa, *One of Ours*, 67
Céline, Louis-Ferdinand, *Journey to the End of the Night*, 58
Chaplin, Charlie
 Modern Times, 59, 60
 The Pawnshop, 59
children's fiction, 201n
chronometers and chronometry, 11, 39, 40, 52, 57, 104, 136, 160, 204, 214, 217, 219, 237, 238
 nautical, 28, 30–3, 36–41, 46, 55, 89, 217, 224, 237
chronotope, 24, 110
chronotype, 24–5, 26, 45, 46, 66, 89, 99, 109, 148, 150, 153, 155, 159, 172
Churchill, Winston, 68

cinema *see* film and cinema
Civil War, the, 150, 153
clock-making, 10, 52, 58, 230–1
clocking-in, 53, 54, 59, 187
clocks
  atomic, 6, 190
  digital, 14, 17–18, 195
  household, 39, 40, 70–1, 77, 115, 118, 130, 157, 158, 199, 224, 230, 232, 233
  public (town, church), 8–9, 11–13, 16, 35, 40, 53n, 68n, 71, 74–5, 77, 104, 118, 129, 142, 158, 191, 204, 207–8, 214, 230; *see also* Big Ben
  railway station, 5–6, 10–11, 14, 15, 17, 66, 223; *see also* railway time
  speaking, 61, 211
  striking, 16, 19, 20, 25, 45, 47, 73, 118, 119, 130, 145, 164, 185, 214, 235; *see also* Big Ben
  three-handed, 11–12, 26
  see also chronometers and chronometry; Doomsday Clock, the; measured (clock) time; Strasbourg Clock, the; watches
Cold War, the, 163, 164n, 178, 205
colonialism and empire, 71, 72, 74, 75, 192, 211, 216, 217–18
computers, 195, 197, 220, 221
concentration camps *see* Holocaust, the
Connolly, Cyril, 112, 124, 128
Connor, Steven, 236
Conrad, Borys, 33, 65
Conrad, Joseph, viii, 27–46, 55, 65, 76, 77, 78, 80, 88–9, 108, 112, 121, 186, 198, 204, 218, 224, 236
  Chance, 27, 29
  'Geography and Some Explorers', 36
  Heart of Darkness, 38, 44
  'Karain: A Memory', 37–8, 41, 236, 237, 238
  Last Essays, 27, 36

  Lord Jim, vii, 27, 38–9, 44, 45, 52, 237
  The Nigger of the 'Narcissus', 33
  Nostromo, 39–40, 44, 52
  'Outside Literature', 27–8, 35, 36, 37, 39, 88
  A Personal Record, 29, 35, 36
  The Secret Agent, 4, 5, 39n, 40–4, 45, 46, 47, 60, 71, 76–7, 78, 89, 119, 120, 218, 236
  'The Secret Sharer', 38
  The Shadow-Line, 40, 65, 66–7, 198, 218
  Under Western Eyes, 40, 45
Cook, Thomas, 11
Co-ordinated Universal Time, 6, 190
cosmology *see* astronomy and cosmology
Cuban Missile Crisis, the, 178
Currie, Mark, 22
  About Time, vii–viii, 86n

Darwin, Charles, 66, 203
  On the Origin of Species, 131
Daylight Saving Time *see* Summer Time
Debord, Guy, 194, 213
  The Society of the Spectacle, 190
'deep' time, 130–2, 137, 139, 186, 194
Delambre, Jean-Baptiste, 2n, 219
DeLillo, Don, 21, 225, 228, 237
  Cosmopolis, 226, 229
  Point Omega, 190, 225, 226, 237
  Underworld, 190, 226
Dick, Philip K., 202
  Time Out of Joint, 205, 206
Dickens, Charles, 149, 150, 157
  David Copperfield, 63
  Dombey and Son, 11, 149
  Hard Times, 17
Donaldson, Ian, 'The Clockwork Novel', 231n
Donnie Darko (film), 208
Doomsday Clock, the, 163–4
Doyle, Arthur Conan, 16–17
  The Valley of Fear, 16

Dunne, J. W., 120–1, 124–9, 143, 154, 157, 178, 188, 197, 209, 210
  An Experiment with Time, 120–1, 124–9, 154
duration (narrative), 23, 78, 81, 86, 116, 122, 190, 202, 232
durée (Bergsonian) 96, 97, 100, 105, 107, 116, 120, 185; see also Bergson, Henri
Durrell, Lawrence, 174
  The Alexandria Quartet, 173–4, 185

Echenoz, Jean, 7
  Le Méridien de Greenwich, 6
Eco, Umberto, *The Island of the Day Before*, 3, 6n
Eddington, Arthur, 91, 94, 110, 111, 128
Edenic retrospection, 144–8, 150, 152, 154, 156, 180, 206–9, 219; see also nostalgia
Eichmann, Adolf, 178, 180
Einstein, Albert, 91–6, 98, 99, 100, 103, 104–5, 107–11, 117n, 126, 128–9, 135, 197, 200, 208, 210, 227; see also Relativity
Eisenstein, Sergei, 188–9, 206
Eliot, George, 150
  Felix Holt, 149
  Middlemarch, 149
Eliot, T. S., 24, 76, 86, 102, 103–4, 125, 186, 188
  Four Quartets, 125, 188, 237–8
  'Rhapsody on a Windy Night', 60–2, 76, 100–1, 102, 104
  'Tradition and the Individual Talent', 24n
  '"Ulysses", Order and Myth', 75
  The Waste Land, 68
empire *see* colonialism and empire
Engels, Frederick, *The Condition of the Working Class in England*, 52–3
Enlightenment, the, 166–8, 217–18, 229–30

eternity, 40, 42, 47, 48, 49, 51, 59, 77, 89, 112, 119, 125, 128, 133, 137, 138, 193, 212, 226, 229, 237; see also timelessness

fabula/sjuzet distinction, 22–3, 24–5, 26, 44, 66, 232
fantasy, 110, 112, 116, 122, 185, 199, 200, 201, 203, 204, 209, 211, 212–13, 214; see also science fiction
Faulkner, William, 102, 170
  'The Bear', 237
  The Sound and the Fury, 65, 102, 120, 135–6, 235
Faust, legends of, 145, 164–5
Felski, Rita, *Doing Time*, 193
feminist criticism, 192–4
Fielding, Gabriel, *The Birthday King*, 179
Fielding, Henry, 233, 234
  Tom Jones, 231, 232
film and cinema, 19, 59, 60, 114, 169, 180, 187, 188–9, 190, 206–9, 212, 225, 226, 231n
Finney, Jack, 'The Third Level', 205
First World War, the *see* Great War, the
Fitzgerald, F. Scott, *The Great Gatsby*, 155
Ford, Ford Madox, 27, 44–5, 86, 111, 135
  The Good Soldier, 45, 77, 173
  Joseph Conrad: A Personal Remembrance, 77, 80
  Parade's End, 45, 64, 77–80, 84, 116, 117, 120, 138, 140–1, 161
Ford, Henry, 58–9
Forster, E. M., 23–4
  Aspects of the Novel, 20–1, 22, 23–4, 110
Foucault, Michel, 196n
Fowles, John, 183
  The French Lieutenant's Woman, 172, 185
  The Magus, 171–2
Free Indirect Discourse/Style, 78, 83, 138

French Revolution, the, 2–3, 153, 214n, 219, 221
Freud, Sigmund, 98–9, 117, 120
Friedan, Betty, *The Feminine Mystique*, 193
Fry, Roger, 80
Fussell, Paul, 154

Galison, Peter, *Einstein's Clocks, Poincaré's Maps*, 104–5
Gallagher, Catherine, 208
Galsworthy, John, *The Forsyte Saga*, 63
Gastev, Alexei, 56
Gell, Alfred, 191–2
Genette, Gérard, 23, 24, 232
 Narrative Discourse, 23, 81, 172
geography, viii, 191–2, 197, 210–11, 222; *see also* cartography; Greenwich (Prime) Meridian; navigation
geology, 131, 137
Gerhardie, William, *Of Mortal Love*, 126
Gibbon, Lewis Grassic, 134, 146, 156
 A Scots Quair, 137–9, 212, 213
 Three Go Back, 138n, 202
Gibson, William, *Neuromancer*, 17–18, 195–6, 214, 216
Gleick, James, *Time Travel: A History*, 209n
Glennie, Paul, 28
 Shaping the Day: A History of Timekeeping in England and Wales 1300–1500, 230
globalisation, 4, 7, 17, 176, 190–6, 214, 218–19, 220
Godden, Rumer, *A Fugue in Time*, 157
Golding, William, 182–3
Gray, Alasdair, *Lanark*, 213–15, 218
Great War, the, 48, 62–72, 74–5, 77–85, 89, 90, 94–5, 105, 116, 119–20, 123, 127, 130, 134–48, 150, 153–8, 161, 164–7, 177, 179, 205, 206
Green, Henry, *Back*, 142, 161

Greene, Graham, 126
 The Confidential Agent, 126
 The End of the Affair, 126, 173
Greenwich Mean Time (GMT), 3–6, 7, 9, 11, 13, 16, 17–18, 26, 28, 31, 32, 33, 36, 37, 38, 41, 42, 46, 55, 68, 69, 72n, 74, 89, 104, 108, 186, 190, 191, 192, 195, 219, 236, 237
Greenwich (Prime) Meridian, the, 3–4, 5, 6, 11, 12, 28, 31, 36, 41, 42, 46, 55, 89, 179, 186, 192, 219
Greenwich Observatory, 3, 4, 5, 6, 9, 12, 40, 41, 42, 43, 46, 104, 108, 219, 224
Griffiths, Jay, *Pip Pip*, 191n
Guedj, Denis, *The Measure of the World*, 2n, 218–19
Gurdjieff, George, 128

Hardy, Thomas, 64, 134, 150, 157, 198
 The Mayor of Casterbridge, 149–50
 A Pair of Blue Eyes, 131
 The Return of the Native, 8–9, 11, 13
 Tess of the d'Urbervilles, 8
 Two on a Tower, 132
Harrison, John, 31–3
Hartley, L. P., 156
 Eustace and Hilda, 147
 The Go-Between, 147, 157
 The Shrimp and the Anemone, 147
Hawking, Stephen, *A Brief History of Time*, 198, 199
Heidegger, Martin, *Being and Time*, 124n
Heinlein, Robert A., 207n
Heise, Ursula, *Chronoschisms*, 171, 196n
Heppenstall, Rayner
 The Connecting Door, 170–1
 Two Moons, 171
l'heure definitive, 2, 17, 72
l'heure de la gare, 8, 14

Hilton, James, *Random Harvest*, 143, 157
Hinton, C. H., 200n
history, modes of experiencing/configuring, viii, 23–6, 64–6, 75, 79, 84–5, 89, 107, 116, 131–4, 136–48, 153, 156, 158–9, 162–7, 172, 175–84, 185, 197, 203, 205–6, 208–9, 211, 212–13, 216, 224–5, 236; *see also* nostalgia
Hitchcock, Alfred, 225
Hitler, Adolf, 133, 165, 167, 171, 183, 209; *see also* Nazism
Holocaust, the, 159, 162–3, 164, 165n, 167, 178–9, 180, 182, 207, 216, 223, 225
Horkheimer, Max, 214
 'The Concept of Enlightenment', 166–7
Howard, Elizabeth Jane, *After Julius*, 179
Hoyle, Fred, 205
 October the First is Too Late, 205–6, 214
Hubble, Edwin, 132
Hughes, Richard, *The Fox in the Attic*, 179
Hugo (film), 231n
Husserl, Edmund, 98
Hutcheon, Linda, *A Poetics of Postmodernism*, 183–4
Hutton, James, 131
Huxley, Aldous, 111, 134, 136, 137, 156
 Antic Hay, 111
 Brave New World, 58–9, 60, 136
 Eyeless in Gaza, 136, 145
 Point Counter Point, 111
Huyssen, Andreas, *Twilight Memories*, 196n

l'incroyable pique-nique, 1–2, 7, 218–19, 220
Industrial Revolution, the, viii, 52, 150, 230
industry and industrialisation, viii, 17, 23, 47–62, 66, 72, 89, 101, 107, 130, 139, 167, 175, 186–7, 191–2, 195, 210–11, 213, 214, 215, 230, 237; *see also* railways and their influence; reification
interior monologue, 76, 130, 136, 138, 146; *see also* Free Indirect Discourse/Style; stream of consciousness
internet, the, 195–6, 220
Isherwood, Christopher, 134–6, 137, 153, 156
 The Memorial, 134–6, 137, 139, 148, 152

James, Henry, 45–6, 64, 66, 153, 154, 166
 The Sense of the Past, 157
James, William, 98, 99, 100, 105
 The Principles of Psychology, 98
Jameson, Fredric, 45, 89, 108–9, 177, 196, 222, 236
 'The End of Temporality', 185–6, 196
 The Political Unconscious, 25–6, 175, 236n
 Postmodernism, or, the Cultural Logic of Late Capitalism, 175–6, 183, 185, 196, 218
Jeans, Sir James, 132
Johnson, B. S.
 Albert Angelo, 171
 The Unfortunates, 171
Johnson, Samuel, 231
Joyce, James, 100, 106, 111, 115, 117, 118, 119, 125, 160, 170, 171
 Finnegans Wake, 116–17, 120
 A Portrait of the Artist as a Young Man, 17, 87, 114
 Ulysses, 9, 65, 75, 77, 86–9, 100, 103, 104, 109, 112, 114, 116, 117, 118, 120, 139, 146, 187–8, 189, 221, 237
 'Work in Progress', 116–17

Kafka, Franz, 170
Keegan, John, 154
Kenner, Hugh, 66, 153

Kermode, Frank, 23, 24, 25, 63, 149, 153, 172
  The Sense of an Ending, 20–2, 24, 122
Kern, Stephen, 99, 109
Kipling, Rudyard, 'On the Gate', 116
Kristeva, Julia, 'Women's Time', 193

Lawrence, D. H., viii, 55, 47–8, 61–3, 102, 129, 138, 153, 154, 234
  Fantasia of the Unconscious, 109, 111
  Kangaroo, 64
  Lady Chatterley's Lover, 64, 121
  'Nottingham and the Mining Countryside', 55
  The Plumed Serpent, 101
  The Rainbow, 47–50, 51, 52, 56, 59, 62–3, 65, 66, 101, 138, 187, 211, 212, 213
  Sons and Lovers, 63
  The Trespasser, 101
  Women in Love, 15, 47–8, 50–2, 55–6, 57, 58, 59–60, 62–3, 66, 71, 101, 120, 133, 187, 203, 211, 233
Lehmann, Rosamond, 142, 144, 156
  The Ballad and the Source, 145
Lenin, Vladimir, 56
Lerner, Ben, 225
  10:04, 189–90
Levenson, Michael, 99–100
  'The time-mind of the twenties', 133
Lewis, Wyndham, 94, 96, 97, 99, 103–4, 106, 108, 109, 113–17, 124, 126, 128, 129
  Blast, 62n
  The Childermass, 112n, 115–17, 122, 202, 215
  Tarr, 113–14
  Time and Western Man, 95–6, 100, 103–4, 110–17, 126
  The Wild Body, 103
  'You Broke My Dream, or An Experiment with Time', 126
licensing laws, 13, 67–8, 72, 104, 112
Lightman, Alan, 199–200, 204
  Einstein's Dreams, 200
Lively, Penelope, 179
  City of the Mind, 194–5, 197, 198
  Moon Tiger, 179, 181, 194
Lloyd, Christopher, 207
Locke, John, *An Essay Concerning Human Understanding*, 231
Lowry, Malcolm, 146–7
  Under the Volcano, 145–7, 159, 164–5
Luckhurst, Roger, 200
Lukács, Georg, 72, 111, 175, 176, 190, 213
  'The Ideology of Modernism', 107
  'Reification and the Consciousness of the Proletariat', 57–8, 59, 107
  The Theory of the Novel, 20, 21, 229
Lumière brothers, 188, 189
Lyell, Charles, 131
Lyotard, Jean-François, 167–8

Macaulay, Rose, 112, 153
  Potterism, 110–11, 151
McEwan, Ian, 179
  Atonement, 184
  Black Dogs, 179, 181, 182
  The Child in Time, 199
Mach, Ernst, 111, 227
  The Science of Mechanics, 95
Machen, Arthur, 'The Bowmen', 155
Mackenzie, Compton, *Sinister Street*, 64
Mackenzie, John M., 10, 13
McTaggart, John, 97, 125, 227–8
  The Nature of Existence, 97, 125
Mann, Thomas, 20, 23, 166, 186
  Doctor Faustus, 164–6, 167, 168
  The Magic Mountain, 18–19, 20, 25, 64, 78, 165–6, 168
Manning, Olivia, *The Balkan Trilogy*, 179

Marinetti, F. T., 'The Founding and Manifesto of Futurism 1909', 106
Márquez, Gabriel García, 217
  One Hundred Years of Solitude, 212–13
Marryat, Captain F., 27, 36
  Mr Midshipman Easy, 27
  Peter Simple, 27
Marvell, Andrew, 234
  'Upon Appleton House', 150
Marx, Karl, 57, 66
  Capital, 53n
Maskelyne, Nevil, 3
Matheson, Richard, *Somewhere in Time*, 128n
Maugham, Somerset, *Cakes and Ale*, 134, 151
measured (clock) time, vii, viii, 2, 12–21, 26, 28, 39–41, 44, 45, 47, 48, 51–61, 66–74, 77, 82, 89, 91, 93–7, 100–2, 105, 109, 112, 113, 117–23, 129–30, 133, 136, 146, 160–1, 184–94, 197, 203–4, 210–17, 220–38; *see also* chronometers and chronometry; clocks; Greenwich Mean Time; 'monumental time'; railway time; Summer Time; watches
Méchain, Pierre, 2n, 219
Melville, Herman, *Pierre, or, the Ambiguities*, 46
memento mori, 68, 133
memory
  nature of, 19, 66, 76, 79, 81–3, 90, 97–9, 100, 102–3, 120–1, 123, 134, 136, 151–2, 156, 158–9, 170, 175, 178, 180–1, 182, 185, 187, 194, 195, 202, 224–5, 229
  literary uses of, 44, 61, 78–91, 101, 102–3, 117, 118, 134–48, 170–1, 173, 182, 188, 194, 197, 206, 212, 215, 223–5
  see also Edenic retrospection; nostalgia; remembrance
Mendilow, A. A., *Time and the Novel*, 196

Meyerhoff, Hans, *Time and Literature*, 18
Michelson, Albert, 95
millennium, the, 1, 218–22
Milton, John, *Paradise Lost*, 150
modernism, 15, 18, 26, 28, 45, 46, 48, 59, 62, 75–123, 129, 131, 134, 135, 138–9, 146, 160, 170, 171, 173, 175, 176, 184, 185–6, 194, 195, 196, 197, 202, 203, 204, 215, 222, 223, 225, 229, 234, 235, 236
modernity, viii, 45, 122, 138, 150, 154–5, 166–8, 170, 200–1, 208, 210, 212–13, 214, 217–18, 230, 237; *see also* Enlightenment, the; Industrial Revolution, the; industry and industrialisation; railways and their influence; technology and its influence
Modern Times (film) *see* Chaplin, Charlie
Montague, C. E., 153
  Disenchantment, 140, 152
  Rough Justice, 72n
'monumental time', 72–5, 84, 89, 90, 91, 93, 108, 123, 135
Moorcock, Michael, 204, 213
  'The Time Dweller', 203–4
  The Time Dweller, 203
Morley, Edward, 95
Mumford, Lewis, 107, 190
  Technics and Civilization, 52, 53, 186–7
Musil, Robert, *The Man Without Qualities*, 121
myth, 25, 75, 87, 145, 148, 181–2, 208, 212, 217, 227

Nabokov, Vladimir, *Ada*, 128n, 210
Nahin, Paul J., *Time Machines*, 209n
Nanni, Giordano, 192
narrative theory (narratology), vii–viii, 19–26, 66, 81, 149, 172, 168–70, 202, 229, 231–3, 235–6, 238; *see also* chronotype; *fabula/sjuzet* distinction

'natural' (solar) time, 9–14, 48–51, 61–2, 66, 68–70, 101, 120, 130, 138, 191, 192, 215, 217, 225–6, 235, 237–8
navigation, 3–4, 29–36, 38–9, 40, 41, 46, 55, 65, 88–9, 108, 112, 198, 217–19, 224, 236
Nazism, 165, 167, 178, 179, 180, 182, 223, 225
Nesbit, E., 201n
Newby, P. H., *The Retreat*, 147
Newton, Isaac, 91, 94, 95, 108, 111, 198, 230
Newton, John, 29
Newton's Guide to the Board of Trade Examinations, 29, 30, 32–3, 34, 41
Nietzsche, Friedrich, 98, 99, 105
Norfolk, Lawrence, 179, 182, 225
In the Shape of a Boar, 180, 181–2, 183, 184
nostalgia, 119, 134–47, 148–59, 186, 205, 206, 208, 214; see also Edenic retrospection
nouveau roman, the, 168–72, 176, 177, 178
nuclear weapons see atomic age, the

Odle, E. V., *The Clockwork Man*, 110, 202–3
Orwell, George, 134, 144, 153, 154, 156
Coming up for Air, 139–40, 141, 143, 144, 149, 151, 152–3
Nineteen Eighty-Four, 214
Osborne, John, 156
Look Back in Anger, 150–1, 156
Ouspensky, P. D., 128

Paris meridian, the, 1–3, 6, 219
Paris Observatory, the, 1–3, 6, 9
philosophy, 95–106, 107, 109, 112–13, 115, 124n, 125, 128, 133, 198, 209n, 210, 227–8, 230–1
photography, 136, 187–8, 224
Pinero, Arthur Wing, *The Magistrate*, 4, 17–18
Pinker, Stephen, 191

Plautus, *The Boeotian Women*, 234–5
Plowman, Max, 141
Poe, Edgar Alan, 'A Predicament' ('The Scythe of Time'), 13n
postcolonial criticism, 192
postmodernism and postmodernity, 166–77, 182–4, 185, 195–6, 212, 215, 217, 218, 219
Poulet, Georges, 230–1
Studies in Human Time, 229
Powell, Anthony, *A Dance to the Music of Time*, 177–8
Powys, John Cooper, *A Glastonbury Romance*, 128
Powys, T. F., *Mr Weston's Good Wine*, 112, 128
Priestley, J. B., 70, 154, 201
Dangerous Corner, 127
I Have Been Here Before, 127
Man and Time, 127–8, 197
Margin Released, 64–5
Time and the Conways, 127, 141
Prime Meridian Conference, the, 3–4, 5, 7, 9, 11, 17, 46, 95, 192, 195
Proust, Marcel, 14, 15, 53, 80–2, 83, 85, 97, 99–100, 101, 102, 103, 109, 112, 113, 118–19, 123, 132, 139, 160, 170, 171, 177, 186, 202, 203, 205, 222, 224, 225, 235
À la recherche du temps perdu (*Remembrance of Things Past*), 14–15, 16, 66, 80–2, 85, 100, 101–3, 106, 120, 121, 123, 222n, 235
pub closing times see licensing laws
Pynchon, Thomas, 189, 195
Against the Day, 148n, 188, 226–8, 229
Mason & Dixon, 217–19, 226, 227, 229, 238
V., 5, 7, 8, 9, 14, 17, 215–16, 217, 226

Quantum Theory, 198, 199
Quennell, Peter, *A Letter to Mrs Virginia Woolf*, 141, 152
Quin, Ann, *Three*, 189

railway time, 5, 8, 10, 11–14, 16, 17, 61, 67, 68, 237
railway timetables, 8, 9–10, 13, 15, 16, 53, 57, 66, 75, 100, 108, 223; see also Bradshaw's railway guides
railways and their influence, 4n, 7–17, 23, 48–9, 53, 61, 67, 104, 106, 108, 130, 132, 149–50, 167, 191, 208, 212, 223–4, 235, 237
Randall, Bryony, *Modernism, Daily Time and Everyday Life*, 193n
Reed, Henry, *The Novel since 1939*, 144
reification, 49, 50–62, 72, 175, 213–16
Relativity, 91–6, 104–5, 108–12, 115–16, 123, 128–9, 132, 133, 174, 197, 199, 200, 201, 205, 222n; see also Einstein, Albert
remembrance, 74, 80, 90–1, 94, 100, 119, 123, 135, 137, 143, 159; see also memory; Remembrance Day (1919); war memorials
Remembrance Day (1919), 71–2, 89–93
Richards, Jeffrey, 10, 13
Richardson, Dorothy, 109
 Pilgrimage, 109, 118–19
Ricoeur, Paul, 73, 74, 233
 Time and Narrative, vii, 72
Robbe-Grillet, Alain, 168–72, 175, 196
 'The Case for the New Novel', 169–70
 Dans le labyrinthe, 170
 The Erasers, 169
 Jealousy, 169
 'Time and Description in Fiction Today', 168–9
 The Voyeur, 170
romance, 27–8, 36–8, 89, 126, 128, 140, 151, 200n, 237
Romanticism, 49, 59, 121
Rushdie, Salman, *Midnight's Children*, 211–12

Russell, Bertrand, 105, 111
 The ABC of Relativity, 93–4, 108
Russian Formalism, 22, 23, 24, 110, 204

Sarraute, Natalie, 169
Sassoon, Siegfried, 70
 Siegfried's Journey, 70–1
Satie, Eric, 14, 17
Sawday, Jonathan, 234
Sayers, Dorothy L., 112
 The Documents in the Case, 110–11
Schivelbusch, Wolfgang, 15n
 Disenchanted Night, 61
science and its influence, 1, 2, 7, 88, 95, 97, 109, 128, 129, 131, 132, 166, 167, 197–200, 217–18, 219, 227–8; see also astronomy and cosmology; Relativity; technology and its influence
science fiction, 110, 128n, 195–6, 199, 200–10
Scott Moncrieff, C. K., 80
Sebald, W. G., 188, 228
 Austerlitz, vii, 188, 223–5, 229
Second World War, the, 127, 132–3, 139–47, 154, 156, 157, 159, 160–7, 170, 171, 173, 176–84, 205, 209, 225, 229
Shakespeare, William, 27, 130
 As You Like It, 222, 225, 234
 Henry IV, 12–13, 234
 Macbeth, 161, 163, 234
 The Sonnets, 234
Shklovsky, Viktor, 110, 204n
Slosson, Edwin E., *Easy Lessons in Einstein*, 93
Smith, Zadie, 179
 White Teeth, 179–80, 184, 220
Snow, C. P.
 The Light and the Dark, 177
 Strangers and Brothers, 177–8, 180
Sobel, Dava, *Longitude*, 31–3
solar time see 'natural' (solar) time
Spark, Muriel, *The Mandelbaum Gate*, 178, 184

'specular time', 169, 170, 172, 174, 180, 185, 205, 209, 212, 215
Spender, Stephen, 163, 234
　'Time, Violence and Macbeth', 161–2
Spenser, Edmund, 'Mutability Cantos', 234
Sterne, Laurence, 234
　The Life and Opinions of Tristram Shandy, 232–3
Stoker, Bram, *Dracula*, 16
Strasbourg Clock, the, 231
stream of consciousness, 76, 86, 89, 98, 100, 102, 103, 111, 113–14, 116–17, 118, 120, 123; *see also* interior monologue
subjective time *see* 'time in the mind' and subjective time
Summer Time, 68–70, 72, 191
sundials, 137, 204, 234–5
Swift, Graham, 182, 183, 225
　Shuttlecock, 181
　Waterland, 179, 181, 182
Swift, Jonathan, *Gulliver's Travels*, 192, 203

Tanpinar, Ahmet Hamdi, *The Time Regulation Institute*, 210–11
Taylor, Frederick Winslow, and Taylorism, 53–8, 67, 187, 204
technology and its influence, viii, 6, 7, 10, 61, 89, 99, 104–5, 106, 122, 166, 167, 186–90, 195, 197, 200–1, 203, 212, 218, 220, 223, 225, 226, 228, 230, 237
television, 125, 189; *see also* video and DVD
tense, grammatical, 22, 141, 191
The Terminator (film), 206–8[1]
Thompson, E.P., 'Time, Work-Discipline, and Industrial Capitalism', 230, 233
Thrift, Nigel, 28
　Shaping the Day, 230
time *see* 'deep time'; Greenwich Mean Time; measured (clock) time; memory; 'monumental time'; 'natural' (solar) time; railway time; 'specular time'; 'time in the mind' and subjective time; women's time
'time in the mind' and subjective time, 18–22, 26, 45, 59, 62, 75, 76, 81, 82, 86, 89, 98, 107, 116, 118, 122, 124n, 133, 136, 171, 195, 198–9, 214–15, 223, 235; *see also durée*; memory
time travel, 138n, 201–9, 217, 227–8
timelessness, 39, 79, 98, 101, 112, 117, 120, 122, 125, 126, 161–2, 227, 237–8; *see also* 'deep time'; eternity
time-zones, 4, 5, 6, 9, 191, 203, 205–6, 214–15
Tolkien, J. R. R., 61n
Tomashevsky, Boris, 22
travel, 106, 191
　air, 10, 108, 124, 190, 191, 220
　road, 106, 108, 123, 149, 157, 194–5
　see also navigation; railways and their influence

Updike, John, *Toward the End of Time*, 199

Verne, Jules, 200n
Vico, Giambattista, 116, 117
video and DVD, 189–90, 195, 225
Vonnegut, Kurt, 201n
　Slaughterhouse-Five, 180, 189, 208–9

war memorials, 74, 135, 137
watches, 8–9, 11, 18, 40, 54–5, 58, 67, 94, 101, 102, 113, 116, 120, 122, 142, 161, 170, 172, 185, 192, 201n, 203, 204n, 211, 216, 223, 224, 225, 227, 230, 234, 237; *see also* clocks; chronometers and chronometry; measured (clock) time
Watt, Ian, *The Rise of the Novel*, 231

Waugh, Evelyn, 156
  Brideshead Revisited, 142, 144–5, 147, 157
Wells, H. G., 124, 125, 203
  'The Chronic Argonauts', 201
  The Time Machine, 201, 202, 203, 227
West, Rebecca, *The Return of the Soldier*, 68, 119–20, 121, 140, 142, 144
Whitehead, Anne, 159
Whorf, Benjamin Lee, 191
Willett, William, 68, 70
Williamson, Henry, 156
  A Chronicle of Ancient Sunlight, 148, 156, 177–8
  The Golden Virgin, 148, 155
Wilson, Angus, 156
  Anglo-Saxon Attitudes, 148
  Late Call, 148
  No Laughing Matter, 148
Winterson, Jeanette, 191, 194, 200
  Sexing the Cherry, 191, 198–9
Wittenberg, David, *Time Travel: The Popular Philosophy of Narrative*, 202
Wodehouse, P. G., *The Small Bachelor*, 112
women's time, 192–4, 215
Woolf, Virginia, 19, 20, 64, 70, 73–7, 79, 80, 82–5, 86, 93, 97, 101, 102, 109, 111, 112, 113, 119, 124, 129–33, 134, 135, 136, 137, 140, 141, 159, 186, 193–4, 198

Between the Acts, 70, 129–31, 132–3, 143
Jacob's Room, 73, 74
'The Leaning Tower', 133
'Modern Fiction', 76, 83, 101
'Modern Novels', 75–6, 77, 83
Mrs Dalloway, vii, 16, 65, 70, 73–5, 76, 77, 79–80, 82–4, 86n, 100, 101, 104, 108, 117–18, 119, 120, 122, 129, 130, 131, 133, 136, 146, 235
Night and Day, 17, 73, 131–2
Orlando, 15–16, 18–19, 25, 45, 82–3, 89, 116, 122, 123, 129, 194, 202
'A Sketch of the Past', 202
To the Lighthouse, 65, 84–5, 101, 119, 121, 130, 131, 136, 139
The Waves, 129, 130, 131, 133, 237
The Years, 129, 133

Yeats, W. B., 'The Second Coming', 220–1

Zamyatin, Yevgeny, 57n
  We, 57, 58
Zemeckis, Robert, 207
Zeno of Elea, 105
'zero hours' contracts, 187n
Ziolkowski, Theodore, 18, 25, 122

EU representative:
Easy Access System Europe
Mustamäe tee 50, 10621 Tallinn, Estonia
Gpsr.requests@easproject.com